D0915949

WITHDRAWN

A Dictionary of Philosophy of Religion

A DICTIONARY OF PHILOSOPHY OF RELIGION

EDITED BY

Charles Taliaferro and Elsa J. Marty

continuum

NEW YORK • LONDON

2010

The Continuum International Publishing Group
80 Maiden Lane, New York, NY 10038
The Tower Building, 11 York Road, London SE1 7NX

www.continuumbooks.com

Copyright © 2010 Charles Taliaferro, Elsa J. Marty and contributors

All rights reserved. No part of this book may be reproduced, stored
in a retrieval system, or transmitted, in any form or by any means,
electronic, mechanical, photocopying, recording, or otherwise,
without the permission of the publishers.

Library of Congress Cataloging-in-Publication Data
A catalog record for this book is available from the Library of Congress.

ISBN: 978-1-4411-1238-5 (hardback)
        978-1-4411-1197-5 (paperback)

Typeset by Newgen Imaging Systems Pvt Ltd, Chennai, India
Printed in the United States of America by Sheridan Books, Inc

Contents

Acknowledgments

To our editor, Haaris Naqvi, our many thanks for his guidance and encouragement. Thanks also go to Tricia Little, Sarah Bruce, Kelsie Brust, Valerie Deal, Elizabeth Duel, Elisabeth Granquist, Michael Smeltzer, Cody Venzke, and Jacob Zillhardt for assistance in preparing the manuscript. We are the joint authors of all entries with the exception of those scholars we invited to make special contributions. We thank Pamela Sue Anderson, Oxford University (Feminist Philosophy of Religion, Lacan, Lyotard, Ricoeur); Benjamin Carter, University of Durham (Florentine Academy, Glanvill, History, Lessing's Ditch, Mendelssohn); Robin Collins, Messiah College (Fine-Tuning Argument); Brian Davies, O. P., Fordham University (Divine Simplicity); Paul R. Draper, Purdue University (Bayes' Theorem); Kevin Flannery, S. J., Gregorian University, Rome (Aquinas, Aristotle); Ian Gerdon, University of Notre Dame (Pelagianism, Roman Catholicism, Transubstantiation); John J. Giannini, Baylor University (Analogy); Paul J. Griffiths, Duke Divinity School (Augustine, Lying, Reading); Harriet Harris, Oxford University (Evangelicalism, Evangelism, Fundamentalism, Prayer); Victoria Harrison, University of Glascow (Holiness, von Balthasar); William Hasker, Huntington College (Intelligent Design, Molinism, Open Theism); Douglas Hedley, Cambridge University (Neoplatonism, Plotinus, Sacrifice); James N. Hoke, University of Chicago Divinity School (Basil, Chrysostom, Dion Chrysostom, Gregory Nazianzus, Gregory of Nyssa, Paul); Dale Jacquette, University of Bern, Switzerland (Schopenhauer); Mark Linville, Clayton State University (Moral Arguments for Theism); Robert MacSwain, The School of Theology, University of the South (Farrer, Lewis); Elizabeth Palmer, University of Chicago Divinity School (Luther); David L. O'Hara, Augustana College (Bishop, Heraclitus, Maimonides, Parmenides, Peirce, Pneuma, Providence, Ptolemaic, Reality, Sacrament, Satan, Separation of Church and State, Suspicion, Symbol, Syncretism, Thales, Transcendentalism, Zeno of Citium); Stephen R. Palmquist, Hong Kong Baptist University (Kant); Paul Reasoner, Bethel University (Bodhisattva, Reincarnation, Sincerity, Transfer of Merit); Dan N. Robinson, Oxford University (Reid); Lad Sessions, Washington and Lee University (Honor); Michael Swartzentruber, University of

Acknowledgments

Chicago Divinity School (Hermeneutics, Liberal Theology, Schleiermacher); David Vessey, Grand Valley State University (Gadamer, Husserl, James, Levinas, Maritain, Pragmatism); Jerry Walls, University of Notre Dame, Center for Philosophy of Religion (Eschatology, Heaven, Hell, Purgatory, Resurrection, Salvation, Universalism); and Matthew Lon Weaver, Independent Scholar (H. Richard Niebuhr, Reinhold Niebuhr).

We are especially grateful for colleagues at St. Olaf College: Calista Anderson (Duns Scotus, Primum Mobile), Charles Biskupic (Idol/Idolatry, St. Francis of Assisi, Irony), Hilary Bouxsein (Angels, Pseudo-Dionysius), Katherine Chatelaine (Anti-Theodicy), Samuel Dunn (Chaos Theory), Elizabeth Duel (Animals, Buddha, Dalai Lama, Heaven (Non-Christian Conceptions), Hell (Non-Christian Conceptions), Icons/Iconoclasm, Karma, Native American Traditions, Sorcery, Teilhard de Chardin, Wicca), Katie Duwell (Derrida, Postmodernity/Postmodernism), Bob Entenmann (Cheng Hao, Cheng Yi, Confucianism/Confucius, Huainanzi, Huayan School, Laozi, Mencius, Neo-Confucianism, Qi, Shintoism, Xiong Shili, Xuanzang, Xunzi, Zhang Dongsun, Zhang Zai, Zhu Xi, Zhuangzi), Jeanine Grenberg (Humility), Katherine Hagen (Gandhi, Vedas), Paul Hamilton (Berlin, Radhakrishnan), Eric Larson (Dominicans, Justice), Linnea Logas (Calvinism, Transmigration), Thomas Marti (Atomism, Time), Erik Olson (Averroes, Diogenes Laertius, Diogenes of Sinope, Spinoza), Anthony Rudd (Fichte, Schelling, Schiller), Jamie Schillinger (Falsafa, Jihad), Jason Smith (Julian of Norwich, Rahner, Soteriology), Alexander Sommer (Durkheim, Tillich), Jamie Turnbull (Kierkegaard), Sirvydas Vebra (Einstein, Socrates), Jacob Zillhardt (Hell (Non-Christian Conceptions)).

Finally, we thank our families and friends for their continued support and encouragement.

Preface

Some of the earliest recorded philosophy in the West and East concerns matters that are of central religious significance: the existence of God or gods, the holy, the soul, good and evil, the afterlife, the meaning and nature of birth, growth and maturity, the relationship of the individual to the family or tribe or community, sacrifice, guilt, mercy, and so on. And from the beginning philosophers have expressed a passionate commitment to understanding the meaning of the words we use in exploring such terrain. So, Confucius gave central importance to what he is said to have refered to as the "rectification of names." And the earliest recordings we have of Socrates show him engaged in a vigorous inquiry into whether his fellow Athenians know what they are talking about when they appeal to such concepts as holiness, duty to the gods, justice, courage, goodness, friendship, beauty, art, and so on.

This dictionary is in this old tradition of seeking to attain clarity and understanding through attention to words, names, and titles. One thing we re-discovered in the course of our work is the importance of community and conversation in the practice of philosophy of religion (historically and today). Sometimes scholarship can be a solitary affair, but while some solitude can provide some enviable time for creative reflection, scholarship is most vibrant when it is a shared activity. We are reminded of the story of the explorer Sir Henry Morton Stanley who took on his disastrous journey to the Belgian Congo a host of great books such as the complete collection of Shakespeare. But with no African conversation partners to discuss such books (and partly this was his fault), the bare existence of the books became a pointless burden. In fact, he had to leave all of them except Shakespeare which some Africans insisted he actually burn as they had become concerned it had become an ill totem of sorts. Without conversation and community, the best of books can be dull companions (unless you happen to be Robinson Crusoe).

We began this dictionary in conversation about the meaning of some terms in contemporary philosophy of religion. It was more of an argument than a conversation, but it led us to join forces in the broader, constructive enterprise of working together on this systematic, ambitious project. As noted in the acknowledgments, this undertaking involved others as well. We highlight the importance of conversation and exchange in this preface, as it is our earnest desire that this book might function as something of a companion or an assistant in cultivating or helping inform conversations among our readers. Our hope is to enrich dialogue rather than to substitute for it in any way, for these definitions are only the beginning of philosophical exploration.

Introduction

Philosophy of religion is the philosophical examination of the central themes and concepts involved in religious traditions. It involves all the main areas of philosophy: metaphysics, epistemology, logic, ethics and value theory, the philosophy of language, philosophy of science, law, sociology, politics, history, and so on. Philosophy of religion also includes an investigation into the religious significance of historical events (e.g., the Holocaust) and general features of the cosmos (e.g., laws of nature, the emergence of conscious life, and the widespread testimony of religious significance). In this introduction we offer an overview of the field and its significance, with subsequent sections on the concept of God, arguments for the existence of God, the problem of evil, the challenge of logical positivism, and religious and philosophical pluralism. At the outset, we address philosophy of religion as chiefly studied primarily in so-called analytic departments of philosophy and religious studies in English speaking countries, but we conclude with observations about so-called continental philosophy of religion. The qualification of "so-called" is added because the distinction between analytic and continental is controversial.

The Field and its Significance

The philosophical exploration of religious beliefs and practices is evident in the earliest recorded philosophy, east and west. In the West, throughout Greco-Roman philosophy and the medieval era, philosophical reflection on God or gods, reason and faith, the soul, afterlife, and so on were not considered to be a sub-discipline called "philosophy of religion." The philosophy of God was simply one component among many interwoven philosophical projects. This intermingling of philosophical inquiry with religious themes and the broader enterprises of philosophy (e.g., political theory, epistemology, and so on) is apparent among many early modern philosophers such as John Locke and George Berkeley. Only gradually do we find texts devoted exclusively to religious themes. The first use of the term "philosophy of religion" in English occurs in the seventeenth-century work of Ralph Cudworth. He and his Cambridge University colleague Henry Moore produced philosophical work with a specific focus on religion and so, if one insisted on dating the beginning of philosophy of religion as a field, there are good reasons for claiming that it began (gradually) in the mid-seventeenth century.

Today philosophy of religion is a robust, intensely active area of philosophy. The importance of philosophy of religion is chiefly due to subject matter: alternative beliefs about God, Brahman, and the sacred, the varieties of religious experience, the interplay between science and religion, the challenge of non-religious philosophies, the nature and scope of good and evil, religious treatments of birth, history, and death, and other substantial terrain. A philosophical exploration of these topics involves fundamental questions about our place in the cosmos and about our relationship to what may transcend the cosmos. It requires an investigation into the nature and limit of human thought and explores embedded social and personal practices. A vast majority of the world population is either aligned with religion or affected by religion, making philosophy of religion not simply a matter of abstract theory but also highly relevant to practical concerns. Religious traditions are so comprehensive and all-encompassing in their claims that almost every domain of philosophy may be drawn upon in the philosophical investigation of their coherence, justification, and value.

Philosophy of religion also makes important contributions to religious studies and theology. Historically, theology has been influenced by, or has drawn upon, philosophy. Platonism and Aristotelianism have had a major influence on the articulation of classical Christian doctrine, and in the modern era theologians frequently have drawn on work by philosophers (from Hegel to Heidegger and Derrida). Philosophy strives to clarify, evaluate, and compare religious beliefs. The evaluation has at times been highly critical and dismissive, but there are abundant periods in the history of ideas when philosophy has positively contributed to the flourishing of religious life. This constructive interplay is not limited to the West. The impact of philosophy on distinctive Buddhist views of knowledge and the self has been of great importance. Just as philosophical ideas have fueled theological work, the great themes of theology involving God's transcendence, the divine attributes, providence, and so on, have made substantial impacts on important philosophical projects.

At the beginning of the twenty-first century, a more general rationale for philosophy of religion should be cited: it can enhance cross-cultural dialogue. Philosophers of religion now often seek out common as well as distinguishing features of religious belief and practice. This study can enhance communication between traditions, and between religions and secular institutions.

The Concept of God

Most philosophy of religion in the West has focused on different versions of theism. Ancient philosophy of religion wrestled with the credibility of monotheism and polytheism in opposition to skepticism and very primitive naturalistic schemes. For example, Plato argued that the view that God is singularly good should be preferred to the portrait of the gods that was articulated in Greek poetic tradition, according to which there are many gods, often imperfect and subject to vice and ignorance. The emergence and development of the Abrahamic faiths (Judaism, Christianity and Islam) on a global scale secured the centrality of theism for philosophical inquiry, but the relevance of a philosophical exploration of theism is not limited to those interested in these religions and the cultures in which they flourish. While theism has generally flourished in religious traditions amid religious practices, one may be a theist without adopting any religion whatever, and one may find theistic elements (however piecemeal) in Confucianism, Hinduism, some versions of Mahayana Buddhism, and other traditions. The debate over theism also has currency for secular humanism and religious forms of atheism as in Theravada Buddhist philosophy.

Traditionally, theists have maintained that God is maximally excellent, necessarily existent, incorporeal, omniscient, omnipotent, omnipresent, eternal or everlasting, and essentially good. Theists have differed over whether they regard God as impassable (not subject to passion) or passable. There is not space to address these issues in detail here; however, the nature of these divine attributes and their relationship to one another have been the subject of much reflection within philosophy of religion.

Two concerns arise when articulating the concept of God and the divine attributes. First, some argue that there is a tension between the God of philosophy and the God of revelation. If scripture definitively portrays God as loving and just, then scriptural narratives in which God appears neither loving nor just must either be interpreted as reflecting a projection of fallible human lovelessness and injustice, or theologians need to show how the God of revelation is nevertheless consistently loving and just. Those adopting the first approach invoke the concept of *progressive revelation*, whereby God has been increasingly revealed over time. Precepts in Hebrew scripture that allow slavery, for example, are judged to be primitive, merely-human projections that eventually give way to the purity and nobility of ethical monotheism as evidenced in prophets such as Isaiah, Jeremiah, and Amos. Other philosophers respond by using the biblical understanding of God to shape the philosophy of God. Thus, while some traditional theists have believed God to be eternal, changeless, and impassable, other philosophers use biblical texts to defend the idea that God is in time, subject to change and God has passions (e.g., love of the good). Again, some traditionalists have held that

xiii

God is not subject to passive states and thus God is not subject to a love that involves suffering. Others ask why suffering love has to be seen as a passive state of being subject to creation. Perhaps love (whether it is sorrowing or joyful) can be understood as supreme action, perhaps even a reflection of a supreme, great-making excellence. This new discussion opens opportunities for the scriptural portrait of God to inform the philosophy of God, bringing a more affective dimension to the philosophy of God.

A second issue arising from philosophical reflection on the concept of God concerns the extent to which human thought and language can form an intelligible concept of God. God is beyond both insofar as God (the reality) is not a human thought or term; if God exists, God pre-exists all human and any other created life. In this sense, God's thoughts are (literally) different from any human thought. Theists seek to balance positive claims about God (technically referenced to as cataphatic theology) with an acknowledgment of the importance of negation or negative claims (apophatic theology). Defenders of a strict, apophatic philosophy of God sometimes assume that conceptual and linguistic limitations are in some sense religiously confining or subjugating. But without concepts or some language, deep religious practices like loving or worshiping God would be impossible. To love X, you have to have some concept or idea of X. How would you know whether you were or were not worshiping X if you had no idea whatsoever about X? At least in theistic traditions, some language and concept of God seems essential. Also, there is a difference between claiming that God is more than or greater than our best terms and concepts and the claim that God is not less than our best terms and concepts. So, one may assert that God is omniscient and analyze this in terms of God knowing all that can possibly be known. One may well grant that, and yet go on to claim that how God possess this knowledge and what it would be like to be omniscient surpasses the best possible human imagination.

A significant amount of work on the meaningfulness of religious language was carried out in the medieval period, with major contributions made by Maimonides (1135–1204), Thomas of Aquinas (1225–1274), Duns Scotus (1266–1308), and William of Ockham (1285–1347). This work built on the even earlier work on religious language by Philo (20 BCE–50 CE), Clement (150–215) and Origen (185–259) of Alexandria. In the modern era, the greatest concentration on religious language has taken place in response to logical positivism and to the latter work of Wittgenstein (1889–1951).

The Challenge of Logical Positivism

Logical positivism promoted an empiricist principle of meaning which asserted that for a propositional claim (statement) to be meaningful it must either be about the bare formal relations between ideas such as those enshrined in mathematics and analytic definitions ("A is A", "triangles are three-sided") or there must in principle be perceptual experience providing evidence of whether the claim is true or false. This delimited meaningful discourse about the world and meant that ostensibly factual claims that have no implications for our empirical experience are empty of content. In line with this form of positivism, A. J. Ayer (1910–1989) and others claimed that religious beliefs were meaningless.

Empiricist challenges to the meaningfulness of religious belief are still raised, but are now deemed less impressive than they once were. In the history of the debate over positivism, the most radical charge was that positivism is self-refuting. The empiricist criterion of meaning itself does not seem to be a statement that expresses the formal relation of ideas, nor does it appear to be empirically verifiable. How might one empirically verify the principle? At best, the principle of verification seems to be a recommendation as to how to describe those statements that positivists are prepared to accept as meaningful. But then, how might a dispute about which other statements are meaningful be settled in a non-arbitrary fashion? To religious believers for whom talk of "Brahman" and "God" is at the center stage of meaningful discourse, the use of the principle of empirical verification will seem arbitrary and question-begging. If the positivist principle is tightened up too far, it seems to threaten various propositions that at least appear to be highly respectable, such as scientific claims about physical processes and events that are not publicly observable. For example, what are we to think of states of the universe prior to all observation of physical strata of the cosmos that cannot be observed directly or indirectly but only inferred as part of an overriding scientific theory? Or what about the mental states of other persons, which may ordinarily be reliably judged, but which, some argue, are under-determined by external, public observation? A person's subjective states—how one feels—can be profoundly elusive to external observers and even to the person him or herself. Can you empirically observe another person's sense of happiness? Arguably, the conscious, subjective states of persons resist airtight verification and the evidence of such states does not meet positivism's standards.

The strict empiricist account of meaning was also charged as meaningless on the grounds that there is no coherent, clear, basic level of experience with which to test propositional claims. The experiential "given" is simply too malleable (this has been called "the myth of the given"), often reflecting prior conceptual judgments and, once one appreciates the open-textured character of experience, it may be proposed that virtually any experience can verify or provide some evidence for anything. Not every philosopher has embraced such an epistemological anarchy, but the retreat of positivism has made philosophers more cautious about identifying a sensory foundation for testing all claims to meaningful language.

One of the most sustained lessons from the encounter between positivism and the philosophy of religion is the importance of assessing the meaning of individual beliefs in comprehensive terms. The meaning of ostensible propositional claims must take into account larger theoretical frameworks. Religious claims could not be ruled out at the start but should be allowed a hearing with competing views of cognitive significance.

Arguments for and against the Existence of God

One of the main issues in philosophy of religion concerns arguments for and against the existence of God. Naturalists argue that the cosmos itself, or nature, is all that exists. Strict naturalists, or eliminativists, believe that reality consists only of what is described and explained by the ideal natural sciences, especially physics, and therefore they deny the reality of subjective experiences or consciousness, ideas, emotions, morality, and the mental life in general. Broad naturalists affirm the possibility or plausibility of the mental life and ethical truths, but reject the existence of God. Appealing to Ockham's razor, the thesis that one should not posit entities beyond necessity, strict and broad naturalists argue that atheism ought to be the presumption of choice.

Theists respond by appealing to four significant, interconnected arguments for the existence of God: the ontological, cosmological, and teleological arguments, and an argument from religious experience. The ontological argument contends that reflections on the idea and possibility of God's existence provides a reason for thinking God actually exists. The cosmological argument contends that it is reasonable to think that our contingent cosmos must be accounted for, in part, by the causal creativity of a necessarily-existing being. Teleological arguments contend that our ordered, complex cosmos is better explained by theism rather than naturalism. And the argument from religious experience argues that the widespread reports by persons across time and culture who experience a transcendent, divine reality provide grounds for thinking there is such a reality. Some theists also make arguments based on miracles and morality. These arguments are considered mutually reinforcing, so that, for example, the cosmological argument may be complemented by a teleological argument, thereby providing reasons for thinking the necessarily-existing being is also purposive. Few philosophers today advance a single argument as a proof. It is increasingly common to see philosophies— scientific naturalism or theism—advanced with cumulative arguments, a whole range of considerations, and not with a supposed knock-down, single proof.

One reason why the case for and against major, comprehensive philosophies are mostly cumulative is because of discontent in what is often called foundationalism. In one classical form of foundationalism, one secures first and foremost a basis of beliefs which one may see to be true with certainty. The base may be cast as indubitable or infallible. One then slowly builds up the justification for one's other, more extensive beliefs about oneself and the world. Many (but not all) philosophers now see justification as more complex and interwoven; the proper object of philosophical inquiry is overall coherence, not a series of distinguishable building operations beginning with a foundation.

One way of carrying out philosophy of religion along non-foundationalist lines has been to build a case for the comparative rationality of a religious view of the world. It has been argued that the intellectual integrity of a religious world view can be secured if it can be shown to be no less rational than the available alternatives. It need only achieve intellectual parity.

The Problem of Evil

The problem of evil is the most widely considered objection to theism in both Western and Eastern philosophy. If there is a God who is omnipotent, omniscient, and completely good, why is there evil? There are two general versions of the problem: the deductive or logical version, which asserts that the existence of any evil at all (regardless of its role in producing good) is incompatible with God's existence; and the probabilistic version, which asserts that given the quantity and severity of evil that actually exists, it is unlikely that God exists. The deductive problem is currently less commonly debated because it is widely acknowledged that a thoroughly good being might allow or inflict some harm under certain morally compelling conditions (such as causing a child pain when removing a splinter). More intense debate concerns the likelihood (or even possibility) that there is a completely good God given the vast amount of evil in the cosmos. Consider human and animal suffering caused by death, predation, birth defects, ravaging diseases, virtually unchecked human wickedness, torture, rape, oppression, and "natural disasters." Consider how often those who suffer are innocent. Why should there be so much gratuitous, apparently pointless evil?

In the face of the problem of evil, some philosophers and theologians deny that God is all-powerful and all-knowing. John Stuart Mill took this line, and panentheist theologians today also question the traditional treatments of Divine power. According to panentheism, God is immanent in the world, suffering with the oppressed and working to bring good out of evil, although in spite of God's efforts, evil will invariably mar the created order. Another response is to think of God as being very different from a moral agent. Brian Davies and others have contended that what it means for God to be good is different from what it means for an agent to be morally good. A more desperate strategy is to deny the existence of evil, but it is difficult to reconcile traditional monotheism with moral skepticism. Also, insofar as we believe there to be a God worthy of worship and a fitting object of human love, the appeal to moral skepticism will carry little weight. The idea that evil is a privation of the good, a twisting of something good, may have some currency in thinking through the problem of evil, but it is difficult to see how it alone could go very far to vindicate belief in God's goodness. Searing pain and endless suffering seem altogether real even if they are analyzed as being philosophically parasitic on something valuable.

In part, the magnitude one takes the problem of evil to pose for theism will depend upon one's commitments in other areas of philosophy, especially ethics, epistemology and metaphysics. If in ethics you hold that there should be no preventable suffering for any reason, no matter what the cause or consequence, then the problem of evil will conflict with accepting traditional theism. Moreover, if you hold that any solution to the problem of evil should be evident to all persons, then again traditional theism is in jeopardy, for clearly the "solution" is not evident to all. Debate has largely centered over the legitimacy of adopting some position in the middle: a theory of values that would preserve a clear assessment of the profound evil in the cosmos as well as some understanding of how this might be compatible with the existence of an all-powerful, completely good Creator. Could there be reasons why God would permit cosmic ills? If we do not know what those reasons might be, are we in a position to conclude that there are none or that there could not be any? Exploring different possibilities will be shaped by one's metaphysics. For example, if you do not believe there is free will, then you will not be moved by any appeal to the positive value of free will and its role in bringing about good as offsetting its role in bringing about evil.

Theistic responses to the problem of evil distinguish between a defense and a theodicy. A defense seeks to establish that rational belief that God exists is still possible (when the defense is employed against the logical version of the problem of evil) and that the existence of evil does not make it improbable that God exists (when used against the probabilistic version). Some have adopted the defense strategy while arguing that we are in a position to have rational beliefs in the existence of evil and in a completely good God who hates this evil, even though we may be unable to see how these two beliefs are compatible. A theodicy is more ambitious, and is typically part of a broader project, arguing that it is reasonable to believe that God exists on the basis of the good as well as the evident evil of the cosmos. In a theodicy, the project is not to account for each and every evil, but to provide an overarching framework within which to understand at least roughly how the evil that occurs is part of some overall good — for instance, the overcoming of evil is itself a great good. In practice, a defense and a theodicy often appeal to similar factors, such as the Greater Good Defense, which contends that that evil can be understood as either a necessary accompaniment to bringing about greater goods or an integral part of these goods.

Some portraits of an afterlife seem to have little bearing on our response to the magnitude of evil here and now. Does it help to understand why God allows evil if all victims will receive happiness later? But it is difficult to treat the possibility of an afterlife as entirely irrelevant. Is death the annihilation of persons or an event involving a transfiguration to a higher state? If you do not think that it matters whether persons continue to exist after death, then such speculation is of little consequence. But suppose that the afterlife is understood as being morally intertwined with this life, with opportunity for moral and spiritual reformation, transfiguration of the wicked, rejuvenation and occasions for new life, perhaps even reconciliation and communion between oppressors seeking forgiveness and their victims. Then these considerations might help to defend against arguments based on the existence of evil. Insofar as one cannot rule out the possibility of an afterlife morally tied to our life, one cannot rule out the possibility that God brings some good out of cosmic ills.

Religious Pluralism

In contemporary philosophy of religion, there has been a steady, growing representation of non-monotheistic traditions, involving fresh translations of philosophical and religious texts from India, China, Southeast Asia, and Africa. Exceptional figures from non-Western traditions have an increased role in cross-cultural philosophy of religion and religious dialogue. There are now extensive treatments of pantheism and student-friendly guides to diverse religious conceptions of the cosmos.

The expanded interest in religious pluralism has led to extensive reflection on the compatibilities and possible synthesis of religions. John Hick is the preeminent synthesizer of religious traditions. Moving from a broadly based theistic view of God to what he calls "the Real," a noumenal sacred reality, Hick claims that different religions provide us with a glimpse or partial access to the Real. He sees religious traditions as different meeting points in which a person might transcend ego-driven, selfish desires and be in relation to the same reality or the Real. While Hick is reluctant to attribute positive properties to the Real in itself (he leaves undetermined whether the Real is personal or impersonal), he holds that all persons will evolve or develop into a saving relationship with the Real after death. One advantage of Hick's position is that it undermines a rationale for religious conflict. If successful, this approach would offer a way to accommodate diverse communities and undermine what has been a source of grave conflict in the past.

The response to Hick's proposal has been mixed. Some contend that the very concept of "the Real" is incoherent or not religiously adequate. Indeed, articulating the nature of the real is no easy task. Some think that Hick has secured not the equal acceptability of diverse religions but rather their unacceptability. In their classical forms, Judaism, Islam, and Christianity diverge. If, say, the Incarnation of God in Christ did not occur, would not Christianity be false? In reply, Hick has sought to interpret specific claims about the Incarnation in ways that do not commit Christians to the "literal truth" of God becoming enfleshed. The "truth" of the Incarnation has been interpreted in such terms as these: in Jesus Christ (or in the narratives about Christ) God is disclosed. Or: Jesus Christ was so united with God's will that his actions were and are the functional display of God's character. Perhaps as a result of Hick's challenge, philosophical work on the incarnation and other beliefs and practice specific to religious traditions have received renewed attention.

An interesting new development in philosophy of religion concerns the concept of evidence and the justification for religious (and secular) beliefs. How much (if any) evidence is needed to justify a person in holding a religious or secular worldview? If one has *some* evidence of the truth of one religion, is the evidence compromised when (or if) one realizes that someone else has what appears to be equally good evidence that a different religion is true?

In addition to the expansion of philosophy of religion to take into account a wider set of religions, the field has also seen an expansion in terms of methodology. Philosophers of religion have re-discovered medieval philosophy and there is now a self-conscious, deliberate effort to combine work on the concepts in religious belief alongside a critical understanding of their social and political roots (the work of Foucault has been influential on this point). Feminist philosophy of religion has been especially important in re-thinking what may be called the ethics of methodology, questioning respects in which gender enters into traditional conceptions of God and in their moral and political repercussions. Feminist philosophy advances a concept of method that focuses on justice and human flourishing, arguing that a mark of legitimation of philosophy should be the extent to which it contributes to human welfare. Another key movement that is developing has come to be called Continental Philosophy of Religion, for it approaches issues such as the concept of God, pluralism, religious experience, metaphysics, and epistemology in light of Heidegger, Derrida, and other continental philosophers.

There are many points at which continental philosophy can be seen as complementing classical and mainstream philosophy of religion, but some elements of continental thought are pitted against traditional philosophy of religion which is sometimes called "onto-theology." The latter privileges the theoretical clarity, explanations of the cosmos, divine attributes, rules of evidence, and so on. Merold Westphal is a representative of those working in the continental tradition who believes that philosophy of religion should be so structured that it privileges *the practical life of faith*. Westphal develops his position as a Christian inspired by Martin Heidegger:

> the goal of theology "is never a valid system of theological prepositions" but rather "concrete Christian experience itself." . . . [B]ecause its goal is the *praxis* of the believer as a distinctive mode of existence, "*theology in its essence is a practical science*." Unlike onto-theology, theology properly understood is "innately homiletical" . . . It is as if Heidegger is saying, I have found it necessary to deny theory in order to make room for practice.[1]

Westphal further articulates his position in connection with a novel by C. S. Lewis (*Till We Have Faces*) in which a main character loses her beloved (the god, psyche) because she seeks knowledge about the beloved.

> The challenge of faith is the same: the believer is called upon to sustain a beautiful and loving relationship through trust in a lover about whom she remains significantly (though not totally) in the dark and who, though he gives himself to her freely, is not at her disposal. The relationship is destroyed when the beloved . . . insists on Enlightenment, on the dissipating the darkness of mystery with the light of human knowledge, on walking by sight and not by faith.
>
> To be able to resist this temptation, faith must deny theory, or, to be more precise, the primacy of insight. For such faith, Plato's divided line and Hegel's modern vision thereof as the movement "beyond faith" to knowledge are not the ascent from that which is inferior . . . to that which is superior . . . ; they are rather the withdrawal from the site at which alone is possible a loving, trusting relation with a God before whom one might sing and dance . . .
>
> This love, this trust, this relationship—these are the practice for the sake of which it was necessary to deny theory. This is not to abolish theology. It is to see that theology's task is to serve this life of faith, not the ideals of knowledge as defined by the philosophical traditions.[2]

This position calls for several observations. First, philosophy of religion has demonstrated that, as a field, it is wide enough to include diverse projects, including Westphal's. Second, Westphal advances his preferred model of theology and philosophy as a Christian. In a field with a plurality of religions represented, philosophers will find it difficult to abandon questions of knowledge, inquiry about the truth or plausibility of theological propositions, and only serve the "life of faith." Finally, it is hard to grasp how one can focus upon the religious or secular "beautiful and loving relationship through trust" in God or the sacred or a beloved human without having a theoretical commitment to the reality of God, the sacred or the beloved human and concepts of that beloved, assumed reality. We suggest that proposals like Westphal's will find it difficult to supplant (though they may complement) traditional and contemporary philosophy of religion.

Conclusion

At its best, the philosophy of religion is about openness to serious dialogue and respectful argument across religious, cultural, and other boundaries. This kind of careful, disciplined thinking provides one of the best ways to engage other religions, and to engage those who reject religion, in a way that can bring deeper understanding of and sympathy for others. There is some resistance to acknowledging the way philosophy of religion should promote what is best described as the pursuit of such wise exchanges between different parties. A Christian philosopher Michael Rea recently signaled his resistance to the idea that philosophy of religion (or theology) should promote wisdom.

> But I cannot resist noting that, despite the superficial attractiveness of the idea that philosophers and theologians ought to be aiming in the direction of wisdom and moral improvement, Christian philosophers as such, and theologians as well, might in fact have some reason for resisting this idea. Recently, a student from another (religious) university emailed me and asked, among other things, what philosophy books or articles I'd recommend for the purpose of helping him to grow in wisdom. My answer was that I wouldn't recommend philosophical texts for that purpose at all; rather, I'd recommend scripture. If philosophy as a discipline (or theology) were to aim its efforts at the production of a self-contained body of wisdom, or at a general theory of right living, it would (I think) be aiming at the production of a *rival* to scripture. And that is a project that I think Christian philosophers and theologians ought to try to avoid. Indeed, to my mind, this sort of project involves just as much hubris as onto-theology is said to involve. Thus it seems to me that the right *theoretical* task for Christian philosophers and theologians to pursue is in fact one that involves clarifying, systematizing, and model-building - precisely the sort of project that analytic philosophers are engaged in.[3]

We are far from suggesting that philosophy of religion should aim at a "self-contained body of wisdom" or produce a sacred scripture, but we suggest by way of reply two points.

First, no scripture in any tradition (including the Christian Bible) is best described as "self-contained wisdom." All sacred scriptures are linked with religious communities, histories, traditions of interpretation, and so on. Second, although Rea is an outstanding, highly gifted philosopher of religion, we suggest that he seems to underestimate how respectful dialogue, joint inquiry into multiple religious and their secular alternatives (with all the involved "clarifying systematizing, and model-building"), can be foundational for a life that involves the love of wisdom which is, after all, the etymological root of the term "philosophy" (from the Greek *philo* for love and *sophia* for wisdom).

Resources

Philosophy of religion is represented in virtually all the main philosophy journals, but it is the specific focus of *The International Journal for Philosophy of Religion, Religious Studies, Faith and Philosophy, Philosophia Christi, Philosophy and Theology, Sophia, American Catholic Philosophical Quarterly* (formerly *New Scholasticism*), *American Journal of Theology and Philosophy, European Journal for Philosophy of Religion,* and *The Thomist.* Theology journals also carry considerable philosophy of religion, especially *The Journal of the American Academy of Religion, The Journal of Religion, Theological Studies, The Journal of Religious Ethics, Heythrop Journal, The Annual of the Society of Christian Ethics, Theology Today, New Blackfriars, Modern Theology, Harvard Theological Review,* the *Scottish Journal of Religious Studies,* and the *Scottish Journal of Theology.* Philosophy of religion can also be found in some cross-disciplinary journals like *Law and Religion, The Journal of Law and Religion, Literature and Theology, The Journal of Humanism and Ethical Religions,* and *Christian Scholar's Review.*

Several scholarly presses produce series of books in philosophy of religion. Continuum publishes a series in philosophy of religion under the editorship Stewart Goetz. Cornell University Press publishes *Cornell Studies in the Philosophy of Religion,* Indiana University Press publishes *The Indiana Series in the Philosophy of Religion,* Kluwer Academic Publishers publishes *Studies in Philosophy and Religion,* and the State University Press of New York publishes *Toward a Comparative Philosophy of Religions.* University presses such as Oxford, Cambridge, Notre Dame, Pennsylvania State, and Temple regularly publish work in philosophy of religion. Prometheus Books produces a substantial number of works in philosophy of religion, most of them highly critical of theism.

Topics in the philosophy of religion are indexed in the *Philosopher's Index,* published by the Philosophical Documentation Center, Bowling Green State University. Entries are listed under such titles as "God," "Religious Experience," and "Buddhism." This is a highly valued tool for writing papers, whether these be for a class or for making a contribution to the field. The *Philosopher's Index* offers brief abstracts summarizing the main tenets of books and articles. It is available on CD covering works published from 1940 to the present thought DIALOG Information Services. Philosophy of religion is also indexed in yearly publications of the *Religion Index* (in two volumes). These are produced by the American theological Association, Evanston, Illinois, USA, and are also available on CD. Books in philosophy of religion are also regularly reviewed by in the journal *Philosophical Books*.

There are regular sessions on the philosophy of religion on the programs of the annuals meetings of the three divisions of the American Philosophical Association, as well as on the program of the annual meeting of the American Academy of Religion. Societies and institutions focusing on the philosophy of religion include: the British Society for the philosophy of Religion; the Society for the Philosophy of Religion; the Society of Christian Philosophers; the Philosophy of Religion Society; the American Catholic Philosophical Association; Boston University Institute for Philosophy of Religion; the American Humanist Association; the American Maritain Association; the fellowship of Religious Humanists; the Jesuit Philosophical Association; the Society for Medieval and Renaissance Philosophy; and the Society for Philosophy and Theology. Addresses for most of these organizations are listed in the *Directory of American Philosophers,* a publication of the Philosophy Documentation Center, Bowling Green State University.

There is a Center for Philosophy of Religion at the University of Notre Dame which offers fellowships to undertake research in the field. Information about the center is noted in the journal *Faith and Philosophy*. St. Olaf College is the site of the Kierkegaard Library, a Publication and Study Center dedicated to the Danish philosopher Søren Kierkegaard (1813–1855) who made an enormous contribution to the philosophy of religion. Fellowships to study at the Center are available. The website "www.infidels. org" is a wonderful and easily accessible database for journal articles exploring the philosophy of religion from the atheist school of thought. The Stanford Encyclopedia of philosophy also exists as an outstanding source for the study of the philosophy of religion.

Notes

1. Merold Westphal, *Overcoming Onto-Theology: Toward a Postmodern Christian Faith* (New York: Fordham University Press, 2001), 16.
2. Ibid., 27.
3. Michael Rea, *Analytic Theology: New Essays in the Philosophy of Theology* (Oxford: Oxford University Press, 2009), 18–19.

Chronology

(c.= circa, signifying approximate dates)

c. 2600 BCE	Indus Valley Civilization
c. 1812–c. 1637 BCE	Abraham
c. 1500–1200 BCE	Development of Brahmanism. Likely composition of Hindu Vedas.
c. 1300 BCE	Moses and the Ten Commandments
c. 1000 BCE	Kingdom of Israel begins
c. 950 BCE	Pentateuch is written
c. 800–400 BCE	Likely composition of early Hindu Upanishads
c. 600–583 BCE	Zoroaster (Zarathustra), founder of Zoroastrianism in Persia
c. 599–527 BCE	Mahavira Jeni, founder of Jainism
586–587 BCE	Babylonians conquer Jerusalem; Israelites taken into captivity
c. 570–510 BCE	Lao Tzu, founder of Taoism
c. 570–495 BCE	Pythagoras of Samos
c. 570–480 BCE	Xenophanes of Colophon
566–486 BCE	Siddhartha Gautama (Buddha), founder of Buddhism
c. 551–479 BCE	Confucius, founder of Confucianism
531 BCE	Siddhartha attains Enlightenment
c. 500–450 BCE	Parmenides of Elea, Greek Eleatic philosopher
c. 500 BCE	Founding of Shintoism in Japan
490–480 BCE	Persian Wars
c. 469–399 BCE	Socrates, his death has a profound effect on Plato
431–404 BCE	Peloponnesian War; End of The Golden Age of Greece
427–347 BCE	Plato
c. 400–c. 325 BCE	Diogenes the Cynic
c. 387 BCE	Plato founds the Academy
384–322 BCE	Aristotle

c. 380–370 BCE	Plato's *Republic*
c. 372–289 BCE	Mencius, Confucian philosopher
367 BCE	Aristotle enters the Academy
c. 365–c.275 BCE	Pyrrho the Sceptic
c. 343–339 BCE	Aristotle tutors Alexander
341–270 BCE	Epicurus, founder of Epicurean philosophy
c. 336 BCE	Aristotle founds Lyceum
c. 333–264 BCE	Zeno of Citium, founds Stoic school
323 BCE	Death of Alexander the Great
221 BCE	Great Wall of China built
206 BCE– 220 CE	Han Dynasty
200–100 BCE	Buddhism splits into Theravada and Mahayana
106–43 BCE	Marcus Tullius Cicero
27 BCE	End of the Roman Republic
c. 4 BCE–c. 30 CE	Jesus of Nazareth, founder of Christianity
c. 1 BCE–65 CE	Lucius Annaeus Seneca
c. 55–135	Epictetus of Hierapolis
70	Destruction of Jewish temple in Jerusalem
100–165	Justin Martyr
121–180	Marcus Aurelius
c. 150–200	Nagarjuna, founder of Madhyamika school of Buddhism
c. 200	Sextus Empiricus
205–c. 269	Plotinus, founder of Neoplatonism
c. 215–276	Mani, founder of Manicheaism
325	Council of Nicaea
c. 338–397	St. Ambrose
354–430	St. Augustine of Hippo
380	Christianity becomes the official religion of the Roman Empire
410	Fall of Rome
451	Council of Chalcedon
c. 475–524	Anicius Manlius Severinus Boethius
570–632	Muhammed, prophet of Islam
610	Muhammed receives his first revelation from God in a cave during Ramadan
613	Mohammed begins preaching about his revelations
c. 650	Qur'an written
c. 788–c. 820	Adi Shankara, founder of Advaita Vedanta Hinduism

789	Beginning of the Viking Expansion
c. 801–866	Al-Kindi, Islamic philosopher
c. 870–950	Al-Farabi, Islamic philosopher
962	The Holy Roman Empire is established
980–1037	Avicenna (Ibn Sina), Islamic philosopher
1017–1137	Ramanuja, founder of Vishishtadvaita Vedanta Hinduism
1033–1109	St. Anselm of Canterbury
1059–1111	Al-Ghazali, Islamic philosopher
1079–1142	Peter Abélard
1101–1164	Héloïse
1126–1198	Averroes (Ibn Rushd), Islamic philosopher
1135–1204	Moses Maimonides
c.1181–1226	St. Francis of Assisi
1214–1292	Roger Bacon
1215	Magna Carta signed
1221–1274	Bonaventure of Bagnoregio
1221–1327	Mongol Invasion of India
1225–1274	Thomas of Aquinas
1254–1324	Marco Polo
1265–1321	Dante Alighieri
c. 1266–1308	Duns Scotus
c. 1285–c. 1349	William of Ockham
c. 1299	Birth of the Ottoman Empire
c. 1304–c. 1576	The Renaissance
c. 1308–1321	Dante writes the *Divine Comedy*
1337	The Hundred Years War begins
c. 1400–64	Nicholas of Cusa
1433–99	Marsilio Ficino
1440	Guttenberg invents the printing press
1453	Constantinople falls to the Ottomans, ending the Byzantine era
1466–1536	Desiderius Erasmus
1469–1527	Niccolò Machiavelli
1478–1535	Thomas More
1483–1546	Martin Luther
1492	Columbus' Voyage; The expulsion of the Jews from Spain
1498	Leonardo DaVinci paints *The Last Supper*
1509–1564	John Calvin
1513	Machiavelli writes *Il Principe*

1517	Luther nails his *Ninety-Five Theses* to the castle church door in Wittenberg, Germany
1517–1648	The Reformation
1533–1592	Michel de Montaigne
1548–1600	Giordano Bruno; accused of heresy and burnt by Inquisition
1548–1607	Francisco Suárez
1561–1626	Francis Bacon
1571	Battle of Lepanto
1575–1624	Jakob Böhme
1588–1679	Thomas Hobbes
1588	Defeat of the Spanish Armada
1592–1655	Pierre Gassendi
1596–1650	René Descartes
1599–1658	Oliver Cromwell
1609–1683	Benjamin Whichcote
1614–1687	Henry More
1617–1688	Ralph Cudworth
1618	The Thirty Years War begins
1623–1662	Blaise Pascal
1625	Grotius publishes *The Laws of War and Peace*
1632–1677	Spinoza; publishes *Ethics* 1677
1632–1704	John Locke
1638–1715	Nicolas Malebranche
1641	Descartes publishes *Meditations*; Beginning of English Civil War
1644	Descartes publishes *Principles of Philosophy*
1646–1716	Gottfried Wilhelm Leibniz
1651	Hobbes publishes *Leviathan*
1668–1744	Giovanni Battista Vico
1671–1713	Lord Shaftesbury (Anthony Ashley Cooper)
1677	Spinoza publishes *Ethics*
1685–1753	George Berkeley
1690	Locke publishes *An Essay Concerning Human Understanding*
1694–1778	Voltaire (François-Marie Arouet)
1703–1758	Jonathan Edwards
1710–1796	Thomas Reid
1711–1776	David Hume
1712–1778	Jean-Jacques Rousseau
1713–1784	Denis Diderot

1723–1790	Adam Smith
1724–1804	Immanuel Kant
1729–1797	Edmund Burke
1739–1740	Hume publishes *A Treatise of Human Nature*
1741	Roman Catholic Church condemns slavery
1748–1832	Jeremy Bentham
1759	Voltaire publishes *Candide*
1768–1834	Friedrich Daniel Ernst Schleiermacher
1770–1831	Georg Wilhelm Friedrich Hegel
1775–1854	Friedrich Wilhelm Joseph von Schelling
1788–1860	Arthur Schopenhauer
1789–1799	French Revolution
1804–1872	Ludwig Andreas Feuerbach
1806–1873	John Stuart Mill
1806	The Holy Roman Empire dissolves
1809–1882	Charles Darwin
1813–1855	Søren Kierkegaard
1815	End of the Napoleonic Wars
1817–1892	Bahá'u'lláh, founder of the Baha'i faith
1818–1883	Karl Marx
1819–1850	The Báb, preached the coming of Bahá'u'lláh the prophet
1833	Slavery abolished in the British Empire
1838–1900	Henry Sidgwick
1839–1914	Charles Peirce
1842–1910	William James
1844–1900	Friedrich Nietzsche
1844–1921	'Abdu'l-Bahá, son of Bahá'u'lláh, consolidated the foundation of the Baha'i faith
1846–1924	F. H. Bradley
1856–1939	Sigmund Freud
1859	Darwin publishes "Origin of Species"
1859–1941	Henri Bergson
1859–1952	John Dewey
1861–1865	American Civil War
1861–1947	Alfred North Whitehead
1861	Serfdom abolished in Russia
1866	Mary Baker Eddy founds Christian Science
1868	End of Feudal Rule in Japan

1869–1937	Rudolf Otto
1873–1970	Bertrand Russell
1874–1948	Nikolai Berdyaev
1883–1885	Nietzsche publishes *Thus Spake Zarathustra*
1884–1976	Rudolph Bultmann
1886–1965	Paul Tillich
1889–1951	Ludwig Wittgenstein
1889–1966	Emil Brunner
1889–1976	Martin Heidegger
1892–1971	Reinhold Niebuhr
1899	Freud publishes *The Interpretation of Dreams*
1904–1984	Karl Rahner
1905–1980	Jean-Paul Sartre
1906–1945	Dietrich Bonhoeffer
1909–1943	Simone Weil
1910–1989	A. J. Ayer
1914–1918	World War I
1929	Whitehead publishes *Process and Reality*; Great Depression begins
1939–1945	World War II
1948	Bonhoeffer publishes *The Cost of Discipleship*
1956	Tillich publishes *Dynamics of Faith*

A

A POSTERIORI. Latin, "from later." A posteriori knowledge stems from experience or observation and so cannot be known beforehand by pure reason or conceptual analysis. We know a posteriori, for example, that Socrates was executed in 399 BCE. Some traditional arguments for God's existence such as the teleological and design arguments are developed a posteriori.

A PRIORI. Latin, "from earlier." A proposition is known a priori when it is known without employing empirical observations or experience. Arguably, one may know a priori that there cannot be a square circle.

ABDUCTION. From the Latin *ab + ducere*, meaning "to lead away." Abductive reasoning explains phenomena on the grounds of prior probability or reasonability. For example, one might argue for theism on the grounds that if theism is true, it is more probable that there would be an ordered cosmos with conscious, valuable life, than if a non-theistic alternative is assumed to be true, such as secular naturalism. Abductive reasoning is most often employed in comparing a limited number of alternative theories. The earliest theistic design arguments in English were abductive in structure as opposed to inductive. Henry More reasoned that the cosmos was akin to what appears to be language; if we assume there is a creator, the cosmos is (as it seems) intelligible, whereas it does not seem intelligible if there is no creator.

ABELARD, PETER (1079–1142). Abelard is best known for his metaphysics, ethics, and understanding of atonement. In metaphysics, he adopted a form of conceptualism, a position midway between Platonism and nominalism. In ethics, he greatly stressed the role of intentions and desires. He thereby put stress on the moral relevance of our interior life. If Abelard is correct, then an ethic that focuses exclusively on external action is inadequate. In theology, he is attributed with what is sometimes called a subjective theory of the atonement, wherein the saving work of Christ is accomplished by sinners being subjectively transformed by Christ's heroic, loving self-sacrifice. Abelard did emphasize such subjective transformation, but there is reason to think he also accepted a traditional Anselmian account of the atonement. Abelard carried out an extensive correspondence with Heloise, which reflected on their love affair and its tragic end. The correspondence includes debate over marriage, romantic love, and the vocation of a philosopher. His principal works are: *On the Divine Unity and Trinity* (1121), *Yes and No* (1122), *Christian Theology* (1124), *Theology of the "Supreme Good"* (1120–1140), and *Know Thyself* (1125–1138).

ABJURATION. An act of renunciation, e.g., the repudiation of an opinion or a vow now deemed spurious.

ABORTION. Intentional termination of pregnancy. Religious and moral arguments against abortion tend to stress the value of the fetus or unborn child as a person, potential person, human being, or sacred form of life. Some religious denominations and traditions contend that the decision to abort in the early stages of pregnancy should be a matter left to individual conscience and not subject to strict prohibition.

ABRAHAMIC FAITHS. Christianity, Judaism, and Islam are called Abrahamic because they trace their history back to the Hebrew patriarch Abraham (often dated in the twentieth or twenty-first century BCE). Judaism, Christianity, and Islam each see themselves as rooted in Abrahamic faith, as displayed in the Hebrew Bible, the Christian Old Testament (essentially the Hebrew Bible) and New Testament, and the Qur'an.

Since the seventeenth century, "theism" has been the common term used in English to refer to the central concept of God in the Abrahamic faiths. According to the classical forms of these faiths, God is the one and sole God (they are monotheistic as opposed to polytheistic) who both created and sustains the cosmos. God either created the cosmos out of nothing, that is, ex nihilo, or else it has always existed but depends for its existence upon God's conserving, creative will (some Islamic philosophers have claimed that the cosmos has always existed as God's sustained creation, but the great majority of philosophers in these three traditions have held that the cosmos had a beginning). Creation out of nothing means that God did not use or require anything external from God in creating everything. The cosmos depends upon God's conserving, continuous will in the same way light depends on a source or a song depends on a singer. If the source of the light goes out or the singer stops singing, the light and song cease.

Traditionally, creation is not thought of as a thing that an agent might fashion and then abandon; the idea of God making creation and then neglecting it—the way a person might make a machine and then abandon it—is utterly foreign to theism.

In these religions, God is said to exist necessarily, not contingently. God exists in God's self, not as the creation of some greater being (a super-God) or force of nature. God is also not a mode of something more fundamental, the way a wave is a mode of the sea or a movement is a mode of the dance. The cosmos, in contrast to God, exists contingently but not necessarily—it might not have existed at all; God's existence is unconditional insofar as it does not depend upon any external conditions, whereas the cosmos is conditional. Theists hold that God is, rather, a substantial reality: a being not explainable in terms that are more fundamental than itself. God is without parts, i.e., not an aggregate or compilation of things. Theists describe God as holy or sacred, a reality that is of unsurpassable greatness. God is therefore also thought of as perfectly good, beautiful, all-powerful (omnipotent), present everywhere (omnipresent), and all-knowing (omniscient). God is without origin and without end, everlasting or eternal. Because of all this, God is worthy of worship and morally sovereign (worthy of obedience). Finally, God is manifest in human history; God's nature and will are displayed in the tradition's sacred scriptures. Arguably, the most central attribute of God in the Abrahamic traditions is goodness. The idea that God is not good or the fundamental source of goodness would be akin to the idea of a square circle: an utter contradiction.

Theists in these traditions differ on some of the divine attributes. Some, for example, claim that God knows all future events with certainty, whereas others argue that no being (including God) can have such knowledge. Some theists believe that God transcends both space and time altogether, while other theists hold that God pervades the spatial world and is temporal (there is before, during, and after for God).

ABSOLUTE, THE. From the Latin *absolutus*, meaning "the perfect" or "completed" (as opposed to the relative). "The absolute" is often used to refer to God as the ultimate, independent reality from which all life flows. Although philosophers and theologians as far back as Nicholas of Cusa have used the term in reference to God (e.g., Nicholas of Cusa argued that God is both the Absolute Maximum and the Absolute Minimum), today the term is primarily associated with idealist philosophers of the nineteenth century such as Ferrier, Bradley, Bosanquet, and Royce. The term—in its modern idealist sense—originated in the late eighteenth century in the writings of Schelling and Hegel and was transmitted to the English through Samuel Coleridge's *The Friend* (1809–1810). Russian philosopher Vladimir Soloviev used the term to refer to reality, which he conceived of as a living organism. The term has also been embraced by some Eastern philosophers, such as Sri Aurobindo, who considered "the absolute" as an appropriate alternative to the name *Brahman*. It is most commonly used in the fields of metaphysics, value theory, and natural philosophy.

ABSOLUTION. From the Latin *absolvo*, meaning "set free." Absolution is the forgiveness of sins and the removal of any connected penalties. It refers primarily to a Christian practice in which a priest or minister absolves the sins of people in the name of God following their confession, but it may also be used simply to refer to God's direct forgiveness without any human intermediary.

ABSURD. That which is untenable or beyond the limits of rationality. When associated with existentialism, the absurd refers to there being a lack of any meaning inherent within the real world or in our actions. It gained currency in popular culture via Samuel Beckett's theatre of the absurd and works by Sartre and Camus. A phrase famously (and erroneously) attributed to Tertullian claimed that faith in an incarnate God was absurd: *credo quia absurdum est*—"I believe because it is absurd." The actual quotation from Tertullian is: *credibile est, quia ineptum est*—"It is credible because it is silly." (*De carne Christi* 5.4). Tertullian is sometimes taken to thereby valorize irrationality, but his thesis was instead that the truth of Christianity was absurd only in relation to Stoic, non-Christian philosophy. If Tertullian is correct, the tenability of Christianity is not contingent upon external, philosophical inspection.

ACADEMY. The name of the educational, philosophical community founded by Plato in 387 BCE. Its name is derived from the location in northwest Athens, which was named after the hero Academus, where Plato met with other philosophers and students. There have been various academies that have played a role in the history of philosophy of religion and theology. The most well known is the Florentine Academy, a fifteenth-century center for Christian Platonism.

ACCESSIBILITY. In analytic philosophy in the twentieth century, much attention was given to accessibility relations. Is our access to the surrounding world immediate and direct or indirect and mediated by sensations? Bertrand Russell identified two significant modes of accessibility: one may have access to something either by *acquaintance* (experiential awareness) or *description*. In philosophy of religion, the question is often addressed of whether

God or the sacred may be directly experienced or perceived or may only be known descriptively or via metaphorical and analogical descriptions.

ACCIDIE. Also written as *acedia.* A state that inhibits pleasure and causes one to reject life. One of the Seven Deadly Sins. Often translated as sloth, *accidie* historically refers to a very different concept. Athanasius called it the "noon day demon" (cf. Psalm 91:6), and Thomas of Aquinas referred to it as the torpor of spirit that prevents one from doing any good works (*Summa Theologiae,* IIa 35.1). According to Aquinas and other medieval Christians, we are surrounded by abundant reasons for joy. Thus, *accidie* is the intentional refusal of joy as opposed to "sloth," which today may refer simply to being lazy or negligent.

ACOSMISM. From the Greek *a* + *kosmos,* meaning "not world." Hegel coined the term in referring to Spinoza's thought, which in Hegel's (erroneous) interpretation is that the world is unreal and only God exists. This interpretation, however, would fit better as a description of the pantheism of the Hindu philosopher Shankara.

ACTION AT A DISTANCE. A causal relationship between two objects or events that are not contiguous or in spatial contact. The denial of action at a distance vexed modern accounts of the mind-body relationship, for if the mind is not spatial, it cannot causally affect spatial objects like the body, for the two are not in spatial proximity. Contemporary physics no longer posits spatial contiguity as a necessary condition for causation. Classical theism posits God as omnipresent and thus not distant from the cosmos with respect to causation. While God is thereby believed to be present at all places in terms of causally sustaining all spatial objects, God is not thereby considered to be spatial.

ACTS AND OMISSIONS DOCTRINE. At the heart of deontological ethics and in contrast to act-consequentialism, the acts and omissions doctrine asserts that an act has a greater moral significance than a failure to act (that is, an omission). Hence, killing someone would be worse than letting someone die. Those upholding a form of utilitarianism tend to discount such a distinction. For utilitarians, it is often the case that failing to rescue someone is the moral equivalent of killing that person.

ACTUALITY AND POTENTIALITY. A dichotomy originally introduced in Aristotle's *Metaphysics* concerning topics of substance and matter that was later adopted into theology by thinkers such as St. Thomas of Aquinas. In Thomism,

God is described as pure act: an eternal, immutable, supremely excellent being. God has no unrealized potentiality. Other forms of theism that see God as temporal and subject to change allow for divine potentiality. Some attention is given to potentiality and actuality in the moral debate over abortion. Some philosophers contend that at early stages of fetal development there is a potential but not actual person.

ACTUS PURUS. For Thomists, God is *actus purus*, in the sense that God is pure act, fully complete, and without potentiality. On this view, God's action in creation and revelation unfolds temporally and successively, but this is due to God's supreme, nontemporal will and nature.

AD INFINITUM. A series is ad infinitum if it is without end. The concept of the infinite plays an important role in arguments for the existence of God. Cosmological arguments frequently assert the impossibility of there being an infinite, actual series, but allow for potential, yet never complete infinites. In the latter case, there could be, in principle, a calculator that begins adding numbers, one per second, from now on ad infinitum, but it would never complete the series and reach the greatest possible number. Some philosophers believe there could never be such a complete, infinite series as in the children's limerick:

Big fleas have little fleas,
Upon their backs to bite 'em.
While little fleas have lesser fleas,
And so on ad infinitum.

ADIAPHORON. Greek, "indifferent." That which is morally indifferent, neither morally required nor prohibited, or, more specifically, that which is not explicitly required for the maintenance of orthodox faith but arguably could be permissible. During the Reformation, the Adiaphorists were the Protestants who sided with Melanchthon in believing that the Catholic sacraments of confirmation and veneration of saints, although without scriptural warrant, should be allowed for the sake of maintaining the unity of the church and would not endanger the believer's soul. The Adiaphorists were opposed by the Flacianists, stricter Protestants who sided with Matthias Flacius in believing that anything that was not explicitly allowed in the Scriptures was forbidden.

ADOPTIONISM. Rather than considering Jesus Christ to be the human incarnation of the second member of the trinity, adoptionists believe that Jesus was a human being who was designated by God as a divine agent or presence on earth. In this unorthodox theology, Jesus' sonship with God the Father has been seen in terms of Jesus' development of "God consciousness," a moral and spiritual unity with God. Functional Christologies

AESTHETICS

resemble adoptionism; Christ is human and divine insofar as Christ functions as God in the world, revealing to all followers God the Father. On this view, Jesus' human person and life is adopted by God to represent or embody the Father's love and character in creation.

ADVAITA VEDANTA. Sanskrit, "nonduality" + "end of the Vedas." One of the main schools of thought within Orthodox Hinduism, *Advaita Vedanta* claims that *Brahman* (God or the life-force) and *atman* (the soul) are "not two." Shankara (c. 788–c. 820 CE) was its leading proponent. Hinduism includes substantial teachings and philosophy other than Advaita, but the Advaita tradition has received the most philosophical attention in the West. *See also* VEDANTA.

ADVENTITIOUS. An idea or concept is adventitious when it comes to a person from an external source. Descartes argued that his idea of God as a perfect reality had to have its source in God rather than for it to have been created by him, an imperfect, finite being. If Descartes is correct, then some concepts derive their meaning and origin from an external reality. If the concept of God is adventitious, it would be akin to the concept of sunburn: you cannot have a sunburn unless the burn was somehow caused by the sun.

AENESIDEMUS OF CNOSSOS (1st century BCE). A Greek skeptical philosopher, Aenesidemus is most famous for his Ten Tropes (*tropoi*) or Modes of Skepticism. These ten tropes consist of equally defensible but inconsistent claims about facts. Aenesidemus broke from the Academy (while it was under Philo of Larissa) and defended Pyrrhonism. His *Pyrrhonian Discourses* influenced Sextus Empiricus.

AESTHETICS. Originally from the Greek, meaning "sensations," and coined first as referring to art in the eighteenth century by the German philosopher, Alexander Baumgarten, from "*ästhetisch*." Aesthetics includes philosophy of art, a study of beauty and ugliness, and reflection on the emotive features of objects or events; e.g., the elegant gesture or the melancholy and wistful storm. Philosophers and theologians have sometimes argued for the congruence of beauty and morality (Platonists), but others separate them (some Kierkegaardians). Religious experiences have been likened to the aesthetics of the sublime. A range of themes in philosophical aesthetics have a bearing in philosophy of religion: when does the meaning of a work of art or a passage in scripture depend upon the intention of the artist or writer? Is there *a test of time* that can be used in both art and religion as a mark of authenticity, truth, or value? What is the imagination? Does the imagination play a parallel role in creating art and in religious thought?

7

AFRICAN PHILOSOPHY. Today, this term covers a host of distinct philosophical traditions, which could be variously categorized as theistic, polytheist, panpsychic, pantheist, and materialist. The concept of "Africa" as a united continent is itself a problematic category, for while it may reflect a European classification and thus a colonial point of view, it may also reflect a pan-African point of view that marks the postcolonial era. Philosophers of religion in the twentieth and twenty-first century have addressed some of the following ideas in an African context: the concept of "religion," the relationship between the divine and nature, reverence of ancestors, the concept of "race," authenticity (is there an *essential* African point of view? Is colonial African philosophy inauthentic? When is philosophy postcolonial?), the moral and religious significance of future generations, the ethics of famine relief, the relationship between the individual and community, slavery, repentance, and duties of reparation.

AFTERLIFE. *See* **LIFE AFTER DEATH.**

AGAPĒ. Greek, "love." An important concept in Christian ethics, agape is usually defined as unconditional fraternal or filial love and set in opposition to *eros*, or sexual love. Kant called it "practical love." The corresponding word in Latin is *caritas*, which is generally translated as "charity." Originally, however, the term referred to the Christian "love-feast," a meal related to the Eucharist and designed to celebrate and promote Christian solidarity. Agapeistic love is thought of as unconditional and not dependent on the passing, contingent qualities of persons. Twentieth-century poet William Butler Yeats playfully observed the difficult and perhaps divine quality of such love: "Only God, my dear, could love you for yourself alone, And not for your yellow hair." One of the more sustained defenses of agape is the two volume work, *Eros and Agape* by the Swedish Protestant theologian Anders Nygren (published first in Sweden, 1930–1936).

AGATHOLOGY. Theories of the good, from the Greek *agathos* (good) and *logos* (word).

AGATHON. Greek, "the good." When applied to human beings, it implies virtue. Aristotle referred to it as that which fulfilled a person's *telos*, that is, one's purpose or end.

AGATHOS. *See* **AGATHON.**

AGNOSTICISM. From the Greek *a* + *ginoskein*, meaning "to not know." An agnostic about God is someone who claims not to know whether or not God exists. A more radical form of agnosticism claims that *no one* knows whether or not God exists. The latter claim is more ambitious because it entails that, if there is a God, not even God knows that God exists. In the twentieth century some argued that agnosticism amounts to a practiced form of atheism, but while some agnostics might be deemed atheists or non-theists insofar as their lives are not informed by theistic convictions, an agnostic (unlike some atheists) may live as though the existence of God is a bona fide possibility. An agnostic may even engage in theistic practices (such as prayer and worship) on the grounds that if God exists such practices have great value.

AKRASIA. Greek, "without power." *Akrasia* refers to weakness of the will. One has *akrasia* when one knows an action is morally required but lacks the will power or resolve to perform the act. People who knowingly do what they sincerely believe to be wrong also have *akrasia* insofar as they lack the power to resist wrongdoing. Socrates, Plato, Aristotle, as well as rationalists like Descartes denied *akrasia*, but a natural interpretation of Romans 7:14–25 gives reason to believe St. Paul affirmed *akrasia* as a very real, personal weakness.

AL-FARABI, ABU NASR (or Abunaser) (c. 870–950). An important contributor to the Baghdad School, he sought to reconcile Platonic and Aristotelian philosophy with Islamic faith. Among several arguments for the existence of God, he developed an elegant cosmological argument to infer the existence of God as a necessary being based on the contingency of the cosmos. He thought that the world was without origin, though it always has and always will depend on its Creator. He contended that intellectual perfection is a religious goal. Al-Farabi gave a central place to logic in his work and developed a robust concept of the proper role of humans: to live cooperatively in community, cultivating a life of knowing. His chief works include *On the Principles of the Views of the Inhabitants of the Excellent State* or *The Ideal City*, *Commentary on Aristotle*, *Philosophy of Plato and Aristotle*, *Short Commentary on Aristotle's Prior Analytics*, and *The Fusul al-Madani*, *Aphorisms of Statesman of al-Farabi*. Al-Farabi is sometimes referred to as the "Second Teacher" in Arabic tradition, Aristotle being the "First Teacher."

AL-GHAZALI, ABU HAMID MUHAMMAD (1058–1111). An Islamic intellectual opposed to what he saw as the errors of philosophical reasoning about religion in the work of Al-Farabi and Avicenna, al-Ghazali promoted religious faith and stressed the importance of a mystical awareness of God over against rationalist philosophy. He held that the Qur'an has an authority for Muslims that supersedes independent philosophical inquiry. Al-Ghazali also believed that the cosmos was created in time ex nihilo by God. His chief works include *The Aims of Philosophers, The Incoherence of the Philosophers, The Standard Measure of Knowledge in the Art of Logic, The Just Balance, The Revival of the Religious Sciences, Deliverer from Error,* and *The Beginning of Guidance.*

ALBERTUS MAGNUS, St. (a.k.a. Albert the Great) (c. 1200–1280). Born in Bavaria, Albertus taught at the University of Paris (where Thomas of Aquinas was his student) and at Cologne. He had a complementary view about the role of philosophy in theology, drawing upon Aristotle in his philosophical theology as well as Neoplatonism. He also had a high view of empirical inquiry. While maintaining that God's nature cannot be known directly and that we cannot prove that the world had a beginning in time, he developed several arguments for the belief that God exists as the necessarily existing Creator of the cosmos (God's essence and existence are identical). His chief works include *Summa Theologiae, Commentary on the Sentences of Peter Lombard* (1240–1249), *Handbook on Creatures* (1240–1243), *Commentary on the Pseudo-Dionysius* (1248–1254), *On the Unity of the Intellect* (c. 1256), and an unfinished *Handbook of Theology* (1270–1280).

ALEXANDER, SAMUEL (1859–1938). Alexander advanced a naturalist, scientifically informed view of nature in which the mind arises as an emergent entity. A Jewish philosopher (the first Jew ever to be appointed as a fellow at Oxford University; the year was 1882) who described Spinoza as being a great influence, Alexander thought of God as emerging from natural cosmic forces. His chief works include *Moral Order and Progress* (1889), *Space, Time, and Deity* (1920), *Spinoza and Time* (1921), *Art and Instinct* (1927), *Beauty and Other Forms of Value* (1993), and *Philosophical and Literary Pieces* (ed. J. Laird, 1939).

ALEXANDRIAN SCHOOL (310 BCE–642 CE). A Platonic institute that included Hierocles, Hermias, Hypatia, John Philoponus, and Olypiodorus. Two of the most prominent early theologians to flourish in Alexandria were Clement of Alexandria (150–215) and Origen (185–254). Both developed a theology of creation that gave a central role to redemption.

ALIENATION. *See* **MAX WEBER.**

ALLAH. Arabic for "God." *See also* ISLAM.

ALLEGORY. An allegory is an extended metaphor. An allegorical reading of scripture was promoted by the Alexandrian

School in order to deal with problems (from the perspective of Greek philosophy) such as anthropomorphic descriptions of God. Philo of Alexandria promoted an extensive allegorization of the Hebrew Bible. One of the obstacles Augustine faced when he was deciding whether to convert to Christianity was the literal reading of the Old Testament. The realization that many (though not all) biblical narratives may be read as allegories brought him closer to the faith that he finally accepted. Later, in response to ecclesiastical abuses, Protestant reformers such as Luther, Melanchthon, and Calvin rejected allegorical readings of scripture as subjective and unreliable.

ALTRUISM. From the Latin *alter,* meaning "the other." An altruistic act is one that is done for the sake of the other or for the good of the other. Some philosophers have argued that all motives are, at base, self-interested, even acts of altruism. Do people aid others only when it gives them personal satisfaction? One reply is that a person would not receive satisfaction from acting altruistically unless she believed that seeking the good of others was good in itself and not merely good because it made her feel satisfied or happy.

AMBROSE, St. (c. 340–97 CE). A skilled Roman administrator and statesman, Ambrose became Bishop of Milan in 374 and remained in the position until his death. He is considered to be one of the four original "doctors of the church" along with Augustine, Jerome, and Gregory the Great. Ambrose was an accomplished orator and his sermons profoundly influenced the young Augustine, whom he baptized in 387.

AMOR FATI. Latin, "love of fate." The willing love or acceptance of one's fate in life. The expression was used frequently by Friedrich Nietzsche to favorably describe the attitude of one who sees all events as part of one's destiny and affirms them all, including any suffering, as facts integral to one's identity rather than as objects of deep regret or remorse. *Amor Fati* is related to Nietzsche's myth of the eternal return: one must live one's life as if one would willingly live that exact same life again. Christian accounts of redemption sometime incorporate an affirmation of the past—even with its sin—insofar as such a past provided the occasion for redemption and great good. But Christian teaching about sin and repentance also promotes the idea that past sins are to be the object of regret and remorse, not affirmation.

AMOUR DE SOI. French, meaning "self-love." One of two forms of self-love Jean-Jacques Rousseau describes in *Emile* (*On Education*), which he characterizes as a natural, healthy form of self-love that is independent of how we relate to others. The other form of self-love, *amour propre*, does depend upon comparing oneself to others and the perception of superiority, which Rousseau considered negative and unnatural. How we ought to view ourselves—either independently or as compared with others—has been a large topic of interest in philosophy of religion (for an example, *see* HUMILITY). Also, Christian theologians have struggled to agree upon what they deem as ordinate as opposed to excessive self-love. Is it permissible or commendable to love God because, in part, one desires the benefits or blessings that are generated by such love? Or should one love God regardless of whether any personal benefits are offered?

ANALOGY. From the Greek *ana* + *logos*, meaning "according to ratio / proportion." A rhetorical device used to relate two things by virtue of a similarity or resemblance between them. When "the Lord" is described as being a shepherd (Psalm 23), this implies that the Lord has certain attributes comparable to those of a shepherd (e.g., he exercises vigilant care).

As set forth by St. Thomas of Aquinas, analogy is a use of language distinct from either the univocal or the equivocal. Equivocal language uses a word in such a way that it has different meanings in different contexts, e.g., "I'm going to the bank" illustrates an equivocal use of the word "bank"—for, given the sentence's context, the word may either mean I'm going to a river bank or a financial bank. Conversely, univocal language uses a word in such a way that it has the same meaning in multiple contexts, e.g., "A rose is a flower" and "That red rose has thorns" shows a univocal use of "rose."

Analogous language uses a word so that its meaning is related to that of the same word in other contexts, in a manner neither entirely different nor entirely the same. For example, when one says, "Black clothes are hot," the meaning of the word "hot" is not the same as when one says, "The fire is hot." Black clothes do not generate heat, but the meaning is related: on sunny days black clothes can make one feel hot, just as a fire can. Aquinas suggested analogy as a solution to the problem of how our language applies to God, since both other types of usage seemed problematic: if our statements about God were univocal it would degrade God to the level of other temporal objects, while if equivocal, our statements about God would be useless. *See also* RELIGIOUS LANGUAGE.

ANALYTIC PHILOSOPHY. A school of philosophy emphasizing conceptual clarity, greatly influenced and developed by the work of G. E. Moore and Bertrand Russell. Today what counts as analytic philosophy is not limited to conceptual analysis, but may include phenomenology and broad appeals to experience and intuition. In the late twentieth century some distinguished analytic philosophy of religion (represented by Alvin Plantinga and Richard Swinburne) has been recognized as using a different model of philosophy than continental philosophy of religion (represented by Jean-Luc Marion and John Caputo).

ANALYTIC STATEMENTS. Propositions whose denial involve a contradiction; for example, "A square has four right angles." The universal consistency of an analytic statement is most often due to its definitional nature, that is, it does not add anything new but rather describes the subject involved. A controversial topic relevant to philosophers of religion is whether or not the statement, "God is good," is analytic.

ANAXAGORAS (499–422 BCE). An ancient Greek philosopher and early proponent of viewing nature as evolving. He thought that small particles create the generation and destruction of gross, macro-bodies like animals and plants. His chief work is *On Nature*, which only survives in fragments.

ANAXIMANDER (610–547 BCE). An ancient Greek philosopher who taught that the cosmos receives its definition and life from that which is boundless and indeterminate (the *apeiron*).

ANAXIMENES (588–524 BCE). An ancient Greek philosopher, credited with viewing air as the fundamental, divine, cosmic principle. He is one of the major pre-Socratic thinkers who gave a central role to philosophy of the natural world.

ANGELS. From the Greek *angelos*, meaning "messenger." Angels have played an important role in the scriptures of Judaism, Christianity, and Islam. Angels are generally understood as spiritual beings created by God; they are immortal and superior to humans in both knowledge of the divine and goodness. The Hebrew word for angel in the Bible is *mal'ak*, which also means messenger, but it was not until the Hellenistic period of Judaism that a developed "angelology" began to emerge in which angels were differentiated from human messengers and God.

Angels serve manifold purposes: they are God's heavenly court, standing in adoration around God's throne throughout eternity; they convey commands and guidance to God's human servants; and, according to Thomas of Aquinas, each baptized soul acquires one "guardian angel," an image which has become engrained in popular culture over the years. According to Pseudo-Dionysius the Areopagite, there are nine distinct choirs of angels, namely (in descending order of rank) seraphim, cherubim, thrones, dominions, virtues, powers, principalities, archangels, and angels. It is commonly believed that fallen angels, including

Lucifer (Satan), were expelled from heaven by God because of rebellion, and that they now control the powers of evil and reside in hell. Other than Satan, there are only four angels named in the Bible (Michael, Gabriel, Raphael, and Uriel), two of whom are only in the apocryphal books of Tobit and Enoch. Muslims believe that the Qur'an itself was revealed to Muhammad by the angel Jibril (Gabriel).

The existence of angels has been advanced on the basis of scriptural authority, experiential testimony (ostensibly credible narratives of the appearance of angels), and an appeal to the principle of plenitude. According to the latter, God is essentially good and of limitless power. The principle of plenitude is that the very nature of goodness is self-diffusive (its character is generative and productive rather than insular) and variety is itself good (*bonum variationis*). Given these premises, it has been argued that God would create all manner of different orders of good beings. Such beings could very well include incorporeal agents, hence angels.

ANGST. A term frequently used by existentialists referring to the anxiety one encounters in the face of death or meaninglessness (*see* ABSURD). Kierkegaard focused on anxiety or dread as a sign of our alienation from God.

ANIMA MUNDI. Latin, "world-soul." The idea, originating in Plato's *Timaeus*, that the world is comprised of a soul or spirit and functions as a living organism.

ANIMALS. Historically, animals have functioned in world religions as symbols of the divine, sacred, or even that which is evil; they have been used as sacrifices to the divine; they have been seen as part of karmic reincarnation whereby a soul might transmigrate, at one time enduring a human and then a nonhuman life; they have also been identified as sacred, protected beings who should not be killed or consumed as food. Some traditional indigenous religions held a sacred place for the very animals they hunted, such as the buffalo for the Sioux.

Religions take different views on animals and how they ought to be treated. Christianity's forerunner in advocating kindness to animals is St. Francis of Assisi, the patron saint of animals. Some Christian churches have special services for the blessings of animals where families bring in their pets for blessing. Pope John Paul II said, "Animals possess a soul and men must love and feel solidarity with our smaller brethren . . . [they are] the fruit of the creative action of the Holy Spirit and merit respect . . . [they are] as near to God as men are."

Most religions, Christianity and Islam for example, say that because animals are God's creatures, they deserve respect and kindness; yet while there are Christian advocates for vegetarianism, generally the Christian tradition holds that it is

14

morally and even divinely permissible to raise and eat animals. Judaism and Christianity historically recognized animals in terms of distinct species (as opposed to coming from a common origin, à la Darwin). While this may be in tension with contemporary biology, it was also part of a general theology that saw intrinsic value in diversity or multiplicity.

Some religions consider certain animals sacred, such as the cow in Hinduism or the dove in Christianity. Many Buddhists and Hindus are vegetarians out of respect for animals. Many Jains wear cloths over their mouths so they can avoid breathing in (and thereby killing) any living organisms. Some Native American traditions believe that when humans pick their totem animal—an animal that possesses traits similar to the person—that animal gains a spiritual or religious significance.

The relationship of humans and non-human animals has occupied a great deal of philosophy of religion since Darwin in the nineteenth century and the modern environmental movement, which, in the late twentieth century, challenged religious traditions to practice greater stewardship over the natural world.

ANIMISM. From the Latin *anima* ("soul"), animism is the belief that animals, plants, and even non-living entities have souls or spirits. It has often been used to refer to indigenous religions, although some scholars find it a pejorative gloss. There is, however, nothing intrinsically derogatory about a worldview that recognizes spirit or experience as a widespread component in the physical world. Early twenty-first century philosophers have re-engaged the prospects of a pan-psychist view of reality, the view that experience or the mental is laced throughout what is typically assumed to be an inanimate world. Galen Strawson is a contemporary defender of pan-psychism.

ANOMIE. Broken limits. An anomic person is one who is in a state without norms or rules. In some religions, suicide is considered an anomic act for it breaks the foundational norm of self-preservation and integrity.

ANONYMOUS CHRISTIAN. *See* **KARL RAHNER.**

ANSCOMBE, GERTRUDE ELIZABETH MARGARET (1919–2001). An early follower of Wittgenstein. Along with Alistair MacIntyre she helped stimulate a revival of virtue theory in the late twentieth century. The use of the term "consequentialism" in analytic philosophy comes from one of her articles, "Modern Moral Philosophy" (1958). She converted to Roman Catholicism while an undergraduate student and was not afraid to publicly defend her faith (she was arrested twice for protesting in front of abortion clinics). Anscombe famously opposed C. S. Lewis in a debate on his theistic argument based on reason. Her chief works include *Intention* (1957), *An Introduction to Wittgenstein's* Tractatus (1959), *Three Philosophers* (1961, with P. T. Geach, on Aristotle, Aquinas, and Frege), *Causality and Determination* (1971), *Times, Beginnings and Causes* (1975), *The Collected Philosophical Papers of G. E. M. Anscombe (3 vols.)*: (1) *From Parmenides to Wittgenstein,* (2) *Metaphysics and the Philosophy of Mind,* (3) *Ethics, Religion and Politics* (1981), and *Human Life, Action and Ethics: Essays* (2005).

ANSELM OF CANTERBURY, St. (1033–1109). He is most famous for his ontological argument for the existence of God based on the idea that God is that than which nothing greater can be thought or conceived (*aliquid quo nihil maius cogitari potest*). Subsequent philosophy of God that gives a central role to God's unsurpassable excellence is often termed "Anselmian."

Anselm articulated and defended a view of the atonement in which human sin creates a debt to God that cannot be repaid except through the incarnation and vicarious suffering of the perfect God-Man, Jesus Christ. As both God and man, Jesus is able to offer to God (the Father) a perfect sacrifice to atone for the sins of the world. Anselm was appointed as the Archbishop of Canterbury in 1093. He is the author of *Proslogion, Monologion,*

De Grammatico, On Truth, and *Why the God-Man?*

ANTHROPOCENTRISM. From the Greek *anthropos* + *kentron,* "human being" + "center." The view that humans are the central and most important form of life in the universe. The term "anthropocentrism" is sometimes used pejoratively. Humanism is a more positive term for those who believe humans are of foundational ethical importance.

ANTHROPOMORPHISM. From the Greek *anthropos* + *morphe,* "human being" + "form." In the form of a human being; the taking on of human characteristics by a nonhuman entity. The claim that a viewpoint is anthropomorphic implies that the attribution of human properties is in some sense problematic or, at best, metaphorical. Anthropomorphism is discussed in relation to the philosophy of God (is it anthropomorphic to think of God as a person?) and of nonhuman animals (is it a mere human projection to think some nonhuman animals are persons?).

ANTI-REALISM. Also called non-realism. A strong version in Christian theology holds that "God" is not a term that is referential to a being that may or may not exist. These anti-realists treat religious anguage about God as expressive of attitudes (e.g., to profess belief in God is to be understood as professing to practice compassion) rather than making propositional claims about reality.

ANTI-SEMITISM. Disdain, denigration, or disrespect of Jews. Some early Christian philosophers such as Justin Martyr explicitly promoted the credibility of Christian faith while seeking to discredit Judaism, arguing that Christians were "the true Israel" and the inheritors of divine revelation and beatitude. With the establishment of Christianity in the late Roman Empire and Medieval Europe, Jews were excluded from philosophical and theological institutions. Jews were allowed (in places) to train in law and medicine, but not theology in European universities. Christian-Jewish dialogue was effectively annihilated in the late fifteenth century with the expulsion of Jews from Spain (in the fourteenth century Jews had been expelled from England). Technically, anti-semitism refers to the Jewish race, while anti-Jewish refers to the religion of the Jews; however, the terms are frequently used interchangeably.

ANTI-THEODICY. Coined by Zachary Braiterman in *(God) After Auschwitz* (1998), the term "anti-theodicy" refers to a particular protesting response to the problem of evil that may be found in biblical and post-Holocaust Jewish thought that intentionally refuses to explore the relationship between God, evil, and suffering. An anti-theodicy operates in opposition to a theodicy, which attempts to reconcile belief in an omnipotent, omniscient, and benevolent God given the magnitude of evil and suffering in the world. By refusing to justify the relationship between God and evil, the author of an anti-theodicy places full blame on God for the horrendous evils she may experience in her life. This protest must arise from an individual's love for God and belief in the existence of a relationship between God and evil. Faith gives rise to and sustains this protest that may be raised on account of one's individual suffering, such as in the biblical book of Job, or collective suffering, examples of which are present in Elie Wiesel's works, including *Night* (1958), *The Trial of God* (1979), and *Ani Maamin: A Song Lost and Found Again* (1973).

ANTICHRIST. The "antichrist" often is referred to in an eschatological fashion and is treated as synonymous with the devil. In the New Testament, however, the antichrist is not someone who attempts to assume the place of Christ, but rather someone who turns *against* Christ. During the Reformation, the Protestants, especially Wycliffe and Luther, vehemently attacked the papacy as the antichrist. Today, the term's primary usage is to personify evil.

ANTINOMIANISM. From Greek *anti* + *nomos*, meaning "against law." The view that Christians who are saved by grace are no longer subject to law.

ANTINOMY. An antinomy is created by two arguments for contrary positions. Immanuel Kant, in his *Critique of Reason*, famously advanced a series of antimonies, for example, arguing that the world did and did not have a beginning. Kant developed antinomies as part of a demonstration of the failure of metaphysical reasoning. According to Kant, metaphysics leads us to embrace incompatible positions.

APATHY. From the Greek *a* + *pathos*, meaning "privation of passion." Often used synonymously with *indifference*. In some schools of Greek philosophy, such as stoicism, apathy is considered a valued state of serene indifference or detachment. Others, such as Descartes, believed apathy, i.e., the freedom of indifference, to be a sorry or even blameworthy state, since one is not motivated toward any action.

APEIRON. Greek, "boundless." The fundamental substance in Anaximander's cosmological theory, which is indestructible, unlimited, and the origin of everything in the cosmos.

APOCALYPSE. From the Greek *apoka lyptein,* meaning "disclosure, revelation unveiling." Strictly speaking it refers to a literary genre wherein heavenly secrets are disclosed or the events of the end of the world are described (for example, the biblical books of *Daniel* and *Revelation*). In contemporary culture it is often used to refer to the imminent end of the world. Apocalyptic literature often includes a radical critique of the cultural and religious status quo, especially of the political elites.

APOCATASTASIS. Greek, "to set up again." The idea that while those creatures who choose evil will perish, at the end of time the creation itself will be restored. Origen favored this theology, but it was not accepted by the church (the Council of Constantinople in 553 rejected Origen's thesis).

APOCRYPHA. From the Greek *apokruphos,* meaning "hidden, unknown." Extrabiblical literature such as the books of *Tobit* and *1 Maccabees* that were present in the Septuagint and the Vulgate but not the Hebrew Bible are considered to be apocryphal.

APOLLINARIANISM. A fourth-century teaching (later condemned as unorthodox) that the incarnation involved the *logos* assuming a human body. Apollinarian Christologies did not acknowledge the full humanity of Jesus Christ.

APOLOGETICS. A defense of the truth of a position or religion. For Christians, apologetics names the practice of setting forth reasons for accepting the Christian faith.

APOLOGY. A defense. The classic model is Socrates' defense of himself in Plato's *Apology*. A well-known apology in the nineteenth century is John Henry Newman's *Apologia pro Vita Sua* (1865–1866).

APOPHATIC THEOLOGY. Also known as negative theology, apophatic theology emphasizes God's radical transcendence to the effect that only negative properties may be attributed to God. God is not material, not spatial, not temporal, not finite, and so on. Some advocates of apophatic theology go so far as to claim that even "existence" cannot be attributed to God; on this view, God may be said to be beyond existence or being. *See also* RELIGIOUS LANGUAGE.

APOSTASY. From the Greek *apostasia*, meaning "a defection." Traditionally an apostate is someone who once professed a traditional religious faith but has since

renounced it. The term is pejorative, implying infidelity, betrayal, or a blameworthy faithlessness. For instance, it would be hyperbolic or misleading to call someone an apostate who was a Christian in her youth, but rejected Christian faith in college in the process of adopting Zen Buddhism.

AQUINAS, St. THOMAS OF (1225–1274). The most influential medieval philosopher and theologian who shaped much (but not all) of Roman Catholic philosophy and theology. He refined the Neoplatonic-influenced Christianity of Augustine by way of Aristotle. So, rather than Augustine's clear distinction of soul and body, Aquinas argued that the soul is the form of the body. Although Aquinas affirmed an individual afterlife, he asserted that the soul and body constituted a unity in this life (and also in the afterlife, after the resurrection of the body). The idea that the soul is the form of the body is called hylomorphism.

Although Aquinas thought that we cannot directly grasp God's essence, he held that there were five compelling arguments to justify the belief that God exists (sometimes called "the five ways") and that God may be known through analogy. Aquinas developed an extensive philosophy of the divine attributes, the incarnation and the trinity, human action and virtues, the atonement, sacraments, the church, history, and politics. His chief works include *On Being and Essence*

(1242–1243), *On Truth* (1256–1259), *On Potency* (1259–1263), *Summa Contra Gentiles* (1259–1263), *On the Divine Names* (1261), *On Evil* (1263–1268), *Summa Theologica* (1265–1272), *On the Eternity of the World* (1270), *On Separate Substances* (1271) and numerous commentaries on works of Aristotle. Aquinas' prolific work amounts to the greatest repository of medieval philosophy by a single thinker.

ARENDT, HANNAH (1906–1975). Jewish political theorist from Germany. She studied under Heidegger and Jaspers and developed a profound critique of social and political injustice in the twentieth century. Her analysis of cruelty in *The Origins of Totalitarianism* (1951), *The Human Condition* (1958), and *On Violence* (1970) build a strong case for a nonviolent democratic culture.

ARETĒ. Greek, "excellence, virtue, goodness." The qualities that constitute a good human being: wisdom (*phronēsis*), moderation (*sōphrosynē*), courage (*andreia*), justice (*dikaiodikaosynē*), etc. Discussion of these virtues was the core of classical Greek ethics and philosophy. Plato, famously, maintained the unity of the virtues. If one lacks the virtue of wisdom, for example, one cannot be said to have the virtue of courage. Some modern virtue theorists question this thesis and allow for a fragmentation of virtues.

Historically virtue theory addresses such questions as: Can virtue be taught? Is there a difference between moral and intellectual virtues? For example, are there significant differences between intellectual courage and courage involving physical action such as bravery on a battlefield? Can utilitarianism allow for the good of virtues? How do religious or secular worldviews inform the theory of virtues? For example, in religions that involve a Creator, it seems that gratitude for the creation is a virtue, whereas in worldviews with no Creator such gratitude would not be a virtue.

ARIANISM / ARIAN HERESY. The belief (espoused by Arius, the Presbyter of Alexandria (256–336 CE), from whom the heresy takes its name) that the Father and the Son (Jesus) are *not* of the same substance. Arianism has the effect of subordinating the Son to the Father. This view was deemed heretical at the Council of Nicaea in 325 CE. In the context of this disagreement, the doctrine of the trinity was formulated. The orthodox view was established as *homoousias*: the three persons of the trinity are of the same substance (*ousia*). *See also* ATHANASIUS.

ARIUS. *See* **ARIANISM / ARIAN HERESY.**

ARISTOTLE (384–322 BCE). Aristotle and Plato are the two most influential ncient philosophers of European philosophy and theology until the eighteenth century and perhaps even to the twentieth century. Aristotle was Plato's student for nearly 20 years. Aristotle had a deep background in medicine and biology, and he devoted much of his work to a philosophy of the natural world. His affirmation of God as pure thought and creator of a world without beginning had a major impact on subsequent cosmology. His understanding of human nature may prohibit individual life after death, though commentators disagree. His account of reason, passion, desire, logic, art, and wisdom were of enormous importance to late medieval thinkers and to the twentieth-century revival of Thomism and virtue theory. Bertrand Russell, in *History of Western Philosophy* (1945), provocatively described Aristotelianism as Platonism purified by common sense. The works attributed to Aristotle include *Categories, On Interpretation, the Prior and Posterior Analytics, Topics, On Sophistical Refutations, Physics, On the Heavens, On Generation and Corruption, Meteorology, History of Animals, On the Parts of Animals, On the Movement of Animals, On the Soul, Parva Naturalia, The Metaphysics, Nicomachean Ethics, Magna Moralia, Eudemian Ethics, Politics, Constitution of Athens, Rhetoric,* and *Poetics.* In modern philosophy of religion Aristotle's work on the virtues, human nature, and his realism have had a salient role. *See also* PHILOSOPHER, THE.

ARNAULD, ANTOINE (1612–1694). A French philosophical theologian who (like Pascal) defended Jansenism. He was also an important critic of Descartes. He is the author of *The Art of Thinking* (with Pierre Nicole), which is also known as *Port Royal Logic* (1662), and *Concerning True and False Ideas* (1683).

ASCETICAL THEOLOGY. Reflection on purgation (the *via purgativa*) through a discipline of sensations, desire, and appetites. The Desert Fathers such as St. Anthony set an important example of a holy ascetic life which greatly influenced Augustine and was one of the reasons for his inquiry into the possible truth of Christian teaching. Ascetical theology was of prime importance in early Christian monasteries, especially for the Desert Fathers.

ASCETICISM. The practice of self-discipline, often through self-denial or the mastering of desires (fasting involves control over the desire for food, a vigil involves control over the urge to sleep) for a religious end such as repentance, worship, the cultivation of virtue, or union or communion with God. Asceticism is widespread among religious traditions, theistic and non-theistic. Buddhist ascetic practices are closely linked with the purging of desire and seeing through the illusory nature of ourselves as substantial individual beings.

ASEITY. From the Latin *aseitas,* meaning "from or by oneself (or itself)." A being has aseity if its very nature is existence or if the ground of its existence is part of its essence. In theism, God possesses aseity because God's existence is not derived from any external source.

ATHANASIUS (300?–373). Bishop of Alexandria from 328 onward, Athanasius was a staunch opponent of Arianism and boldly argued that the Father and Son are of the same essence. He advocated a Trinitarian theology popularized as "The Creed of St. Athanasius." His principal works include *Against the Gentiles, On the Incarnation, Orations against the Arians, Apology against the Arians,* and *On Doctrine.*

ATHEISM. From the Greek, meaning "without God." Atheism is the denial that there is a God. Historically, the term achieved currency as a denial of theism, but the term today is broader and is often used as the denial of either a theistic or non-theistic view of God. *See also* AGNOSTICISM.

ATMAN. Sanskrit for "self." In Hindu traditions, *atman* refers to the self or the soul. There are a variety of philosophical schools of thought within Hinduism, which disagree on the relationship between atman and *Brahman* (God or the Ultimate Reality). The *Advaita Vedanta* school of thought supports a strict non-dual perspective, in which atman is Brahman.

ATOMISM. From the Greek *atomos* for indivisible, the view that the material world is composed of indivisible things. The theory, originally developed by Leucippus and Democritus in the fifth century BCE, that all matter is made up of indivisible atoms which are separated by the void. Ancient atomism asserts that there is a smallest piece of matter that cannot be divided. The only characteristics that such atoms have are shape and size. However, the way that atoms are oriented and the way they combine with other atoms also has an effect on the macroscopic scale. Color, sound, smell, taste, and temperature are merely ways that we perceive different atoms interacting.

Ancient atomism had a revival in the seventeenth century with thinkers such as Boyle and Descartes. These philosophers emphasized the mechanical nature of the universe that atomism implies. If all atoms are governed by the same laws, it means that all future locations of atoms are predetermined by their preceding locations. On the assumption that everything that exists is made up of atoms, all events in the past and the future could be derived if all locations and motions of all atoms were known at one given time. Thus, this view results in determinism and is incompatible with free will. While atomism is often deterministic, one can be an atomist and allow for indeterminism.

ATONEMENT, THEORIES OF. Christian theologians have advanced multiple accounts of how God brings about an atonement or at-one-ment with God. A long standing tradition associated with Anselm of Canterbury holds that sinful humanity dishonors God by sin and is subject to punishment. The ultimate punishment for sin is death. Because of humanity's original sin or perpetuation of sin, mere human moral and religious virtue is not able to avoid the deadliness of sin. Only if God becomes incarnate so that the perfect Jesus Christ, fully human and yet fully God, lives a perfect life and then assumes the punishment of sin can there be atonement. If God were simply to cancel the debt or punishment for sin without sacrifice, there would be no honoring of divine justice. Because of Jesus' suffering and death, Jesus' sacrifice is *vicarious*, taking the place of others. On this model, sometimes called the Anselmian or Juridical or Satisfaction theory, Jesus' death is substitutionary.

On a subjectivist or exemplar view of the atonement, Jesus' life, suffering, death, and resurrection constitute atonement between God and creatures when creatures recognize the cost of sin and the outpouring of God's self-sacrificing love in Christ.

Another model, Christus Victor, combines elements of both theories. On this view, Christ's birth, life, teaching, passion, death, and resurrection are to be truly transforming (as affirmed by the subjectivist account) and Christ's work also provides a means by which the penalty of sin can be overcome through the resurrection of the dead. The Christus Victor model thereby holds (with the Anselmian theory) that the atonement involves more than subjectivity, but its emphasis is on Christ's providing a means of overcoming evil (opening the way to an afterlife of redemption) and not providing a sacrifice that placates the Father or substitutes a perfect innocent life for our own in a juridical framework. Swedish theologian Gustaf Aulen (1879–1977) was an important recent proponent of the Christus Victor model. For Eastern Orthodox Christians, the process of atonement is consummated by *theosis*, the transformation of the soul into likeness to or union with God.

ATTRIBUTES, DIVINE. In theism, the chief divine attributes include omnipotence, omniscience, essential goodness, omnipresence, necessary existence or aseity, eternity or everlasting, and simplicity. Attributes that are also represented in theistic tradition include being worthy of worship and obedience, immutability (not subject to change), impassibility (not subject to passion), beauty, and personality. "Personality" is controversial; some classical theists worry that it reflects anthropomorphism, even though traditional

Christians believe the Godhead consists of three persons.

AUGUSTINE, St. (354–430 CE). Augustine Aurelius Augustinus, more familiarly known as Augustine and dignified by the Catholic Church with the twin titles of "saint" and "doctor of the Church," was born in 354 CE in North Africa, and died there in 430 as Bishop of Hippo Regius, a small Roman town in what is now Algeria. He was born to Monica and Patricius, poor but middle-class Roman citizens with high ambitions for their oldest son, which led them to secure the best possible education for him. Augustine, by his own account, profited from this education, and by his early 30s had been appointed official rhetor to the city of Milan, a position which would ordinarily have led to further advancement in the Roman civil service. Unsatisfied, however, he sought a deeper and more meaningful understanding of life and the world, became convinced that Christianity was true, and in 387 was baptized in Milan. He spent the rest of his life in the service of the church as priest and then bishop, preaching and writing on almost every topic of lively intellectual concern at the time. Most of his work—an enormous corpus—survived him (he took good care that it should), and through it he became the single most important influence on Western thought for at least a millennium.

He made significant contributions in at least four areas of thought. The first, in response to the Manicheans, was the appropriation and development of strands of Platonist thought which made possible the defense of an understanding of God as creator of the cosmos out of nothing, and, concomitantly, of evil as lack. The second, against the Donatists, and the pagans, was the elaboration of a doctrine of the church as a peaceful city opposed in its founding and purpose to the violent human city, and yet at the same time, composed of saints and sinners admixed. The third, against the Pelagians, was a defense of the primacy of divine grace over human effort, while not yet denying human freedom. And the fourth was the elaboration of an understanding of what it means to call God triune, which remains largely determinative for the Christian West to this day. Augustine's key works include *The Confessions* (397–401), *On Christian Doctrine* (396–426), *The Enchiridion on Faith, Hope and Love* (421–424), *On the Trinity* (400–416), and *The City of God* (413–426).

AUTHORITY. A term that has both an evaluative and descriptive use. Evaluatively, a person or institution may be said to be authoritative when it is trustworthy and thus worthy of belief and, perhaps, obedience. One may use the term descriptively when referring to a setting in which a person or institution is deemed trustworthy and thus believed to be worthy of belief and obedience, without thereby implying that the authority itself is legitimate. In the history of religion, two of the more significant disputes over authority involve the papacy (Petrine Authority) in Christianity and disputes over the religious authority in succession to Muhammad (Sunni versus Shi'ite traditions in Islam).

AVATAR. A term used in Indian religions to refer to a divine incarnation or manifestation. *See also* HINDUISM.

AVERROËS (a.k.a. Ibn Rushd) (1126–1198). An Arabic Islamic philosopher, born in Andalusia, who developed a rich natural theology with arguments for God's existence. His cosmological argument conceives of the world as God's creation, but not in time. God as the eternal, necessarily existing creator, has always sustained the world in existence. Sometimes thought of as denying the afterlife, Averroës held that there will be a resurrection though this will not consist of a revitalization of our current bodies. Averroës also wrote on a number of important legal-ethical issues, including the guidelines and standards for waging jihad (from the Arabic, meaning "struggle"; this term can be applied in many contexts such as personal struggles against internal evil, verbal arguments, and wars). His works include *Commentaries of Aristotle's Categories, Posterior Analytics, The Physics, On the Heavens, On Generation and Corruption, On the* *Soul, The Short Physical Treatises, Metaphysics, Politics, Rhetoric, The Incoherence of the Incoherence, A Commentary on Plato's Republic, The Middle Commentary on Porphyry's Isagoge, On the Harmony of Religion and Philosophy, The Distinguished Jurist's Primer,* and a medical encyclopedia titled *Generalities.*

AVICENNA, ABU ALI AL-HUSAYN (a.k.a. Ibn Sina) (980–1037). A Persian Islamic philosopher and physician, Avicenna reconciled Aristotelian and Neoplatonic thought with Islamic philosophy. Avicenna defended the belief in an afterlife for individual souls and he argued that, for God, essence and existence are one (the very meaning of God is that which necessarily exists). His works include *The Book of Healing, The Canons of Medicine, Remarks and Admonitions,* an autobiography, *The Life of Ibn Sina,* and many other treatises.

AXIOLOGY. From the Greek *axios* + *logos,* meaning the study or theory of values. Axiology is therefore broader than ethics, for it includes the theory of values that do not directly relate to ethics, such as the value of artistic creativity. Hedonism is the value theory that pleasure and pleasure alone is good. Natural law is the theory of values which locates the value of good of things in their nature.

25

AXIOM. From the Greek for "to think worthy." An axiom is a proposition that is assumed to be true, not being based on the knowledge of other propositions. An axiom may be regarded as intuitively obvious or self-evident, but not justified or demonstrated to be true by other propositions. For example, "everything is itself and not something else."

AYER, ALFRED JULES (1910–1989). In philosophy of religion, Ayer is best known for his argument that religious propositions about God have no cognitive content or meaning because they cannot be verified empirically. Ayer was the chief popular defender of logical positivism. He later thought his theory of meaning was deeply problematic. Just before he died, he reported having an out of body experience, which became a public sensation but did not impact his thinking about religion. His works include *Language, Truth, and Logic* (1936), 2nd ed. (1946), *The Foundations of Empirical Knowledge* (1940), *Philosophical Essays* (1954), *The Problem of Knowledge* (1956), *Philosophy and Language* (1960), *The Concept of a Person* (1963), *The Origins of Pragmatism* (1968), and *Russell and Moore* (1971). *See also* EMPIRICISM and RELIGIOUS LANGUAGE.

B

BACON, FRANCIS (1561–1626). He developed an elegant case for empirical, scientific inquiry that was free from superstition and based on applying inductive reasoning to empirical observations. He warned readers against the ways in which popular fashion can shape one's beliefs. Clear thinking was a religious duty and to become prey to untrustworthy methods was a form of idolatry. He promoted science as a cooperative, communal task motivated by Christian charity. Bacon argued that while some philosophy can lead one away from God, further philosophy will return one to God. His chief works include: *Essays* (first published 1597), *Two Books on the Advancement of Learning* (1605), *The New Organon* (1620), and *The New Atlantis* (1627).

BACON, ROGER (c. 1214–1294). English philosopher who advanced a high view of mathematics and experiential-experimental inquiry. He also believed there was a role for divine, inner illumination. His works include *Opus Maius* (1267), *Opus Minus* (1267), *Opus Tertium* (1267), *Compendium of Studies in Philosophy* (1271), and *Compendium of Studies in Theology* (1292). He is sometimes known as the admirable doctor (Latin: *doctor abmirabalis*).

BAD FAITH. Originally from the French, *mauvaise foi*. A term introduced by Jean-Paul Sartre in *Being and Nothingness* (1943), having to do with the state of lying to oneself, or self-deception. A general description of this concept would be treating oneself as the other, even dissociating oneself from one's own actions, which is abhorrent to Sartre and his view that individuals are a "single project," not divided into parts and certainly not into unknown parts. Christian philosophers such as Merold Westphal have given a central role to exposing cases when believers as well as skeptics are prey to bad faith or self-deception. *See also* FAITH, SELF-DECEPTION.

BAGHDAD SCHOOL. A Muslim center for scholarship, philosophy, and theology

27

established in 832 CE. The Baghdad School also translated the works of Greek philosophers such as Plato, Aristotle, and Plotinus into Arabic.

BAHÁ'Í FAITH. From the Arabic *Bahá*, meaning "glory" or "splendor." A monotheistic religion that teaches the unity of all religions and has a strong humanitarian focus. Bahá'ís believe that God's will has been progressively revealed through a variety of messengers (including Abraham, Krishna, Buddha, Jesus, Muhammad, Zoroaster, and so on), the most recent of whom is Bahá'u'lláh.

The Bahá'í faith emerged out of Shi'a Islam. In 1844, Siyyid `Alí-Muhammad of Shiraz, Iran, claimed to be "the Báb" (Arabic for "the Gate") and announced the coming of a Messianic figure. His followers were persecuted by the Islamic clergy, and the Báb himself was executed in 1850. In 1863, one of the Báb's followers, Mírzá Husayn `Alí Núrí, declared himself to be the messenger foretold by the Báb and took the title Bahá'u'lláh. He was banished to `Akká, an Ottoman penal colony in what is now Israel, where he remained until his death in 1892. Bahá'u'lláh's son, `Abbás Effendi (known as `Abdu'l-Bahá or "Servant of Bahá"), became the next leader of the Bahá'í community, followed by his grandson, Shoghi Effendi.

The Bahá'í faith is now a world religion, with over five million adherents in 247 countries and territories. Bahá'ís are the largest religious minority in Iran and often face persecution from the Islamic majority.

BARTH, KARL (1886–1968). Swiss theologian who stressed the radical otherness of God, the limitations of natural theology, and the revealed sovereignty of the world of God disclosed through scripture. He stressed that a believer's realization of God's truth is the result of grace rather than rational inquiry. His commentary on Romans was heavily influenced by Kierkegaard. Deeply suspicious of natural theology, he emphasized the "otherness of God" and the primacy of the Word of God as revelation. Barth's work (sometimes referred to as neoorthodoxy) is deeply opposed to the liberal theology associated with Rudolf Bultmann whose demythologized Christianity seemed (in contrast) to have little theological content. Barth is the author of *Epistle to the Romans* (1919), *Word of God and Word of Man* (1928), *Anselm* (1931), *Church Dogmatics* 4 vols. (1932–1953), *Credo* (1935), *Dogmatics in Outline* (1947), and *Evangelical Theology: An Introduction* (1962).

BASIL THE GREAT, St. (a.k.a. Basil of Caesarea) (c. 330–379). One of the great fathers of the early Christian church. Basil is the most well known of the "Cappadocian Fathers," a group of church fathers (also including Gregory of Nazianzus and

28

Gregory of Nyssa) who served as bishops and wrote multiple works in the central region of modern Turkey. Basil, the older brother of Gregory of Nyssa, was raised in a prominent Christian family and was sent to Athens to be schooled in rhetoric and the classical tradition. He later devoted himself to Christianity becoming a Christian ascetic, and he founded one of the earliest monasteries. After becoming bishop of Caesarea, Basil became a central figure in combating Arianism and was responsible for appointing anti-Arian bishops including Gregory of Nazianzus and Gregory of Nyssa. Basil's works focus primarily on defining and maintaining orthodoxy as set forth at the Council of Nicaea (325 C.E.) (e.g., *On the Holy Spirit*). His writings on monastic life led to the development of the "Rule of St. Basil," which came to define Eastern monasticism.

BAYES' THEOREM. According to Bayes' theorem,

$$\text{Pr}(h/e) = \frac{\text{Pr}(h) \times \text{Pr}(e/h)}{\text{Pr}(e)}$$

If Pr(e) is not equal to zero, then Pr(h/e)

In English, this says that if *e* is not certainly false, then the probability that *h* is true given that *e* is true is equal to the probability that *h* is true times the probability that *e* is true given that *h* is true divided by the probability that *e* is true.

Bayes' theorem is often used to assess the effect of evidence on a hypothesis. If *h* stands for some hypothesis and *e* stands for a statement reporting a piece of evidence, then Bayes' theorem tells us that the probability that the hypothesis *h* is true given the evidence *e* [Pr(h/e)] depends on three things. First, it depends on how probable *h* is prior to discovering the evidence: the higher Pr(h), the higher Pr(h/e). Second, it depends on how well *h* predicts (or "retrodicts") *e*: the higher Pr(e/h), the higher Pr(h/e). And third, it depends on how surprising the evidence is: the lower Pr(e), the higher Pr(h/e). In short, hypotheses that are initially plausible and successfully yield data that would otherwise not be expected are themselves very probable given that data.

Some philosophers of religion believe that Bayes' theorem is the key to assessing the epistemic status of the "hypothesis" that God exists. Others think that it is often misapplied to issues in philosophy of religion and that it is popular because of a sort of scientism that dominates analytic philosophy. Strangely, both of these views are correct.

BAYLE, PIERRE (1647–1706). Bayle was a skeptic about rationalist philosophy and theology. He defended the use of faith in assenting to fundamental Christian truths, but he was opposed to those who taught that faith or reason could settle disputes between Roman Catholics and Protestants. He defended tolerance with wit. He is the author of *The Historical and Critical Dictionary* (1697, 1702), known for its subversive criticism of human pretensions.

BEAUTY. Beauty is a central object of interest for Platonists and a recurring theme in Platonic forms of Judaism, Christianity, and Islam. Beauty has been defined as an inherent objective property (perfect symmetry) or as a relational property (something is beautiful if it should generate pleasure or delight). In the modern era, some philosophers have promoted non-normative and non-cognitive concepts of beauty, but beauty persists as an ongoing theme in normative accounts in which God, justice, human love, and so on, are considered beautiful. Beauty is also one of the main topics in contemporary aesthetics.

BEAUVOIR, SIMONE DE (1908–1986). Her critique of patriarchy in religious and secular culture helped promote feminist philosophy of religion, as well as expose the vices of male-dominated institutions and personal, oppressive practices. She is the author of *The Second Sex* (1949) and a variety of other works including philosophical novels and an autobiography.

BEHAVIORISM. A movement that seeks to replace subjective and introspective psychology with an analysis of overt and implied action or behavior. Behaviorism is often part of an overall naturalist philosophy of nature that is materialistic.

BEING. While logical positivists eschewed the intelligibility of being as a concept, being has been an object of philosophical inquiry since Parmenides. Some identify God as being itself or as the ground of being (e.g., Paul Tillich).

BEING, THE GREAT CHAIN OF. The intellectual historian, A. O. Lovejoy, employed this term to refer to the hierarchical relationship between levels of reality with God at the highest point of this order. The material world is at the lowest level with plants, animals, human persons, and angels in an ascending order. These interwoven stages or levels may be found in medieval philosophy but came under attack in modern science. The Great Chain of Being was a teleological (purposive) order as distinct to a non-purposive, mechanical view of nature. *See also* LOVEJOY.

BELIEF. In philosophy, belief is usually treated in propositional terms. To believe that God exists is to hold (or accept or maintain) that it is true that God exists or, technically, that the proposition "God exists" is true. Some philosophers and theologians also recognize types of belief that are not propositional in a narrow sense. For example, one might believe in a person (and thereby have trust in her) or believe in a cause (and thereby hold that the cause is worthy). Some philosophers argue that there is always evidence for beliefs on the grounds that if you believe something to be the case, it appears to you to be the case. If something appears to you to be the case, then you have evidence that it is the case. The latter rests on a principle that appearances can themselves count as evidence. Some theologians disagree and claim that one can have beliefs even in the face of strong counter-evidence.

BELIEF, ETHICS OF. Laws or principles of evidence received the greatest attention in early modern philosophy (Descartes and Locke) but Plato and Aristotle also had views on when beliefs are or are not justified. In the nineteenth century William Clifford advanced a stringent ethics of belief, arguing that it is always wrong to hold a belief on the basis of insufficient evidence. His views have been critiqued because of his lack of a clear criterion for distinguishing sufficient from insufficient evidence. Philosophers like Williams James have questioned whether Clifford had sufficient evidence for his criterion of sufficient evidence.

BELIEF-IN. Some philosophers claim that *belief in* something is different from *belief that* something is the case. Inspired by Wittgenstein, the American philosopher Norman Malcolm once held that he could believe *in* God but not that God exists.

BENEVOLENCE. From the Latin *bene + volens* ("well wishing"), benevolence involves action that benefits others and is the opposite of acting in narrow self-interest. It is central to the ethics of Jonathan Edwards, David Hume, and Henry Sidgwick, among others.

BENTHAM, JEREMY (1748–1832). Bentham was a prominent exponent of hedonistic utilitarianism. He held that an act is right if there is no other act available that will produce greater happiness. Bentham also argued for substantial social reform and, being an avowed atheist, he argued against the historical reliability of the New Testament. He observed that he never lost his religious faith as he never had such faith to lose. Bentham is the author of *A Fragment on Government* (1776), *Principles of Morals and Legislation* (1789), *An Introduction to the Principles of Morals and Legislation* (written 1780, published 1789), *Handbook of Political Fallacies* (1824), *Rationale of Judicial Evidence* (1827), *Outline of a New System of Logic* (1827), and *Deontology or the Science of Morality* (1834).

BERDYAEV, NICOLAI ALEXANDROVICH (1874–1948). A Russian, Christian philosopher who stressed the freedom and creativity of God and humanity. He argued that evil stems from the human misuse of freedom and that human fulfillment is to be found in creative community. Human beings share with God's creative power and are called by God to be loving co-creators. Human time spent not in accord with God's will is false and unintegrated, whereas human time spent in accord with God's will and nature is eternal. Berdyaev's works include *The Meaning of History* (1923), *The Destiny of Man* (1931), *Freedom and the Spirit* (1935), *Solitude and Society* (1939), *Slavery and Freedom* (1940), *The Beginning and the End* (1947), *The Russian Idea* (1949), and *Dream and Reality* (1951).

BERGSON, HENRI (1859–1941). French philosophy professor who influenced Sartre and Beauvoir. Central to his philosophy is the thesis that the future is open for God and creatures. He championed a non-mechanistic understanding of nature and posited a life-force which he thought essential in accounting for the fecundity of life. He further defended the existence of freedom, creativity, and the foundational importance of our experience of time as a matter of duration rather than as a matter of instants, measurable as clock time. Bergson saw temporality as foundational to human experience. Rather than accept the Cartesian framework in which subjects are things that think (*je suis une chose qui pense*), he held that subjects are things that continue (*je suis une chose qui dure*). He won the Nobel Prize for Literature in 1927. Bergson's works include *Time and*

Free Will: An Essay on the Immediate Given of Awareness (1889), *Matter and Memory* (1896), *Laughter: An Essay on the Meaning of the Comic* (1900), *Creative Evolution* (1907), *The Two Sources of Morality and Religion* (1932), and *The Creative Mind* (1946).

BERKELEY, GEORGE (1685–1753). An Anglo-Irish philosopher, Berkeley (pronounced "Barclay") developed an idealist philosophy that construed the natural world in terms of sensations or ideas, souls, and the mind of God. Berkeley is famous for his thesis: to be is to be perceived (*Esse est percipi*). The world continues always to exist (even when we are not immediately sensing it) because it is constantly being perceived by God.

Berkeley argued against the distinction Locke (as well as others like Galileo) made between primary and secondary qualities via *reduction ad absurdum* arguments. Locke thought that primary qualities are mind-independent (e.g., solidity) whereas secondary qualities (e.g., color) are not. Berkeley argued that primary qualities are also mind-dependent. Berkeley's works include *A New Theory of Vision* (1709), *Treatise Concerning the Principles of Human Knowledge* (1710), *Three Dialogues between Hylas and Philonous* (1713), *De Motu* (1721), *Alciphron* (1732), *The Theory of Vision or Visual Language, Vindicated and Explained* (1733), *The Analyst* (1734), *Siris* (1744), *The Querist*

(1735), and *Commonplace Book* (1930). Berkeley had aspirations to build a theological school in Bermuda, and the city, Berkeley, in California is named after this thinker.

BERLIN, SIR ISAIAH (1909–1997). A Jewish philosopher and scholar, Berlin was a historian of ideas and considered one of the twentieth-century's leading liberal thinkers. Influenced by Kant, Rousseau, and Hegel, and having witnessed the political upheaval caused by World War II and the Cold War, Berlin spent his career defending liberalism and value pluralism. Berlin was staunchly opposed to any form of political extremism. In *Historical Inevitability* (1955) he attack determinism in defense of individual moral responsibility.

Berlin is best known for his lecture "Two Concepts of Liberty" (1958) in which he creates a distinction between positive and negative liberty. In the lecture, Berlin favors negative liberty and identifies positive liberty as a major factor in the rise of nationalism and communism during the nineteenth century. Much of the rest of Berlin's career was spent fine-tuning the concepts of positive and negative liberty in the face of both criticism and praise. His work is central to any discussion regarding the defense of civil liberties.

In 1957, Berlin became Professor of Social and Political Theory at the University of Oxford. In 1967, he became President of Wolfson College at Oxford. Berlin's works include *Karl Marx* (1939, 4th ed. 1978), *Four Essays of Liberty* (1969), *Vico and Herder* (1976), *Russian Thinkers* (1978), *Concepts and Categories: Philosophical Essays* (1978), *Against the Current: Essays in the History of Ideas* (1979), *The Crooked Timber of Humanity* (1990), and *The Magus of the North: J. G. Hamann and the Origins of Modern Irrationalism* (1993).

BERNARD OF CLAIRVAUX (1090–1153). Abbot of Clairvaux, Bernard was highly influential in promoting mystical and revealed theology, while discouraging philosophical theology that appeared to give too much authority to human reason (e.g., Abelard). His *Sermons on the Song of Songs* (1135–1153) are an extraordinary blend of erotic meditation and theology. His other works include *On the Love of God* (1126), *On Grace and Free Will* (1127), and *On Contemplations* (1150–1152).

BEST OF ALL POSSIBLE WORLDS. Leibniz held that as a perfect being God would create only the best possible world. While lampooned in Voltaire's *Candide* and criticized by some who likened the best of all possible worlds to the notion of there being the greatest possible number, some contemporary philosophers defend Leibniz's position.

BHAGAVAD GĪTĀ. Sanskrit, *gita* + *Bhagavat*, "song of the blessed one." The Bhagavad Gita is the most famous section of the great Hindu epic poem, the *Mahabharata*, which is highly esteemed among Hindus. At the heart of the poem, the warrior Arjuna is counseled about his duty, the soul, and the divine by his charioteer, Lord Krishna. *See also* HINDUISM.

BHAKTI. Sanskrit, "devotion." A devotional movement in Hinduism that flourished in South India beginning in the seventh century CE and in North India during the twelfth and thirteenth centuries. It rejected the sacrificial ritualism and *Brahminical* (upper-caste) hegemony of the Vedic tradition, opening the door for women and members of lower castes to engage in devotional music and dance in pursuit of a mystical union with the divine. *See also* HINDUISM.

BIBLE. From the Greek *biblia* for "book." The Jewish Bible, or *Tanakh*, consists of the *Torah* ("Teaching"), the *Nevi'im* ("Prophets"), and the *Ketuvim* ("Writings"). The Christian Bible includes the aforementioned books (which it calls the Old Testament) as well as the Gospels, Acts of the Apostles, and the Epistles (which together comprise the New Testament).

BISHOP. A member of the Christian clergy consecrated for the governance of a diocese. Bishops have authority over priests and are often themselves governed by archbishops. The English word "bishop" is derived from the Greek *episkopos*, meaning "overseer" or "supervisor." *Episkopos* is used in the earliest Christian writings, but the development of the offices of pastoral ministry occurred unevenly in the first centuries of Christianity. Many well-known philosophers have also been bishops, including St. Augustine of Hippo, Clement of Alexandria, Robert Grosseteste, Anselm of Canterbury, Joseph Butler, William Paley, and George Berkeley.

BIVALENCE, PRINCIPLE (OR LAW) OF. Every proposition is either true or false. The principle is sometimes symbolized as everything is either A (where "A" stands for any predicate such as "red" or "student") or—A (not A), whereas the law of identity is A is A, and the law of non-contradiction is A is not—A (i.e., not not A). The principle has relevance in debates over divine omniscience. Some argue that God's knowledge does not extend to the future because with respect to future contingent events (e.g., those involving free choices) prior to those events propositions about them are neither true nor false. Some philosophers also object to the principle on the grounds that some concepts and propositions are vague; e.g., it may not be true or false that "a person is middle aged" because "middle aged" is not precisely defined.

34

BODHISATTVA. A Sanskrit term that, in Buddhism, refers to a being who is on the way to becoming a Buddha. Various traditions within Buddhism offer different paths toward release from suffering and enlightenment. The bodhisattva path is one aimed at the highest form of enlightenment (to be a Buddha) and begins with the formation of a compassionate intention to assist all sentient beings. Traditionally, a vow was taken in the presence of a Buddha to enter upon the bodhisattva path. This path includes basic moral purification, meditative practices, and the development of various disciplines until certain non-retrogressive states are reached. Part of the purpose of the path is to accumulate merit, which can then be used to assist all sentient beings. Bodhisattvas, then, are chiefly characterized by compassion for all sentient beings and wisdom to see into the true nature of all reality. They are often seen as compassionate savior figures, particularly in the Mahayana tradition (although they are present in earlier forms of Buddhism as well). Important examples are *Maitreya* (the Buddha to come), *Avalokitesvara* (the bodhisattva of compassion—in Tibetan Buddhism the Dalai Lama is an incarnation of this bodhisattva), and *Manjusri* (the bodhisattva of wisdom).

BOEHME, JACOB (a.k.a. Jacob Behmen) (1575–1624). A German mystic who stressed the unity and primordial nature of God. The deepest level of all reality is God, who Boehme referred to as the Abyss, or *Ungrund*. The trinity emerges from *Ungrund*, which in turn creates the cosmos. Boehme's works include *Aurora, or The Dawn* (1612), *De Tribus Principiis, or Description of the Three Principles of Divine Being* (1619), *De Triplici Vita Hominis, or Concerning the Three Divisions in the Lives of Men* (1620), *The Signature of All things* (1622), and *The Great Mystery or An Explanation of the First book of Moses* (1623).

BOETHIUS, ANICIUS MANLIUS SEVERINUS (c. 475/480–524/6). A Roman philosopher who defended an atemporal concept of God, arguing that God does not exist sequentially. Rather, God enjoys an absolute simultaneity or completion. Boethius wrote his most important book, *The Consolations of Philosophy*, in prison prior to his execution. This work is considered a model of natural theology and it includes a critique of wordly fame and the pursuit of earthly glory. His other works include *De topicis differentiis* (The Theory of Topics), five *Opuscula sacra* (short theological treatises), and *On the Difference of Nature and Person.*

BONAVENTURE, St. (GIOVANNI DI FIDANZA) (1221–1274). A French philosophical theologian who defended the ontological argument. Bonaventure was a devoted follower and promoter of St. Francis of Assisi. According to Bonaventure, human beings possess innate ideas of God, virtue, and the good. The life of faith involves illumination and a living out of the ontological argument whereby one comes to a living relationship with God. He is the author of *Commentary on the Sentences of Peter Lombard* (1250–1251), *On Christ's Knowledge* (1253–1257), *On the Mystery of the Trinity* (1253–1257), *On Charity and the Last Things* (1253–1257), *The Mind's Journey to God* (1259), *Two Lives of St. Francis* (1267), *On the Ten Commandments* (1267), *On the Seven Gifts of the Holy Spirit* (1268), and *On the Six Days of Creation* (1273).

BONHEOFFER, DIETRICH (1906–1945). German theologian who was a key leader of the confessing Church (those who spoke out against Adolph Hitler) in Nazi Germany. Implicated in an attempt to assassinate Hitler, he was killed shortly before the end of World War II. Bonheoffer taught that, rather than promote a cheap view of grace, Christians need to live in radical dependence on Christ. The primacy of Christ even subordinated "religion" to Christ's Lordship so that, paradoxically, Bonheoffer promoted a "religionless" form of Christianity. His works include *The Communion of Saints* (1930), *Act and Being* (1931), *The Cost of Discipleship* (1937), *Ethics* (1949), and *Resistance and Submission* (1951).

BOWNE, BORDEN PARKER (1845–1910). A founding member of a group of philosophers who came to be known as personalists. Over against the impersonalism of utilitarianism and the modern nation state, Bowne stressed the personal nature of God. His chief works include *Metaphysics* (1882), *Philosophy of Theism* (1887), *The Theory of Thought and Knowledge* (1897), *Theism* (1902), and *Personalism* (1908). *See also* PERSONALISM.

BOYLE, ROBERT (1627–1691). An English natural philosopher, Boyle defended the argument from design. His chief works include *The Origin of Forms and Qualities* (1666), *The Excellency and Grounds of the Mechanical Hypothesis* (1674), *The Excellency of Theology* (1674), *The Notion of Nature* (1686), *Final Causes* (1688), and *The Christian Virtuoso* (1690).

BRADLEY, F(RANCIS) H(ERBERT) (1846–1924). A British idealist, Bradley defended the idea that reality is most fundamentally an Absolute, a unified reality behind the world of appearances. Truths that are not seen in relationship to the whole or Absolute reality are partial. In ethics, Bradley defended the idea that human fulfillment is to be found in self-realization. He also saw community life as essential to moral and philosophical development. He is the author of *Appearance and Reality* (1893), *Principles of Logic* (1883), and *Ethical Studies* (1876).

BRAHMAN. In Hinduism, *Brahman* is the ultimate reality, limitless and unchanging. *Advaita Vedanta* teaches a form of monism, in which Brahman and *atman* (the self or soul) are identical (*Advaita* is Sanskrit for "not two"). *See also* ADVAITA VEDANTA.

BRAITHWAITE, R(ICHARD) B(EVAN) (1900–1990). He defended a non-cognitive, non-realist (*see* ANTI-REALISM) view of religious language. Commanding someone to love God is to be analyzed as recommending that the person live in a way with love toward all creation. He is the author of *Scientific Explanation* (1953), *Theory of Games as a Tool for the Moral Philosopher* (1955), and *An Empiricist's View of the Nature of Religious Belief* (1957).

BRENTANO, FRANZ (CLEMENS) (1837–1917). A theist who defended a non-materialist view of persons, the goodness of God, and an objective order of values. He is the author of *Psychology from and Empirical Standpoint* (1874) and *Our Knowledge of the Origin of Right and Wrong* (1889).

BRIDGEWATER TREATISES. A series of treatises published in the early nineteenth century by the Reverend Francis Henry Egerton, the eighth Earl of Bridgewater, arguing for the wisdom, power, and goodness of God based on our knowledge of, and inferences from, the natural world.

BRIGHTMAN, EDGAR SHEFFIELD (1884–1952). A member of the personalist movement who stressed the personal nature of God and ethics. For reasons that stem from the problem of evil, Brightman held that God is finite in power, rather than omnipotent. Brightman (along with fellow personalists Borden Bowne and Peter Bertocci) taught at Boston University, which is why personalism is sometimes referred to as Boston personalism. His chief works include *An Introduction to Philosophy* (1925), *A Philosophy of Ideals* (1928), *The Problem of God* (1930), *A Philosophy of Religion* (1940), *Nature and Values* (1945), and *Person and Reality* (ed. P. A. Bertocci 1958). *See also* PERSONALISM.

BROAD, CHARLIE DUNBAR (1887–1971). A British philosopher who defended a non-reductive view of human persons and realism in ethics. He opposed ethical and psychological egoism. He was agnostic about whether there was life after death and had a lively interest in parapsychology. Broad's meticulous critique of McTaggart constitutes a high water mark in analytic philosophy. He is the author of *Scientific Thought* (1923), *Five Types of Ethical Theory* (1930), *The Mind and Its Place in Nature* (1925), *Examination of McTaggart's Philosophy,*

2 vols. (1933–1938), *Ethics and the History of Philosophy* (1952), *Religion, Philosophy, and Psychical Research* (1953), and *Lectures on Psychical Research* (1963).

BRUNNER, EMIL (1899–1966). A Swiss theologian who was midway between the neoorthodoxy of Barth and the liberal theology of Bultmann. Brunner held that we posses a natural openness to God and Christian revelation. The latter takes us beyond reason alone to an ethic and religious life that values persons preeminently. Brunner's works include *The Symbolical in Religious Knowledge* (1914), *The Mystic and the Word* (1924), *The Philosophy of Religion of Evangelical Theology* (1927), *The Mediator* (1927), *The Divine Imperative* (1932), *Man in Revolt* (1937), and *Christianity and Civilization,* 2 vols. (1948–1949).

BRUNO, GIORDANO (1548–1600). An Italian Dominican, Bruno wrote in favor of Copernicus' astronomy and pantheism, for which he was burnt as a heretic in Rome.

BUBER, MARTIN (1878–1965). Buber stressed the primacy of personal over against impersonal relations, which he formulated in terms of "I-You" or "I-Thou" relations rather than "I-it." The relation to God is a high form of the "I-Thou" relation. In 1925, he translated the Hebrew Bible into German, in collaboration with Franz Rosenzweig in Frankfurt. His works include *I and Thou* (1922), *Religion and Philosophy* (1931), *The Kingdom of God* (1932), *Between Man and Man* (1936), *The Prophetic Faith* (1942), *The Tales of the Hasidim,* 2 vols. (1947–1948), *The Prophetic Faith* (1950), *Two Types of Faith* (1950), *Good and Evil* (1952), *The Eclipse of God* (1953), *Hasidism and Modern Man* (1958), and *The Origin and Meaning of Hasidism* (1960).

BUDDHA, THE (c. 560–c. 480 BCE). The Buddha was born Siddhartha Gautama in Nepal to a royal family. The legends about his life generally include the following.

When Siddhartha Gautama was born, astrologers predicted that he would become a spiritual leader, much to his father's displeasure. In attempting to prevent the prediction from coming true, Siddhartha's father kept him surrounded by luxury and wealth, secluded from the world. During this time, Siddhartha married and had a son. In his late teens or early twenties (after his marriage and the birth of his son), Siddhartha desired to see how people outside the palace lived and arranged to leave the palace walls. While going through the streets of Nepal, he encountered suffering for the first time in the form of the Four Sights. He saw an elderly man, a diseased man, and a corpse. Shocked by this suffering, Siddhartha realized that one day he would become like these sights. He then encountered a monk and was impressed by the man's peacefulness. Siddhartha decided to renounce his life as a royal prince and become like the monk.

Siddhartha left the palace, shaving his head and wearing only monastic robes. For six years, he met with monks and practiced asceticism, trying to control his bodily needs by nearly starving. Realizing that asceticism was bringing the suffering he was trying to avoid, Siddhartha developed the Middle Way, between overindulgence and self-deprivation, by eating only what was necessary. Finding a tree to sit under, Siddhartha entered a deep meditation in which he battled temptations and desires, emerging victorious over them. At this time, Siddhartha became the Buddha, the Enlightened One or the Awakened One.

After attaining Enlightenment, the Buddha began teaching people about the Middle Way, suffering, and the alleviation of suffering. The people that followed him became the beginning of the *sangha*, or community. The Buddha and the *sangha* traveled out of Nepal into India spreading the *dharma*, or teaching, and gathering more followers.

When the Buddha's father heard of this, he sent some of his guards out to bring the Buddha home, but upon hearing the *dharma*, they became followers. Soon, the Buddha's wife and son joined the *sangha* as well. His wife formed a group of nuns following the Buddha.

When he was around 80 years old, the Buddha fell ill. Before he died, he asked his disciples if they had any unresolved doubts or questions, which they did not. He then told them not to follow any leader, but rather to follow his teachings. After he died, he was cremated and the Buddhist tradition continued with his followers.

BUDDHISM. Buddhism emerged from Hinduism, tracing its origin to Gautama Sakyamuni, who lived in northern India sometime between the sixth and fourth centuries BCE and came to be known as the Buddha ("Enlightened One"). His teaching centers on the Four Noble Truths; (1) life is full of suffering, pain, and misery (*dukka*), (2) the origin of suffering is in desire (*tanha*), (3) the extinction of suffering can be brought about by the extinction of desire, and (4) the way to extinguish desire is by following the Noble Eightfold Path. The Eightfold Path consists of right understanding, right aspirations or attitudes, right speech, right conduct, right livelihood, right effort, mindfulness, and contemplation or composure.

Early Buddhist teaching tended to be non-theistic, underscoring instead the absence of the self (*anatta*) and the impermanence of life. In its earliest forms, Buddhism did not have a developed metaphysics (that is, a theory of the structure of reality, the nature of space, time, and so on), but it did include belief in reincarnation, skepticism about the substantial nature of persons existing over time, and either a denial of the existence of *Brahman* or the treatment of *Brahman* as inconsequential. This is its clearest departure from Hinduism. The goal of the religious life is *nirvana*, a transformation of human consciousness that involves shedding the illusion of selfhood.

Schools of Buddhism include Theravada Buddhism, the oldest and strictest in terms of promoting the importance of monastic life; Mahayana Buddhism, which emerged later and displays less resistance to Hindu themes and does not place as stringent an emphasis on monastic vocation; Pure Land Buddhism; and Zen Buddhism.

BULTMANN, RUDOLF (1884–1976). German theologian who argued that to be credible, Christianity needed to be "demythologized," renouncing any appeal to miracles. The core teaching of Christianity (its message or *kerygma*) is the encounter with Christ's word, but this word is not so much a matter of a historical God-incarnate. Christ's message is, rather, our need to take our freedom seriously and to live in a contingent world authentically, not caving into a self-deception that masks anxiety (angst). Bultmann's works include *Jesus and the Word* (1926), *Belief and Understanding*, 2 vols. (1933, 1953) "The New Testament and Mythology" in *Kerygma and Myth*, vol. 1 (1948), *Theology of the New Testament*, 2 vols. (1948–1953), *The Question of Demythologizing* (with Karl Jaspers) (1954), *History and Eschatology* (1957), and *Jesus Christ and Mythology* (1958). *See also* DEMYTHOLOGIZE.

BURKE, EDMUND (1729–1797). A British statesman who was suspicious of the Enlightenment claims about reason. He believed in the vital role of tradition and culture in matters of politics, culture, and religion. Burke argued that the French Revolution was disastrous (he condemned the regicide of Louis XVI) because there was no stable moral culture to inhibit the political chaos and violence. He is also known for his high view of the sublime. He is the author of *Philosophical Enquiry into the Origin of our Ideas of the Sublime and the Beautiful* (1757) and *Reflections on the Revolution in France* (1790).

BUTLER, JOSEPH (1692–1752). A foremost defender and practitioner of natural theology in his day. He defended the compatibility of faith and reason, and he developed a powerful argument against psychological egoism. His works include *Fifteen Sermons* (1726), *Dissertation on the Nature of Virtue* (1936), and *Analogy of Religion* (1736).

C

CABALA. From the Hebrew, meaning the "received" or "traditional." The Cabala is a varied set of teachings and literature that emerged from pre-Christian Judaism through the fourteenth century and is outside of the Hebrew Bible. Cabala teaching reflects Neoplatonic influence in its portrait of creation in terms of emanation. Sin is separation from the source of being, God, and salvation is to be found in union with God. Cabala teaching is un-orthodox; for example, some Cabala tradition posits that God exists beyond the God of orthodoxy.

CALVIN, JOHN (1509–1564). French Protestant who flourished in Geneva, Switzerland, and whose teaching became central to Reformed churches and Presbyterians. Calvin stressed the sublime sovereignty of God as the gracious, just, and provident Lord of creation. The created order is the result of common grace, while the redeemed order of those called to salvation through Christ is a function of special grace. Salvation is not merited by good works but by unmerited grace. Calvin saw human history as a theater of God's glory in which human beings are saved from their fallen state of total depravity. His work brought together a legal, systematic methodology as well as a zeal that helped shape European, reformative culture. Calvin is the author of *Institutes of the Christian Religion* (final version 1560).

CALVINISM. Calvinism is a set of theological beliefs adapted by followers of John Calvin's teachings. Calvinism has been accepted by some Protestant churches as a doctrine which stresses predestination, the need and want for God's grace, and the sovereignty of God. Calvinism began in the sixteenth century as a thought system stressing God as the key reference point in everything that takes place, both on a human and a cosmic level. Under this assumption, humans are completely dependent upon God for common and special grace leading to salvation. The key points of Calvinism can be summarized with the acronym TULIP: Total Depravity, Unconditional

Election, Limited Atonement, Irresistible Grace, and Perseverance of the Saints.

The Fall (1956), and *Reflections on Capital Punishment* (1960).

CAMBRIDGE PLATONISTS. A movement of philosophers, theologians, poets, and priests in the seventeenth century that promoted the good, the true, and the beautiful in their philosophy of God and religion. They promoted religious tolerance and the existence of free will over against predestination. They firmly advanced a non-materialist view of human nature in opposition to Hobbes' materialism. They produced the first philosophical treatment of the design and ontological arguments in English. Members included Benjamin Whichcote, Henry More, Ralph Cudworth, and John Smith. It is likely that Cudworth was the first in English to use the term "philosophy of religion." Many of the terms in philosophy of religion today (such as "theism" and "materialism") can be traced back to Cambridge Platonist writings.

CAMUS, ALBERT (1913–1960). An Algerian French philosopher, novelist, and playwright. Camus' work challenged the idea that atheism was of little moral or personal significance. He defended the notion that we should act boldly out of basic human decency, even if there is no God or if life is an apparent absurdity. His works include *The Myth of Sisyphus* (1943), *Letters to a German Friend* (1945), *The Plague* (1947), *The Rebel* (1951),

CARDINAL VIRTUES. The four virtues highlighted in Plato's *Republic*, Book IV: practical wisdom (or prudence), courage, justice, and temperance (or self-control). These were later incorporated into Christian theology. Christian theologians have traditionally held that knowledge of these virtues does not require special revelation.

CARTESIANISM / CARTESIAN. The system of Descartes / a follower of Descartes. *See* DESCARTES.

CASUISTRY. From the Latin, *casus*, "a case." The science of applying general rules to particular moral cases. Assessing whether to break a code of conduct (do not bring beverages into the library) may call into play more than one principle (keep a promise to complete a dictionary, which requires coffee). Casuistry is the practice of discerning which principles are more stringent. Because of the perceived abuse of casuistry in early modern Europe, the term was sometimes used to suggest mere maneuvering to justify some desired end. In this sense, it has been used disparagingly to refer to abstruse, pointless reflection on moral cases, but its traditional, more respectful use refers to the practice of determining when certain cases fall under general moral precepts involving prohibitions and requirements.

CATEGORICAL IMPERATIVE. A categorical imperative commands some action, unlike a hypothetical imperative, which merely states that if you want X you will need to do Y. (If you want to see Big Ben, you ought to go to London.) A categorical imperative therefore states a duty that is not contingent on anyone's particular desires. Kant not only argued that properly moral requirements must be categorically imperative in form, but he also held that they could all be derived from one fundamental principle, which he therefore called the Categorical Imperative. He gave two main formulations of the principle (which he claimed were equivalent.) The first involves an appeal to maxims. A maxim is the general principle which I at least presuppose when I act. (e.g., "If I need money, and can only get it by making false promises, I will make them.") Kant held that we should only act on maxims that we can will to be universal. Kant held that this challenge of universalizing exposed why we could not endorse the maxim above; if it was accepted universally, the whole practice of making promises would collapse. But this is not a utilitarian appeal to consequences; rather, it shows that we are attempting to make a moral exception of ourselves by acting in a way that we necessarily wish others to avoid. Kant's

second formulation is that we should treat the rational nature in a person (including ourselves) as an end in itself, and not merely as a means to our own ends. On this view, we may use other persons as means (e.g., using a waiter to get some coffee) but we should never treat them merely as means, that is in a way that does not respect their value in themselves. Persons are not to be treated as mere instruments.

CATEGORIES. One of the main tasks of metaphysics is to identify the general categories of reality; for example, in metaphysics one may distinguish between substance, property, event, facts, and so on. Two of the greatest philosophers who engaged in systematic categorizing of what exists (or how we conceptualize the world as we experience it) are Aristotle and Kant.

CATHOLIC / CATHOLICISM. From the Greek *kath* + *holou*, meaning "about whole." While sometimes used generally to mean "universal," the English term is often treated as an abbreviation for being a Roman Catholic. However, technically all Christian traditions that accept the Nicene Creed believe that they too are part of the catholic (or universal) Church. Anglicans and Lutherans, for example, sometimes describe themselves as catholic *and* reformed. *See also* ROMAN CATHOLICISM.

CAUSE, CAUSATION. Causation is relevant in philosophy of religion in accounts of the cause of the cosmos itself, the nature of causation between physical events, and the causation of physical events by mental events and vice versa. The concept of a causal explanation is central to natural theology, as well as to secular, naturalistic projects designed to explain religious life as no more than human projections, faulty reasoning, and so on.

CERTAINTY AND DOUBT. Apparent contraries. To be certain that X is not to be in doubt that X. But can one be certain that X by faith and yet have doubts that X by reason? *See also* DOUBT.

CH'ENG I. *See* **CHENG YI.**

CHANG TSAI. *See* **ZHANG ZAI.**

CHANG TUNG-SUN. *See* **ZHANG DONGSUN.**

CHANGE. Change has been an important topic in philosophy of religion. Classical Buddhism teaches that everything is in a state of change. Some theistic arguments claim that change requires a changeless cause (for Aristotle, the unmoved mover). Some theistic philosophers hold that to attribute change to God is to treat God as imperfect or less than perfect. It has been argued that if God changes, God changes due to some imperfection, otherwise God would not change. Still other theists hold that a God of perfect love would change in God's response to changing values and events in creation.

CHAOS THEORY. Chaos, from the Greek *khaos*, meaning "vast chasm or void" or "confusion." Chaos theory is a branch of mathematics that deals with extremely complex dynamic systems that appear to be random, but are actually the result of an extreme sensitivity during initiation to error. If one were to compare two identical chaotic systems, and then slightly alter one of them in an earlier stage, the two systems would be vastly different at a later stage. A popular example of a chaotic system involves time travel into the past where even the death of a single insect can change the course of the future in inexpressible ways (popularly known as the "butterfly effect"). The theory relies upon a physical universe that is governed by the laws of physics in which every action has a consequence. Chaotic systems are the subject of research in ecology, economics, and mathematics.

CHARITY, PRINCIPLE OF. One should presume that others are intelligent and well-meaning unless there are strong reasons for thinking otherwise. The principle

44

may be used in reference to texts; acting on the principle leads one to interpret a text in the best light, revealing a plausible thesis.

CHENG HAO (a.k.a. CH'ENG HAO) (1032–1085). Cheng Hao, along with his brother Cheng Yi (1033–1107), was a pioneer in the development of Neo-Confucian philosophy. A student of Zhou Dunyi (1017–1073), Cheng Hao accepted the dualism of *li* (principle) and *qi* (matter or material force), but unlike his brother, he emphasized *li*. Cheng Hao developed the concept of *Tianli* (principle of Heaven), a term that appears in the *Book of Rites* (*Liji*), as something akin to natural law. Unlike his brother, Cheng Hao emphasized the unity of humanity and the cosmos, and he believed that introspection was the means of uncovering this truth. Influenced by Buddhist meditation, Cheng Hao was a strong influence on the development of the idealist strain in Neo-Confucianism, culminating in the philosophy of Wang Yangming (1472–1529).

CHENG YI (a.k.a. CH'ENG I) (1033–1107). Cheng Yi, along with his brother Cheng Hao (1032–1085), was a pioneer in the development of Neo-Confucian philosophy. Both brothers studied with Zhou Dunyi (1017–1073), who refined the concept of the dualism of *li* (principle) and *qi* (matter or material force).

Unlike Cheng Hao, Cheng Yi emphasized empirical observation rather than introspection as a means of attaining knowledge of *li*. His school came to be known as the School of Principle (*Lixue*). Cheng Yi emphasized participation in human affairs, particularly public service. Although he declined high office, he criticized politically powerful officials, for which he was twice censured and twice pardoned. He greatly influenced the great Neo-Confucian synthesizer Zhu Xi (1130–1200), and the orthodox school of Neo-Confucianism came to be known as the Cheng-Zhu School.

CHI'I. *See* **QI.**

CHISHOLM, RODERICK (1916–1995). A Platonist, a defender of libertarian freedom, and an opponent of reductive materialism and utilitarianism. Chisholm also outlined ways in which theism could envision God defeating evil. His works include *Perceiving* (1957), *Realism and the Background of Phenomenology* (1960), *The Ethics of Requirement* (1964), *Theory of Knowledge* (1966), *The Problem of the Criterion* (1973), *Empirical Knowledge* (ed. with R. J. Swartz 1973), *Person and Object* (1976), and *The First Person* (1981).

CHRIST. (Gk. *christos*) A translation of the Hebrew term *Messiah*, which means "anointed one." Although traditionally applied to Roman Emperors, it is now most commonly associated with Jesus of Nazareth, the central figure of Christianity. Some distinguish the earthly Jesus from the cosmic Christ.

CHRISTIANITY. With over two billion adherents today, Christianity is the world's largest religion. Christians accept the Hebrew scriptures and Judaism's understanding of God's action in history, but interprets it as foreshadowing the later incarnation of God as Jesus Christ (a person who has both divine and human natures), whose birth, life, teaching, miracles, suffering, death, and resurrection are believed to be the principle means by which God delivers creation from its sin (moral and spiritual evil) and devastation. As part of its teaching about the incarnation, Christianity holds that while God is one, God is constituted by three persons in a supreme, singular unity called the trinity.

Traditional Christianity asserts that through God's loving mercy and justice, individual persons are not annihilated at death, but either enjoy an afterlife in heaven or suffer in hell. Some Christians have been and are universalists, holding that ultimately God will triumph over all evil and there will be universal salvation for all people, though a greater part of the tradition holds that God will not violate the free will of creatures and that if persons seek to reject God, then those persons will be everlastingly separated from God.

Some unity of Christian belief and practice was gradually achieved in the course of developing various creeds (the word comes from the Latin *credo*, "I believe," with which the creeds traditionally began) that defined Christian faith in formal terms. The Nicene Creed, most of which was written and approved in the third century CE, is the most famous and most widely shared of these.

At the heart of traditional Christianity is a ritual of initiation (baptism) and the Eucharist, a rite that re-enacts or recalls Christ's self-offering through sharing blessed bread and wine (sometimes called communion or mass). What unity Christianity achieved was broken, however, in the eleventh century with the split between the Western (now the Roman Catholic Church) and Eastern, Byzantine Christianity (now the Orthodox Churches), and broken again in the sixteenth century with the split between the Roman Catholic Church and the Protestant churches of the Reformation. Many denominations emerged after the Reformation, including the Anglican, Baptist, Lutheran, Methodist, and Presbyterian Churches. Since the middle of the twentieth century, greater unity between Christian communities has been pursued with some success.

Some Christians treat the Bible as infallible and inerrant in its original form (free from error), while others treat the Bible as authoritative and inspired, but not free from historical error or fallible human influence. *See also* ABRAHAMIC FAITHS.

CHRISTOLOGY. The study of Christ and his nature. A *high Christology* or *Christology from above* emphasizes Christ's divinity whereas *low Christology* or *Christology from below* stresses the humanity of Jesus. Relative to this distinction, creedal Christology in, say, Chalcedon, seeks the golden mean between the high and low. *See also* JESUS and TRINITY.

CHRYSOSTOM, JOHN (c. 347–407). One of the great fathers of the early Christian church. Chrysostom was raised in Antioch and schooled in the Greek classical tradition and in the "Antiochene school" of biblical exegesis. He became a priest in Antioch and was famous for his preaching; he was known as "John of the golden tongue." In 398, he was appointed patriarch of Constantinople, though he had to be kidnapped from Antioch out of fear that the people of Antioch would prevent his removal from the city. Though his preaching was just as popular in Constantinople as it was in Antioch, Chrysostom made enemies with the wealthier classes of the great city, particularly due to his opposition to the theater, horse races, and other luxuries enjoyed by the wealthy. His most notable enemy was the Empress Eudoxia. Chrysostom was eventually exiled from Constantinople before his death. Chrysostom is best known for his many homilies, and his other key works include *On Wealthy and Poverty, Letters to Olympias,* and his *Easter Sermon.*

CHU HSI. *See* ZHU XI.

CHUANG TZU. *See* ZHUANGZI.

CHURCH. In Greek the word for church was *ekklesia,* from *ek + kaleo* ("out" + "called"), which meant a gathering or an assembly. Today the term can be used to refer to a building for worship, a local Christian community, a denomination, or all Christians worldwide.

CICERO, MARCUS TULLIUS (106–43 BCE). A statesman, lawyer, and philosopher whose appreciative work on Plato led Augustine to become deeply influenced by Plato, ultimately paving the way for Augustine's conversion to Christianity. Cicero wrote on many topics in politics and culture, and he also developed an argument for God based on the apparent design of the cosmos. Cicero defended a form of natural law. His works include *On the Nature of the Gods, On Duties, On Divination, On the Greatest Good and Evil, On Friendship, On the Republic,* and *On Laws.*

CLARKE, SAMUEL (1675–1729). He developed an influential version of the cosmological argument for God's exis-tence. He also defended Newton's view of nature and God in a correspondence with Leibniz. His works include *A Demonstration of the Being and Attributes of God* (1706), *A Discourse concerning the Unchangeable Obligations of Natural Religion and the Truth and Certainty of Christian Revelation* (1706), and *Scripture Doctrine of the Trinity* (1712).

CLEMENT OF ALEXANDRIA (c. 150–215 CE). An outstanding synthesizer of Christianity and Platonism, Clement developed a cosmic Christology in which the incarnation is seen as the fulfillment of world history. He is the author of *Protrepticus, A Hortatory Address to the Greeks*, and *The Teacher Stromata (Patch-Work)*.

COLERIDGE, SAMUEL TAYLOR (1722–1834). Along with fellow Roman-tic poet, William Wordsworth, Coleridge opposed rationalism and the mechanistic materialism of his age, arguing for the indispensability and value of the imagi-nation in inquiry. He was in the Christian, Cambridge Platonist tradition. His works include *Biographia Literaria* (1818), *Aids to Reflection* (1825), and *Confessions of an Inquiring Spirit* (1840).

COLLINGWOOD, ROBIN GEORGE (1889–1943). A British philosopher who contributed to many areas, especially the philosophy of history in which he argued for the indispensability of placing your-self subjectively in the position of relevant agents. His works include *Essay on Philosophical Method* (1933), *Autobiography* (1939), *The Principles of Art* (1938), *The Idea of History* (1946), and *The Idea of Nature* (1945).

COMMON CONSENT ARGUMENTS. Principally an argument for theism, but it can also be used to support other views. "If all people or most believe there is a God, that is some reason for thinking there is a God." The argument is not a demonstration. It is possible everyone is wrong, but it may also be argued that if theism is true, one would expect many (but perhaps not all) persons to believe it. A contemporary argument against Christian theism reverses the common consent argument and proposes that the God of Christianity would make Godself manifest to all people everywhere. Thus, because there is no such global manifes-tation, some argue that Christianity is false. Some anti-skeptical arguments are also akin to common consent arguments: e.g., Is it plausible to believe that universal convictions about there being moral truths are false?

COMMUNITARIANISM. A late twentieth-century ethical movement that stresses the essential role of the community in moral decision-making. A communitarian may address a moral dilemma about abortion or physician-assisted suicide in terms of specific community values rather than appeal to a general, abstract theory of human rights.

COMPASSION. Literally "feeling with," a compassionate person is one who empathizes (or sympathizes) with those believed to be harmed and who is disposed to go to their aid.

COMPATABILISM. The thesis that determinism can allow for freedom. For example, it has been argued that a person is free if she does what she wants and is not being coerced or manipulated by other agents, if she is not constrained by physical shackles, and so on. Such freedom seems compatible with determinism, according to which the "free person's" acts are necessary, given the laws of nature and antecedent and contemporary causes.

COMPOSITION / DIVISION, FALLA-CIES OF. The fallacy of arguing that a whole has every property of its parts and vice versa. If every human person has a mother, it does not follow that humanity as a whole has a mother. Reasoning from parts to whole is not always a fallacy, however. If every part of a table is made out of wood, then we may infer that the table as a whole is made out of wood. This fallacy

and the debate over whether it is a fallacy has a role in the literature on the cosmological argument.

COMTE, AUGUSTE (1789–1857). An important defender of positivism, an anti-theistic movement that celebrates human power and achievements. He promoted a religious form of humanism. His works include *Course on the Positive Philosophy* 6 vols. (1830–1842), *System of Positive Polity* 4 vols. (1851–1854), *Catechism of Positivism* (1852), and *The Subjective Synthesis* (1856).

CONCEPTUAL RELATIVISM. *See* **RELATIVISM.**

CONCEPTUALISM. The belief that properties like *being a number* or *being human* have no existence independent of minds. This is a denial of Platonism. One of the problems facing conceptualism is that it appears that there are truths about properties quite independent of (at least created human) minds. Thus, it appears that 1+1 = 2 is true, whether or not any mind ever thought mathematically.

CONDORCET, JEAN ANTOINE (1743–1794). A French philosopher who advocated a philosophy of history that was essentially progressive, where human beings move from being hunters to farmers and eventually achieve a perfection in which all inequalities between persons are overcome. Despite his extraordinary optimism, his early hope in the French revolution was not justified: he was arrested and condemned to death, but died while in prison. His works include *Essay on the Application of Analysis to the Probability of Majority Decisions* (1785), *Life of Turgot* (1786), *Life of Voltaire* (1787), and *Sketch for a Historical Picture of the Process of the Human Mind* (1794).

CONFESSION. The acknowledgment of sin or guilt. The New Testament commands confession: "confess your sins to one another, that you may be healed" (James 5:16). Some religions (Christianity and Buddhism, for example) have rites of public confession and promote the practice of self-examination as a prelude to confession.

CONFUCIANISM / CONFUCIUS (a.k.a. K'ung fu-tzu) (551–479 BCE). Confucianism is a social and political philosophy originating in China that has also profoundly shaped Japan, Korea, and Vietnam. It takes its name from Confucius, the Latinized form of Kong Fuzi ("Master Kong"), the most important figure in East Asian intellectual history.

Confucius was born during the Spring and Autumn Period, when China was politically divided and the Zhou dynasty was in decline. His disciples compiled his teachings in the *Lunyu* or *Analects*. Confucius taught that social and political order depended on individual self-cultivation, behavior regulated by *li* or ritual, and a hierarchical social order based on age, gender, and status. Through self-cultivation one develops the virtues of humaneness, righteousness, propriety, and wisdom, manifested in *li*. *Li* originally referred to religious behavior—proper ceremony and rites—but came to refer to ritualized behavior between people according to their status. *Li*, for example, reinforced the proper relationship in the five bonds between ruler and subject, father and son, husband and wife, elder brother and younger brother, and friend and friend. *Li* was intended to inculcate the proper attitudes of loyalty and obedience toward superiors and benevolence toward inferiors.

Although Confucius assumed a ruler would inherit his position from his father, a ruler's legitimacy depended on his ruling morally. The purpose of government is to promote the subjects' welfare, and a ruler is expected to serve as a moral exemplar for his subjects. His rule is ultimately entrusted to him by a mandate from Heaven (*tian*), a transcendent moral order.

Confucianism was further developed by Mencius (c. 372–289 BCE) and later generations, and it was adopted by the Han dynasty (206 BCE–220 CE). The commentaries of Zhu Xi (1130–1200 CE) on the classical Confucian canon became the orthodox interpretation of Confucianism. Orthodoxy was enforced by the civil service examination system, the principal means of recruiting government officials from the seventh century to 1905, when the Confucian civil service examinations were abolished.

CONSCIENCE. The power to discern what appears to be morally right or wrong, a virtue or vice. Religious ethicists debate the extent to which a person's conscience is normative: if a person's conscience leads her to think X is morally required, does she have a duty to do X? Problem cases include cases when a person's conscience may be disordered but not due to any blameworthy act of the person herself.

CONSCIOUSNESS. Widely acknowledged as difficult to define, the English term "consciousness" was employed by Ralph Cudworth in the seventeenth century to designate the state of awareness or experience that persons have when awake, as when persons think, feel, sense, emote, desire, intentionally act, and so on. In modern philosophy, controversy arises over whether consciousness is a real state distinct from bodily states and processes or whether it is a configuration of nonconscious states and not a genuinely distinct, irreducible property. The philosophy of consciousness has relevance for a great deal of philosophy of religion:

theists argue, for example, that they offer a better account of consciousness than naturalists, while some naturalists seeks to explain consciousness in exhaustively scientific, nonconscious terms and argue that they offer a better account than theists. Some Buddhist and Hindu philosophers have developed sophisticated accounts of consciousness to bolster either no-self theories of human nature or for the articulation of the relationship between *Brahman* and *atman*.

CONSEQUENTIALISM. Theories that determine the value of an act by its effects: if doing an act will result in greater good than harm, a consequentialist will see doing the act as possessing a greater value than omitting to do the act. Foremost among consequentialist theories are versions of utilitarianism. Consequentialism, and utilitarianism in particular, are often viewed as secular ethical theories, but they have different religious advocates. Jeremy Bentham, who is commonly seen as the father of modern utilitarianism, was preceded by theistic utilitarians. William Paley was a leading theistic consequentialist. *Contrast with* DEONTOLOGY.

CONTEMPLATION. The practice of meditative reflection on a subject, e.g., on the divine. Religious orders are sometimes *contemplative*, when such a practice is central, as opposed to *active*, when the order is focused on acts of mercy and justice in the world.

CONTINENTAL PHILOSOPHY. Philosophy that is influenced by Husserl, Heidegger, Sartre, Camus, Foucault, Derrida, Irigary, Adorno, Ricoeur, Gadamer, and those philosophers who resemble them. In the early and middle twentieth century "continental philosophy" came to be distinguished by phenomenology (a methodology that stresses the study of appearances or lived experience) as opposed to the perceived aridity and merely apparent rigor of Anglo-American analytic philosophy associated with Bertrand Russell, G. E. Moore, J. L. Austin, Gilbert Ryle, et al. Later twentieth-century philosophy has blurred this distinction with "analytic philosophers" employing phenomenology and some "continental philosophers" forswearing phenomenology for linguistic and structural methodologies.

CONTINGENT. A state of affairs is contingent if it does not obtain or does not necessarily obtain. "The cat is on the mat" is contingent as it is not a necessary truth that any cat is on any mat. Objects are contingent when they do not necessarily exist.

CONWAY, ANNE FINCH (1631–1679). A student and close friend of Henry More, the Cambridge Platonist. She sought to develop a more immanent view of God's relation to the world than in classical Christian theism. She is among the early Quaker (or Society of Friends) philosophers. She is the author of *The Principles of the Most Ancient and Modern Philosophy* (written in the early 1670s, published posthumously in 1690).

COOPERATION WITH EVIL. Cases when a person aids or does not prevent an evil. Cicero advanced the concept of passive injustice, when a person does not object to or protest an evident evil. Traditional moral theology distinguished between *formal cooperation* (in which a person consents or agrees with an evil) versus *material cooperation* with or without consent (for example, a person sells or gives to a burglar tools needed for a robbery).

COSMOLOGICAL ARGUMENT. An argument for theism based on the contingency of the cosmos. The cosmological argument holds that without a necessarily-existing (not contingent) being, the existence of a contingent cosmos is unexplained and we must posit an infinity of contingent explanations. According to this argument, as long as the cosmos is still seen to be contingent there will be a failure to reach a complete or full explanation of the cosmos unless we posit the existence of God to ground or form basis for our explanations of things within the cosmos. Cosmological arguments are sometimes formulated to justify the belief that the cosmos requires a necessary cause in time (a First Cause), but they are often articulated in terms of the cosmos requiring a necessary cause at every (and thus any) time it exists. Some forms of the cosmological argument are formulated not in terms of necessity and contingency, but in terms of causal dependence and independence. Some philosophers argue that our cosmos of dependent causation in which events are accounted for (and depend on) other events, requires an independent being to account for its existence and continuance.

COSMOLOGY. Accounts of the origin and nature of the cosmos. Some philosophers of religion minimize cosmology and stress religion as a social, cultural phenomena, whereas others hold that cosmology bears centrally on questions about God, the soul, the afterlife, and ethics.

COSMOS. From the Greek *kosmos*, meaning "order, ornament, world, or universe." Classical theism regards the cosmos as created, if not at a first moment in time, then at least continuously held in being through God's causal conservation at every moment. Naturalists regard the cosmos as uncreated and without temporal beginning. Pantheists view the cosmos as in some measure divine, either as a reality that is identical with God or as a reality that constitutes but is not identical with God.

COUNTERFACTUALS. A conditional proposition (If A, then B) in which the antecedent, A, is false or did not occur. For example, consider the claim that if Camus had not died so young, he would have become a Roman Catholic. The status of counterfactuals is currently in dispute, especially the counterfactuals of freedom. Is it true or false now that if you are offered a theology professorship at Fordham University in the future, you will freely accept the position? Molinists think such a question admits of a truth value and that God knows all counterfactuals, whereas open theists claim there is no truth *now* of what free creatures will do under conditions that have yet to occur or may never occur.

COURAGE. Ancient, medieval, and some modern uses of the term in English presuppose that courage involves the perceived risk-taking for a good, or at least an ostensibly good cause. Risk-taking that is not for the good has customarily been described with other terms such as *boldness* or *recklessness* in the context Aristotle uses in describing an excess that fails to achieve a golden mean (moderation). Current usage in English is vague and ambiguous.

COVENANT. From the Latin *convenire*, meaning "to come together." The covenant is a key element in Judaism, which traces its lineage and inheritance to the covenant between Abraham and God. There are also covenants between Adam and Eve and God, Noah and God, and a renewal of covenantal relations with Judah and Moses. A covenant is sometimes distinguished from a *contract*. A covenant tends to define the life of the participants who internalize their role in a covenantal relationship. Contractual relations can be less definitive of one's identity and refer to more impersonal agreements.

CREATIO EX NIHILO. Latin for "creation from nothing." Classical Judaism, Christianity, and Islam have affirmed that the creation is created by God and not from some pre-existing material. This is often referred to as *creatio ex nihilo*, though the expression can be misleading insofar as it suggests God made the creation from some thing (in which "nothing" is taken to refer to something). The classical theistic claim about creation may also be expressed in terms of creation from God.

CREATION. In religious traditions, creation refers to all that is created. For monotheists, creation includes everything except God. In classical theism, God's creation is seen as originative (the cosmos has a beginning) and ongoing insofar as the cosmos exists due to the continuous conserving power of God as Creator. To describe the natural world as a creation implies that it has one or more creators. The idea that God created the cosmos also suggests a strict distinction between creator and creation.

CREATIONISM. Popular term for the view that all species on earth were created separately by God rather than diverse species evolving from simpler, common organisms. A "literal" reading of Genesis 1 appears to support creationism, while Genesis 1 may alternatively be read as affirming the goodness of diverse kinds in a created order compatible with evolution. This latter view sees creation as good, in part, for its diversification in keeping with the medieval precept *bonum est multiplex* (good or goodness is multiple or is a multitude). *See also* INTELLIGENT DESIGN and SCIENCE AND RELIGION.

CREATOR. God is conceived of as the creator of the cosmos in theistic religious traditions. In classical Jewish, Christian, and Islamic theology God creates freely and therefore God is not necessarily a creator, though some classical theologians claim that God is essentially good, it is of the nature of goodness to be self-diffusive, and therefore God's nature strongly inclines or makes fitting God's being the creator.

CREDO QUIA ABSURDUM EST. Latin, "I believe because it is absurd." A phrase famously (and erroneously) attributed to Tertullian. Tertullian held that the Christian faith is not in harmony with reason as conceived of in non-Christian philosophy. If pagan philosophy deems Christianity absurd, that is no reason to reject it. In fact, the kind of apparent absurdity of Christianity from a pagan vantage point reveals its credibility for Christianity ultimately makes better sense of the cosmos. Kierkegaard later incorporates such an absurd dimension of faith in discussing the teleological suspension of the ethical. *See also* ABSURD.

CREDO UT INTELLIGAM. Latin, "I believe in order to understand." Anselm's maxim (based upon a saying of Augustine) that faith helps one to understand and know about God, the world, and the self. This suggests that accepting Christian faith or assuming it as a presupposition or a first step in inquiry allows one to have a richer, evident comprehension of God and the creation. As a purely intellectual endeavor, this may be analogous to some scientific reasoning, e.g., if we accept theory T, then certain data is intelligible, whereas the data seems utterly inexplicable without T. And yet Anselm may be read as identifying more than an intellectual orientation: an initial trusting openness to God intellectually as well affectively is an important step toward coming to authentically understand God, the soul, and the world.

CREEDS. A statement of belief. From the Latin *credo*, meaning "I believe," with which the creeds used in worship traditionally begin. Examples in the Christian tradition include the Apostle's Creed, the Nicene Creed (325, 381), the Creed of Chalcedon (451), the Athenasian Creed, and the Creed of the Sixth Ecumenical Council against the Monothelites (680). The Apostle's Creed and Athenasian Creeds have undetermined dates because of their uncertain origins, but the former is traditionally attributed to the original apostles of Jesus Christ when inspired by the Holy Spirit (during Pentecost), while the latter creed is named after Athanasius.

CRITICAL REALISM. Critical realism holds that you are seeing this dictionary, but that this process occurs through a medium of sensation. In contrast, direct realism is the view that under ordinary, good conditions, you are seeing a dictionary right now in an unmediated fashion. Critical realists insist on the fallibility of our perception, and hence the need to treat ostensible or apparent perceptual claims with cautious scrutiny. Philosophical approaches (positive or negative) to religious experience in the medieval as well as modern era tend to be in terms of critical realism rather than dogmatic skepticism or uncritical acceptance.

CRITICISM. Kant called the Enlightenment the age of criticism. Subsequent Romantic philosophers set out to criticize criticism. In theology, "lower criticism" has focused on textual authenticity, determining, for example, the more reliable primitive texts making up the New Testament. "Higher criticism" takes up more comprehensive questions about the meaning, historical and theological significance, of scripture.

CUDWORTH, RALPH (1617–1688). A major contributor to Cambridge Platonism and the first to use the term "philosophy of religion" in English. Cudworth offered one of the earliest accounts of how in free agency a subject steps back from his current character and desires to elect which desires, and thus what character, he wishes to embrace. In the midst of the English civil war (1641–1651), Cudworth counseled the House of Commons to be mindful of a Platonic view of goodness: God loves goodness because it is good; goodness is not a matter of God's capricious will. He defended libertarian free will, tolerance, innate ideas, and natural theology as a whole. His works include *True Intellectual System of the Universe* (1978), *Eternal and Immutable Morality* (1731), and *A Treatise of Free Will* (1838).

CULTURE. From the Latin *colere*, meaning "to cultivate or till." The term "culture" has more of a use in sociology than philosophy of religion, but from its origination philosophers have addressed what they take to be the good and evil of the beliefs and practices of their society. Insofar as "culture" stands for a community or group's set of beliefs, practices, and history, then philosophers from Socrates to Rawls have questioned the moral integrity of the cultures of their day. Augustine's *The City of God* may be read as a Christian critique of pagan Greco-Roman culture. In the twentieth century, Christian theologians such as the Niebuhrs wrestled with the extent to which authentic Christian faith could be lived out in contemporary culture.

CULVERWEL, NATHANAEL (c. 1618–1651). A Cambridge Platonist who stressed the concord (even the amicable relationship) between faith and reason. Culverwel held that philosophical inquiry into theology required a loving, wise search for truth. His works include *Spiritual Opticks* (1651) and *An Elegant and Learned Discourse of the Light of Nature* (1652).

D

DALAI LAMA. *Dalai* is Mongolian for "Ocean" and *Lama* means teacher or guru, so the full title refers to a teacher with a spirituality that is as deep as an ocean. Tibetan Buddhists believe that the Dalai Lama is a reincarnation of a *bodhisattva*, of which there have been 14. The original incarnation of the Dalai Lama, Gedun Drupa, was born in 1391. Tenzin Gyatso, born in 1935, is the 14th Dalai Lama.

Each time a Dalai Lama dies, a new one must be found. Traditionally, the direction in which the Dalai Lama's head falls when he dies is the direction the monks should search for the next reincarnation. If the Dalai Lama is cremated, sometimes the direction of the smoke indicates the direction of the next reincarnation. After consulting with the Oracle (a man who is an advisor to the Dalai Lama), the monks begin their search, which can sometimes take up to four years. The reincarnation, however, is born within two years after the death of the previous Dalai Lama. Typically, the search for all of the Dalai Lamas has been in Tibet, but the 14th Dalai Lama has said

that it is possible he will be reincarnated outside of Tibet if it is in China's control.

The High Lamas, in charge of finding the Dalai Lama, first go to Lhamo Lhatso Lake to receive a vision of where to begin the search. When they find the boy they believe is to be the next Dalai Lama, they give him a series of tests, including identifying the past Dalai Lama's artifacts out of a set of identical objects. If multiple boys equally pass the tests, the High Lamas put the boys' names in an urn and a name is drawn out in public. The 14th Dalai Lama says that as a child looking through the Potala Palace, where he was educated in the Tibetan Buddhist tradition, he recognized the rooms and the objects in them from his previous life, although he says he has no memory of his previous lives as a whole.

When the Dalai Lama is discovered, he almost immediately begins his training. He is educated in logic, Tibetan art, Tibetan culture, Sanskrit, medicine, Buddhism, poetry, music, drama, astrology, phrasing, and synonyms. He is allowed to receive gifts from his family and see them. The 14th Dalai Lama's brother was even allowed to go with him to the palace and study. The 14th Dalai Lama was the fifth of 16 children and was born in a small village. When he turned 15, he was formally initiated as the Dalai Lama because of the Chinese invasion of Tibet. In 1959, he fled to India to escape Chinese persecution. Both the head of state and the spiritual leader of Tibetan Buddhism, the 14th Dalai Lama currently lives in exile in India, traveling the world and teaching loving-kindness and peace.

DANTE ALIGHIERI (1265–1321). Italian poet and author of the *Divine Comedy* (first printed edition in 1472), the narrative of Dante the Pilgrim on a journey. Beginning with his being lost in the middle of his life and culminating in a vision of God in which his will and desire are captured by the love that moves the sun and other stars, the journey takes Dante through limbo, hell, purgatory, and finally to paradise. The poem and Dante's other works, such as *On Monarchy* (1309) and *Vita Nuova* (New Life) (1292) involve a host of philosophical themes. Dante holds that earthly loves (such as his love for a young woman named Beatrice) can be a reflection of the transcendent love of God. His poem the *Divine Comedy* is built on an extensive framework in which reason (represented by Virgil) acts in collaboration with faith (Beatrice). His other works include *On Plebeian Eloquence* (c. 1305) and *The Banquet* (1308).

DAOISM. A Chinese philosophy articulated by Laozi in the *Daodejing* and by Zhuang Zhou in the *Zhuangzi* that seeks harmony by means of passivity and humility. Dao means "road" or "way" and refers to the processes of life which flow back and forth in a correlative pattern between yin and yang. It is used as both a noun and a verb. Although the *dao* is ultimately inaccessible to human minds, the "true person" (*zhen ren*) may seek unity with the *dao* through effortless action (*wu wei*), accepting the flow of reality between yin and yang. One ought not to draw moral (good vs. bad) or aesthetic (beautiful vs. ugly) distinctions, for these human forms of ordering the world interrupt the *dao*.

DARWIN, CHARLES ROBERT (1809–1882). Co-discoverer of the theory of biological evolution, Darwin and Alfred Russel Wallace, working independently, advanced a theory of evolution at the same time. Darwin argued that current and extinct organisms developed through a process of natural selection and elimination. Rather than species being separately created by a provident God, diverse kinds of living things developed from simpler life forms. At first Darwin advanced evolution as the way God shaped life on earth, and he did not include human evolution in his purview. Partly due to Darwin's assessment of the pain and apparent violence of nature involved in evolution and his assessment of a common mammalian ancestry for human and nonhuman mammals, Darwin took leave of Christianity. His stance near the end of his life was agnosticism. His works include *The Origin of Species* (1859), *The Variation of Animals and Plants Under Domestication* (1868), and *The Descent of Man* (1871). The latter work contains Darwin's case for human evolution.

DARWINISM. Darwin influenced biology as well as philosophy as a whole and even economics and politics. His work has tended to support a secular, naturalistic description and explanation of human life as part of the natural world. The issues of significance for philosophy of religion that arise as part of the legacy of Darwin's work include: Is evolutionary biology alone sufficient to account for the emergence of consciousness, moral and aesthetic values, and religion? Does Darwinian evolutionary biology undermine an ethic of compassion and justice? For example, would a human being have a compelling moral reason to be compassionate or act justly if such an act would undermine his survival and / or the survival of all those in his genetic family? Can naturalism or theism better explain why there is a world in which evolution takes place? While evolutionary biology has been interpreted as undermining a theistic argument from design, evolution could not take place without the stable laws of chemistry and physics. An argument from design can therefore take place at a deeper level of explanation: How is one best to account for the cosmos as a whole, replete with evolution? *See also* SCIENCE AND RELIGION.

DEATH. The cessation of life. Philosophical questions on death include, centrally, the question of whether death is final and irreversible. Can persons survive biological death? Different beliefs about the surmounting of death include belief in a resurrection of the body, survival of the soul as an immaterial reality, reincarnation, or the complete re-creation of a person after a period of nonexistence. The latter is described as a gap-inclusive life as it involves a person coming into life, living, ceasing to be, and then coming back into being. The criterion of death has been controversial: Should it be marked by irreversible loss of brain activity? Or should it involve multiple conditions and include other organs?

Arguments over whether death is bad if it involves nonexistence go back to ancient Greco-Roman philosophy. Arguably, if something is bad, it must be bad for someone or something. If you die, this will be bad for those who mourn your loss, but if you perish (so it is argued), your state of death cannot be bad for you because there is no you. Some philosophers counter that absences, such as your absence from life after your death, can be bad even if death is not bad for you. Some forms of Daosim see death as natural, whereas Christianity has typically viewed death (along with sin) as evil and believed that redemption occurs when death and sin are overcome.

DECONSTRUCTION. A practice made popular by Derrida in which a text is shown to implode or collapse in virtue of its structure or entailments. Some texts have implicit assumptions in conflict with their stated objective, such as the liar paradox in which "a liar claims to be a liar," or Plato's *Phaedrus*, which contains important arguments against writing (we only know the case against writing today because it was transmitted by writing). Deconstruction as a literary or philosophical tool works on less obvious cases, e.g., Descartes on the self. Some theologians see Kierkegaard as deploying a technique of deconstruction against Hegelianism and Danish Christianity.

DEDUCTION. An argument involving necessary entailment. From the thesis "No humans are immortal," one may deduce, "No immortal is human."

DEGREES OF PERFECTION ARGUMENT. Aquinas' fourth proof for the existence of God on the grounds that there are degrees of perfection in the world. Some things vary in terms of goodness, truth, and nobility. This, in turn, suggests a scale in which there is something that is the highest or greatest good, truth, or nobility. Aquinas further held a view of causation according to which the greatest thing in a genus is the cause of lesser things. In the science of his day, it was thought that heat was ultimately caused by the greatest heat, namely an ultimate fire. Aquinas contended that there is something that is the cause of all existing things and of the goodness and perfection of all things— and this (he argued) we call God.

This argument and his analogy about fire may have little plausibility today, but his reasoning may suggest ways in which God as a supremely perfect being can be conceived. Philosophical theologians in the Anselmian tradition hold that God is maximally excellent, which they treat as the thesis that God has the greatest possible set of great-making properties. As we examine the goods or excellences of the world, arguably we discover varying degrees of such goods as thoughts or consciousness, knowledge, power, moral virtue, and so on. Theists may use the kind of reasoning behind the fourth proof to build up a conception of that which is truly or maximally perfect. Other arguments such as the ontological argument would then be needed to argue further that this maximally excellent being exists.

DEISM. The tradition believing that the cosmos is created by God, but God is not revealed through miracles in human history and does not play an active, sustaining role in creation. Some deists believe in the goodness of God and an individual afterlife. Some deists historically engaged in strenuous anti-Christian polemics (Voltaire and Thomas Paine), whereas others sought to make deism compatible with Christian practice (Thomas Jefferson's Christianity embraced Christ's moral teaching but he expunged all miracle narratives from his Bible).

DEMIURGE. Plato's term for the divine force that shapes the world of matter based on the world of forms. The demiurge, which is featured in Plato's *Timaeus*, entered into Gnostic popular belief the idea that the world was made by a lesser god, a malevolent or at least sub-benevolent force, and that salvation is to be achieved by knowing the God beyond the god (or demiurge) of this earthly realm.

DEMOCRITUS (460–370 BCE). The philosopher and pupil of Leucippus (an influential Atomist pre-Socratic) who maintained that the material world is composed of indivisible, tiny objects or atoms. Known as the laughing philosopher, he is traditionally thought to have no fear of death: for at death he said, since we cease to be, we have no reason to fear death.

DEMYTHOLOGIZE. A practice popularized by Rudolf Bultmann (1884–1976) in which one seeks to find the essence of Christianity by looking behind or through supernatural stories of miracles and heaven. For example, a demythologized view of Christ may deny that Christ was the incarnation of the incorporeal Creator God of the cosmos, but it may take the Christian teaching of Christ's life as advancing a radical call for persons to live a courageous life of compassion in the pursuit of justice and mercy.

DEONTOLOGY. Theories that moral duties or requirements and moral prohibitions are binding and not contingent on their consequences, especially in terms of utilitarian calculations. Cases may arise when doing an immoral act (e.g., framing an innocent person) that might bring about some good or avoid suffering (e.g., preventing a race riot). A deontologist will not condone the evil act, regardless of the consequences. *Contrast with* CONSEQUENTIALISM.

DERRIDA, JACQUES (1930–2004). Derrida is best known for being a French philosopher and postmodernist, the founder of deconstruction, and the author of *Of Grammatology* (1967). He is also known for his work on "The Gift" and became very popular during the 1970s. He was born in Algeria and studied and taught philosophy for more than 20 years at the *Ecole Normale Superieure*. "The Supplement" is one of Derrida's well-known key terms that challenges Western metaphysics—it is a unified body of thought in the philosophical quest for a simple origin that favors presence as a self-sufficient source. "The Trace" is another of his key terms that challenges conventional thought when he says "a past that has never been present" to explain the priority of presence. Derrida's work with deconstruction criticizes literary texts, philosophical texts, and political institutions. Derridean deconstruction tries to re-think differences that divide self-consciousness in an effort to bring about justice, even though it may be impossible to achieve. In the 1990s Derrida's writing seemed to go in two directions, the first being politics and the second being religion. Much of Derrida's work draws upon traditions of Husserl and Heidegger. Some of his other well-known writings are *Speech and Phenomena* (1967), *Writing and Difference* (1967), *Margins of Philosophy* (1972), *Dissemination* (1972), *Glas* (1974), *The Post Card* (1980), *Given Time* (1991) and *The Politics of Friendship* (1994).

DESCARTES, RENÉ (1596–1650). Through a strict methodology, Descartes offered two arguments for theism. One was an ontological argument to the effect that the possibility of God's necessary existence entails God's actual existence. The other is an argument that the best explanation of our idea of God as a

perfect being must be the actual existence of God as a perfect being. He also defended the certain existence of the self, the distinction between the self and the body, and the general reliability of our senses. His argument that the self is not identical with its body is based on the thesis that it is possible for the self to exist without its body. If it is possible for the self to exist without its body, the self and body are not identical.

In theology and philosophy of religion, two aspects of Descartes' work have received the most attention:

First, his methodology was shaped principally by an excoriating skepticism. What can be doubted? Descartes set out to build a foundation of indubitable knowledge, a project that has come to be known as foundationalism. The presumed failure of his foundationalism has led some thinkers to believe that the overall project of the Enlightenment to achieve impartial certain knowledge independent of tradition is a failure.

Second, Descartes' case for the distinction of the mind and body has received unrelenting criticism on the grounds that he left unexplained how the mind and body interact, and he also (implicitly) subordinated the value of the body to the mind. Especially to feminists, this represents an offense to the wholeness and integrity of personal identity. Defenders of Descartes (called Cartesians) counter that Descartes' foundationalism can be reconstructed rigorously (see work by

Roderick Chisholm): the interaction of mind and body is no less strange than the causal interrelationship of events, particles and fields in contemporary physics, and that unless feminists wish to embrace behaviorism or deny the existence of consciousness, some recognition of the difference between the mental and physical is unavoidable.

"Dualism" is the current term to describe the view that the mind and body are distinct, but this term was not used by Descartes or by other earlier "dualists" such as Plato and Augustine. Although the term "pluralism" has other established usages, it would be fitting to see Descartes not so much as a dualist (embracing two-ism), but as embracing a plurality of kinds of things and thus (in metaphysics) a pluralist. Descartes is the author of *Rules for the Direction of the Mind* (1628/9, never completed), *The World* (1634), *Discourse on the Method* (1637), *Meditations on First Philosophy* (1641, 2nd ed. 1642, published with the *Objections and Replies*), *Principles of Philosophy* (1644), and *The Passions of the Soul* (1649).

DESIGN, ARGUMENT FROM OR TO. Some philosophers argue first that the cosmos *appears* to be designed or that it is the kind of reality that would be designed, and then argue from that that the cosmos is indeed designed. Arguments from design can be found in works by Cicero, Aquinas, Cudworth, Paley, and others.

DETERMINISM. Determinism is the view that all events necessarily occur given all contemporaneous and antecedent events and the laws of nature. A shorthand way of defining determinism is that it asserts that there is only one possible future, given all events and laws in the past and present. Some theists embrace determinism of the created world but not God, while some see God and nature in indeterministic terms. Spinoza thought God or nature (*Deus sive natura*) is determined. Determinism is incompatible with libertarian freedom. *See also* FREE WILL.

DEUS ABSCONDITUS. Latin, "Hidden God." Some theologians contrast the hidden God with the God of revelation (*Deus revelatus*). Some hold that God must be at least partly hidden, otherwise creatures could not act freely with any kind of autonomy independent of God's sovereign power.

DEUS EX MACHINA. Latin, "god from the machine." A device in Greek theater whereby a god may be introduced to resolve a theatrical problem, e.g., the tragedy *Medea* ends when a god rescues Medea after she has killed her children and rival. A god would be lowered onto the stage by way of an elaborate machine. Aristotle, famously, lamented this artificial device.

DEUS SIVE NATURA. Latin, "God or Nature," the slogan of Spinoza's panentheism. Spinoza recognized God and nature as equivalent. Some have thereby seen Spinoza as divinizing all reality (hence Spinoza's being labeled as the "god-intoxicated philosopher") or as naturalizing the divine.

DEVIL. *See* **SATAN.**

DEWEY, JOHN (1859–1952). An American pragmatist who opposed what he judged to be overly abstract and theoretical ideals found in Plato and Descartes. Dewey commended a religious way of life, but he did not thereby intend any institutional or theistic practice. Dewey has been interpreted as advancing a non-dogmatic reverence for the natural world and an understanding of personal growth and maturity in terms of lifelong learning through wise experimentation. Dewey defended a secular form of pragmatism in which knowledge and values are achieved through experiential testing. His works include *Psychology* (1887), *Studies in Logical Theory* (1903), *Ethics* (with Tufts, 1903), *How We Think* (1910), *Essays in Experimental Logic* (1916), *Reconstruction in Philosophy* (1920), *Experience and Nature* (1925), *The Quest for Certainty* (1929), *Art as Experience* (1934), *A Common Faith* (1934), *The Teacher and Society* (1937), *Experience and Education* (1938),

Logic: The Theory of Inquiry (1939), and *Theory of Valuation* (1939).

DHARMA. Sanskrit, "carrying / holding." A term in Indian religions used to refer to right action. It is sometimes used as a translation of term religion. *See also* HINDUISM.

DIDEROT, DENIS (1713–1784). Unlike Voltaire and Rousseau who retained deistic or modified theistic philosophies, Diderot advanced a thoroughgoing naturalism. He was the principle architect of the ambitious encyclopedia that sought to systematize all secular knowledge. Diderot was stridently opposed to slavery, clerical power, and censorship. His works include *Encyclopédie* (1750–1765), *Philosophical Thoughts* (1746), *Letter on the Blind* (1749), *Thoughts on the Interpretation of Nature* (1754), *Letter on Deaf Mutes* (1759), and *Rameau's Nephew* (written 1761, published 1805).

DILTHEY, WILHELM (1833–1911). An early proponent and practitioner of what became the field of sociology. His sociology of religion focused on the construction of alternative worldviews in light of cultural realities. His works include *Introduction to the Sciences of the Spirit* (1883), *Studies on the Foundation of the Sciences of the Spirit* (1905), *Experience and Poetry*

(1905), *The Essence of Philosophy* (1907), and *The Types of World View* (1911).

DIOGENES LAERTIUS (3rd century CE). Regarded not as a philosopher in his own right, his extant work *Lives of the Philosophers* is nevertheless one of the most important secondary sources for the thought of many Greek and Latin philosophers. In particular, he is an invaluable source for the writings of Epicurus, leading some to believe that he was an Epicurean, though this is uncertain.

In his work, he divides philosophers into Ionic and Italic schools, with the former derived from Anaximander and the latter from Pythagoras. After Socrates, the Ionic philosophers are further divided into three branches: Plato and the Academics through Clitomachus, the Cynics through Chrysippus, and Aristotle through Theophrastus. The Italic school consists of Telanges, Xenophanes, Parmenides, Zeno of Elea, Leucippus, Democritus, and others through Epicurus. Diogenes is also known for his own humorous (though presumably mostly fictional) poetry regarding the illustrious deaths of the philosophers of his day.

DIOGENES OF SINOPE (a.k.a. Diogenes the Cynic) (404/412–323 BCE). While many stories are told about his life, one thing that we do know is that he lived in a tub or *pithos* in Athens. His principle

that if an act is not shameful when done in private, it is not shameful if done in public led him to such exploits as eating in the marketplace (contrary to custom) and masturbating there—lamenting that it was not as easy to satisfy his belly by rubbing it—defecating in the amphitheater, and urinating in public.

Diogenes is sometimes viewed as standing for rationality and common sense against lofty metaphysics, as illustrated by his act of bringing a plucked chicken to Plato's Academy, exclaiming that it was Plato's man, since Plato had defined man as a featherless biped. As with other Cynics, Diogenes believed that reason consisted of living in accordance with nature, rather than the pretentious standards of civilization. He experienced great difficulty in trying to find a person who met such a standard, and he is said to have traveled with a lit lantern during the day in search of a truly honest person.

DION CHRYSOSTOM (c. 40–c. 120 CE). Dion, also known as Dio of Prusa, was a first century orator well known for his rhetorical speaking abilities (hence, the label of "Chrysostom," or "gold mouth"). Dion fell out of favor with the Roman emperor Domitian because he was a friend of a member of Domitian's family who had angered the emperor and had been killed; as a result, he was exiled around 82 CE. During his exile, he traveled widely through lands north of Asia Minor, including the land of the Getae, about which he later wrote and spoke. After Domitian's death in 96 CE, Dion was able to return and continue his life as an orator. Being well-schooled in both classical Greek traditions and philosophical schools, Dion makes multiple references to and offers critiques of both. He is also one of the few sources in existence on the Greek mystery cults. Unfortunately, most of Dion's discourses have been lost (including his complete discourse on the Getae). A total of 80 of his discourses currently exist; the most famous of these are his Olympic Discourse and his four discourses on Kingship. The details of Dion's death are unknown, but he was certainly alive and involved in a lawsuit with Pliny the Younger in 112 CE.

DIRTY HANDS. A popular term for the problem of persons who have done ill in the process of bringing about some presumed desirable ends. In the fourth century CE, Basil the Great did not excommunicate or punish Christians who were soldiers (and who thus killed during war), although he held that their unclean hands made them unable to take communion until three years after their military service. Modern philosophers have wrestled with the question of whether some honorable practices (governance) inevitability involve dirty hands and that to deny this involves an impractical moral rigorism.

DISSENT. An important religious and moral category, whereby a person may claim allegiance to a religious community or tradition and yet protest or not consent to some community or traditional rule or teaching. For example, one may claim to be a faithful Roman Catholic and yet dissent on church teaching about the celibacy of priests or the impermissibility of female priests.

DIVINE. *See* **GOD.**

DIVINE ATTRIBUTES. *See* **ATTRIBUTES, DIVINE; and GOD, CONCEPTS AND "ATTRIBUTES" OF.**

DIVINE COMMAND THEORY. The belief that moral truths can be analyzed in terms of God's approval or disapproval. Strong versions hold that moral truths *consist* of what God commands, whereas moderate versions claim that moral truths can be analyzed in terms of God's approval or disapproval. On this view, X is morally wrong entails God disapproves of X. Some object to the strong version on the grounds that an atheist can have a clear comprehension of moral truths while denying the existence of God. This alone does not seem decisive, for one can have a clear comprehension of some things and properties (from water to the concept of truth) without knowing or while even denying their underlying structure.

Divine command theories face the worry that God's commands may be free and unconstrained. If God approved of rape or murder or the sacrifice of a child (see Genesis 22:1–19, the narrative of Abraham and Isaac), would such acts be morally required? Some reply by modifying their account to make explicit God's essential goodness. In this framework, God would not command murder, et al. Some theists claim that God's commands have normative force due to God's role as Creator. If God creates and conserves a good cosmos, do not creatures in some sense belong to God and owe some allegiance to the Creator? On this view, God's commands have normative force due to divine ownership.

DIVINE DISCOURSE. A term made popular by Nicholas Wolterstorff to designate God's revelation through human language. Wolterstorff sees divine discourse as a phenomenon distinct from revelation as a broader category in which God may be disclosed without the use of prepositions or sentences.

DIVINE SIMPLICITY. The teaching that God is simple can be found in the writings of authors such as Augustine of Hippo, Anselm of Canterbury, and Thomas of Aquinas. It was formally ratified by the Fourth Lateran Council and the First Vatican Council. In this context, "simple" means "non-composite."

Defenders of divine simplicity typically (though not always) note three ways in which something might be thought to be composite. In Aquinas' terminology (Aquinas being a particularly famous and systematic defender of divine simplicity) (1) it might be composed of "form" and "matter," (2) it might be composed of "individuality" and "nature," or (3) it might be composed of "essence" and "existence." The teaching that God is simple (and even when expressed in terms other than those used by Aquinas) denies that God is composite in any of these ways. It claims, therefore, that God is not a physical body, not something which undergoes any kind of change, not something belonging to a natural kind of which there could be more than one member (and, therefore, not something distinguishable from its nature, or sharing its nature with anything), and not something owing its existence (or way of existing) to anything in any way.

Critics of the teaching that God is simple commonly suggest that it involves some absurd identity claims or that it conflicts with the biblical account of God. Its defenders argue that it is actually implied by the biblical account and is chiefly to be construed as a piece of negative theology (an account of what God is *not*) rather than an attempt to describe God in positive terms. The "big idea" behind the teaching can be stated thus: as the absolutely perfect source of the *existence* of everything, God cannot be *part* of a *dependent world*; God must be the *uncreated* source of *all* distinguishable things in *all* their many forms. As the source of all creaturely perfection, God must be absolutely perfect and, therefore, non-composite.

DOCETISM. From the Greek *dokeo,* meaning "to seem." The view that God only *appeared* to assume human nature in the incarnation. Some Gnostics adopted docetic views of Christ. Some passages in the New Testament appear to explicitly rule out docetism, e.g., descriptions of Jesus' bleeding and the depiction of Jesus as dying in all four gospels.

DOCTA IGNORANTIA. Latin, "learned ignorance." A concept found in Nicholas of Cusa's concept of the mystical ascent to God. In the final stages of seeking union with the divine, the soul must put aside the desire for clear intelligibility and recognize the awesome incomprehensibility of God.

DOGMA. From the Greek, *dogma,* "that which seems to one, opinion or belief" (which in turn comes from the Greek verb, *dokeo,* "to think, to suppose, to imagine"). An authoritative belief or doctrine. While technically the term is synonymous with doctrine, it is often used negatively to refer to a rigid belief that is held without any evidence.

DOMINICANS. The Dominican order was founded by St. Dominic in France in the early thirteenth century; the official name is the *Ordo Praedicatorum,* or Order of Preachers (OP). This is an order of Catholic nuns, sisters, friars, priests, and laity, whose primary purpose is to preach the gospel and teach right principles. The order has a very strong academic past and is the order of St. Albert Magnus, St. Thomas of Aquinas, and many others. The order focuses on teaching, and as such, it found great success in setting up schools and missions throughout and beyond the bounds of Christendom during the Middle Ages. The order works hard to combat heresy and paganism; in fact, the first Grand Inquisitor of Spain was a Dominican, as well as many other officials throughout the history of the Church. The order prides itself on its strong intellectual past, and having produced the likes of Albert Magnus and Thomas of Aquinas, it is apparent that the order has a good foundation for this claim. And yet the order has also produced a strong mystic tradition. "German Mysticism" is also known as "Dominican Mysticism" and included such mystics as St. Catherine of Siena and Meister Eckhart.

The order spread quickly around Europe after its foundation, and yet its

DOUBLE EFFECTS, PRINCIPLE OF

birthplace in France was threatened greatly during the French Revolution, but around the same time the Order started a strong presence in America. In more recent times the order has continued its strong academic tradition with the foundation and continuation of numerous schools throughout the world, including *École Biblique et Archéologique française de Jérusalem* founded in 1890 which published both editions of the Jerusalem Bible. The Order of Preachers focuses much more on community involvement, a trait that distinguishes it quiet markedly from Augstan orders. The order is also known as the the Blackfriars (England), Jacobins (France), and followers often use the abbreviation O.P. after their names.

Many people believe that St. Dominic was the originator of the practice of saying the rosary, a practice which uses a necklace-like string of prayer beads to guide one through a series of 68 prayers and allows one to focus on five mysteries of the life of Jesus.

DOSTOEVSKY, FYODOR (1821–1881). A Russian novelist, short story writer, and journalist, whose work has been influential in philosophy of religion. His *Notes from the Underground* (1864) wrestles with determinism, freedom, and individual agency. *Crime and Punishment* (1866) involves trenchant themes of guilt, confession, punishment, grace, and redemption. *The Idiot* (1868–69) raises questions about goodness and the person

of Jesus. *The Brothers Karamazov* (1879–1880) is rife with arguments and counter-arguments about atheism, the problem of evil and redemption, and its narrative contains important developments that portray the mystical Christian life, as articulated in the context of the Russian Orthodox Church.

DOUBLE EFFECTS, PRINCIPLE OF. A principle of medieval theology that is still used to warrant acts that have ill as well as good effects. An act like giving a large dose of morphine to a patient may be permissible if it is intended to control or eliminate pain even if it has the foreseen consequence of suppressing the patient's breathing and thus causing her death. Stringent conditions in biomedical ethics would have to be met for this to be unproblematic: the patient must be terminally ill, the use of morphine is in accord with the consent of the patient, and so on.

Formally, the principle condones action with ill effects under four conditions: (1) The action from which ill is caused must be either good itself or neutral. (2) The agent's intention must be to do good. (3) The good and evil or ill is causally immediate so that the evil is not a means for the good. (4) There must be grave, good reasons for permitting the evil or ill. The principle is designed to block a straightforward utilitarianism calculation in which the end justifies the means, but it is difficult to rule out some

69

utilitarian use of the principle, especially in light of the fourth condition.

A controversial use of the principle would allow a Roman Catholic physician to terminate a pregnancy but only indirectly and if it was an essential, necessary consequence of saving the mother's life. Under such conditions, the intent must be to save the mother and not to perform an abortion, viz. A strict Roman Catholic cannot save the mother by means of the abortion, but thus allows (without requiring) action that may terminate pregnancy under highly stringent (and increasingly rare) conditions.

DOUBT. The belief in the improbability of a proposition or the lack of belief about the certainty of a proposition. One doubts a proposition to the extent that one either believes the proposition is false or implausible. Doubt may be compatible with belief so long as the belief is not completely implausible. Given that when a person believes X to be true, it appears to the person that X is true, it seems impossible for a person to believe X if there is incontrovertible evidence known to the person that X is false (for X would then appear not to be true). Even so, evidence and belief can function on multiple levels. A belief that X may endure despite there being both evidence known for and against its truth. Doubt may also come into play in contexts that are not confined to propositional beliefs as when one doubts a person's integrity or ethical

trustworthiness. *See also* CERTAINTY AND DOUBT.

DUALISM. Today, the term either refers to substance dualism (the soul or mind or person is distinct from her body) or property dualism (being conscious or being mental is distinct from being physical). In contemporary theology, the term is almost invariably treated as a term of disapprobation as it is linked to a value theory that denigrates the body. There is no such entailment, however, from the thesis that the mental or mind and the physical or body are distinct realities to any negative valuation of the body per se. Classical defenders of dualism include Plato, Augustine, and Descartes. Modern dualists include Mark Baker, Stewart Goetz, William Hasker, Howard Robinson, Daniel N. Robinson, Richard Swinburne, and Peter Unger.

DUNS SCOTUS, JOHN (c. 1266–1308). A Scottish Franciscan philosopher-theologian. He was ordained to the priesthood in 1291, studied theology at Oxford, and later lectured in Paris. After being temporarily banned from France in 1303 for siding with the Pope in a dispute with King, Phillip the Fair of France, Duns Scotus was allowed back into the country. Returning to Paris, he then took up the position of Franciscan regent master in theology. In 1307, Duns Scotus was transferred to Cologne where he died in 1308.

The writings of Duns Scotus are characterized as extremely complex and lengthy, which earned him the nickname "Subtle Doctor." The term "dunce" also originated as a play on his name. An example of his dense writing style can be seen in his attempt to prove God's existence, which emphasizes how God can only be known a posteriori. His proof is acclaimed as one of the most comprehensive and meticulous proofs made for God's existence during the Middle Ages.

Duns Scotus' theological writings emphasized the divine will, but he also devoted considerable time to writings on the process of redemption and the Virgin Mary. Although Duns Scotus was a theologian, he was highly dedicated to using philosophy to understand God and the world. In the field of philosophy he is greatly venerated for his work in logic, but he is best known for his contributions to metaphysics. Some of his most well-known works include the *Ordinatio, Quaestiones Quodlibetales, Quaestionnes Subtilissimae in Metaphysicam,* and *Collationes.*

DURKHEIM, ÉMILE (1858–1917). Durkheim is widely considered the father of sociology, with his sociology seamlessly running into philosophy. Durkheim was highly interested in the way societies maintain cohesion. He posited the importance of social facts, that is, phenomena that exist independent of and external to individuals. Social facts are much more useful and powerful than individual actions, according to Durkheim, because they are more objective and reflect a collective consciousness. His analysis of religion stressed the social function of beliefs and rites in establishing codes of what is acceptable and forbidden. His works include *The Rules of Sociological Method* (1895), *The Division of Labour in Society* (1893), *Suicide* (1897), *The Elementary Forms of Religious Life* (1912), *Education and Sociology* (1922), *Sociology and Philosophy* (1924), *Moral Education* (1925), and *Lessons of Sociology* (1950).

DUTY. From the Latin *debere* for "to owe." In moral theory, duties and obligations (the terms are not used synonymously) are sometimes contrasted with virtues and vices. Obligations involve states of character and emotions (passions, the disposition to pleasure or sorrow), whereas duties are sometimes thought to have normative authority no matter what one's emotions or character.

E

ECKHART, MEISTER (c. 1260–1327). German Christian theologian and mystic whose philosophy of the relationship between God and the soul bordered on a unitive pantheism. His work may exhibit the way in which theism can allow for deep pantheistic insights without embracing monism. His works include *Three Part* (1314), *Parisian Questions* (1302–1303), and *German Sermons.*

ECUMENISM. From the Greek *oikoumene*, meaning "the inhabited world." Ecumenism is the movement to promote religious unity. Although sometimes used to refer to unity between religions, ecumenism refers primarily to efforts for unity *within* a religious tradition, e.g., between Catholics and Protestants.

EDICT OF MILAN. The proclamation declaring the toleration of Christians and the restoration of their property in 313 CE by Constantine the Great and Licinius.

EDWARDS, JONATHAN (1703–1758). An American idealist, compatabilist, and defender of virtue theory and the beauty and glory of God. His public reputation today is largely built around his extraordinary preaching, especially the paradigm of fire and brimstone sermonizing in "Sinners in the Hands of an Angry God," but his broader philosophical and theological work deserves more attention. Edwards was one of the first European-American philosophers. He was appointed as president of the College of New Jersey (eventually Princeton College and the University). His works include *Notes on the Mind* (c. 1720), *Religious Affections* (1746), *Freedom of the Will* (1754), *Original Sin* (1758), and *True Virtue* (published posthumously, 1765). He was influenced by George Berkeley's case for idealism and the Cambridge Platonist view of virtues.

EGOISM. Psychological egoism is the view that persons by nature always act ultimately upon some perceived self-interest.

Ethical egoism is the view that one ought to act out of self-interest if one fully understands a situation. Such an ethical type was popularized in the twentieth century by Ayn Rand in her essays and novels. Some philosophers deny that egoism should be recognized as an *ethical theory*, as ethics involves impartial, disinterested inquiry. A reply to this charge is that egoism can (at least in principle) be defended on the grounds of impartial reflection. In the worn but useful phrase, "A rose that beautifies itself, beautifies the whole garden." One of the most prominent and forceful critics of psychological and ethical egoism was Bishop Joseph Butler in the eighteenth century. Also, Dostoevsky criticized the popular secular egoism of Western Europe according to which, if one pursues one's own best interests, the best interests of society will also be pursued (notably his work, *Notes from the Underground*, 1864, first English edition 1918).

EIGHTFOLD PATH. The ideal way of living according to the Buddhist faith that leads to enlightenment: right view, right intention, right speech, right action, right livelihood, right effort, right mindfulness, and right concentration.

EINSTEIN, ALBERT (1879–1955). German theoretical physicist, best known for his theory of relativity and of mass-energy equivalence ($E = mc^2$). His theories of general and special relativity redefined how time and space are viewed today. The idea that time could be relative to human beings rather than absolute has brought up unresolved debates regarding how God could exist in all time. Einstein personally agreed with Spinoza, regarding God as harmony and beauty rather than involved in human affairs. He argued that science and religion could strengthen each other rather than conflict. He claimed that if religion was motivated by fear it would only clash with science after bringing up false axioms; however, if religion was motivated by awe and mystery it would help one to fully experience the world. He discusses this concept in "Science and Religion," an article published in the journal *Nature* in 1940. He also summarizes his view in *Out of My Later Years* (1950): "Science without religion is lame, religion without science is blind."

In 1921, Einstein received the Nobel Prize in Physics. His chief works include *A Contemporary Viewpoint on the Production and Transformation of Light* (1905), *Electrodynamic Bodily Movement* (1905), *Toward a Theory of Brownian Motion* (1906), *Theory of Light Production and Absorption* (1906), *The Principle of Relativity and its Deducible Consequences* (1907), *Sketch of a General Theory of Relativity and a Theory of Gravitation* (1913), *Groundwork of the General Theory of Relativity* (1916), *On the Special* and General Theories of Relativity: A Popular Exposition (1917), Cosmological Considerations of General Relativity Theory (1917), The Meaning of Relativity (1921), On the Method of Theoretical Physics (1933), Motion of Particles in General Relativity Theory (with Infeld, 1949).

ELIADE, MIRCEA (1907–1986). Philosopher and historian of religions, Eliade sought a unified understanding of religions. He is best known for his understanding of myth and for his distinction between the sacred and the profane. He interpreted religious experience as based upon "hierophanies," or manifestations of the sacred, and he advanced a theory of Eternal Return, wherein myths and rituals not only commemorate but also participate in hierophanies. His works include Cosmos and History: The Myth of the Eternal Return (1954), The Sacred and the Profane (1957), Yoga, Immortality and Freedom (1958), Rites and Symbols of Initiation (Birth and Rebirth) (1958), Patterns in Comparative Religion (1958), The Sacred and the Profane: The Nature of Religion (1959), Myths, Dreams and Mysteries: the Encounter between Contemporary Faiths and Archaic Realities (1960), Images and Symbols: Studies in Religious Symbolism (1961), Myth and Reality (1963), Shamanism: Archaic Techniques of Ecstasy (1964), The Two and the One (1965), The Quest: History and Meaning in Religion (1969), and A History of Religious Ideas, 3 vols., (1978, 1982, 1985).

He was also the editor in chief of the 17 volume Encyclopedia of Religion (1987).

ELIMINATIVISM. In philosophy of mind, the thesis that the final, true theory of reality will eliminate any reference to or role for some features of our mental life. Candidates for elimination include beliefs, desires, and consciousness itself. Eliminativists sometime disparage talk of beliefs and so on as folk psychology. They have gone on to argue that traditional theism involves an illicit projection of folk psychology. Eliminativism is usually connected with strict forms of naturalism and materialism.

EMERSON, RALPH WALDO (1803–1882). An important transcendentalist, Emerson defended a non-theistic, immanent view of the divine. Emerson was deeply opposed to what he saw as a mechanized, dehumanizing popular materialism of his day. He championed independent, experience-based education and reflection. Emerson offered popular lectures in New England that attributed to all human persons a spark of the divine. This Neoplatonic outlook supported a philosophy of education that saw great value in leading students to awaken to the divine (and the protean, good potential) within. He was close friends with Henry David Thoreau and supported Thoreau's experiment in living narrated in Walden Pond. Emerson's works include Nature (1836),

Essays (2 vols., 1841, 1844), *Poems* (1846), *Representative Men* (1850), *English Traits* (1856), *The Conduct of Life* (1860), *May Day and other Pieces* (1867), *Society and Solitude* (1870), and *Letters and Social Aims* (1876).

EMOTION. Emotions (e.g., anger, love, hate, happiness) are sometimes distinguished from reason in ethical theory and thought to be in tension with it, though more recent works by Robert Solomanson and others treat emotions as essentially involving reason. Anger, for example, involves a person condemning or feeling rage on the basis of reason, e.g., a belief that a wronged injury has occurred. In religious ethics, there is debate over the voluntariness of emotions (e.g., Is a person responsible for their emotions?), the relationship of emotions and action (e.g., perhaps one can have a duty to engage in loving action, but it is more problematic to suppose that a person can have a duty to feel love as an emotion), and the ethical status and definition of emotions (e.g., what is the difference between love and lust?).

EMPEDOCLES (c. 490–430 BCE). Greek, pre-Socratic philosopher who held that nature itself is constituted by a mix of love and strife. He is the author of *On the Nature of Things* and *Hymns of Purification*. Both works are poems, with several hundred lines of each surviving.

EMPIRICISM. A method that gives primacy to experiential and sensory evidence. While empiricism is chiefly associated with British philosophers such as John Locke, George Berkeley, and David Hume, one can find proto-empiricist dictums in Roger Bacon that privilege sensory experience as well.

ENGELS, FRIEDRICH (1820–1895). German social scientist and philosopher who, along with Karl Marx, helped develop communism as a social ideal to be achieved at the end of a long history of class conflict. Engels defended a form of philosophical materialism and atheism as foundational to his political philosophy. True emancipation of persons is not to be found in individualist (bourgeois) acts of freedom, but in a coordinated community with common property. Engels' chief works include *Herr Eugen Dühring's Revolution in Science (Anti Dühring)* (1878), *Socialism: Utopian and Scientific* (1883), *The Origin of the Family, Private Property, and the State* (1884), *Ludwig Feuerbach and the Outcome of Classical German Philosophy* (1888), *Principles of Communism* (1919), and *Dialectics of Nature* (1925).

ENLIGHTENMENT. An intellectual, cultural, and philosophical movement in the eighteenth century, which emphasized human reason and freedom from tradition, especially religious tradition. Kant offered as a motto of the Enlightenment:

"Dare to know" (Latin: *sapere aude*). Contemporary philosophers are not united in assessing the achievement of the Enlightenment. Thinkers during the Enlightenment seemed to advance the case for human rights (*see* HUMANISM), but thinkers such as Hume and Kant also appear to be guilty of racism, Locke (paradoxically given his other convictions) seemed to allow slavery, and the Enlightenment's concept of reason has been critiqued as culture-specific and not (as Kant and others hoped) universal. Enlightenment can also refer to the Buddhist concept of liberation or *nirvana*, an escape from the cycle of death and rebirth (*samsara*).

ENS REALISSIMUM. Latin for "the most real being." Kant held that God is the most real being.

ENTAILMENT. Entailment is a logical relationship that warrants inference. For example, given the thesis "If A, then B," and "A," then "B" is entailed.

EPICTETUS (c. 55–c. 135 CE). A Greek Stoic philosopher and, at least at one time, a slave. Epictetus taught a spirit of content resignation in the face of forces that we cannot control. His works include *Discourse of Epictetus* (8 books extant) (c. 101 CE) and *Enchiridion* (a "handbook" summarizing the doctrines of the *Discourse*) (c. 135 CE).

EPICURUS (341–270 BCE). An ancient Greek philosopher who founded the school of thought called Epicureanism. Epicurus articulated a form of hedonism, according to which all and only things that give rise to pleasure are good. However, Epicurus did not endorse hedonism in the popular, "spring break" sense. Rather, a life of deep and refined pleasure involves diligent moderation and philosophical reflection. He argued that we should have no fear of death for insofar as death is annihilation, we will not exist after death and thus will not be in any state to have fear. Some 300 works have been attributed to Epicurus. The fraction of his work that survives includes *On Nature* (in 37 books, fragments of nine extant), the *Canon*, and letters to Herodotus, Pitocles, and Menoeccus.

EPIPHENOMENALISM. The thesis that the physical world affects the mind or the mental, but not vice versa. On this view, the mental is like the sparks caused by a machine or the suds of a beer or the foam of a wave in which the key causal contributor is the machine, the beer, or the water.

EPISTEMOLOGY. From the Greek *epistēmē*, meaning "knowledge." Epistemology is the study of or theories about knowledge. One may also use the term "epistemic" as an adjective to refer to that which pertains to knowledge; e.g., do we have epistemic access to the will of

God? In epistemology one also studies theories of evidence, justification, and warrant. What are the possible modes or ways of knowing the world, ourselves, morality and the divine? Questions that bear specifically on the justification of religious beliefs are addressed in *religious epistemology*.

Some philosophers identify epistemology as *the* distinguishing mark of modern philosophy, beginning with Descartes. It is very difficult to do epistemology, however, without also doing metaphysics (which concerns theories and accounts of what exists). A question such as "Can we trust our sensory experience?" presupposes that there are such things as sensory experience, trust, and (most obviously) ourselves. Modern philosophy may rightly be seen as privileging epistemology, but not in such a way that completely overshadows metaphysics.

EQUIPROBABILISM. The thesis that if a precept (a prohibition of some liberty) is equally probable as the probability that liberty is permissible, an agent may act in liberty. Imagine there is some reason for an agent on moral or religious grounds to be celibate as part of his vocation, but he also has some reason to pursue a licit sexual relationship. Equiprobabilism would allow liberty in this case. It is grounded on the assumption that "possession is the better claim" (*melior est conditio possidentis*). Given that persons possess liberty, there is a presumption that exercising liberty is permissible unless overridden by good reasons.

EQUIVOCAL. Terms are used equivocally when they are used in different senses, but this is not made clear contextually, often resulting in false conclusions. Example: A ham is an amateur radio operator. People eat ham. Conclusion: People eat ham radio operators. In philosophy of religion, some have thought that good is used equivocally in these two statements: "God is good" and "Some human beings are good." *See also* ANALOGY and RELIGIOUS LANGUAGE.

ERASMUS, DESIDERIUS (c. 1467–1536). Christian humanist, outstanding scholar, and Augustinian monk. A contemporary of Martin Luther, he chose not to join the Reformers despite his sympathy with them in regards to protesting ecclesiastical abuses. Erasmus' translation of the New Testament provoked serious debate over the extent to which one can find a doctrine of the trinity in scripture.

Erasmus was a close friend of Thomas More. Arguably, Erasmus and More can be seen as paradigmatic Renaissance philosophers in Northern Europe. They both (like the Florentine Platonists) welcomed the Christian engagement with non-Christian classics. Erasmus' works include *The Contempt of the World* (1490), *Chiliades Adagidrum* (1507), *In Praise of Folly* (1509), a Greek text of the New

Testament (1516), a series on the Church Fathers, including Jerome, Cyprian, Pseudo-Arnobius, Hilarius, Irenaeus, Ambrose, Augustine, Chrysostom, Basil, and Origen (1516–1536), *Diatribe on Free Will* (1524), and *The Epicurean* (1533).

ERIUGENA, JOHN SCOTTUS (a.k.a. Erigena) (c. 810–c. 877). An Irish Neoplatonist philosopher and theologian, Eriugena taught grammar and dialectics in France under Charles the Bald at the Palatine School near Laon. A master of classical Greek, he translated and interpreted the works of Dionysius the Areopagite, Maximus the Confessor, and Gregory of Nyssa.

His chief work, *Periphyseon* (also known as *On the Division of Nature*), sought to integrate Neoplatonism and Christianity. In this five-volume work, he divided nature into four categories: (1) that which is not created but creates (God as source), (2) that which is created and creates (the primordial causes, i.e., divine ideas), (3) that which is created and does not create (the creation), and (4) that which is not created and does not create (God as end). Eriugena, moved by the Neoplatonic vision of progression and regression, saw creation as emanating from and returning to God. Although he saw God and creation "as one and the same thing" because of God's superessentiality, he also maintained that God was above being and distinct from creation, thereby avoiding pantheism.

Eriugena was the first major influence of Neoplatonism in the West since Boethius (480–524/5), and his early followers included Remigius and Heiric of Auxerre and Pope Sylvester II. His work also influenced Christian mystics such as Meister Eckhart, Nicholas of Cusa, and Giordano Bruno. Councils at Vercelli (1050), Rome (1059), and Paris (1210 and 1225), in addition to a bull by Honorius III (1225), however, condemned his work as pantheistic.

ESCHATOLOGY. From the Greek *eschatos,* meaning "last." Accordingly, it designates the branch of Christian theology that deals with the last things. Traditionally, it has focused on four topics: death, judgment, heaven, and hell.

Personal eschatology focuses on the ultimate fate of individuals after their personal death and judgment, which is why heaven and hell receive so much attention in the field. Cosmic eschatology broadens the horizon to consider the final resolution and outcome of the entire created order. Eschatology is thus concerned with the "end" of the world in the teleological sense as well as the temporal. It seeks to discern the purposes for which God created the world and how God will accomplish them.

Although eschatology has sometimes been treated as a mere appendage to systematic theology, the reality is that it is integral to the Christian message, and any sound version of theology must be thoroughly eschatological. This is evident from the pregnant line Christians repeat when they celebrate the Eucharist: "Christ has died; Christ is risen; Christ will come again." The resurrection of Christ is itself an eschatological event that portends his coming again and the final judgment.

The resurrection also points out one of the main tensions and matters of debate, namely, the relationship between "realized eschatology" and "futurist eschatology." The former focuses on life with God in the here and now, and the transformation the gospel has already accomplished. The latter, by contrast, anticipates things yet to come. A fully adequate eschatology includes both elements, recognizing that eschatology has been inaugurated, but not consummated. As it is often put, there is an "already" as well as a "not yet" dimension to eschatology. God's Kingdom is indeed present, but it is not yet here in its fullness. Christians still pray for the day when God's will is fully done on earth as it is in heaven.

Interest in eschatology was at a low point in the nineteenth and early twentieth centuries when belief in human progress was at its height, and many believed utopia could be brought to earth by education and technology. The later twentieth century and early twenty-first century, by contrast, witnessed an explosion of renewed interest in the field. No doubt a major factor in this development was the emergence in popular culture of fundamentalist eschatology through several best selling books. These books not only promulgated the theory of the "rapture" of the church, followed by the great tribulation, and then the millennial reign of Christ, but also correlated these predictions with certain political events, particularly involving Israel and the Middle East.

Another fascinating development in contemporary eschatology is the conversation between theologians and cosmologists, particularly as these relate to scientific predictions of how the world will end. Scientific accounts of the end of the world point to ultimate cosmological futility with all life being destroyed either in a universe that grows ever colder as it continues to expand, or in a dramatic implosion that will turn the universe into a melting pot. These discussions underline the reality that any meaningful eschatology requires a God beyond the natural order, who has the power to raise the dead and make all things new.

ESSENCE. The term is often used to describe the core concept of a being. Thus, for classical theists, the essence of God is existence. On this view, the very core concept of God is of a being who exists and (for most Muslim philosophers and for Christian philosophers who follow Anselm) exists necessarily.

ETERNAL. A term used to describe something that is either everlasting (without beginning or end temporally) or timeless (nontemporal).

ETERNAL RETURN / RECURRENCE. Events A, B, and C have and will reoccur infinitely, in the same order and involving exactly the same things. For the Stoics, given the perpetual, rational, and providential nature of divine activity, the same causal principles will be re-applied in the world time and time again, resulting in eternal return.

Nietzsche also famously employed the concept of eternal return in his work, arguing that given an everlasting finite universe there must be exact recurrences. It is debatable whether Nietzsche actually believed this to be a true property of the cosmos or rather used it simply as a thought experiment to delimit the authenticity of life. If you had to live your life over and over again for all eternity, would you still affirm it?

More broadly speaking, eternal return can also refer to an understanding of time as cyclical. Understood in this sense, much Eastern philosophy would follow this doctrine, as would some ancient Greek philosophers (e.g., Heraclitus) and medieval theologians (e.g., Eriugena).

ETERNITY. Something (God, values, ideal forms) is eternal if it is not subject to temporal change. A value like justice may be thought of as eternal if it is not subject to change; it remains a fixed reference point for all of time. The concept of "eternal life" has sometimes been used to refer to a life lived in orientation to eternal values as opposed to preoccupation with temporal goods like fame or reputation. In the philosophy of God, "eternity" has been used to refer to God being timeless: there is no past, future, or successive change for God.

Boethius and some other philosophers (Augustine, Aquinas) held that God's eternality helps account for the capability of what (for us) is divine foreknowledge of future free action. If God is eternal, there is a sense that what for us is past and future is present to God eternally. If God is eternal, God does not act successively (first willing one thing, then another). Rather, God wills (eternally) successiveness; e.g., from all eternity God willed that God would be revealed first to Abraham, then to Moses. God's eternity also accords with the conviction that God created temporality or time. Some moderns hold a different view, claiming that God is a dynamic, personal reality who is temporal and yet not somehow governed or trapped by time (as a necessarily existing being, God does not age, weaken or decompose over time).

ETHICS. The domain of virtues and vices, right and wrong action. In ethical theory, one seeks to understand the nature, justification, and structure of ethical values. Can one rank the virtues, identifying which virtues are more foundational? In applied ethics, philosophers seek to address the virtues, vices, right and wrong action of specific practices such as abortion, euthanasia, duties to relieve suffering and so on. Ethics is sometimes studied or carried out with respect to particular traditions (one can practice Buddhist ethics or Christian ethics). Significant questions in philosophy of religion concern the foundation of ethics and methodology. Can ethics as a practice be normative if naturalism is true? If theism is true, how does this impact ethics? Philosophy of religion includes work in ethical theory as well as in applied ethics, with attention to religious values that are in play with medical practices, politics, environmental practices, sexual ethics, and so on.

EUCHARIST. From the Greek for "thanksgiving," the Eucharist is the central Christian rite of sharing consecrated bread and wine in remembrance of Christ's life, passion, death, and resurrection. It is also called the Mass, Holy Communion, or the Lord's Supper. Christian theologians have advanced different accounts of the consecrated bread and wine. Sacramental realists affirm that Christ is truly present in these elements or in the elements plus the full Eucharistic rite as a whole. *See also* TRANSUBSTANTIATION.

EUDAIMONIA. Greek for "happiness, well-being, or success." A central claim of Aristotle and those influenced by him is that human flourishing (*eudaimonia*) is a fundamental good. Eudaimonian ethics are often a part of natural law, a theory

that goodness consists in the fulfillment of nature. On this view, there is such a thing as *human nature* and a set of goods and excellences that comprise a fulfilled human being.

EUTHYPHRO PROBLEM / DILEMMA. Is X right because the gods approve of X? Or do the gods approve of X because X is right? This question emerges in Plato's dialogue *Euthyphro*. Plato himself seems to hold that the gods love the good because it is good.

EVANGELICALISM. The term "Evangelical" has been used of Protestant churches since the Reformation, reflecting these churches' claims to base their teaching pre-eminently on the Gospel (*evangelion* being Greek for Gospel). In Germany and Switzerland, "Evangelical" (*evangelisch*) has been used of Lutheran churches in contradistinction to Calvinist bodies. However, since 1945 all Protestant churches in Germany have been designated as part of the Evangelical Church in Germany. The evangelical wing of the Anglicanism is that which most identifies with Protestant teaching, including emphases on verbal inspiration and sole authority of scripture, personal conversion and salvation by faith, substitutionary atonement, and evangelism and revival. In this respect it is part of a pandenominational, global evangelicalism which has roots in the Methodist revivals of the eighteenth century. This pan-denominational evangelicalism includes Pentecostal and charismatic Christianity, which is the fastest growing part of the Church today.

EVANGELISM. The proclaiming of the Gospel (*euangelion*). The term "evangelist" is used three times in the New Testament (Acts 21.8; Eph 4.11; 2 Tim 4.5), alongside other designations of ministry or gift. The Apostles are also said to have "evangelized." Today the term "evangelism" is used particularly to refer to methods of proselytization performed by Evangelicals, which can include rallies with key speakers, beach missions, dissemination of tracts, and the development of certain dynamic styles of worship (using contemporary media and music, for example) that seem continuous with other aspects of people's lives.

EVERLASTING. Without a temporal beginning or end. Some theists contend that while God is everlasting, God is not atemporally eternal or timeless.

EVIDENCE. In most theories of knowledge historically, evidence is a normative concept of reason that can justify, entitle, or warrant a belief. Some naturalists have proposed non-normative accounts, according to which evidence is that which supports reliable beliefs for human beings whose cognition has developed through evolution.

EVIDENTIALISM. The view that beliefs are not justified unless supported by evidence. This position is thought to have reached its zenith in Descartes, Locke, Hume, and W. K. Clifford. Clifford (1845–1879) held that it is a sin to ever hold a belief without sufficient evidence. Unfortunately, he never defined what constitutes sufficient evidence.

EVIL, THE PROBLEM OF. If there is an all-powerful, all-good, and all-knowing God, then why is there evil? This is the classical theistic problem of evil that comes in the form of either a deductive or a probabilistic argument. Deductive arguments contend that there is a strict logical incompatibility between theism and the existence of evil. Probabilistic arguments usually concede that it is logically possible for God and evil to co-exist, but they argue that, given the amount of evil that exists, it is unlikely or improbable that God exists. A theodicy attempts to justify the apparent problem of the existence of evil in God's creation. *See also* ANTI-THEODICY; THEODICY.

EVOLUTIONARY ETHICS. Ethics as derived from evolutionary theory. This faces the difficulty that evolutionary theory does not seem to provide a reason to believe that if a form of life survives natural selection, it is ipso facto good or virtuous or more ethical than organisms that perish. Darwin proposed that in human beings compassion and ideals of justice will tend to promote survivability, but he also conceded that it might not do so. Some environmental ethicists claim that Darwinian and neo-Darwinian evolution can provide reasons for thinking that nonhuman animals deserve greater moral attention (given our mutual ancestral descent) than if one adopts the view that species are all separately created. While some philosophers think evolutionary theory and ethics are incompatible with Christianity (Richard Dawkins), others (Michael Ruse) see no essential conflict.

EX NIHILO NIHIL FIT. Latin for "from nothing, nothing comes." If this precept holds, something has always existed rather than there being a time in the past when there was nothing. Aristotle, for example, believed in an uncreated cosmos (one that has always existed).

EXCELLENCE. A term often used to refer to a good-making property; e.g., wit may be an excellence in oratory.

EXCLUSIVISM. In Christianity, a term used to refer to the position that belief (or trust) in Jesus Christ is essential for salvation. More moderately, an exclusivist may hold that salvation comes only through Jesus Christ even if this does not involve explicit belief or trust in Christ. Philosophers of other religions may make similar assertions about the exclusivity of their truth claims.

EXISTENCE. Some philosophers treat "existence" as a property and distinguish between the properties of existing contingently and existing necessarily. Other philosophers resist thinking of "existence" as a property and claim that it is dispensable in our descriptions and explanations of the world; e.g., rather than affirm "Lions exist," we should say "There are lions."

EXISTENTIALISM. A philosophical and literary movement that emerged in Europe (most notably in France) following World War II. Nineteenth century writers such as Soren Kierkegaard, Fyodor Dostoevsky, and Fredrich Nietzsche foreshadow many of the themes that existentialists later picked up on and further developed. The existentialist movement itself encompassed a vast array of thinkers, both theistic (e.g., Gabriel Marcel) and atheistic (e.g., John-Paul Sartre). Some consider existentialism to be more of a general "mood" than a systematic school of thought, making it a difficult term to decisively pin down. In general, existentialism was highly critical of essentialism and the search for an abstract, universal "human nature," focusing instead on the plight of the concrete individual in his or her quest for authenticity, that is, responsibility (as opposed to anonymity) for one's actions and values. Existentialists typically ascribed a radical freedom to individuals, and they often wrote of *angst* or anxiety in the face of death and meaninglessness, questioning why they had been "thrown" into existence. Many considered "nothingness" to be a basic category. Key existentialists include Lequier, Berdyaev, Buber, Rilke, Camus, Beauvoir, Merleau-Ponty, Kierkegaard, Nietzsche, Unamuno, Ortega, Heidegger, Jaspers, Bultmann, Marcel, Tillich, Sartre, and Kafka.

F

FAITH. May refer either to what is believed (religious teachings or creeds) or the act of believing itself. The latter has a subjective dimension, whereas the former is often thought to be objective in the sense that its truth or falsehood does not rest on the believer's subjective state. Philosophers and theologians have advanced competing models of faith. Fideists claim that religious faith does not require external evidential justification. Some hold that faith is evidentially justified (Richard Swinburne is a prime example). Norman Malcolm distinguished between *faith in* (as in "faith in God") versus *faith that* (as in "faith that God exists"), claiming that one can have the first without the second. Roger Trigg has countered that it makes no sense to have faith in God unless one believes (hopes or assumes) God exists. Some theologians describe "faith" as a gift, conferred through God's mercy. *See also* BELIEF-IN.

FALL, THE. Traditional Christian theology affirms that there was an initial, historical act of disobedience in which human beings turned away from God. In Genesis, the first humans (Adam and Eve) are created in a state of harmony and fecundity in the Garden of Eden and are then exiled from Eden due to disobedience to God. This is a fall from a state of blessing. Although the story of the fall is in both the Christian Old Testament and Hebrew Bible, Christian theology has tended to give more attention to the fall, in part due to the teaching that Jesus Christ is the New Adam, reversing the disobedience of Adam. Mary, the mother of Jesus, is also sometimes depicted as reversing Eve's fall.

FALLIBILISM. The thesis that human beliefs are capable of error, in opposition to the idea that some beliefs or texts are incapable of error, or are infallible. Some philosophers historically and today have held that some human beliefs are infallible (the self exists, there are sensations), but many philosophers today are content to argue that such convictions about the self and so on are justified but not established as infallible knowledge. If a belief is infallibly known, it is incorrigible (not subject to correction), but it is possible (logically) for a belief to be incorrigible without being infallible.

FALSE. See **TRUTH & FALSEHOOD.**

FALSAFA. An Arabic word derived from the Greek *philosophia.* ("Philosopher" translates as *Faylasuf,* sg., *Falaasifa,* pl.) In the Islamic context, *falsafa* originally referred to the intellectual practices and arguments encountered in Aristotelian and Neoplatonic schools of the Byzantine and Sassanian lands conquered by Muslims, though these schools and their texts were understood by many Muslims of the era to be continuous with questions, concerns, and principles found in the sources of Islamic revelation. Beginning in the eighth century, significant numbers of logical, linguistic, metaphysical, and ethical texts were translated into Arabic, and when drawn into conversation with pre-existing ideas and commitments, this gave rise to intense debates and intellectual development in centers of learning such as Baghdad. Though not all philosophers of this era were Muslims, the Islamic cultural and intellectual context framed the development of the tradition. This initial watershed gave rise to the achievements of philosophers such as al-Kindi, Avicenna, al-Farabi, Averroës, and al-Suhrawardi. Among the philosophers, some who claimed to be Muslim

were accused of being *kuffar* (sg., *kafir*), or unbelievers, and strong, though not necessarily hegemonic, currents within Islamic thought have been aggressively antagonistic toward the rationalism of the philosophers. *Falsafa* as a discipline distinct from theology did not flourish much beyond the twelfth century in Western Islamic lands, though many of its methods and commitments were absorbed by theology as well as Sufi mystical thought. In the East, particularly Persia and India, *falsafa* has maintained a more robust identity.

FALSIFIABILITY. Karl Popper proposed that an essential condition of meaningful scientific statements was their liability to falsifiability. On Popper's view, Freudian psychoanalysis was suspect because it seemed incapable of being shown to be false. In the 1950s and 1960s Anglophone philosophers questioned whether religious beliefs were falsifiable. Paradoxically, a prominent non-theistic philosopher Moritz Schlick claimed that the existence of an afterlife is not falsifiable (the living will never know if the dead survive in some other realm) but it is verifiable if true. *See also* TRUTH & FALSEHOOD.

FARRER, AUSTIN MARSDEN (1904–1968). British philosopher, theologian, biblical scholar, and Anglican priest, primarily known for his metaphysics, view of divine action, and theory of revelation.

Farrer's first book, *Finite and Infinite* (1943) was written, by his own admission, while he was "possessed by the Thomist vision, and could not think it false." But Farrer's relation to Thomism was complex and indirect, and he is perhaps best thought of as an original metaphysician who used—for his own purposes—certain Thomistic themes such as the uniqueness of God and the consequent need for analogy in reference to deity, the technical language of being and substance, and a preference for cosmological over ontological reasoning. Farrer's second major philosophical text, *The Freedom of the Will* (1958), was less Thomistic and more indebted to contemporary British linguistic philosophy, although his arguments against determinism and in defense of libertarian free will were distinctive. *Love Almighty and Ills Unlimited* (1962) put forward a theodicy for natural evils, and *A Science of God?* (1966) defended the compatibility between theistic belief and science, particularly biological evolution. Farrer's last book, *Faith and Speculation* (1967), attempts to summarize and revise his previous work in light of criticism and further reflection. Among many themes, it is perhaps most noted for articulating a "double-agency" view of divine action, in which God acts through created finite agents without compromising their own character and integrity. In terms of theology, Farrer belonged to the Anglo-Catholic wing of the Church of England and wrote numerous essays on various doctrinal topics.

Perhaps his most creative book in this area was *The Glass of Vision* (1948), in which he articulated a theory of divine revelation through images (rather than propositions or events) and which also contains an important defense of the role of imagination and "wit" in human reason.

FATE / FATALISM. One's fate is one's destiny, and fatalism is the view that one's fate is fixed or predetermined so that any acts to alter the inevitable future are done in vain. *See also* DETERMINISM.

FEMINIST PHILOSOPHY OF RELIGION. "Feminist" is an attribute increasingly applied to both women and men who are bound together in gender mappings of the Anglo-American field of philosophy of religion across the boundaries of different religions, and between theism and atheism. Feminist philosophers of religion seek greater philosophical, religious, and gender integrity in all argumentation, engaging women philosophers, not only men. A gap remains between the dominant works in philosophy of religion and the new directions taken in feminist philosophy of religion. For instance, feminist debates about the injustice of our epistemic practices remain hidden from the philosophical mainstream, while the latter can appear blind to salient material and social differences in their own philosophical thinking.

The "new" in twenty-first century feminist philosophy of religion includes greater attention to moral psychology and virtue epistemology. So, the philosophical attention of feminists has turned to the motivations for religious practices, including the reasons or causes for passions in different religions. In addition, feminist philosophers are considering novel metaphysical issues; they generate new core concepts—like "transcendence incarnate"—encouraging philosophers of religion in debates about material reality, bodily existence, and spatial locations.

In 1994, Nancy Frankenberry and Marilyn Thie broke ground for feminist philosophers in co-editing the first special issue on "Feminist Philosophy of Religion" in a prominent Anglo-American philosophy journal (*Hypatia: A Journal of Feminist Philosophy* [Fall] 9:4). It took another four years before the first two monographs, following Frankenberry and Thie, applied feminist critiques to the field of Anglo-American philosophy of religion (Pamela Sue Anderson, *A Feminist Philosophy of Religion: the Rationality and Myths of Religious Belief* (1998), and Grace M. Jantzen, *Becoming Divine: Towards a Feminist Philosophy of Religion* (1998)). It was another six years before a volume of feminist essays in the same spirit appeared co-edited by Pamela Sue Anderson and Beverley Clack, *Feminist Philosophy of Religion: Critical Readings* (2004). The most recent collection of major work in this field is edited by Pamela Sue Anderson, *New Topics in*

Feminist Philosophy of Religion: Contestations and Transcendence Incarnate (2009). At each of these stages, progress has been made in critical argumentation bridging traditional theism and feminist philosophy. The hope is that the next generation is assimilating the very best philosophical argumentation by feminists into the global mainstream of philosophy of religion.

FEUERBACH, LUDWIG ANDREAS (1804–1872). German materialist philosopher and critic of religion, Feuerbach was born in Bavaria and studied theology at Heidelberg and Berlin. In Berlin, he studied under Hegel and Schleiermacher, receiving his doctorate in 1828. Feuerbach is best known for his theory of projection, wherein he reversed the Hegelian dialectic and asserted that "God" is nothing more than a projection of humanity's self-alienated essence. He argued that theology is actually (and ought to be reduced to) anthropology, because God worship is actually self-worship. An atheist who denied an individual afterlife, Feuerbach held that human emancipation lies in an affirmation of this life while renouncing false supernatural projections. His work heavily influenced Karl Marx. The novelist known as George Eliot translated and was influenced by his works. Feuerbach's chief works include *Towards a Critique of Hegel's Philosophy* (1839), *The Essence of Christianity* (1841), *Principles of the Philosophy of the Future*

(1843), and *The Essence of Religion* (1846).

FICHTE, JOHANN GOTTLIEB (1762–1814). German idealist philosopher. A supporter of the French Revolution and an admirer of Kant, Fichte taught at Jena from 1794 until his dismissal in 1799 on charges of promoting atheism. His publications and teachings in this period had a huge influence on a generation of German thinkers and writers. Aiming to develop Kant's critical philosophy into a rigorous and thoroughgoing system of idealism ("*Wissenschaftslehre*"—Science of Knowledge), Fichte attempted to derive all of reality from the "self-positing" activity of the Ego. But he also argued that this idealism could not be made fully comprehensible on a purely theoretical level and must be taken up as a practical demand for an infinite striving to realize the ideal in the real. Thus idealism becomes a practical philosophy of ethics and politics. In his own way, therefore, Fichte maintained the Kantian thesis of the primacy of practical reason. His later writings were mostly political, and he became a leading spokesman for German nationalism. His works include *Critique of all Revelation* (1792), *Foundation of the Science of Knowledge* (1794), *The Foundation of Natural Rights* (1796), *A System of Ethics* (1798), *The Vocation of Man* (1800), *Characteristics of the Present Age* (1804), *Way to a Blessed Life* (1806), *The Closed Commercial State* (1800), and *Speeches to the German Nation* (1807–1808).

FICINO, MARSILIO (1433–1499). An important advocate of a Platonic understanding of Christianity, Ficino translated and commented on Plato's *Symposium* and advocated a high view of divine love spiritually. His works include *Commentary on Plato's Symposium* (1469), *On the Christian Religion* (1474), *Platonic Theology* (1482), as well as a translation of Plato's works (1483) and a translation of Plotinus (1492).

FIDEISM. From the Latin, literally meaning "Faith-ism." A radical form of fideism holds that evidence is of no relevance to the nature and integrity of faith. Less radical forms of fideism allow for some justificatory reasons through religious experience, for example, but resist rationalist or empiricist methodologies and what some call evidentialism (the thesis that for a belief to be licit it must be supported by available evidence).

FILMER, SIR ROBERT (c. 1588–1653). An English political writer, Sir Robert Filmer was educated at Cambridge and later knighted by Charles I. He is best known for his efforts to develop a doctrine of the divine right of kings rooted in the Bible and Christian faith. In his posthumously published *Patriarcha* (1680), he rooted patriarchalism in the authority given by God to Adam, applying this analogously to contemporary kingship. He also sought to trace a succession from the Hebrew patriarchs to the contemporary kings of Europe. His other works include *Freeholder's Grand Inquest* (1648), *Anarchy of a Limited and Mixed Monarchy* (1648), *Observations* (1652), and *The Power of Kings* (1680).

FINE-TUNING ARGUMENT. The fine-tuning argument is a version of the teleological argument for the existence of God based on the so-called fine-tuning of the cosmos for life. "Cosmic fine-tuning" refers to the widely accepted claim that the laws and certain fundamental numbers (i.e., constants) of physics, along with the initial conditions of the universe, must have been set with enormous precision in order for life to exist, particularly embodied conscious beings of our level of intelligence. For example, it is commonly claimed by physicists that if the cosmological constant—a fundamental number that influences the rate at which the universe is expanding—were not within one part in 10^{120} (i.e., 1 followed by 120 zeroes) of what physicists consider its natural range of values, the universe would have expanded too rapidly, hence practically eliminating the possibility of life evolving.

There are three basic responses to this fine-tuning. First, some appeal to some sort of transcendent cause—such as God—to explain the existence of a life-permitting universe. Second, advocates of the so-called multiverse hypothesis claim there are an enormous number of regions of space-time, with a wide variety of different constants, initial conditions, or even laws, and hence it is likely that at least one region would have just the right combination for life. Finally, some say that the existence of a life-permitting universe was just an extraordinarily lucky accident and that there is no further explanation for our existence.

Although many advocates of the fine-tuning argument claim that God is the best explanation for the existence of a life-permitting universe, they need not make this claim. For example, Scottish physicist and mathematician, John Leslie speculates that the transcendent cause is some Platonic principle of "ethical requiredness," whereas Robin Collins, an American philosopher, prefers to think of the fine-tuning argument as only providing confirmation for theism, not as claiming that theism offers the best explanation of our universe.

FIRST CAUSE ARGUMENT. A version of the cosmological argument, according to which the cosmos had a first cause either in time (in which case the cosmos has a beginning) or in the order of being. In the latter case, the cosmos may have had no beginning but its nature and being is possible only because of the reality and activity of a first cause. Arguments for a first cause deny there can be an actual infinity of explanations or causes.

FIVE WAYS, THE. The customary term for Aquinas' five arguments for the existence of God. These conclude that there is (1) a first mover, (2) a first efficient cause, (3) a necessary being, (4) a maximally perfect being, and (5) a designer.

FLORENTINE ACADEMY. A key movement in the Renaissance reclamation of classical sources driven particularly by the writings of Marsilio Ficino and Giovanni Pico Della Mirandola, whose work first brought the Platonic tradition and Platonic translations systematically into Western philosophy. Their philosophy is typified by the syncretic claim that, although Christian revelation is the primary model of God's revelation, pagan philosophical systems could reveal something of the truth of God. The greatest of these pagan traditions was the Platonic, particularly as understood in the Neoplatonic formulations of Plotinus and his followers.

FOREKNOWLEDGE. Ability to know the future. Given an omniscient God (in a strong, unrestricted sense of omniscience), foreknowledge is often thought to be essential to the very nature of God. For God to be omniscient, God cannot be ignorant of the future. Foreknowledge does raise paradoxes, however. If God knows you will freely read this entry in 2011, could you have done otherwise? Most monotheists hold that God is eternal and that God only foreknows what

you will do from our point of view, whereas to God all times are present to God's eternal presence. Some moderns (often called open theists) deny divine foreknowledge and understand omniscience as covering all that is possible for God (or any being) to know. They thereby restrict omniscience to not including all future acts.

FORGIVENESS. The traditional definition of forgiveness is that it involves a person forswearing (or moderating) resentment directed at a presumed wrong-doer. The forgiver is one who has been either directly or indirectly wronged; it would make no sense for someone to forgive a person unless that person is believed to have wronged the forgiver. Questions arise about the relationship of forgiveness and mercy, whether forgiveness can be wrong, and the extent to which forgiveness must be relational. Is forgiveness conditional on the wrong-doer confessing and reforming?

FOUCAULT, MICHEL (1926–1984). A French thinker who employed philosophical methods in treating culturally and politically significant institutions and practices. Foucault's work is in the Nietzschean spirit of unmasking so called impartial, objective principles and institutions as being actually motivated by very particular forces. He has been influential on feminist philosophers of religion and others seeking to expose implicit or disguised forms of control, repression, and development. His works include *The Order of Things* (1969), *The Archaeology of Knowledge* (1969), *Discipline and Punish* (1975), and *History of Sexuality*, 3 vols. (1976, 1984).

FOUNDATIONALISM. All of our justified beliefs have their justification because of their relationship to a base of justified (perhaps even self-justified) beliefs. Descartes was a prominent foundationalist. An alternative epistemology appeals to coherence and mutual support. On this view, there is not a single, prestigious base of certain knowledge, but a web of beliefs that are (ideally) mutually supportive and self-correcting.

FRANCIS OF ASSISI, St. (1182–1226). Francis of Assisi is best known in the Christian faith as the Patron Saint of Animals and the founder of the Franciscan order. He is also a Patron Saint of the environment and of Italy. St. Francis was the son of a wealthy merchant and in his youth seemed destined to a life in the upper class. However, his engagements in merriment and military service were soon overpowered by his desire to help the poor. In his quest for spiritual enlightenment, he gradually withdrew from his carefree lifestyle. Eventually Francis renounced all of his worldly possessions, despite his father's vehement protests.

Within a year Francis had 11 followers and was granted permission by Pope Innocent III to found a new religious order. Francis was never ordained as a priest, so he and his followers were originally known as the Order of Friars Minor.

Today members of this order are commonly referred to as Franciscans. Members of the order take a vow of poverty and usually own no property. They live a communal lifestyle with the members of their order, striving to live as true to Jesus' teachings as possible in accordance with the Rule of St. Francis. Interestingly, the first documented case of stigmata is attributed to St. Francis. In 1224, during a 40-day fast, the vision of an angel with six wings overcame Francis. The angel, a seraph, gave Francis the five wounds of Jesus Christ as a gift.

FREE WILL. The most stringent form of free will is called libertarianism and holds that a subject freely does X when she does X but could have done otherwise, even given all prior and contemporaneous events and the prevailing laws of nature. Less stringent forms of free will held by thinkers such as Locke and Hume hold that freedom involves simply a subject acting upon given desires (whose origin is not of concern). The latter is compatible with determinism—insofar as the desires an individual wills to fulfill may be completely determined—this view is sometimes called compatibilism.

FREE WILL DEFENSE. A term popularized by Alvin Plantinga for arguing that atheism is not entailed by the existence of a good, omnipotent God and the existence of evil. Plantinga argued that it is possible that an all-good, all-powerful God may allow evil due to the free action of creatures. He presented this argument as a *defense*, rather than a theodicy. The latter involves arguing that it is reasonable to believe theism is true notwithstanding world evil, whereas a defense argues that it is not unreasonable to accept theism and world evil. The Free Will Defense has an important role in the logical form of the problem of evil.

FREEDOM, POSITIVE / NEGATIVE. Freedom *to* versus freedom *from* acting upon a predicate. One has positive freedom when one has the ability and opportunity to speak. One has negative freedom when one is not restrained by, for example, chains or prison. Negative freedom can occur without positive freedom, but positive freedom requires at least some minimal negative freedom. *See also* ISAIAH BERLIN.

FREGE, GOTTLOB (1848–1925). He held that propositions exist necessarily, e.g., 7+5 = 12. Some proponents of the ontological argument appeal to Frege's Platonism to offset claims by Humeans that all of reality is contingent. His works include *Conceptual Notation* (1879), *Foundations of Arithmetic* (1884), and *Basic Laws of Arithmetic* (1893, 1903).

FREUD, SIGMUND (1856–1939). Austrian neurologist, psychologist, and the founder of psychoanalysis. In philosophy of religion, Freud's work constitutes an important naturalistic account of the emergence and power of religion in terms of guilt, the placation of a father figure, and wish-fulfillment. An atheist and materialist, Freud's work paradoxically supported a nonreductive account of human persons, preserving the idea that human beings are purposive animals. Freud's concept of the unconscious has also served as a model for some accounts of religious experience in which persons consciously may be said to be influenced by deeper layers of experience. His works include *Studies in Hysteria* (1895), *The Interpretation of Dreams* (1899), *The Psychopathology of Everyday Life* (1904), *Humor and its Relation to the unconscious* (1905), *Totem and Taboo* (1913), *Introductory Lectures in Psychoanalysis* (1916–1918), *The Ego and Psychoanalysis* (1916–1918), *The Ego and the Id* (1923), *The Future of an Illusion* (1927), *Civilization and its Discontents* (1930), *The Problem of Anxiety* (1936), and *Moses and Monotheism* (1939).

FRIENDSHIP. An important concept going back to Plato and Aristotle. Friendship has been largely conceived of as a reflexive, reciprocal relationship (love or affection between friends is to be mutual), and one that is particular rather than general. That is, it is customarily believed that both parties in a friendship deserve or merit preferential treatment by each other. The particularity of friendship vexed medieval monastic tradition as it was thought of as incompatible with Christ's command to love all persons. Aelred of Rievaulx (c. 1110–1167) launched a successful defense of preferential friendships in *Spiritual Friendships*.

Important questions in a philosophy of friendship include: Can a good person be friends with someone wicked? Can one be friends with someone who possesses far greater power? If a friendship ends in enmity, was it ever a *bona fide* friendship? Does friendship consist in or give rise to moral duties? Can a friendship be considered analogous to a work of art? Is friendship a basic good or something that is good for other reasons, e.g., it leads to happiness? Can one be friends with God?

FUNDAMENTALISM. The label "fundamentalist" was coined in 1920 by Curtis Lee Laws, a Northern Baptist in the U.S., to name those who were doing "battle royale for the fundamentals" of the faith. From there "fundamentalism" became the title of an unofficial coalition of evangelicals who found common cause in defending the authority of the Bible against higher criticism and liberal theology.

This coalition included: members of the Prophetic and Holiness movements, dominant among whom were premillennial dispensationalists; scholars, most notably those from Princeton Theological Seminary; and anti-evolution crusaders. Throughout the 1920s fundamentalists fought the modernists in their denominations, and many left to form their own churches. The main issues over which they fought are sometimes referred to as the "five points of fundamentalism": the inerrancy of scripture, the Virgin Birth of Christ, his substitutionary atonement, his bodily resurrection, the authenticity of the miracles (the 5th of the Presbyterian points), and premillennialism / the literal Second Coming of Christ (the 5th of the popularly known "Five Points of Fundamentalism" in the 1920s).

Creationism was not a major point of contention until anti-evolution crusaders from the southern U.S. allied themselves with the fundamentalist cause. Then the historic Scopes Trial of 1925, in which a schoolteacher was successfully tried in Dayton, Tennessee for teaching evolution in school, gained such bad press for fundamentalists that they began to retreat from public life. They developed a distinctive doctrine of separation, or purity; keeping themselves separate from worldly activities and attitudes, from non-fundamentalist Christians, and even from anyone who mixes with non-fundamentalist Christians. Politicized fundamentalists, who emerged in the 1970s, mark a turn back toward social engagement, and are criticized by separatist fundamentalists for their compromising cooperation with others.

The doctrine of inerrancy was the hallmark of fundamentalism, and has remained the hallmark of many post-fundamentalist evangelicals within the Anglo-Saxon world, though not without dispute. This doctrine teaches that the Bible in its original manuscripts contained no errors, and that any errors we may find in our texts are errors of copying or translation, and have providentially been kept to a minimum. Fundamentalists usually interpret inerrancy to mean that the Bible contains no factual errors.

They arrive at inerrancy by means of their doctrine of plenary verbal inspiration, according to which God inspired the very words of the Bible and kept them from error.

The term "fundamentalism" has come to refer to this distinctive stance, according to which the Christian faith needs an inerrant Bible as its foundation. When used in this way, it can apply to people outside of the historic fundamentalist movement, and is also applied to people across the world religions who hold significantly similar views with respect to their own faith.

G

GADAMER, HANS-GEORG (1900–2002). A German philosopher who drew attention to the irreplaceable value and importance of tradition in inquiry. His work is juxtaposed to a scientific reductionism as well as the Enlightenment ideal of tradition-free inquiry. Gadamer was deeply influenced by Heidegger, but he was far more concerned with values than Heidegger. Gadamer focused on understanding, instead of knowledge, as the central epistemic category for philosophy. He joins other phenomenologists in not restricting truth to propostions, but shows how it makes sense to speak of works of art and texts as true. He thought that in order to properly understand a text one had to understand how the text answers a question; consequently the best interpretations are those that show how the text could be true. His contributions to philosophical hermeneutics have been influential for theological hermeneutics. His works include *Plato's Dialectical Ethics* (1931), *Truth and Method* (1960), and *The Idea of the Good in Platonic-Aristotelian Philosophy* (1988).

GALILEO GALILEI (1564–1642). Italian astronomer, natural philosopher, and physicist. Galileo famously defended Copernicus' heliocentric theory of the universe as opposed to the Ptolmeic astronomy. Roman Catholic authorities compelled him to renounce his support for heliocentricity. The case of Galileo is often used to support the thesis that religion (or at least institutional Christianity) and science are inevitably in conflict. Famously, Galileo claimed that if you want to get to heaven, you should read the Bible, but if you want to study the heavens you should use a telescope. His key works include *The Starry Messenger* (1610), *The Assayer* (1623), and *Dialogue Concerning the Two Chief World Systems* (1632).

GANDHI, MOHANDAS KARAMCHAND (1869–1948). A political reformer and religious thinker who used collective nonviolent action in order to free India from British colonial rule. Born in India, Gandhi studied law in England and then practiced in South Africa for 20 years before starting his major work in India.

Gandhi believed that humans should not use violence because of their limited knowledge, and instead he encouraged his followers to practice discipline and love of adversaries in their movement of non-cooperation. He called this approach *satyagraha* (Sanskrit: *satya*, "truth," and *agraha*, "force"), which means holding fast to the truth. His method was *ahimsa*, non-violence, based on an ancient Indian concept prohibiting violence, which Gandhi expanded to include not belittling or coercing others. He believed that means and ends are necessarily related. The moral principles of truth and nonviolence guide all "true" religions, according to Gandhi, who held that God is truth. A life-long practicing Hindu, he was also influenced by other religions, such as Christianity, Jainism, and Islam. Gandhi thought that the status of untouchables in the caste system was the greatest problem of Hinduism. Overall, Gandhi demonstrated his beliefs through practice and encouraged others to do the same, for religion at its best was concerned with human community and faith was inextricably tied to social ethics.

GASSENDI, PIERRE (1592–1655). A French philosopher and mathematician, he is celebrated in the history of philosophy as one of Descartes' most perceptive critics. Gassendi subscribed to atomism and opposed Aristotelian treatments of the natural world. While opposed to Descartes' arguments for God and the soul, Gassendi did defend the existence of the soul and natural theology. His works include *Exercises Against the Aristotelians* (1624), *Disquisitio Metaphysica* (1644), *Syntagma philosophicum* (1658), and *Opera Omnia* (1658).

GILSON, ETIENNE HENRI (1884–1978). The most important twentieth-century intellectual historian of the medieval era. Gilson developed a rigorous articulation and defense of Thomas of Aquinas for modern philosophers. His works include *Thomism* (1920), *The Philosophy of Saint Bonaventure* (1924), *Saint Thomas Aquinas* (1927), *Introduction to the Study of Saint Augustine* (1929), *Studies of the Influence of Medieval Thought on the Development of the Cartesian System* (1930), *The Spirit of Medieval Philosophy*, 2 vols. (1932), *Christianity and Philosophy* (1936), *The Unity of Philosophical Experience* (1937), *Heloise and Abelard* (1938), *Dante* (1939), *God and Philosophy* (1941), *The Christian Philosophy of Saint Augustine* (1947), *Being and Essence* (1948), *Being and Some Philosophers* (1949), *John Duns Scotus: Introduction to his Fundamental Positions* (1952), *History of Christian Philosophy in the Middle Ages* (1955), *Painting and Reality* (1955), and *The Spirit of Thomism* (1964).

GLANVILL, JOSEPH (1636–1680). Glanvill was a Latitudinarian divine (priest) and disciple of the Cambridge Platonist Henry More. His early writing supported many of the themes of the Cambridge

Platonists, including attacks on the perceived limits of scholasticism, an advocacy for Cartesian philosophy, and a promotion of the new scientific method of the seventeenth century. In his later writings Glanvill sought to prove the reality of the spiritual world and its compatibility with modern scientific discovery. Most controversially, Glanvill used accounts of witchcraft in support of this argument. His works include *The Vanity of Dogmatizing* (1666), *Essays upon Several Important Subjects in Philosophy and Religion* (1676), and *Saducismus Triumphatus* (1681).

GNOSTICISM. A religious movement originating roughly at the same time as Christianity, combining popular Platonist beliefs with heterodox Jewish and Christian thought. A great deal of Gnostic teaching affirmed that the material creation itself is not the work of God but of a lesser being or a god of this world sometimes identified as Sophia (*see* DEMIURGE). We are souls trapped in this world, not fully aware of our need for our true home, which is in union with the God beyond this world. Our salvation lies partly in knowing this God and our journey to this God through ascetic practices and knowledge.

GOD. In Abrahamic faiths, "God" functions as a descriptive noun referring to a supreme, powerful reality that is the object of religious belief and practice. So, in Judaism, Christianity, and Islam, God is the all good, necessarily existing creator and sustainer of the cosmos. In these traditions, "God" sometimes functions as a proper name referring to the being who is encountered in religious experience as opposed to standing for the descriptive role as, for example, the one who creates, sustains, and redeems. Concepts of God vary across cultures and traditions, some of which are monotheistic while others are polytheistic and pantheistic. Some concepts of God maintain a clear distinction between God and the cosmos (God is not the creation), while others identify God and the natural world (Spinoza).

GOD, ARGUMENTS FOR THE EXISTENCE OF. These include the ontological, cosmological, and teleological arguments, as well as arguments from religious experience and miracles.

GOD, CONCEPTS AND "ATTRIBUTES" OF. As understood in traditional Judaism, Christianity, and Islam, God is the Creator of the cosmos, omnipotent, omniscient, wholly good, omnipresent, everlasting or eternal, necessarily existent, worthy of worship and incorporeal. Other attributes are sometimes thought to be divine simplicity (God is not made up of parts), immutability (not subject to change), and impassability (not subject to emotions or passions). Theists in these traditions sometimes differ in their treatment of the attributes: Is God outside of time? Does omniscience include knowledge of the future?

"God" is also understood differently in traditions that affirm the unity of God and nature. According to pantheism, God is in some sense everything. In panentheism, the world (or nature or "creation") is thought to exist within God. Some nonrealists treat the concept of God noncognitively and believe "God" does not refer to a creator or some other transcendent being. On their view, talk of God is to be understood as a way of cultivating certain values and feelings such as compassion and loving your neighbor.

GOD, DEATH OF. A dramatic metaphorical declaration that the concept of God is no longer legitimate—philosophically, religiously, or theologically. It is most famously traced to Nietzsche's *Thus Spake Zarathustra* (1883–1885), but it was a term used earlier by Hegel and Emerson.

GOD OF THE GAPS. Arguments for God's existence that rely on the explanatory gaps of other theories. If, for example, evolutionary biology cannot explain the emergence of human life from nonhuman animals, a theist may use this as part of a case for creationism.

GOD OF THE PHILOSOPHERS. Pascal once juxtaposed God as conceived of by philosophers with the God of religion. Some believe the former is too intellectual or abstract and not immediately relevant to ordinary believers.

GODDESS. A female god, often associated with indigenous religions and nature or earth worship. Some feminist theologians think that religious practices that were defined by goddess worship were more pacific, collaborative, and matrifocal than the patriarchy linked with the worship of a male god.

GOLDEN RULE. "Do onto others as you would have others do onto you." This ethical command occurs in numerous religious traditions, although usually in the negative form; e.g., Confucius said "What you do not want done to yourself, do not do to others."

GOOD, THE. Most commonly used in a broad, Platonic context to refer to goodness in general or the form or property by which good things are good. Platonists have traditionally held that the goodness of particular things and acts are good in virtue of the property the Good.

GOSPEL. In Greek, *euangelion*, "good news." The Gospels contain accounts of the life of Jesus. Christians recognize four canonical gospels: Matthew, Mark, Luke, and John. The first three are known as the synoptic gospels and have much material in common. Most scholars accept a two-source hypothesis for the relationship between the synoptic gospels, according to which Mark's gospel was written first. Matthew and Luke then drew from Mark's gospel and a second source, called

Q (from *Quelle*, German for "source"). John's gospel was written latter and varies significantly from the other three. There are also many Apocryphal gospels (such as the Gospel of Thomas), which were not included in the canon. *See also* BIBLE.

GOVERNMENT. Philosophers, from Ancient Greece and China onward, have addressed the nature and legitimacy of governance and the proper structure of political communities. In philosophy of religion, inquiry has focused on the extent to which governance and politics requires a religious foundation; the legitimacy of monarchical rule, democracy, and other forms of governance; the relationship of religious and civic duty and virtue; toleration; the freedom to practice religion; and the limits of imposing religious practices among non-religious subjects or citizens. Just War Theory is a domain that many philosophers and theologians have engaged which bears directly on the philosophy of government and politics.

GRACE. Unmerited favor. In theology, grace has been conceived in formal, penal terms (through grace God forgives sins), and as linked to gifts such as God's creation and redemption. Creation itself has been construed as a matter of *common grace* and God's calling of souls to salvation as *special grace*. Infused grace occurs when God instills in the soul the gift of faith or virtue.

GREEK PHILOSOPHY. The term used to refer to Ancient Greek philosophy, from the pre-Socratics to the fifth century CE and the collapse of the Western Roman Empire.

GREGORY OF NAZIANZUS (c. 329–390). One of the great fathers of the early Christian church and one of the Cappadocian fathers along with Basil the Great and Gregory of Nyssa. Gregory was raised in Nazianzus and was schooled in the classical tradition in Athens alongside Basil. Gregory returned to Nazianzus around 359 and began to serve the church there in 361. In 373, Basil appointed him bishop of the small territory of Sasima in an attempt to combat Arianism by appointing anti-Arian friends to high-ranking positions, but Gregory was never happy about this appointment. Gregory spent two years in Constantinople around 380 before returning to Nazianzus. He vigorously emphasized the importance of believing in the trinity in order to be a faithful Christian, claiming that God the Father is the source and cause of the trinity, but nevertheless comprising a unity that is indicative to the doctrine. He wrote poems and letters, but it is his sermons (now published as *Forty-five Sermons*) that are best known.

GREGORY OF NYSSA (c. 335–c. 398). One of the great fathers of the early Christian church. He is the youngest of the Cappadocian fathers (the others being

Basil the Great and Gregory of Nazianzus) and the younger brother of Basil and Macrina the Younger. It appears that Gregory was married at some point in his life, though very few details about this marriage exist. Gregory hailed from a prominent Christian family and is usually seen as having been heavily influenced by his brother Basil, who appointed him bishop of Nyssa in the fight against Arianism.

Gregory is often seen as continuing the work of Basil and defending Basil's positions (e.g., *Against Eunomius* and *On Virginity*), but he also took up ideas of Christian Platonism (e.g., *On the Soul and Resurrection* and *On the Making on Man*) and wrote the lives of saints, including his sister (e.g., *Life of Macrina* and *Life of Moses*). Gregory of Nyssa, along with Gregory of Nazianzus and Basil the Great, developed a doctrine of the trinity, stressing that it was necessary to believe in the three Godheads as being a single God in order to be a Christian follower of the Catholic Church. Gregory also elaborates the idea of giving Jesus to Satan as a ransom in order for salvation. Jesus (the sinless, God-man) is given to Satan as a kind of substitute for us. Jesus thus lures Satan into releasing us from captivity, and then overcomes Satan. This model of the atonement has sometimes been called the mousetrap, as Jesus is used as a kind of bait to trap the evil one.

GROTIUS, HUGO (1583–1645). An important Dutch jurist and philosopher who defended the concept of international law on the grounds of natural law as opposed to contractarianism or utilitarianism. His works include *On the Law of Booty* (1604), *On the Law of War and Peace* (1625), and *On the Truth of the Christian Religion* (1627).

GUILT. One is guilty of a wrongdoing if one is morally responsible for the act and therefore worthy of blame. The state of being guilty differs from the state of feeling guilt. One may be guilty of an act without feeling guilty, and one may feel guilty for an act when one is not guilty. In some moral and religious traditions, internal desires (such as envy or lust) even if not acted upon are deemed worthy of blame and thus can be sources of guilt and guilt feelings. Some religious rites of confession, remorse, repentance, forgiveness, and personal renewal are believed to involve absolution, the removal of guilt. *See also* SHAME.

GURU (Sanskrit, "teacher"). A term used in Indian religions to refer to a teacher, usually of a spiritual nature.

GURU GRANTH SAHIB. The sacred book of Sikh religion, believed to be the tenth and final incarnation of Guru Nanak (the founder of the religion).

H

HABERMAS, JÜRGEN (1929–). An influential German philosopher and sociologist, Jürgen Habermas was born outside of Düsseldorf, Germany and witnessed the fall of the Third Reich as an adolescent. The postwar revelation of the crimes committed under National Socialism had a deep impact on his outlook. In 1954 he finished his dissertation at the University of Bonn and first gained notice (as well as criticism) for his book, published in 1962, about the development and role of the public sphere in Western culture, a subject which forms a major theme in his work. He was a professor first at the University of Heidelberg, then at Frankfurt in 1964, the Max Planck Institute in Starnberg in 1971, and the University of Frankfurt from 1982 until his retirement in 1994.

While writing on a number of topics having to do with philosophy and society, one of Habermas' central philosophical projects was his development of a theory of rationality. His system drew on speech act theories, and he proposed communication resulting in consensus as the primary function of rationality.

He also suggested the importance of an "ideal speech situation," in which communicants can discuss important social issues on the basis of rationality alone, free from inequality or distortion. Truth, in his system, is the consensus that would be reached in this ideal speech situation.

Habermas thus sees the existence of a free and equitable public sphere as vitally important to democratic societies and believes that this function is impaired in contemporary societies by economic forces. Regarding the role of religious reasoning in the public sphere, Habermas draws a line between personal justifications and the justifications offered for public policies. He rejects as too stringent the view held by some philosophers that individuals must only rely on secular reasoning when discoursing in the public sphere, but he also insists that justification for coercive laws must be offered in non-religious language that is equally accessible to all. Ultimately he suggests that the dialogue between religious and secular individuals is mutually informative and of value to both.

HADITH. Sayings ascribed to the prophet Muhammad. The collection is considered the second most holy text in Islam, the Qur'an being the first.

HAECCEITY. A property that can only be possessed by one object. Some hold that individual persons have a haecceity. So, Barack Hussein Obama has the property of *being Barack Hussein Obama,* and no other person can have that property. This bears on the philosophy of creation. If there is a haeceity *being Barack Hussein Obama,* God could have deliberately set out to create *him* rather than someone else who shares all his physical and mental properties.

HARE, RICHARD MERVYN (1919–2002). A defender of impartialism in the ideal observer tradition. He also defended a non-cognitive view of religious belief. His works include *The Language of Morals* (1952), *Freedom and Reason* (1963), and *Moral Thinking* (1981).

HARTSHORNE, CHARLES (1897–2000). A bold American philosopher, influenced by Alfred North Whitehead. Hartshorne defended pan-psychism and a form of theism in which the world is in God but God and the world are not identical (sometimes called process theism or panentheism). Hartshorne mounted a vigorous defense of the ontological argument for the existence of God, as found in the work of Anselm. He did not subscribe to traditional Christian theism on several fronts: he denied that God is omnipotent, for example, and he was skeptical about an individual afterlife. His works include *The Collected Papers of Charles Sanders Peirce* 6 vols. (ed. with Paul Weiss, 1931–1935), *The Philosophy and Psychology of Sensation* (1934), *Beyond Humanism* (1937), *Man's Vision of God and the Logic of Theism* (1941), *The Divine Relativity* (1947), *Reality as Social Process* (1953), *Philosophers Speak of God* (with William L. Reese 1953), *The Logic of Perfection* (1962), *Anselm's Discovery* (1965), *A Natural Theology for our Time* (1967), and *Creative Synthesis and Philosophic Method* (1970).

HEAVEN, CHRISTIAN CONCEPTION OF. The hope of heaven is both the climax of the Christian story and an integral component of the Christian vision of reality. The heart of that vision is the claim that the ultimate reality is the trinity, a God who exists in three persons in an eternal relationship of love. This God is not only the source of all truth, goodness, and beauty, God is also infinitely creative and boundless in God's own happiness and joy.

The Christian story is that human beings were created in the image of the triune God for an eternal relationship with God. Although humans have fallen and gone their own way, it is God's design to restore and perfect that relationship.

The prospect of enjoying such a relationship with God, as God intended all along, is what grounds the hope of heaven. The quality and degree of happiness and fulfillment one may aspire to experience is infinitely greater than anything one may dream of if the most basic constituents of reality are matter and ever dissipating energy.

The hope of heaven has been an animating force in Western culture for the better part of two millennia. It has been a moral source of enormous significance, not only providing grounds to make rational sense of ethics, but also endowing people's lives with ultimate meaning. Moreover, it has inspired some of the greatest artistic achievements, both literary and visual. Two biblical images have been predominant in artistic depictions of heaven, a garden and a city. Cities embody the highest forms of culture and society, and heaven as the New Jerusalem would represent the apex of such achievement. The image of a garden captures the human longing to return to Eden and the primordial fellowship with both nature and God that it represents.

A central component of heaven as traditionally understood by Christians is the beatific vision, the ultimate delight of seeing God that is the epitome of joy and satisfaction. This has sometimes been understood in a highly intellectualist sense, as an experience of contemplating God in timeless bliss. This picture of heaven has little place for relationships with other persons or other aspects of the created order as contributing to the highest human fulfillment.

By contrast, recent New Testament scholarship emphasizes that final redemption includes the entire created order. The book of Revelation pictures this in terms of the New Jerusalem coming down to a renewed earth. God's final purpose is achieved when God's will is done on earth as it is in heaven. The beatific vision is not less important on this view, but here it is anticipated that the glory of God will be perceived throughout the new creation with all its delights and radiant beauty.

In view of this picture, the common claim that one goes to heaven when one dies may need to be qualified. Although the New Testament clearly teaches that those who die are with Christ, they still await the final resurrection when all will be raised in their bodies. It is then that heaven in its fullness will be a reality. As the book of Revelation famously describes this scene, God will dwell with humanity and wipe every tear from our eyes as death, pain, and mourning forever pass away. Those so blessed will look to the future with ever increasing joy as they continue to explore the infinite beauty of God and grow in God's boundless love.

HEAVEN, NON-CHRISTIAN CONCEPTIONS OF. Islam believes that the body and soul of everyone are resurrected but only those who have worshiped Allah alone will go to heaven for eternity. In Judaism, the existence of an afterlife s non-specific in early writings: there are references to earthly punishment for being disobedient to God and a place of the dead, *sheol*, are referenced. There are two main Indian conceptions of heaven: a permanent bliss and happiness, and a temporary state where *samsara* consumes all. It is also seen as infinite, endless, indefinable, complete, and full of pleasures. Some sects of Indian philosophy believe that heaven is a home of the gods and family members who have died. The Buddhist heaven is thought to have sensual pleasures where a person can continue his or her spiritual work. The Chinese philosophies (such as Daoism and Buddhist sects) believe in two heavens: a pre-natal heaven and a later heaven. The pre-natal heaven is the bliss before people are born into the world while the later heaven is the bliss after death. Daoists strive to reverse the birth process so the pre-natal heaven can be achieved again. The two heavens are visible in the *yin-yang*.

HEDONISM. The belief that pleasure or happiness is the only basic good: all other goods derive their goodness directly or indirectly because of pleasure or happiness. Hedonism can allow that there are a host of different levels of pleasure, including refined intellectual and aesthetic pleasures. A hedonist may even defend altruism as a preeminent pleasure. As a theory of the good, hedonists need not see goodness as only a human matter; assuming at least some nonhuman animals experience pleasure or happiness, their well-being should also be considered as being good. *See also* ETHICS.

HEGEL, GEORG WILHELM FRIEDRICH (1770–1831). A philosopher of great significance, Hegel defended a metaphysics and a philosophy of history that sought to render all of reality rational. Two major schools of thought emerged, often called Left wing and Right wing Hegelianism. The latter construes Hegel as a Christian theist, while the former sees Hegel in non-theistic terms and as a heterodox Christian.

Hegel believed that history and thought itself should be seen as a dynamic dialectic. One may represent this in three stages at the outset. Assume the concept of the changeless, as in Parmenides' thesis that there is only being. This thesis invites the anti-thesis associated with Heraclitus that everything changes. This in turn invites a synthesis: some things remain the same, some things change. Hegel's analysis of the master-slave relationship in *The Phenomenology of Spirit* (1807) has been highly influential. By Hegel's lights, the master is dependent upon the slave for his identity and vice versa. According to Hegel, religion is one way that a society becomes self-conscious of its values. Religion is not fully rational, but neither faith nor revelation could be contrary to reason. He also thought religions could only be understood in the context of their concrete practices.

Hegel's other works include *Science of Logic* (1812–1816), *Encyclopedia of the Philosophical Sciences in Outline* (1817), *Foundations of the Philosophy of Right: Natural Right and Political Science in Outline* (1821), and *Lectures on the Philosophy of Religion* (1895).

HEIDEGGER, MARTIN (1889–1976). Heidegger's early work is in phenomenology. He believed that time and temporality are key factors in understanding human nature and that we should live in anticipatory resoluteness toward our own death. Heidegger argued that Western philosophy suffered because of its forgetfulness of being. His later work saw a key role for poetry in the recovery of being. Heidegger was a member of the Nazi party briefly in the 1930s. Despite this regrettable legacy, Heidegger has been profoundly influential in continental philosophy, impacting thinkers such as Sartre and Derrida. His works include *The Theory of Categories and Meaning in Duns Scotus* (1916), *Being and Time* (1927), *What is Metaphysics?* (1929), *Kant and the Problem of Metaphysics* (1929), *On the Essence of Reason* (1929), *The Self-Assertion of the German University* (1933), *Hölderlin and the Essence of Poetry* (1936), *On the Essence of Truth* (1947), *Holzwege: Off the Beaten Path* (1949), *Introduction to Metaphysics* (1952), *What is Called Thinking?* (1954), *On the Question of Being* (1955), *What is Philosophy?* (1956), *Identity and Difference* (1957),

Composure (1959), *On the Way to Language* (1959), *Nietzsche* (1961), *What is a Thing?* (1962), *Views* (1970), and *Phenomenology and Theology* (1970).

HELL, CHRISTIAN CONCEPTION OF. The Christian account of an infinite God of perfect love not only raises the possibilities for human happiness and fulfillment to extraordinary heights, it also implies extreme depths of loss and misery. In particular, human beings may lose out on the eternal relationship with God for which they were created. The doctrine of hell is the elaboration of this frightful possibility.

The traditional account of this doctrine involves three crucial claims: that some persons will never accept the grace of God, and therefore will not be saved; that those who reject the grace of God will be consigned to hell, a place of great misery that is the just punishment for their sins; and that there is no escape from hell, either by repentance or suicide or annihilation.

The claim that eternal misery is the just punishment for sin has often been defended by traditional theologians on the ground that sin is infinitely serious, and therefore demands an infinite punishment. The infinite seriousness of sin is due to the fact that one owes God perfect honor and obedience, so any failure in this regard puts one in infinite debt to God. In the same vein, others have contended that since God is infinite in authority, beauty, goodness, and the like, one's obligation to honor God is likewise infinite. So again, to fail in one's duty is to incur a debt that is serious beyond measure.

The misery of eternal hell is typically said to include two dimensions: the pain of sense and the pain of loss. The pain of sense has traditionally been thought to consist primarily of literal fire that would cause intense agony. The pain of loss refers to the anguish of losing out on the great good of eternal life in relationship to God. This loss produces bitter emotions such as regret and remorse that gnaw at the hearts of the damned. So understood, hell has been construed as a sort of supreme torture chamber in both popular piety and the works of noted classical theologians.

This picture of hell has come under extensive criticism from both philosophers and theologians. The primary objection they have raised is the so-called "proportionality problem" which holds that finite beings can only do finite harm, so infinite punishment is out of proportion to any evil they might do. Eternal hell cannot therefore be defended as a matter of justice for sins committed in this life.

More recently defenders of hell have appealed to human freedom rather than to principles of retributive justice to make sense of the doctrine. That is, they argue that sinners can by their own free choice reject God decisively and thereby confirm their characters in evil so thoroughly that they would never want to repent.

So God respects their choice and leaves them to their self-chosen misery. This view emphasizes the pain of loss much more than the pain of sense. As C. S. Lewis famously characterized this view, "the doors of hell are locked from the inside." It is not that God has chosen to lock people into eternal misery, but they have chosen it for themselves by locking God out of their lives, and that is the essence of hell.

Critics question this strategy for defending eternal hell by challenging the claim that anyone can choose evil so decisively. Evil may be chosen in the short run, they contend, but there is no intelligible motive for choosing eternal misery for oneself. The debate here hinges on whether such a self-destructive choice can make moral and psychological sense.

HELL, NON-CHRISTIAN CONCEPTIONS OF. The belief in hell almost always involves a place or time of suffering and punishment for sins or evils committed in a previous life. As such, Hinduism (although the earliest Hindus did not believe in an afterlife in heaven or hell but rather one in which we return to the earth) holds that souls are punished in *nakara* appropriately for the sins that they had committed until they are purified through suffering and are reborn in balance of their *karma*. The *Bhagavad Gita*, along with other portions of the *Mahabharata*, describes this idea of hell and mentions ways in which it can be avoided. Buddhism also acknowledges a place and function for *nakara* in its ideology, but it strongly emphasizes that its followers strive to escape *samsara* (Sanskrit, commonly meaning "the wheel of suffering") that souls inhabit during all reincarnation cycles before reaching *nirvana*. Some Chinese philosophies (such as Daoism) believe hell to be full of pain and torture; it is a place underground, mimicking an earthly prison, where the sun does not reach, and is meant to be a necessary stage for purging evil before progressing to a different life stage.

Islam has a similar traditional concept of hell as Christianity, believing it to be an inferno of great suffering for souls being punished that have not lived according to God's laws. The Arabic word for hell, *Jahannam*, is closely related the the Hebrew word, *Gehenna*, which is Judaism's word for hell. Judaism's ideas about heaven and hell contrast from the Christian and Islamic ones in that while in *Gehenna* the soul's afterlife involves becoming fully aware of one's past deeds, both good and bad, and that suffering is the direct result from the personal shame of not having lived in full accordance with God's will.

HÉLOÏSE (1101–1164). A student of Abelard. The scandal of their romantic relationship, secret marriage, and then its bitter ending followed by the mutilation of Abelard were important for medieval reflection on marriage, romance, and the vocation of philosophy. Heloise's correspondence with Abelard is an important example of high learning, passion, and an exploration of the tortuous questions to which human beings are prey.

HENOTHEISM. A term coined by Max Müller to describe the worship of a single God, while acknowledging the possibility of the existence of other gods. Henotheism implies a belief that God or gods may have circumscribed domains. This is different from monotheism, according to which God is omnipresent and there is no place where God is not.

HERACLITUS (Flourished ca. 500 BCE). Pre-Socratic philosopher in Asia Minor, native of Ephesus. No complete text of Heraclitus survives; what we know of his philosophy we know from his aphorisms quoted by others, making it difficult to make a definitive statement of his final views. Nevertheless, several of Heraclitus' doctrines were influential on subsequent philosophers. These include his doctrines concerning the *logos,* and *flux*. Heraclitus rejected *polymathy*, or the attempt to understand the world by learning many things, since merely gathering bits of information could lead one to miss the unchanging *logos* that lies behind the cosmos and that the cosmos proclaims. The cosmos is in constant *flux* or change, so wisdom comes from attending to the principle of change, not only to the changing things themselves. This doctrine is associated with the famous statement, attributed to Heraclitus, that it is not possible to step in the same river twice. Sometimes this is taken to mean that nothing is stable, but this is probably not what Heraclitus meant. Rather, the *logos* is stable, and a discerning observer will see that all things become their opposite: e.g., heat becomes cold, wet becomes dry, what is living dies, and what is unliving comes to life. *See also* PRE-SOCRATICS.

HERBERT OF CHERBURY, EDWARD (1583–1648). His theology stressed key Christian teachings that relied minimally on revelation. His work is thereby linked to the deist movement which dispatched with revelation altogether. His work includes *On Truth* (1624), *On the Causes of Errors* (1645), and *The Ancient Religion of the Gentiles* (1663).

HERMENEUTICS. A complex term, hermeneutics is generally about the theory of interpretation. While many histories of hermeneutics begin with the Reformation's emphasis on scripture, the breadth of hermeneutical thinking stretches back to Aristotle and includes medieval scriptural interpretation strategies. Aristotle understood the Greek word *hermeneia* to be articulate speech. His work *On Interpretation* studied articulate speech and the things to which that speech related. Later, Church fathers were forced to wrestle with how to interpret their sacred texts. The concern in the early Church for allegorical readings of difficult passages, in Clement of Alexandria for example, later blossomed into a strategy for interpreting the bible including four levels of meaning: literal-historical, allegorical, tropological, and analogical. With the Reformation, the centrality of Scripture created new energy in exegetical methods and efforts.

The word "hermeneutics" was first used by J. C. Dannhauer in connection with exegesis as the "art of interpretation." Friedrich Schleiermacher generalized the idea of hermeneutics across all disciplines, subsuming biblical exegesis under a more universal hermeneutical methodology. In the twentieth century, Martin Heidegger's "hermeneutics of facticity" changed the course of hermeneutical thought. Hermeneutics moved from textual study and the understanding of an author to the concept of understanding as such. Hans-Georg Gadamer, a student of Heidegger, developed the notion of a "hermeneutical philosophy" which centered on the interpretive and linguistic character of all understanding. The French post-structuralist philosopher Paul Ricoeur extended Gadamer's hermeneutical philosophy to include important insights in ideology critique and critical theory. Jacques Derrida, a student of Ricoeur, developed a deconstructionist project that challenged the ontological dimensions of hermeneutical philosophy. Important texts in hermeneutical philosophy include: Friedrich Schleiermacher's *Hermeneutics and Critique* (1838), Martin Heidegger's

Being and Time (1927), Hans-Georg Gadamer's *Truth and Method* (1960) and *Philosophical Hermeneutics* (1976), and Paul Ricoeur's *Hermeneutics and the Human Sciences* (1981).

HIGHEST GOOD. *See* **SUMMUM BONUM.**

HINDUISM. Hinduism is so diverse that it is difficult to use the term as an umbrella category even to designate a host of interconnected ideas and traditions. "Hindu" is Persian for the name of a river that Greeks referred to as the Indos and the British as the Indus, from which we get the name "Indian". Hinduism names the various traditions that have flourished in the Indian subcontinent, going back to before the second millennium BCE. The most common feature of what is considered Hinduism is reverence for the Vedic scriptures, a rich collection of oral material, some of it highly philosophical, especially the *Upanishads.* Unlike the three monotheistic religions, Hinduism does not look back to a singular historical figure such as Abraham.

According to one strand of Hinduism, *Advaita Vedanta* (a strand that has received a great deal of attention from Western philosophers from the nineteenth century to the present day), this world of space and time is non-different in its essential nature from *Brahman*, the infinite. The world appears to us to consist of discreet diverse objects because we are ignorant, but behind the diverse objects and forms we observe in what may be called the phenomenal or apparent world (the world of phenomena and appearances) there is the formless, reality of Brahman. Advaita Vedanta rejects ontological duality (*Advaita* comes from the Sanskrit term for "non-duality"), arguing that Brahman alone is ultimately real. Advaita does not deny the existence of a diverse world of space and time, but understands the many to be an appearance of the one Brahman. Shankara (788–820) was one of the greatest teachers of this nondualist tradition within Hinduism.

Other, theistic strands of Hinduism construe the divine as personal, all-good, powerful, knowing, creative, loving, and so on. Theistic elements may be seen, for example, in the *Bhagavad Gita* and its teaching about the love of God. Ramanuja (eleventh century) and Madhva (thirteenth and fourteenth centuries) are well known theistic representatives of Hinduism.

There are also lively polytheistic elements within Hinduism. Popular Hindu practice includes a rich polytheism, and for this reason it has been called the religion of 330 million gods (*devas*). There is a strong orientation in the Hindu tradition to understanding the multiple deities as different name and form expressions of the infinite Brahman. This makes it difficult to characterize Hinduism as polytheistic in the generally understood sense of the term.

110

Whether they follow a non-dual or a theistic form of Hinduism, many Hindus believe that a trinity of gods—Brahma, Vishnu, and Shiva—is the cardinal, supreme manifestation of *Brahman*. Brahma is the creator of the world, Vishnu is the sustainer (variously manifested in the world, e.g., as Krishna and Rama, incarnations or *avatars* who instruct and enlighten), and Shiva is the destroyer, the Lord of time and change.

Most Hindus believe in reincarnation. The soul migrates through different lives, according to principles of *karma* (Sanskrit for "deed" or "action"), the moral consequence of one's actions. Karma is often associated with (and believed to be a chief justification for) a strict social caste system. Not all Hindus support such a system, and some Hindu reformers in the modern era argue for its abolition. The final consummation or enlightenment is *moksha* (or release) from ignorance and *samsara*, the material cycle of death and rebirth. In non-dual forms of Hinduism, liberation is achieved by overcoming the false dualism of Brahman and the individual self or soul (*atman*) and discovering their essential identity.

Hinduism has a legacy of inclusive spirituality. It accepts the validity and value of other religions. The one God may be worshiped under a variety of names and forms. In the *Bhagavad Gita*, Krishna declares: "If any worshiper do reverence with faith to any God whatever, I make his faith firm, and in that faith he reverences his god, and gains his desires, for it is I who bestow them" (vii. 21–2). Hinduism has also absorbed and, to some extent, integrated some of the teaching and narratives of Buddhism. Although Hinduism and Islam have sometimes been in painful conflict, there are also many cases of tolerance and collaboration.

HISTORICAL JESUS. A scholarly reconstruction of the historical figure, Jesus of Nazareth. *See also* BIBLE; CHRISTIANITY; GOSPEL; and JESUS.

HISTORICISM. The thesis that the meanings of events are inextricably bound to the time of their occurrence. For example, there could not be a Christian saint in ancient Greece. A radical form of historicism claims that truth itself is relative to time periods, e.g., slavery was morally licit in ancient Rome. This position seems either no more plausible than moral relativism or to lead to an absurdity: if historicism is true, then because there are times when historicism is thought to be false, it is sometimes false.

HISTORY. The term 'history' may refer to what has taken place in the past or to accounts of what has taken place in the past. Philosophers have engaged in both speculative and critical approaches to both.

In terms of developing a general understanding of the past, philosophers have developed speculative theories of the meaning of human history. For example, some theologians have thought of human history in terms of creation, fall, and redemption. Hegel developed a speculative account of history in terms of the life of spirit. Teilhard De Chardin articulated a theological interpretation of evolution, according to which history will culminate in a divine consciousness. These accounts are sometimes considered "speculative" history.

In terms of historical inquiry itself, some philosophers are critical realists, upholding the normative practice of history as a source of knowledge. Other philosophers challenge the idea that there is an objective, discernible true or meta-narrative in human history. This "critical" approach to history looks at history as a series of subjective human accounts of past events. This approach has some similarities with the latter form of speculative history in that it questions the motivations and virtue of humans as historical actors. This critical approach can be traced back to skeptical Enlightenment accounts of religious experience, for instance, Hume's attack on miracles. Recently this critical history has been central to the postmodern critique of meta-narratives which marks out the writings of writers like Foucault.

HOBBES, THOMAS (1558–1679). A British political philosopher who offered a contractarian foundation for society. According to Hobbes, social bonds are justified for without governance we would be in a state of nature and at risk of premature violent death. Hobbes advanced a materialist view of the world and God. He combined a stringent form of hedonism with a case for the establishment of a powerful governing sovereign. His works include *The Elements of Law* (1640), *On the Citizen* (1651), *Leviathan* (1651), *On Body* (1655), and *On Man* (1658).

HOLBACH, PAUL HENRI D' (BARON) (1723–1789). An anti-Christian polemicist and materialist-determinist. He argued that human beings are machines. His works include *Christianity Unveiled* (1767), *The System of Nature* (1770), *Common Sense, or Natural Ideas Opposed to Supernatural Ideas* (1772), *Social System* (1773), *Natural Politics* (1774), and *Universal Morality* (1776).

HOLINESS. Holiness is a central notion within Christian theology and spirituality. Christian conceptions of human holiness are typically organized around the idea of an individual life embodying a special relationship with Jesus Christ through which a person is transformed into the likeness of Christ. Illustrative examples of such lives can be found both in the New Testament and in the stories of the lives of the saints. There are many different views of human holiness, some emphasizing that human holiness is a property achieved as a result of the whole of an exemplary Christian life, others giving more prominence to the idea that to be holy is to be actively engaged in one's own unique relationship with Christ.

Twentieth-century theology featured a lively debate about whether or not it was possible to be a genuine Christian theologian unless one was holy. Some theologians, for example, Hans Urs von Balthasar, have emphasized that human holiness is a necessary condition for knowledge of God; hence a person lacking holiness would thereby lack knowledge of *theos* (God)—the subject matter of theology. Von Balthasar also accorded human holiness a central role in Christian apologetics, arguing that the lives of the saints constitute the best evidence for the truth of Christianity.

The notion of human holiness, however, is not unique to Christianity; many religious traditions identify certain exemplary practitioners who are thought to have a special relationship with the divine. This suggests that the concept "human holiness" has important trans-cultural implications despite the fact that there is little agreement between religious traditions about what exactly makes a particular figure exemplary.

HOLY SPIRIT. The third member of the trinity in the Christian faith. In the words of the Nicene Creed: "And I believe in the Holy Spirit, the Lord and Giver of Life; who proceeds from the Father (and the Son); who with the Father and the Son together is worshiped and glorified; who spoke by the prophets." Controversy occurs between the Western, Latin church (Catholic and Protestant), which sees the Holy Spirit as proceeding from the Father *and* the Son, and the Eastern, Orthodox church, which holds that the Holy Spirit only proceeds from the Father. Some Orthodox Christians claim that the West's addition of the *filioque* clause ("and the Son") resulted in a subordination of the Holy Spirit, which has led the West to have a less stable, more erratic history of spirituality and mysticism. By understanding the Holy Spirit as proceeding from the Father alone, Eastern Orthodox Christians believe they accord a higher role to religious experience.

HOLY WILL. For Kant, the idea of a will that cannot do evil. Kant held that all or most human beings do not have a holy will. Some traditional, Anselmian Christians believe that Jesus Christ had a holy will and could do no evil. This can create tension with the New Testament narrative of Christ undergoing temptation. Some Anselmians reply that you can be tempted to do that which you actually could not carry out. Perhaps Mother Teresa was tempted to steal to help the poor, but she was of such a character that she could not have actually carried out such a robbery.

HONOR. The concept of honor is controversial—vital to some, abhorrent to many, alien to others. It inspires lives of integrity and courage, but also acts of violence and oppression, and some think it has become "obsolescent" (Peter Berger). Some philosophers (e.g., Marilyn Adams), impressed with the anthropological study of so-called "honor cultures," find deep roots for thinking of honor in the Abrahamic sacred texts. But mostly philosophers ignore the concept. This neglect is unfortunate, especially if based on conflating different concepts all labeled "honor" (honor as reputation, recognition, status, achievement, trust, commitment, and the like); even when distinguished, however, these concepts are peripheral to normative work today. Rather, the central concept of honor should be *personal honor*, a Janus-concept facing both inward (an individual's responsibility, rooted in character, for maintaining her own honor) and outward (membership in an honor group, commitment to its publicly-shared code, and special trust in members of the group). Personal honor varies (in both membership and code) from group to group, so that some instances may be noble, others despicable. Such honor is relative and hence not the same as morality, though in some instances honor is at least consistent with morality. Arguably personal honor is nearly ubiquitous in human societies, and not least in our own—in the military, of course, but also in sports, professions, the family, politics, and elsewhere.

In religion, the concept is useful not only for describing religious communities and their members' normative commitments to one another and to the object of their ultimate concerns, but perhaps also in theocentric thinking about God's relations to humanity. In short, although it currently lies fallow, personal honor is a fertile field for philosophical and theological cultivation.

HOOKER, RICHARD (1554–1600). An important Anglican who promoted an influential theory of natural law. Hooker's view that humans are naturally oriented toward law was influential in the minds of the founders of the American republic. His primary work was *Of the Laws of Ecclesiastical Polity: Eight Books* (1593).

HSIUNG SHILI. *See* **XIONG SHILI.**

HSUAN-TSANG. *See* **XUANZANG.**

HSUN TZU. *See* **XUNZI.**

***HUAINANZI* (a.k.a.** *HUAI-NAN TZU*). The *Huainanzi* is a text compiled in the second century BCE under the patronage of Liu An, Prince of Huainan, a member of the imperial family. The *Huainanzi* is a syncretic work, introducing Daoism and cosmological elements into Confucianism. This text is among the first to elaborate a non-theistic cosmogony based on the origin of all things through the interaction of heaven and earth and *yin* and *yang*. The *Huainanzi* also considers the human body a microcosm and describes breathing techniques and physical discipline to prolong life. It helped link philosophical Daoism with the emerging forms of religious Daoism.

HUAYAN SCHOOL (a.k.a. HUA-YEN SCHOOL). The Huayan School of Mahayana Buddhism, known in Japan as the Kegon School, emerged in the early seventh century, growing out of study of the *Avatamsaka Sutra* (Chinese: *Huayan ing*; Japanese: *Kegonkyō*). Using the metaphor of Indra's Net, in which each element of reality is reflected in each other element, the Huayan School teaches the interrelationship and interpenetration of all aspects of reality. The Huayan School had a significant influence of the development of the Neo-Confucian cosmology of the Supreme Ultimate and the dualism of *li* (principle) and *qi* (matter or material force).

HUGH OF St. VICTOR (1096–1141). A highly influential contributor to mystical theology. He charted the ascent of the soul to God though the stages of knowledge, meditation, and contemplation. His theological work on the sacraments was accepted by Peter Lombard who was instrumental in shaping the Roman Catholic late medieval view of liturgy and sacred rites. His works include *On the Sacraments of Christian Faith* (c. 1134), *Didascalion, On the Mystic Ark, On the Union of Soul and Body,* and *On the Soul.*

HUMANISM. A term that today is often thought to imply secularism, but was originally used more broadly to refer to those who gave a central focus and value to human life. Erasmus and Thomas More (now St. Thomas More, since his canonization in 1935) were humanists but hardly secular (except in the older, general sense in that they were not monks).

HUME, DAVID (1711–1776). Scottish empiricist philosopher and historian. In philosophy of religion he is most keenly studied for his critique of natural theology in *Dialogues on Natural Religion* (1779), his case against the rational plausibility of believing that miracles occur, his defense of the moral legitimacy under some circumstances to commit suicide, his case against an afterlife, and his thesis that the internal self is as much a non-rational belief as believing in the uniformity of external nature throughout time. Scholars are divided on Hume's final views on God, but it is likely he held a thin form of deism, acknowledging that the cause and order of the cosmos could very well be due to a force that has some analogy to the human mind. The net effect of his *Dialogues* and other works has been to undermine theistic arguments from design, contingency, miracles, and so on. Hume's other works include *A Treatise of Human Nature* (1739, 1740), *Enquiry Concerning Human Understanding* (1748), *Enquiry Concerning the Principles of Morals* (1751), *History of England* (1754–1762), and *Natural History of Religion* (1757).

HUMILITY. Humility is a virtue with a checkered history. We find reference to it in both the Christian and Jewish traditions as a state of character in which one compares oneself against God and finds oneself lacking. Such proper recognition of human limits through appeal to the distinction between the finite and the infinite, the human and the divine, is at the heart of religious self-knowledge, and versions of the virtue thus understood can be found in writings from Augustine to Aquinas, and from Bernard of Clairvaux to Ignatius Loyola.

Yet such comparisons of oneself to God can lead also to apparently unseemly states of character, as for example, when Ignatius Loyola asserts that, to be humble, one must recognize oneself as "foul," or as "wounds" or "ulcers" who are worthy of nothing. Furthermore, problems can arise about how to understand one's worth vis à vis other persons on the basis of this comparison with the divine. On the one hand, comparison of oneself to the divine seems to be the great equalizing force in human relations: if I am less worthy than a divine being, then so too are all other humans. We are all thus in the same boat, worth-wise. Yet the history of humility shows, on the other hand, that a comparison of oneself with the divine becomes associated with comparing oneself unfavorably against other persons. So, Bernard of Clairvaux asserts that the humble person considers himself inferior to other persons as well as to God, and St. Benedict says similarly in his Rule that the humble person should consider himself lower and of less worth than other people, comparing oneself even to a worm.

Because of such problems that arise when trying to make sense of a virtue centered on appreciating one's own limits, humility has thus also been vigorously rejected. David Hume, most famously, accuses it of being a "monkish" virtue that has no utility and that should, therefore, be excised from the catalogue of virtues. Images of false humility, such as Uriah Heep in *David Copperfield*, only encourage us to this Humean abandonment of humility as a virtue.

Nonetheless, there have also been recent efforts to re-conceptualize this virtue in a way that avoids the excesses of earlier versions of it. Recent, secular accounts of it suggest that humility is simply the virtue of proper self-knowledge, a state in which I accurately understand both my capacities and my limits. Such awareness is, furthermore, achieved for some not so much by a human / divine comparison, but by honest comparison of oneself with other persons. Some of these theorists, keen to avoid the problematic Christian history of the virtue, even seek instead to associate this proper self-knowledge more with Aristotelian magnanimity: a proper self-knowledge of someone who genuinely has flaws would encourage something more akin to traditional accounts of humility; but the proper self-knowledge of someone who really had no flaws and was in fact a perfectly moral person would look more like Aristotle's magnanimous man who knows his worth and knows how to treat himself and other persons in light of that fact.

Other moral theorists, following Kant's suggestion that the comparing of self to the other is more likely to be the source of the worst evils in the world than to have any virtue, have sought a Kantian comparison of self with the demands of morality as the route to acquiring humility. None of us could be without flaws in comparison with the strict demands of morality, so the thought that some of us would emerge from our self-analysis with magnanimity is misguided. Instead, honest assessment of self leads to a humbling of oneself or acts as a restraint on the one hand (because one recognizes that one always falls short of the demands of morality) and, on the other, an abiding respect for oneself (because one recognizes oneself as the source of moral reasons and demands in the first place). Such a secular account of humility, while abandoning the traditional human / divine comparison, retains the traditional belief in the equally limited status of all humans.

HUSSERL, EDMUND (1859–1938). A German philosopher, Husserl is widely acknowledged as a founder of phenomenology. Phenomenology was the attempt to find a new, scientific foundation for philosophy based on careful descriptions of the phenomena of experience. Husserl was born Jewish and converted to Lutheranism at age 27, and he later claimed to be greatly influenced by Rudolf Otto's *Die Heilige* (1917). He himself published almost nothing about religion, but phenomenology has been seen as a promising route to understanding religion, especially religious experience. Edith Stein, Max Scheler, Paul Ricoeur, Emmanuel Levinas, Jean-Luc Marion, and Merold Westphal are all philosophers who are working explicitly in the tradition of Husserlian phenomenology and who have made important contributions to philosophy of religion. His works include *Logical Investigations* (1900/01), *Ideas Pertaining to a Pure Phenomenology and to a Phenomenological Philosophy* (1913), *Cartesian Meditations* (1931), and *The Crisis of the European Sciences and Transcendental Phenomenology* (1936).

HUXLEY, T. H. (1825–1895). An early defender of Darwinian evolution. He denied being an atheist and coined the term *agnosticism*, as describing his own position of not claiming to know either that God exists or that God does not exist. His works include *Man's Place in Nature* (1864), *Hume* (1879), *Collected Essays* 9 vols. (1893–1894), *Scientific Memoirs* 5 vols. (1898–1903), and *Life and Letters* 3 vols. (ed. L. Huxley 1903).

HYLOMORPHISM. The Aristotelian view that objects consist of a form-matter relationship. A horse has matter in the way of bones, flesh, organs, and so on, but the form *horse* is a whole, functioning animal.

117

I

ICONS / ICONOCLASM. The term "icon" comes from the Greek *eikon,* meaning "image." An icon is any image of a religious work, such as a painting or statue, which is used in religious worship. In Christianity, the rosary used for prayer, the crucifix, the statues of Mary the Mother of Jesus, and pictures of biblical events are all icons that are used on a daily basis both in group and individual worship. Buddhists have statues and pictures of the Buddha and pictures of the Dalai Lama. Hindus are most well known for their use of icons (*murtis*): each individual, family, and community have a deity whom they worship and each deity is represented by a statue or picture which is decorated, sacrificed to, and treated like a guest in the house or temple.

Icons, in each of the aforementioned religions, are understood to be a symbol for the deity and not the deity itself: Hindus believe that the God(dess) enters the icon, but the icon is only celebrated as being one of many aspects of the God(dess), and Buddhists do not believe that a statue of the Buddha is the Buddha but rather a reminder of the Buddha.

Although icons sometimes have a negative connotation (they are sometimes associated with idols), they are typically used as an image on which to focus during prayer or reflection.

Iconoclasm (lit. "image breaking"), refers to the disapproval or destruction of any icons considered to be idols, and its practice has often been the result of opposing views about the proper use of icons turning violent. For example, the great iconoclasm of 1556 in Flanders (called Beeldenstorm) saw much Roman Catholic art destroyed by mobs of Protestant reformers emboldened after public sermons.

IDEAL OBSERVER THEORY. This theory analyzes moral judgments in terms of how a subject would form evaluations under heightened conditions. An ideal observer theory can be found in the thought of Adam Smith, Henry Sidgwick, and to some extent Immanuel Kant and J. S. Mill. Ideal moral observation has been described as constituted by ideal forms of impartiality, knowledge of all the facts on the basis of which to form moral judgments, and an affective awareness of all involved parties. One can accept an ideal observer theory while denying that an ideal observer exists, though a theist may claim that God functions as such an ideal judge.

IDEALISM. A general term that has been employed to describe worldviews in which the mind or the mental is foundational in the order of being. George Berkeley is a clear example of an idealist as he held that reality is at base constituted by God, finite spirits, and minds; what we think of as mind-independent matter is constituted by perceptual experiences, human and divine. Berkeley's outlook is sometimes called subjective idealism. More difficult to classify is Hegel who has been described as an objective idealist. Hegel did not think the material world was constituted by minds and their states, but he thought that all of reality reflected a rational structure that is supremely intelligible to mind.

IDOL / IDOLATRY. Treating a person, thing, or event with the praise and allegiance owed to God. Idolatry is the worship of any image or object, and an idol is that which assumes the role of a false God. In monotheistic faiths idolatry is often expanded to encompass the valuing of any person, object, or activity above God. For example, when Moses descended Mt. Horeb with the Ten Commandments, he discovered the Israelites engaged in idolatry, worshiping a statue of a golden calf. Today, idols may consist of wealth, power, *eros*, or any number of objects or acts that can come to control a person's life rather than God or that which is truly sacred.

Idolatry is negative in the Abrahamic traditions because it involves the worshiping of a worldly creation, when it is only the creator that deserves such credit. Certain branches of Christianity, including Roman Catholicism and the Orthodox denominations, allow for the depiction of religious figures, such as Jesus Christ. However, the depiction of religious figures falls under the umbrella of idolatry in fundamentalist Christian denominations, Judaism, and Islam.

Hinduism is sometimes viewed as an idolatrous faith; this is not entirely accurate. Hindu philosophers view all language to be just as representative of the eternal as any image or object. Representing attributes of the divine symbolically is acceptable, although they believe that ultimately *Brahman* is beyond any worldly representation.

IGNORANCE. In Christian ethics, some forms of ignorance are held to vitiate responsibility. Invincible ignorance is an ignorance the agent cannot (at least in current conditions) overcome. Perhaps we are in a state of invincible ignorance when it comes to confident views of the mental states of some animals (do fish undergo morally relevant suffering?). In such a case, a fisherman may be blameless if he is charged with intentionally causing suffering. Vincible ignorance can be overcome, however, and is the result of negligence or prejudice. A slave owner in the early nineteenth century might claim ignorance of whether slavery causes morally relevant suffering, but this does not appear to be exculpatory.

ILLATIVE. A term from the work of Bishop John Henry Newman to refer to an innate awareness we may have of values and the sacred.

IMAGE. From the Latin *imago,* meaning "copy, statue, picture, idea, or appearance." Susanne Langer and some other philosophers have argued that images are central to thinking in science, philosophy, and religion. Arguably, there was a profound shift of images of nature when the West moved from seeing the natural world as a book (creation was God's first book; the Bible was the second) to seeing it as Darwin's tree of life. Some philosophers of religion have proposed instead that the ultimate encounter of the soul with God must be beyond images. *See also* ICONS.

IMAGINATION. A key reference point for philosophers in or influenced by the Romantic movement. There are multiple philosophical uses of this term. According to one use, the imagination is the power to conceive or visualize that

which is not present sensorially. From a narrow, strict point of view, we do not sense the back but only the surface of objects. Nonetheless, it would seem absurd to claim that you only can see the surface of a chocolate chip cookie and not the cookie itself. Some philosophers hold that it is the imagination that allows one to claim she sees more than cookie surfaces. Others use the imagination more broadly to involve the conceiving of that which may or may not exist. Strictly speaking, the imagination refers to a power or faculty of persons, rather than to a thing. Someone may be said to have imagination insofar as she has the power to form mental imagery.

IMMANENCE. From the Latin *immanere,* meaning "to inhabit." The immanence of God is God's presence throughout the creation. Immanence is a feature of God's omnipresence or ubiquity.

IMMANENT. God is thought to be immanent in creation insofar as God is omnipresent. Divine immanence throughout the creation does not entail that God incorporates the cosmos as God's body or that God is materially present; e.g., there is more of God in a large land mass like Australia rather than the comparatively smaller (though lovely) New Zealand.

IMMATERIALISM. A common term for idealist theorists like George Berkeley who denied matter has a mind-independent existence. A thoroughgoing immaterialist denies that matter (and energy) has a reality independent of the mind and various immaterial activities, objects, and states. There is an important difference between idealist theists like Berkely and non-idealist theists. Berkeley thought that matter was not independent of mind because he held that what we recognize as matter is in some sense constituted by divine and created minds, whereas classical theists hold that the material world is dependent upon the divine mind but its reality is not constituted or made up of mental states (divine or human). The latter would therefore only be a moderate form of immaterialism in contrast to a more radical idealist claim.

IMMORTALITY. A person or soul is immortal if it will not perish or cease to be. Some distinguish between an immortality that is innate (a soul by its nature cannot perish) versus conferred (a soul will not perish because of God's love). Arguments for individual immortality have been developed on the grounds that the soul does not contain parts and thus is not subject to dissolution, and on the grounds that if there is an omnipotent God who loves created persons, then that God would lovingly preserve persons through death, transforming them to a higher state (heaven, union with God, and so on). Immortality has also been defended on the grounds of God's justice;

survival of death is essential if there is to be both a concord between virtue and felicity, as well as wickedness and punishment. *See also* LIFE AFTER DEATH.

IMPARTIALITY. A judgment is impartial when it is determined by objective reasons and not by an individual's particular, subjective preferences. Some philosophers contend that impartiality is one of the basic, essential conditions for moral inquiry.

IMPURITY. Concepts of impurity have a role in many religions that demarcate the sacred or the holy from that which is profane or worldly. So, in traditional Judaism, adultery was seen as making the adulterer impure, a state that either called for a capital punishment or for rigorous rites and acts of cleansing. Impurities may stem not just from immoral acts, but from the failure to properly observe rituals. Historically, the concept of impurity is akin to the concept of a pollutant, a toxin that despoils something good or intended to be pure.

INCARNATION. The belief that God assumed human nature. Classical, Chalcedonian Christianity holds that Jesus Christ is fully human and fully God. Some Christians believe this involved the second person of the trinity undergoing a self-limitation (Greek, *kenosis*), whereby God put aside omnipotence, omniscience, and omnipresence to assume a human life of limited power and vulnerability, limited knowledge, and location.

Some theologians do not posit a limitation of these properties: they hold instead that while the second person of the trinity retained all divine properties, the second person of the trinity focused its life as a created mind that became the *person* of Jesus Christ, the child born in Palestine. On this view, sometimes called the two minds theory, Jesus Christ is the embodied mind of God, a mind that exists within the broader divine mind of God. T. V. Morris and Richard Swinburne defend versions of this second account.

INCOMMENSURABILITY. Two values are incommensurate if they cannot be compared in importance or significance on a single scale or framework. For example, what is more important: friendship or art? If we cannot rank these values, they are incomensurate.

INCONSISTENT TRIAD. Three propositions that cannot all be true. According to some (but not all) atheists, the following is an inconsistent triad: God is all good. God is all-powerful. There is evil.

INCORPOREALITY. Nonphysical or disembodied. Classical theists claim that God is nonphysical, and some religions that believe in an afterlife hold that a human being at death becomes disembodied.

INDUCTION. Reasoning is inductive when it proceeds from specific cases to a general conclusion. Inductive reasoning is typically considered fallible: One may reasonably conclude that "All swans are white" having observed thousands and even millions of swans, even though the general statement is false (there are black swans).

INFALLIBILITY. Incapable of being in error. Some Christians, for example, believe the Bible, as the revealed word of God, is infallible. *See also* FALLIBILISM.

INFERENCE. An inference refers to what can be learned, whereas an entailment is an essential, logical relation.

INFINITE. Not finite. Some philosophers deny there can be an actual infinite, but think that there can be potential infinities (sequences that have a beginning but no end). If persons are immortal, they have a potential infinite for a future, for their lives will not have an end-point, but they will never complete an actual infinite (as there can be no greatest possible number).

INSPIRATION. In philosophy of religion, inspiration is most often associated with the concept of revelation. Traditional Christians, for example, believe that scripture is inspired by the Holy Spirit: "All Scripture is God-breathed and is useful for teaching, rebuking, correcting and training in righteousness" (2 Timothy 3:16).

INSTRUMENTALISM. A position in philosophy of science which holds that scientific descriptions and explanations function as instruments to help scientists control and predict events, rather than to reference real objects.

INTEGRITY. Today the concept of integrity is sometimes seen as mere self-consistency; thus, a consistently wicked person (a rigorous Nazi) may be thought of as possessing integrity. But the older concept of integrity (derived from the Latin *integritās* for "wholeness") involved a person being faithful to authentic, good ideals.

INTELLIGENT DESIGN. The intelligent design movement, which has flourished in the U.S. since the 1990s, aims to present a paradigm for the origin and development of life on earth that will provide an alternative to, and can eventually replace, the prevailing Darwinian theory of evolution. Proponents of intelligent design claim to objectively and reliably identify features of biological life that cannot be explained on the basis of randomness in addition to the uniform operation of impersonal natural laws. These features, it is inferred, must be the product of intelligent design.

Intelligent design theory as such does not take a position concerning the identity and characteristics of the designer, so the theory is claimed to be non-religious and suitable for inclusion in public school curricula. At the same time, however, it is clear that much of the motivation for the theory is to provide a religion-friendly replacement for Darwinism, which is perceived as favoring naturalism and atheism.

While the theory has found favor with conservative religious groups and with a small minority of scientists, most scientists (including many that are religious believers) reject it on the grounds that (1) the claims concerning the failure of Darwinism are unfounded or at best premature, (2) the movement presents no constructive scientific alternative; its scientific efforts are almost entirely devoted to criticizing Darwinism, and (3) intelligent design is really a thinly disguised version of creationism, a view that has repeatedly been characterized by the courts as inherently religious and unsuitable for public education. *See also* SCIENCE AND RELIGION.

INTENTION. In Christian moral theory, intention is held to have important moral significance, even if not acted upon. Good intentions may also excuse otherwise bad acts.

INTERCESSION. In the process of liturgical or private prayer a person may petition God to confer a blessing or to do a good work on behalf of another person or people. In this case, a person intercedes on behalf of others.

religious simplicity but not perfection, and history itself is to be seen as a veil of soul-making, whereby humans eventually achieve union with God through Christ.

INTUITION. From the Latin *intueri*, "to look at." Some philosophers claim to know certain truths, especially in ethics, by intuition rather than through discursive reasoning. Some philosophers claim that intuitive knowledge can be gained by recognizing some truths as self-evident (A is A) and not due to an inference from some deeper, additional set of known truths.

INVERTED SPECTRUM, PROBLEM OF. *See* **PRIVATE LANGUAGE ARGUMENT.**

IRENAEUS OF LYON (125–202). An important opponent of Gnosticism, Irenaeus insisted on the foundational goodness of the material world and the Johannine understanding of Jesus as the *logos* incarnate. In twentieth-century philosophy of religion, John Hick has advanced what he calls an Irenaean theodicy in *contrast to* Augustine. For Augustine, human beings are born in an unfallen, perfect state, but then fall from paradise and seek redemption through Christ. Irenaean theodicy does not see the fall in such dramatic terms. Human beings are born in a state of moral and

IRONY. From the Greek *eironeia*, meaning "dissembling." Irony is broken into three main types: verbal, dramatic, and situational. Verbal irony occurs when an individual conveys an idea by intentionally conveying the opposite. Sarcasm is an example of this type of irony.

Dramatic irony refers to narrative forms of media. When a consumer of the media is aware of information that characters in the narrative are unaware of, dramatic irony occurs. In Shakespeare's *Hamlet*, the audience knows Polonius is hiding in Gertrude's bedchamber, but Hamlet thinks it is Claudius.

When one's actions lead to reaching the diametric opposite of what one had intended, situational irony occurs. In *Oedipus Rex*, it is ironic that Oedipus' attempt to not fulfill the prophecy that he will kill his father and marry his mother leads directly to Oedipus killing his father and marrying his mother.

One of the earliest and most famous examples of irony in philosophy comes from Socrates. In fact, Socratic irony is still employed today. In conversation with others, Socrates would feign ignorance, asking many questions. This tactic ironically led to the person who disagreed with him reaching Socrates' intended conclusion seemingly of his own accord.

Soren Kierkegaard employed irony to better articulate his arguments. Kierkegaard wrote many of his works using pseudonyms. Interestingly though, he did not always completely agree with what his pseudonyms said. He would articulate their view points, but Kierkegaard's deeper lessons actually came from the ironies that rose when those viewpoints were followed to their logical conclusions.

More recently, irony has been used to describe perceptions of reality by philosophers such as Richard Rorty. From an ironic view point anything can be made to look good or bad through redescription. For example, Billy says it is good that it is sunny out because he is tired of bad weather, but Suzy says that it is bad because she is distracted from her homework. It is philosophically ironic that both Billy and Suzy are right depending on how one describes the situation. Some ironists reject the idea of any ultimate truths.

ISLAM. The second largest world religion, with over 1.5 billion followers. Islam asserts shared roots with Judaism and Christianity, acknowledging a common, Abrahamic past. The Qur'an (from *Qu'ra* for "to recite" or "to read") was, according to tradition, received by the Prophet Muhammad from the Angel Gabriel as the literal speech and revelation of God (in Arabic, *Allah*). In addition to the Qur'an, Islamic teaching was forged by the sayings (*hadith*) of the Prophet Muhammad (570–632). Islam proclaims a radical monotheism that explicitly repudiated both the polytheism of pagan Arabia and the Christian understanding of the incarnation and the trinity. Central to Islam is God's unity, transcendence, and sovereignty, God's providential control of the cosmos, the importance for humans to live justly and compassionately and to follow set ritual practices of worship.

"Islam" in Arabic means submission, and a follower of Islam is therefore called a Muslim, "one who submits" to God. The Five Pillars of Islam are (1) witnessing that "There is no god but God and Muhammad is his messenger," (2) praying five times a day while facing Mecca, (3) alms-giving, (4) fasting during Ramadan (the ninth month of the Muslim calendar), and (5) making a pilgrimage to Mecca. The two largest branches of Islam are Sunni and Shi'a; their differences began to develop early in the history of Islam over a disagreement about who would succeed the Prophet Muhammad in the leadership of the community. Sunnis comprise a vast majority of Muslims. Shi'ites put greater stress on the continuing revelation of God beyond the Qur'an as revealed in the authoritative teachings of the *imams* (holy successors who inherit Muhammad's "spiritual abilities"), the *mujtahidun* ("doctors of the law"), and other agents. Like Christianity, Islam has proclaimed that a loving, merciful, and just God will not annihilate an individual at death, but provide either heaven or hell.

J

JAINISM. Also known as Jain Dharma, Jainism is a religion that originated in India toward the end of the Vedic period. Jains believe in a timeless history of endless cosmic cycles. These cycles are divided into two halves: a progressive half and a regressive half. In the third and fourth phases of each half of the cosmic cycle, there are 24 *Jinas* (conquerors) or *Tirthankaras* (ford-makers). The 24th Jina of the current cycle was Vardhamana ("increasing"), known as Mahavira ("great hero"), a historical figure who lived near Patna in the state of Bihar and was a contemporary of Siddhartha Guatama, the founder of Buddhism. Historians date Mahavira as living from 497 to 425 BCE, but Jain tradition puts him a century earlier, from 599 to 527 BCE. *Jinas* or *tirthankaras* such as Mahavira are religious teachers who have conquered *samsara* (the cycle of death and rebirth) and can provide a crossing or ford (hence, "ford-maker") for Jains to follow them from *samsara* to liberation.

Jainism, like Buddhism, emerged as a *shramana* or ascetic tradition in response to the ritualism of Vedic religion and the hegemonic role of the priestly *Brahmin* caste. Jainism teaches that all living beings, including plants and animals, have an eternal soul (*jiva*). They therefore strictly adhere to the principle of *ahimsa*, or non-violence, and undertake many ascetic practices. Jains are strict vegetarians and also avoid root vegetables. The aim of life is to shed one's *karma* through these ascetic practices and achieve liberation (*moksha*) from *samsara*.

By the fifth century CE, Jainism had split into two main sects: Digambara ("sky-clad") and Shvetambara ("white-clad"). Digambara Jainism was stricter, teaching that people should not own anything, including clothing, and that only men could attain *moksha*. Shvetambara Jainism was more moderate, allowing people to wear white robes and own a few basic possessions: an alms bowl, a broom (to sweep the ground in front of oneself in order to avoid stepping on any living creatures), and a *mukhavastrika* (a piece of cloth to hold over one's mouth to prevent one from accidentally inhaling, and thereby killing, small insects). Today there are approximately 5 million Jains and many different branches of Jainism, but most of them are associated with one of these two main sects.

Jains are expected to live out five basic vows: *ahimsa* (nonviolence), *satya* (truth), *asteya* (non-stealing), *brahmacarya* (celibacy), and *aparigrapha* (non-possession). The way in which these principles are lived out varies depending upon whether one is a householder or a renunciant. Jains identify 14 stages (*gunasthanas*) of the path to liberation (*moksha marg*). The ascetic vows (*mahavratas*) are taken at the sixth stage. Only ascetics can attain liberation. Because the world is timeless, Jains do not believe in a creator God. However, they consider the liberated soul (*arhat* or *kevalin*) to be divine, and they worship the Jinas.

JAMES, WILLIAM (1842–1910). American philosopher and psychologist, brother of the writer Henry James. William James was one of the main defenders of pragmatism, an American philosophical tradition that appealed to the effect of a belief upon one's actions for the meaning of that belief. According to James' pragmatism, the true beliefs are the ones that work. In his psychological writings he argues against mind-body dualism and is best known for the James-Lange theory of emotions, in which emotions are part of the physiological response to stimuli, not the cause of the physiological response.

James was interested in religious experiences throughout his career. His book, *Varieties of Religious Experience* (1902), looked at the ways that mystical experiences motivate people to believe in a divine power and, in the case of "healthy-minded" experiences, make them better persons. We may judge religious experiences not by the authority that underwrites them, but by their consequences, "not by their roots, but by their fruits." He is careful to say that the experiences do not provide evidence for the existence of God, for we can never tell if they are genuine experiences or mere deceptions, and he thinks they can be reproduced through the use of drugs.

In his essay "The Will to Believe" (1897), he argues against the view that we are only justified in believing something if we have sufficient evidence for it; he instead claims that often we need to believe something first in order for our actions to bring it about. He holds that agnosticism is the same as atheism since they result in the same actions, and he argues that religious believers may be justified even without full evidence for their beliefs. He is the author of *The Principles of Psychology* (1890), *The Will to Believe and Other Essays in Popular Philosophy* (1897), *The Varieties of Religious Experience* (1902), *Pragmatism* (1907), *A Pluralistic Universe* (1909), and *Essays in Radical Empiricism* (1912).

JESUS (c. 4 BCE–c. 30 CE). The central figure of Christianity, Jesus was born and lived in modern-day Palestine in the early first century. He was Jewish but is not considered significant in Judaism. In Islam, Jesus (Isa) is considered one of the true prophets along with Abraham and Muhammad. Many other religious traditions revere Jesus as a great moral teacher.

Jesus was born during the reign of Herod the Great and grew up in the small town of Nazareth in Galilee. The name Jesus (Gk. *Iesous*) is a Hellenized form of the Hebrew *Yehoshua*, that is, Joshua, which means "the Lord rescues / delivers." Our main sources for knowledge about his life are the Gospels (Greek, *euangelion*, "good news") in the Christian New Testament. The attempts of historical Jesus scholars to reconstruct his life agree that that he was a Jewish teacher and healer, baptized by John the Baptist and crucified in Jerusalem by Pontius Pilate.

Christians believe that Jesus is the Christ. The title Christ comes from the Greek *christos*, a translation of the Hebrew *messiah*, which means "anointed one." According to the Hebrew prophets, the Messiah would be a great king who would deliver the people from their oppressors with God's support. The New Testament presents Jesus as a fulfillment of these prophecies, but goes beyond traditional expectations and fashions a new understanding of the role of the Christ. Jesus is portrayed as the Son of God who forgives the sins of the world through his atoning life, death, and resurrection. The Gospels claim that three days after his crucifixion, he was raised from the dead and appeared to his followers, establishing the Church

among them. Christians believe that he then ascended into heaven and will come again to judge the living and the dead.

In the centuries that followed, Christian theologians formulated complex doctrines about Jesus' nature and his relationship to God. A series of seven ecumenical councils (held between 325 and 681 CE) established that Jesus was one person, but had both a fully human and a fully divine nature. This position is called a hypostatic union. The councils also formulated the doctrine of the trinity, according to which Jesus is the second of three persons, all of whom share the same substance.

JEW / JEWISH. *See* **JUDAISM.**

JIHAD. An Arabic word that translates most literally as "to strive" or "to struggle." In the context of Islamic thought, *jihad* refers to striving in the pursuit of divine good, which can take a number of different forms, including but not limited to violent warfare. The Islamic tradition of jurisprudence, which overlaps with Islamic philosophy, contains lively and intricate reflection on questions about what constitutes just cause and competent authority, what is permitted and forbidden in the conduct of war, the place of extreme emergencies, and other topics familiar to Western ethical discussions of war. While in jurisprudence *jihad* has referred primarily to struggle in the form of warfare, in the larger horizon of Islamic thought its reference has always been more broad, including activities such as the struggle to purify one's heart, to strive after knowledge, and to pursue justice through political means other than warfare.

JUDAISM. In Judaism, God's principal manifestation is held to have been in leading the people of Israel out of bondage in Egypt to the Promised Land (Canaan) as recounted in the book of Exodus. This "saving event" is commemorated perennially in the yearly observation of Passover. The tradition places enormous value on community life, which is depicted in the Hebrew Bible as a covenant between God and the people of Israel. The more traditional representatives of Judaism, especially the Orthodox, adopt a strict reading of what they take to be the historic meaning of the Hebrew scripture as secured in the early stages of its formation. Other groups, such as the Conservative and Reformed, treat scripture as authoritative but do not depend on a specific, historically-defined interpretation of that scripture. Although there is presently some lively disagreement about the extent to which Judaism affirms an afterlife of individuals, historically Judaism has included an affirmation of an afterlife. *See also* ABRAHAMIC FAITHS.

JULIAN OF NORWICH (c. 1342– c. 1416). One of the most famous English mystics. Relatively little is known about her life and even her name, which takes its present form from her time as an anchoress at the Church of St. Julian in Norwich. When she was around 30 years old, Julian suffered a period of illness. While on her deathbed, Julian experienced a series of visions of Jesus Christ, which are recorded in *Sixteen Revelations of Divine Love.* The visions themselves are borderline heresy, and many have suggested that Julian was a proponent of universal salvation. Nevertheless, Julian consistently reaffirmed her commitment and adherence to the traditional teachings of the Church. Her experiences had a profound influence on many of those around her, including Margery Kempe. Her visions emphasize the compassion and love of God, and famously evoke feminine, maternal imagery in describing the role of God and Jesus Christ. She is also famous for coining the phrase "All shall be well, and all shall be well, and all manner of thing shall be well." Tod Wodicka used this phrase as the title of his first novel. John Hick mentions Julian extensively in *The Fifth Dimension,* referring to her doctrine of theodicy as a doctrine of "No Theodicy without Eschatology." T. S. Eliot quotes Julian in the fourth of his *Four Quartets.*

JUNG, CARL GUSTAV (1875–1961). Swiss psychologist and early psychoanalyst influenced by Freud until 1913 when he broke with Freud and developed an account of human nature, both consciousness and the collective unconscious. In the latter, Jung posited archetypal patterns that he thought were shared by all humans. Jung's work was more amenable to a positive religious interpretation than Freud's, and his work has some influence in religious treatments of God's relationship to the human conscious and unconscious. Near the end of his life, Jung became deeply concerned with the apparent emptiness of modern materialism and he counseled a recovery of spirituality. His works include *Psychology of the Unconscious* (1912), and *Psychological Types* (1921), *Man and His Symbols* (published posthumously in 1964), and an autobiography, *Memories, Dreams, Reflections* (1961).

JUST WAR THEORY. The topic concerning moral restrictions on warfare that go back to some of the earliest recorded works on war. Just war theory posits the question: is *anything* and thus *everything* permissible in war? Great empires have carried out savage massacres with no regard to noncombatants or prisoners, or whether or not warfare is justified on the grounds of self-defense or divine sanction.

Just War Theory has emerged slowly in the history of ideas and culture and addresses the following conditions: Is nation (or empire or community) A justified in waging war on nation B if (1) there is no other, peaceful alternative, i.e., a last

resort, (2) Nation B has without proper provocation attacked A or attacked another nation C to which A has allegiance, (3) Nation A's intention or goal is restricted to repelling B's illicit, unprovoked attack and securing a stable peace; hence, the ultimate intention or goal of A must be peace, and (4) Nation A does not intend or foresee using illicit means in executing the war (directly killing or torturing noncombatants)? Other conditions have been taken into account such as the likelihood of A defeating B and a calculation of the costs involved.

JUSTICE. Justice is a surprisingly complex and diverse term in the history of philosophy of religion. The ancients saw justice as a virtue; see, for example, Plato's *Republic* and Aristotle's lengthy investigation in the *Nichomachean Ethics*. In the sense of virtue, justice tends to focus on the correct alignment of character in both the person and the state. Socrates' thesis in Plato's *Republic* is that the best way to understand the virtue of justice for an individual is to look at justice in the ideal state. His conclusion is that justice is the right placement of the rational, passionate, and appetitive characteristics of the body in question. Aristotle sees justice as the mean between the extremes of performing injustices upon others as an act of overreaching one's proper place and accepting too many injustices and not receiving one's due.

The concept of justice, however, was not settled by the ancients. Other common disagreements arise from questioning whether justice is a divine command or a principle which guides all other divine commands, as well as the question as to whether justice is a natural virtue or a human construct, perhaps nothing more or less than a mutual agreement between people. The modern view generally divides justice into three distinct types: retributive, distributive, and restorative justice.

Retributive justice centers on giving people what they deserve, often focusing (especially with institutional justice) on punishment for wrong action, but also, to a lesser degree, on rewarding right action in an appropriate manner.

Distributive justice focuses mainly on the proper ways of gaining or maintaining wealth and power. For example, John Rawls (1921–2002) sees justice as primarily concerned with setting up institutions that will give all people equal access to opportunities for wealth and power. Robert Nozick (1938–2002), on the other hand, is far more concerned with the appropriate acquisition and transfer of wealth. An important subset of distributive justice is commutative justice which guides principles of contracts and ownership.

The third major type of justice considered by contemporary philosophers is restorative justice, which strives for a holistic approach to criminal justice in which the victim and the offender are brought together so that each may learn from the other and be fully integrated back into society, which is a good for the victim, for the perpetrator, and for the society as a whole.

Another useful distinction among various conceptions of justice, used by Charles Bonaventure Marie *Toullier* (1752–1835) and other thinkers, is to differentiate between interior and exterior justice: interior justice is concerned with morality while exterior justice deals primarily with jurisprudence.

JUSTIN MARTYR (c. 105 CE–c. 165 CE). Justin argued for Christianity on philosophical terms, in which the love of Jesus was seen as the consummation of philosophy (which literally means the love of wisdom). Justin was martyred under emperor prefect Rusticus. His writings include *Apology* and *Dialogue with Trypho*.

K

KANT, IMMANUEL (1724–1804). Kant challenged the traditional metaphysics and epistemology of his day, creating a new, "transcendental" system that responded to both the rationalists and the empiricists leading up to him. The primary goal of Kant's critical philosophy was to make room for faith by placing limits on human reason's ability to gain knowledge, while avoiding Hume's claims about non-rational belief. His *Critique of Pure Reason* (1781, 2nd ed., 1787) argued that traditional metaphysics fails because the mind contributes forms for all knowledge (namely, space, time, and 12 categories, including causation); empirical knowledge therefore pertains not to things themselves (the noumenal world) but to constructions of the mind (the phenomenal world). The self is a necessary presupposition of all knowledge, yet it cannot be proven to exist. Likewise, theoretical arguments for God's existence all fail; but so must any attempt to disprove God's existence. Theistic *belief* thereby remains a viable option, but stands in need of a new grounding.

Kant's *Critique of Practical Reason* (1788) defended a new moral theory, whereby freedom gives rise to an inwardly manifested moral law (or categorical imperative) that requires universal maxims to be employed in a manner such that persons are respected and treated as ends in themselves. To explain how morally good choices can be rational in the face of our apparently unjust world, one must adopt practical faith in a future life wherein a just God ensures that happiness and virtue will be in concord. While he recognized that this practical argument cannot yield theoretically valid conclusions, Kant thought it effectively grounds practical conviction: whoever tries to be good, while believing moral action is rational, acts as if such a God actually exists.

In *Critique of Judgment* (1790), Kant attempted to bridge the first two *Critiques* by portraying our experiences of purposiveness (e.g., beauty, the sublime, natural organisms) as synthesizing nature and freedom. This paves the way for a teleologically rich moral theology that regards human beings as the final purpose of a divine, creative intelligence. Similarly, *Religion within the Bounds of Bare Reason* (1793) portrays religious symbols as bridging nature and freedom. The problem of radical evil makes moral action impossible without an appeal to God's grace. But believers, too, will inevitably resort to evil and self-deception unless they unite together in a church, guided by internally-legislated principles of virtue. True service of God thus consists of whatever beliefs and actions empower the believer to be good. While he was highly critical of most historical religious faiths, Kant advanced an ideal model of Christianity as the universal religion of humankind.

Kant's other works include *The Only Possible Argument in Support of a Demonstration of the Existence of God* (1763), *An Inquiry into the Distinctness of the Fundamental Principles of Natural Theology and Morals* (1764), *Observations on the Feeling of the Beautiful and the Sublime* (1764), *Dreams of a Spirit-seer* (1766), *Prolegomena to Any Future Metaphysics* (1783), *Foundations of the Metaphysics of Morals* (1785), *Metaphysical Elements of Natural Science* (1786), *Metaphysics of Morals* (1797), and *Conflict of the Faculties* (1798). *See also* CATEGORIAL IMPERATIVE.

KARMA. Sanskrit for "action." A belief in Hinduism, Buddhism, and other Indian religions in which morally good or evil actions come back to the actor; a good action comes back to the actor in benefits and an evil action comes back to the actor in punishments. In Hinduism there are three types of karma: acts in a previous life manifest in this life, acts in this life manifest in this life, and acts in this life manifest in a future life. A good action reaps good karma while evil action reaps bad karma. For example, if I donate a lot of my money to charities, in the next life I may become a queen, but if I cheat on an exam, I may be fired from a job later in this life. A popular expression summarizing karma is "what goes around comes around." The religions that have a divine figure believe that that figure deals out the karma while non-theistic religions believe that karma is simply cause and effect and does not need any sort of judge.

KATHENOTHEISM. From the Greek *kata + hena* ("one by one") + *theism*. The worship of one god at a time. Max Müller (1823–1900) coined the term to describe the polytheism of Vedic religion, where various gods are worshiped in succession, one by one. *See also* HENOTHEISM.

KIERKEGAARD, SØREN (1813–1855). Contemporary Kierkegaard scholars are divided when it comes to the question of whether he is to be considered a great philosopher or a more parochial figure, a theologian of his day and age. Even if the latter is true, Kierkegaard's thought and work had a huge influence on the subsequent direction and development of European philosophy and theology.

Kierkegaard reacted to the Hegelian views prevalent amongst his contemporary Danish theologians, although his views are themselves strongly permeated by Hegelian ideas and assumptions. His work and thought could be characterized as an inversion of Hegel's thought: one that attempts to return to more romantic notions and an alternative conception of the relationship between humanity and divinity. In this regard, Kierkegaard charges Hegelianism with being unable to account for, or having failed to do justice to, human subjectivity. This move is basically an attempt to defend Christian faith against the onslaught of philosophical reason in the manner of Kant.

Kierkegaard takes David Hume's skeptical point, that Christian faith cannot be conclusively justified in virtue of human reason, and he uses this as a point in Christianity's defense. If reason cannot conclusively prove faith, Kierkegaard argued, then neither can it disprove it. In fact, Kierkegaard claimed, the very attempt to consider faith a matter of proof is a misunderstanding of its nature. Christian faith is not a philosophical argument, nor is coming to faith the result of being persuaded of a conclusion. It is rather, Kierkegaard held, a movement undertaken on the basis of the paradox of the Christian message and as such, an irrational leap into the arms of God. Kierkegaard's works include *Either / Or: A Fragment of Life* (1843), *Fear and Trembling* (1843), *Philosophical Fragments* (1844), *Concluding Unscientific Postscript* (1846), *Works of Love* (1847), and *The Sickness unto Death* (1849).

KNOWLEDGE. *See* **EPISTEMOLOGY.**

KUHN, THOMAS S. (1922–1996). An important contributor to twentieth-century philosophy of science, Kuhn challenged the idea that science is practiced in a disinterested fashion. He also analyzed the way in which scientific change occurs. At any given time, science may have a central model or ideal for an explanation (a paradigm), but this can shift due to systematic anomalies. Kuhn has been interpreted as advocating a strict anti-realism, but this is not necessary the case. Some have used Kuhn's model of scientific revolution to chart revolutions in philosophy, religion, and theology. Kuhn's works include *The Copernican Revolution* (1957), *The Structure of Scientific Revolutions* (1962), *The Essential Tension: Selected Studies in Scientific Tradition and Change* (1977), *Black-Body Theory and the Quantum Discontinuity* (1978), and *The Road Since Structure: Philosophical Essays, 1970–1993* (published posthumously, 2000).

L

LACAN, JACQUES (1901–1981). The contribution of Jacques Lacan to philosophy and the human sciences can be summed up in his famous assertion that "the unconscious is structured like language." With this, he brings together Ferdinand de Saussure's conception of language and Sigmund Freud's conception of the unconscious. Lacan's crucial assumption remained that language is a self-regulating system of signs rather than signs or words which refer to an independent reality. Lacan analyzes language in terms of its internal structures, i.e., what language is in itself as a formal system of relations, and not in terms of what language refers to or is about. Lacan insisted that Freud's original insights were distorted by positivist or scientist methods which reduce the unconscious to the behavior of the ego. In the late 1950s Lacan would accuse the International Psychoanalytic Association of reducing (Freudian) psychoanalysis to a mechanical causal behaviorism. He went on to demonstrate that psychoanalysis as tool for understanding the practice(s) of language extends its sphere of influence to

the human sciences and so to the conditions for all meaning and values. In this way, Lacan extends his work and influence to the texts of philosophy, literature, and theology, generating controversy and often troublesome practices. At issue was the Lacanian view that psychoanalysis, or eventually "psycholinguistics," is no more than the science of provoking and seeking to understand the language of the unconscious; it cannot give any promise of a cure. Lacan's controversial theories and practices kept him at the center of debates within and outside of the profession of psychoanalysis, notably in the debates of postmodern philosophers and theorists. In his lecture, "On the Death of God," Lacan claims that Freud himself might be counted among "the great theologians of our century" because he examines the manifestations and deformations of a religious function, that is, the religious form of the commandment to love the Lord God your Father and your neighbor as yourself. In other words, Lacan saw in Freud what we might see in Lacanian psycholinguistics: the persistent life of God, despite claims to "the death

135

of God." The male Father God remains central to Lacan's understanding of the social-symbolic structures of language, and so, the condition of all meaning and values: "His" constitutive role in structuring the language of the unconscious, in turn, constitutes patriarchal authority, gender, and relations of sexual difference. These strongly masculine values lead feminist psycholinguists like Julia Kristeva (*Tales of Love*, 1987) to critical engagement with Lacanian forms of analysis. Lacan's works include a series of his seminars (in 28 vols., 1954–1980) and *Écrits* (1966).

LAMAISM. *See* **DALAI LAMA.**

LANGUAGE. *See* **RELIGIOUS LANGUAGE.**

LANGUAGE-GAMES. A term derived from Wittgenstein who held that there are different domains of discourse with their own set of rules and customs. Some claim that the language game of religion may be said to be different from the language game of science. Talk of language games in the mid-twentieth century was part of a general philosophy that recognized diverse, appropriate forms of discourse and a tendency to displace scientific discourse as the most prestigious and authoritative.

LAOZI (a.k.a. Lao-Tzu) (c. 6th BCE). Laozi ("the Old Master") is the purported author of the *Daodejing*, a text also known as the *Laozi*. He is considered the founder of Daoism. There is no contemporaneous information on Laozi, and his historicity is debatable. The text attributed to him may have had more than one author.

The *Daodejing* evokes a *Dao* ("Way"), an ultimate reality that cannot be described in language or through rational discourse, but can only be grasped intuitively. Using indirect language, particularly paradox and analogy, the *Daodejing* suggests a natural order in opposition to human institutions. Passivity and humility are virtues. Water, for example, is soft and yielding yet able to wear down stone. The *Daodejing* rejects the Confucian stress on ritual, propriety, and moral self-cultivation. Its ideal of *wuwei* ("non-action") eschews purposeful action in favor of simple and natural behavior.

LAPLACE, PIERRE SIMON DE (1749–1827). A French astronomer famous for claiming that in his science he had no need for God as a hypothesis. LaPlace articulated a strong form of determinism. His most influential work is *A Philosophical Essay on Probabilities* (1814).

LEIBNIZ, GOTTFRIED WILHELM (1646–1716). German rationalist and defender of the view that the creation is the best possible world. Leibniz argued for this on the grounds that God is perfect, rational, and omnipotent. Leibniz defended a version of the cosmological argument, the principle of sufficient reason, and promoted European religious tolerance as well as European respect for Chinese culture and philosophy. Leibniz defended the belief in innate ideas against Locke's empiricism. His works include *Dissertatio de Arte Combinatoria* (1666), *Discourse on Metaphysics* (1685), *General Inquiries* (1686), *The New System* (1695), *New Essays on Human Understanding* (1703–1705, but not published until 1765), *Theodicy* (1710), and *Monadology* (c. 1713).

LESSING, GOTTHOLD EPHRAIM (1729–1781). German playwright and thinker who contended that a large "ditch" separates contemporary persons from the original revelation of God in Christ. Some Christian philosophers in reply argued that while "the age of miracles" found in the New Testament has passed, Christ remains a contemporary (a living presence today). Lessing's works include *The Education of the Human Race* (1777–1780) and *Nathan the Wise* (1779).

LESSING'S DITCH. Taken from a phrase in Lessing's essay on *The Proof of the Spirit and of Power*, this argument states that in a time beyond the workings of miracles as described in the New Testament, it has become increasingly difficult to build a faith on the historical claims of miraculous actions which cannot be proven to be historical truths. As a consequence, Lessing argues, there appears an "ugly, broad, ditch" between contemporary personal experiences of faith and the historical experience of God in Jesus Christ.

LEVINAS, EMMANUEL (1906–1995). Often working outside of the academic limelight, Levinas was influential first in introducing Husserl's phenomenology to France, and then in arguing that as subjects we are morally responsible to the needs of others before we are knowing or acting subjects. He calls this insight "ethics as first philosophy." God, the Infinite, is inconceivable and is present to us only as an ethical command. A Lithuanian Jew, Levinas spent World War II in a French prisoner of war camp and published a number of Talmudic interpretations in addition to his philosophical work. His writings include *The Theory of Intuition in Husserl's Philosophy* (1930), *Existence and Existents* (1947), *Time and the Other* (1947), *Totality and Infinity* (1961), *Otherwise than Being or Beyond Essence* (1974), *Difficult Freedom: Essays on Judaism* (1976), *Beyond the Verse: Talmudic Readings and Lectures* (1982), and *Of God Who Comes to Mind* (1982).

LEWIS, CLIVE STAPLES (1898–1963). British scholar, writer, poet, Christian apologist, and lay Anglican theologian, primarily known for his classic series of children's fantasy literature, *The Chronicles of Narnia* (1950–1956). Although Lewis studied and briefly taught philosophy at Oxford, his professional expertise was in medieval and Renaissance literature, which he taught for many years at both Oxford and Cambridge and on which he published numerous scholarly works. However, following his gradual conversion from atheism to idealism to theism to orthodox Christianity (culminating in 1931), Lewis embarked on a remarkable secondary career as an amateur theologian and highly effective apologist. His books *The Problem of Pain* (1940— on theodicy), *The Abolition of Man* (1943—on moral relativism and cultural education), *The Great Divorce* (1945—on free will and personal eschatology), *Miracles* (1947, 2nd ed., 1960—on naturalism and the possibility of special divine action), and *Mere Christianity* (1952—on basic Christian doctrine) are among the most widely read and discussed texts in the second half of the twentieth century. Although Lewis' various arguments are often criticized by professional philosophers and theologians, his thought has proved surprisingly resilient: it continues to fascinate and provoke and find adherents among both academic and general readers. In philosophy of religion, his theistic "argument from reason" (presented in the first edition of *Miracles*, famously critiqued by G. E. M. Anscombe in 1948, and revised in the second edition) is still frequently discussed, as is his imaginative exploration of post-mortem freedom in regard to heaven and hell in *The Great Divorce*.

LEX TALIONIS. From the Latin, meaning "An eye for an eye, a tooth for a tooth" (cf. Lev. 24:17–23). Law prescribing equality between crime and punishment. It is often not appreciated how the *lex talionis* may be understood as establishing a cap on revenge. If someone unfairly destroys an eye, it is not permissible for you to kill the wrongdoer and his city.

LI. *See* **QI.**

LIBERAL THEOLOGY. Also known as "modern theology," the primary assumption of liberal theology is that the content or meaning of religious convictions are separate from the way those convictions are expressed or formulated. In this way, concern for—and the use of—philosophical, cultural, and social discourse is a particular staple of liberal theology. Friedrich Schleiermacher is often considered "the father of modern theology."

LIFE AFTER DEATH. Theistic and many non-theistic religions affirm that human persons do not perish into nothingness (cease to be *in nihilum*) at physical death, but continue to live either on another plane of existence or creation, or they will be re-created at a future resurrection, or that their souls will persist in the lives of other humans or nonhuman animals. The belief in life after death is an ancient concept. Pythagoras, for example, believed in the transmigration of souls whereby a human being could one day be reincarnated as a dog. *See* IMMORTALITY.

LIFE, MEANING OF. Questions about the meaning of life generally concern the value and purpose of human life, but one can ask about the meaning of not just life, but also about the meaning of the cosmos. Possible answers include: human life is intrinsically valuable if led ethically and to maturity; human life is both intrinsically valuable and yet it is also part of a large (boundless?) created order sustained by a God of love; or "man [human being] is a useless passion," which is the last line of Sartre's *Being and Nothingness*. Buddhist accounts of life's meaning differ from Muslim accounts, and so on.

LOCKE, JOHN (1632–1704). A surgeon and important contributor to metaphysics, epistemology, and political theory. Locke was one of the first British empiricists who gave pride of place to the authority of observation, discounting the appeal to innate ideas. He was a theist and defended a consciousness-based account of personal identity. What makes you the same person over time is the fact that your consciousness is continuous between now and your past. He believed that people own themselves and their labor, and he defended the idea that property is an extension of self-ownership and labor. Often accused of promoting an excessive personal individualism, he nonetheless held that persons are responsible for the needy and dispossessed. He defended Jesus as the Messiah and Christian faith as a whole, although he may have denied that God is triune. Locke was an opponent of the divine right of kings and he promoted religious tolerance except in the case of Roman Catholics, whom he believed to be servants of a foreign prince. His works include *Essay Concerning Human Understanding* (1689), *Two Treatises of Government* (1689—published anonymously), *Letter on Toleration* (1689—published anonymously), *Some Thoughts Concerning Education* (1693), and *The Reasonableness of Christianity* (1695).

LOGIC. Formally, "logic" refers to rules of entailment such as the law of identity (A is A), noncontradiction (A is not not A), and excluded middle (either A or not A). Informally, one may refer to the logic of a given position in the case of inquiry about some practice or belief system. The "logic" behind the debate over whether a war is justified, for example, may include the different conditions outlined in the just war tradition.

LOGICAL POSITIVISM. An empiricist movement according to which a proposition is meaningful if and only if it concerns the relation of ideas (definitions) or if the truth or falsehood of the proposition is evident (in principle) empirically. This principle was used by A. J. Ayer and others to argue that religious language was not meaningful. There was great controversy in the middle and late twentieth century about whether the principle is itself meaningful and about the role of empirical evidence. It appears, for example, that there are statements about the future that are meaningful but could (in principle) never, if true, be verified. For example, "There will never be a planet with unicorns and hobbits."

LONERGAN, BERNARD (1904–1984). A Canadian philosophical theologian who defended a nuanced epistemology that gave a central role to insight. In his latter work he recognized an affective dimension to theological inquiry. His chief works include *Insight* (1957) and *Method in Theology* (1972).

LOVE. In Greek, one can identify *eros* as one form of love which involves desire. This may or may not be sensuous or erotic. Another form of love was called *phileo*, which can designate friendship love or the love of a virtue like wisdom. *Agape* love was considered a love that was divine or unconditional, not dependent upon the particular characteristics of the beloved.

Today the term "love" has a wide variety of meanings and it is sometimes used in a way that is morally neutral, e.g., just because someone loves does not entail that the love is virtuous or good, for a person may be said to love cruelty. Be that as it may, Platonic philosophical tradition from Plato to the Florentine academy and the Cambridge Platonists understands love to be the key to the fulfillment of the soul as the soul seeks to love the good, the true, and the beautiful.

Questions in philosophy of love include: Does love have to rest on reasons? What is the relationship between impartial charity and the preferential love of a person? Is loving a person a matter of loving the properties of the person (her wit, intelligence, elegance, and so on) or of loving the person who has these properties but might lose them? Can you love another person too much?

LOVEJOY, ARTHUR O(NCHKEN) (1873–1962). A preeminent historian of ideas who wrote a seminal treatment of medieval European philosophy and its encounter with modern science. He was the first editor of the *Journal of History of Ideas* and his chief works include *The Great Chain of Being* (1936) and *Essays in the History of Ideas* (1948). Lovejoy's work on the great chain of being was a highly influential study of the philosophical and social unravelling of medieval philosophy with the advent of modern science.

LUTHER, MARTIN (1483–1546).

Martin Luther was the son of peasants and born in Eisleben, a small town in Saxon Germany. When he died 63 years later in Eisleben, he was known across Europe as the founder of the theological movement that would later be called the Protestant Reformation. As a young man successfully studying law at Erfurt, Luther was overcome with terror one night while out in a thunderstorm and vowed to his patron saint Anne that if he survived he would become a monk. But the scrupulosity of life as an Augustinian monk burdened Luther, who, even after being ordained a priest, believed that his inability to live perfectly would invoke God's wrath and punishment. To distract Luther from his fears of damnation, his confessor Johann von Staupitz sent him to the newly established university at Wittenberg to gain his doctorate and lecture in Old Testament.

It was in Wittenberg that Luther spent the rest of his life, teaching and preaching as he developed a theology that would both alleviate his fears of God and split the Western church. Although Luther never intended to depart from Catholicism, he found himself fighting for reform as early as 1517, when he wrote and disseminated 95 theses against the selling of indulgences (which absolved the recipient of their sins). By this time Luther had become convinced that the church was abusing its power, swindling the poor, and preaching of a false gospel by which humans could save themselves through good works. When he refused the Pope's command that he recant his writings in 1521, he was excommunicated from the church and declared an outlaw by the emperor, subject to captivity and death. Yet, he survived the political turmoil and social unrest caused by his theology, living for 25 more years, marrying the former nun Katherine von Bora, raising five children, and developing a theology that would spread quickly throughout Europe due to the popularity of his ideas and his use of the newly-invented printing press.

Luther's conception of grace, which became the theological foundation of Protestantism, viewed salvation as a gift of God given to Christians by Christ through faith apart from works. Separating justification from sanctification, Luther attributed salvation to God alone, through the work of Christ, while still allowing for humans to live freely and responsibly, fueled by the Holy Spirit. Against papal authority, Luther located the church's authority in Scripture alone. Against visible church hierarchy, Luther developed the doctrine of the priesthood of all believers and the invisibility of the true church. Against the Eucharistic doctrine of transubstantiation, Luther preached the "real presence" of Christ's body and blood in the bread and the wine.

Luther's translation of the Bible into the vernacular not only made Scripture accessible to the laity but also helped concretize a standardized version of the modern German language. His contributions to hymnody led to the further development of church singing and are still found in hymnals today. Luther wrote with aggressive passion against those who disagreed with his theology—Catholics, Jews, and even other reformers—in a way that Lutherans today consider regrettable. Yet, his theology is still today regarded by many Protestants as being at the heart of Christian truth. His works include *On the Liberty of a Christian Man* (1520), *An Address to the Nobility of the German Nation* (1520), and *On the Babylonian Captivity of the Church of God* (1520).

LYING. The Western tradition of thought about lying has attended principally to two issues. First, what is it to lie? Second, when, if ever, is lying permissible (or required)? As to the definitional question, three elements have been of importance. The first is duplicity: intentionally claiming what you take not to be the case. The second is an utterance intended to deceive or mislead its hearer. And the third is uttering something which is in fact false. Since each of these can be present in an utterance absent the other two (and any two absent the third), these elements may be combined in various ways in defining the lie. The most common definitions have been those that combine the first

and second elements, though with widely differing degrees of emphasis.

As to the second issue, the lie's permissibility: positions here have ranged from an exceptionless ban on the lie, through a relaxed acceptance of its frequent unavoidability, to a defense of its propriety or even its obligatoriness in certain circumstances. The standard Christian position from late antiquity to the Reformation was that duplicitous utterance is never defensible. This was a position argued trenchantly and influentially by Augustine in the fourth century. The difficulty of that position led to a luxuriant casuistry which attempted to preserve the ban on duplicity while yet making it possible to speak deceptively. Immanuel Kant, at the end of the eighteenth century, revived a rigorous ban on the duplicitous lie, though for reasons very different from Augustine's. His position, however, found as little support among Kantians as Augustine's had among Augustinians, and much current discussion of lying is either strictly historical or attentive to the peculiar paradoxes produced by the possibility of lying to oneself.

LYOTARD, JEAN-FRANCOIS (1924–1998). Lyotard is perhaps best known for his epoch-making, "postmodern" argument against philosophers like Kant, Hegel and Marx whose grand "metanarratives," or modern schemas, promise truth and justice at the end of inquiry.

Lyotard argues for a multiplicity of heterogeneous and so, incommensurable language-games with their own immanent criteria. Anyone who rejects this must be thinking from a totalitarian or rigidly doctrinaire standpoint. In *The Postmodern Condition* (1979), Lyotard argues for a postmodern sublime against Kant's argument concerning the unrepresentable aspects of the sublime as "a combination of pleasure and pain: the pleasure that reason should exceed all presentation, the pain that imagination or sensibility should not be equal to the concept." Lyotard stresses the manner in which Kant's critical philosophy is perpetually interrupted by uncontainable moments of excess such as the sublime. In contrast, Lyotard's postmodern sublime "puts forward the unpresentable in presentation itself." Due to incommensurable absolutes, the postmodern sublime cannot privilege consensus: instead Lyotard looks for a means to mobilize difference. Thus Lyotard concludes that the "terror" of modernity's absolute universality is disturbed and to be, continually, disrupted by postmodern difference. Yet later essays, found in his *The Inhuman* (1988), suggest that the sublime of avant-garde painters is also "an event, an occurrence" in the "here and now": this creates "the joy obtained in the intensification of being." Lyotard's works include *Phenomenology (1954), Discourse, figure (1971), Libidinal Economy (1974), The Postmodern Condition* (1979), *Just Gaming* (1979), *The Differend* (1983), *Driftworks* (1984), *Peregrinations* (1988), *Heidegger and "the Jews" (1988), The Inhuman* (1988), and *Lessons on the Analytic of the Sublime* (1991), and two collections, the *Lyotard Reader* (1989) and *Political Writings* (1993).

M

MACKIE, JOHN (1917–1981). An Australian born, Oxford philosopher in the Humean tradition who argued systematically for atheism and a noncognitive view of ethical values. One of his arguments against ethics is that objective ethical properties would be "queer" given our understanding of the natural world. His chief debating partner in print was Richard Swinburne, an advocate of theistic natural theology. Mackie's chief works include *The Cement of the Universe* (1974, 1980), *The Miracle of Theism* (1982), "Evil and Omnipotence," *Mind, 64* (1955), "A refutation of Morals," *Australasian Journal of Philosophy and Psychology, 24* (1946), and *Ethics: Inventing Right and Wrong* (1977).

MAGIC. Christian Old and New Testament sources associate magic with sorcery and devilish arts, but the Renaissance promoted a form of white magic involving alchemy and the development of virtue through enchantment. *See also* WICCA.

MAGICK. *See* MAGIC.

MAIMONIDES (1135–1204). Also known as Moses ben Maimon, Rabbi Moses, and the Rambam (from the initials of "Rabbi Moses ben Maimon"). Maimonides was the most important Jewish philosopher of the Middle Ages and one of the most important Jewish thinkers of all time. He was born in Córdoba, Spain, and spent much of his life fleeing religious persecution. His family fled to Fez in 1148, then to Egypt in 1165. He was a court physician in Cairo until his death. He wrote a number of works in Hebrew and Arabic. His major work, the *Guide of the Perplexed*, is an important work of apophatic theology and one of the most important philosophical works of Judaism. In the *Guide*, Maimonides attempted a rational reconciliation of philosophy and revealed religion. His *Guide* was of interest not just to Jews but also to Christians and Muslims. Albert the Great and Thomas Aquinas were both influenced by Maimonides' attempt to synthesize Jewish monotheism and Aristotelian metaphysics.

Maimonides stresses the importance of law and proper conduct of life. His *Mishneh Torah* was to be an all-encompassing commentary to supplement the Torah. In it, he attempts to show that there is nothing in the Torah that does not serve a rational purpose. Maimonides took the point of the Jewish law to be the betterment of the body and of the soul. Every action prescribed in the Torah is therefore beneficial for both the body and for the soul. His principal works are: *Treatise on the Art of Logic, Commentary on the Mishnah* (1168), *The Guide of the Perplexed* (c. 1190), *Treatise on Resurrection* (1191), and *Letter on Astrology* (1195). *See also* APOPHATIC THEOLOGY.

MALCOLM, NORMAN (1911–1990). Inspired by Wittgenstein, Malcolm defended the intelligibility of religious belief notwithstanding serious doubts about theism. He offered a forceful defense of a version of the ontological argument. Malcolm also famously defended the view that dreaming does not actually involve dream experiences. His chief works include *Knowledge and Certainty* (1963), *Dreaming* (1959), and *Memory and Mind* (1977).

MALEBRANCHE, NICOLAS (1638–1715). A French Cartesian philosopher who understood God to be involved in all causal relations. What accounts for your reading this book is not just your intentions, anatomy, and so on, but also God making it such that these factors have causal agency. This view is sometimes called occasionalism, for causal relations between objects in this world consist of occasions for divine agency. Malebranche's chief works include *The Search after Truth* (2 vols. 1674, 1675), *Treatise on Nature and Grace* (1680), and *Dialogues on Metaphysics and Religion* (1688).

MANICHAEAISM (a.k.a. Manichaenism). An ancient Gnostic religion founded by Mani (c. 210–276 CE) in Babylon, which was then part of the Persian Empire. Manichaeism was a dualistic religion, positing the existence of two great cosmic forces, one good and one evil. These forces play out their cosmic battle in human beings, pitting the soul (composed of light) against the body (composed of dark earth). In order to overcome the evil, material world, one must seek the good, spiritual world. Like other Gnostic religions, salvation comes through knowledge, while ignorance results in sin. Manichaeism thrived between the third and seventh centuries CE, spreading throughout the Roman Empire and as far east as China. Although early Christians were highly critical of Manichaeism and deemed it a heresy, it often influenced their worldview. In *The Confessions*, Augustine recounts how he entertained Manichaeism in his youth, but later rejected it. In 382 CE, the Roman Emperor Theodosius I (who later made Christianity the official religion of the Roman Empire) issued a decree of death for Manichaens. Manichaens were also persecuted by Buddhists and Zoroastrians. Muslims, however, were tolerant of Manichaeism.

MARCION OF SINOPE (c. 85 CE– c. 165 CE). A Gnostic Christian who held that the religion of Yahweh is not of the true God. We are to seek a higher God than the god-creator (a Demiurge) of this world. The higher God sent Christ whom the Demiurge in this world killed. Christ overcame death and Paul was appointed to preach a gospel of liberation and salvation.

MARCUS AURELIUS ANTONINUS (121–180 CE). A philosophically reflective Roman emperor whose private notes were later published as *The Meditations* and have long been treasured as promoting stoical calm and serenity in the midst of sometimes devastating conflict.

MARCUSE, HERBERT (1898–1979). A Freudian Marxist who offered a deep critique of the materialism and shallowness of post-World War II Europe and North America. Marcuse was as deeply opposed to Soviet Marxism as he was to the West's pursuit of military and social power. His chief works include *Eros and Civilization* (1955) and *One-Dimensional Man* (1964).

MARITAIN, JACQUES (1882–1973). French Neo-Thomist, he brought Catholic neo-Thomism into dialogue with many of the leading philosophical movements of twentieth-century France, especially those hostile to Catholicism, such as Sartre's existentialism and Bergson's vitalism. He also recast Thomistic philosophy in light of the advances of modern science and movements in modern art. He defended a form of intellectual intuition distinct from what is found in Husserlian phenomenology and Bergsonian philosophy. His writings include *Art and Scholasticism* (1920), *The Degrees of Knowledge* (1932), *Integral Humanism* (1936), *Existence and the Existent* (1947), *Approaches to God* (1953), *Creative Intuition in Art and Poetry* (1953), and *Moral Philosophy* (1960).

MARX, KARL (1818–1883). The chief architect of communism along with Engels, Marx did not regard himself as a philosopher and yet he promoted a serious philosophy of history, economics, and politics. Marx argued that history is the history of class struggle. He argued that feudalism necessarily led to capitalism and that necessary historical forces will lead to the collapse of capitalism and, through a worker's revolution, to the reign of the proletariat. The latter end-state was not at all akin to the state hierarchy of the Soviet Union but more of a paradisal world of natural concord without exploitation. His stance has been called economic determinism, but it is more often termed historical materialism. When he described religion as the opiate of the people, one might think this is benign as opium use at the time was medicinal, but in fact he regarded religion as a tool for pacifying workers who ought to revolt against the bourgeois. Marx was in the left-wing school of Hegelianism and was strongly influenced by Feuerbach. His works include *The Economic and Philosophical Manuscripts of 1844* (1844), *Theses on Feuerbach* (1845), *The German Ideology* (1846), *The Poverty of Philosophy* (1847), *The Communist Manifesto* (1848), *Grundrisse* (1857–1858, published 1953), and *Das Kapital* (3 vols., 1867, 1885, 1893).

MASHAM, DAMARIS CUDWORTH (1659–1708). The daughter of Cambridge Platonist Ralph Cudworth and close friend of John Locke, Damaris Cudworth Masham defended women's education and a practical life of Christian virtue. Her works include *A Discourse Concerning the Love of God* (1696) and *Occasional Thoughts in Reference to a Virtuous or Christian Life* (1705).

MATERIALISM. A term used synonymously today with physicalism, the view that all that exists is physical. The definition of what counts as physical is unsettled. Are ideas physical? Or time?

MAYA. Sanskrit for "not that" or "illusion." In Hindu philosophy, *maya* refers to the belief that the sensory world is an illusion. *Advaita Vedanta* teaches that the self (*atman*) and the Ultimate Reality (*Brahman*) are "not two." In order to attain liberation (*moksha*) from the cycle of death and rebirth (*samsara*), one must transcend the illusion of physical reality. *Maya* is sometimes personified as a goddess.

McTAGGART, JOHN McTAGGART ELLIS (1866–1925). A British atheist idealist philosopher who argued that temporal passage (past, present, and future) is unreal. Such relations (which he called the B series) can be displaced by what he called the A series and the relations of preceding, simultaneous with, and subsequent to. His early work was on Hegel, but he later articulated an elaborate metaphysics. According to McTaggart, the world is made up of souls related to one another in love. He believed in the immortality of the soul and reincarnation but denied the existence of a personal God. Instead, he conceived of the absolute as the community of souls. His students Bertrand Russell and G. E. Moore, reacting against his neo-Hegelian idealism, went on to found modern analytic philosophy. McTaggart's chief works include *Studies in the Hegelian Dialectic* (1896), "The Unreality of Time" (1908), and *The Nature of Existence* (2 vols., 1921–1927). *See also* TIME.

MEANING. Questions about the meaning of a place, action, or event often involve questions about the cause or consequences of the thing in question or its significance and value. Questions of meaning may therefore be quite broad in philosophy of religion, and include the broadest of all questions: What is the meaning of life? A Buddhist answer to this question will differ from a Christian answer. Questions about the meaning of texts raise theoretical questions about the significance of the original intention of the author(s), the surrounding, historical conditions, and the current conditions in which the text is encountered. The practice (art) of interpreting texts is called hermeneutics (from the Greek *hermenia* for "interpretation" or "explanation"). Theories of meaning that stress the intended meaning by the author or speaker are called internal theories, while theories that stress established public usage are called external theories. *See also* HERMENEUTICS.

MEDIATION. In philosophy of religion, mediation is of concern in the context of religious experience, prayer, Christology, and redemption. In religious experience, philosophers debate whether the experience of God (or the sacred) can be direct or whether it must be mediated by sensory or some other cognitive state. In prayer, some believe that one can pray to a saint or angel to intercede on one's behalf. In Christology, Jesus is traditionally understood to be the mediator between God the Father and the world. In matters of redemption, historically there have been controversies over whether the church needs to function as a mediator between the soul and God and over whether Mary is a proper mediator in a soul's journey to redemption.

MEDITATION. A contemplative state of mind that has a different but sometimes closely related role in different religions. So, in theistic religions, there is a common practice of persons contemplating scripture or icons or a holy teaching in the course of the practitioner opening her mind to the presence of God. In Buddhism, meditation often takes a different course in which the goal of meditation may be to see through the diaphanous, spurious nature of ego-driven desire and to see the unreality of the ostensible substantial self.

MENCIUS (a.k.a. Meng Tzu) (371–289 BCE). Mencius is the Latinized form of Mengzi (Master Meng). Mencius was, after Confucius himself, the most important

Confucian philosopher of the classical Age. His teachings developed two themes found in the *Analects* of Confucius: the goodness of human nature and the ruler's obligation to behave morally toward his subjects. In contrast to the Legalist school of thought emerging at the time, which held that human beings are basically amoral and motivated by self-interest, Mencius argued that everyone is born with a natural propensity toward goodness. This natural inclination, however, must be cultivated through education and example. The purpose of government is to ensure the welfare of the people. The ruler, whose authority is ultimately derived from the moral mandate of Heaven, can lose his legitimacy through misrule. The people, acting as agents of Heaven, then have the right to overthrow the evil ruler. The teachings of Mencius, compiled in the *Book of Mencius* (*Mengzi*), became part of the Confucian canon that formed the basis of the imperial civil service examination system until 1905.

MENDELSSOHN, MOSES (1729–1786). A Jewish philosopher of the German Enlightenment and disciple of Leibniz and Wolff. His work focused on proofs of and for the existence of God. He argues that his own Judaism was not a "revealed religion," but a "revealed legislation," and so religion was not based on the following of certain doctrinal beliefs, but the following of certain actions. This characterization of religion allowed Mendelssohn to reconcile his faith with his own political liberalism. His works include *Philosophical Writings* (1761) and *Morning Hours, or Lectures on the Existence of God* (1785).

MERCY. Mercy involves unmerited or undeserved favor, typically in the context of justice. So one may have mercy on someone who is in trouble when one is not obligated to go to her assistance, and one may have mercy on a criminal when a lesser punishment is imposed or the criminal is pardoned altogether. Philosophers have disputed the relationship of mercy and justice. Does mercy need to be consistent (that is, if you have mercy on one criminal are you then obliged to have mercy on a criminal in similar conditions)? Can mercy be good when it is in conflict with justice? Imagine a criminal genuinely deserves a harsh punishment in the context of retributive justice, but a magistrate thinks (rightly) that pardoning the criminal will bring about great good (e.g., the criminal has repented and will aid in fighting crime). In that case, could it be good that the magistrate does something that is wrong from the standpoint of retributive justice? In theology, some theologians hold that from the standpoint of justice, an all good God would destroy the wicked, but from the standpoint of mercy, God may and has elected to redeem the wicked. Does this involve God doing something that (from the standpoint of retributive justice) should not be done? *See also* JUSTICE.

METAPHOR. From the Greek *metaphora*, meaning "to transfer or transform." Metaphors are typically derived from nonmetaphorical literal language that is transferred to a new context based on a presumed analogy. In the statement "Your dictionary is a breath of fresh air," "fresh air" is a metaphorical attribution. Some distinguish between live and dead metaphors. A dead metaphor, sometimes called a cliché, is a usage that is so common that it fails in terms of vividness, surprise, or the making of a novel connection. For example, "When you left me, you broke my heart." *See also* RELIGIOUS LANGUAGE.

METAPHYSICS. Theories of what exists. Some use the term to designate entities that are posited beyond empirical observation, but such usage is not standard. Metaphysics is difficult to escape. Even to claim, "I doubt the reliability of metaphysics" makes a claim about what exists (the self and doubt, for starters).

METEMPSYCHOSIS. *See* TRANSMIGRATION.

METHOD / METHODLOGY. There are a variety of methods employed in philosophy of religion such as phenomenology and analytical philosophy with its premium on conceptual analysis. Some philosophers make an important distinction between a presupposition in methodology and the truth of that presupposition. For example, someone may embrace methodological naturalism (assume that all explanations are in terms of natural, non-theistic or non-supernatural causes) and yet not accept the truth of naturalism. Historical studies of the Hebrew and Christian Bibles that embrace methodological naturalism typically seek to either explain away or not affirm acts of God or miracles. A non-theistic historian is more likely to treat prophecies about the future (as in Luke 21:20) as cases of *vaticinium ex eventu* (cases of when the writer is predicting an event that has already occurred) than if the historian is a theist who believes that there may be authentic God-inspired knowledge of the future. A historian who is not open to the possibility of divine agency is akin to the natural scientist who rules out libertarian freedom. The latter will never allow the appeal to irreducible free agency to stand.

MIDDLE KNOWLEDGE. The concept of middle knowledge was introduced to account for divine foreknowledge and future free action. Middle knowledge consists of knowing what free agents would decide given certain states of affairs which may or may not obtain. An instance of middle knowledge would consist in God knowing what you would do if you were offered a bribe of a certain amount under certain circumstances. By God knowing those circumstances, God knows what you will freely do. To posit middle knowledge of God involves holding that God knows not only all truths about what for us is the past, present, and future, but also that God knows all that would have occurred or might have occurred under different conditions. Some philosophers opposing middle knowledge are called open theists. They maintain, instead, that God's omniscience covers all that can be known by God who exists in the present, and that future free contingent acts cannot be known until they occur.

MILL, JOHN STUART (1806–1873). British empiricist, utilitarian, and defender of a liberal political theory that gave primary value to human liberty. He defended a modest theism that was far more limited than traditional Christianity. He thought an afterlife was possible, but he did not think God was both all powerful and all good. His chief works include *System of Logic* (1843), *Principles of Political Economy* (1848), *On Liberty* (1859), *Subjection of Women* (1861, published in 1869), *Utilitarianism* (1861 in *Fraser's Magazine*, 1863 as a separate publication), *Examination of Sir William Hamilton's Philosophy* (1865), *Autobiography* (1873), and *Three Essays on Religion* (published posthumously in 1874).

MIND. A term that is sometimes used to refer to a person or soul or, sometimes, more narrowly to refer to a person's psychological or mental life. "Mind" may also refer to one's goal or purpose. When some theists refer to the mind of God they are referring to God's provident purpose or intentions.

MIND-BODY RELATIONSHIP. A common term for the relationship between the mental and physical, the self or subject and her body and bodily processes. Some religious philosophers defend dualist accounts in which the mind (self or the mental) is distinct from the body; others suppose the mind is the body, with a multiplicity of positions in between.

MIRACLE. From the Latin *mirari*, meaning "to wonder at." Famously defined by David Hume as a violation of a law of nature by a supernatural agent. Hume also discusses the importance of trusting the testimony of those who claim to experience the miraculous, demanding of one's faith that such a source has legitimate authority, e.g., believing in Catholic doctrines about the resurrection that trace back to the apostles' testimony. However, this definition fails to appreciate the religious meaning of miracles, for reported miracles are almost always cases in which the miracle serves some religious end. It also employs a peculiar view of nature, implying it is a law of nature that God not act in nature with special intentions. A better definition is that M is a miracle when M would not have occurred without God's agency, when M has religious significance, and when M is not part of God's general willing of cosmic order.

MODAL LOGIC. Entailments involving propositions that are possible, necessary, or impossible. One claim in modal logic is that if X is possibly necessary, X is necessarily necessary. In philosophy of religion, modal logic is most often used in debates over the ontological argument. For example, in some versions of the ontological argument it is argued that God either exists necessarily or that God's existence is impossible. This premise is sometimes supported as part of the thesis that God has every great-making attribute and that necessary existence would be an excellence. Philosophers such as Leibniz then go on to argue that it is possible that God exists. If it is possible that God exists, then God's existence is not impossible. If God's existence is not impossible, it is necessary. Hence, God exists. Some detractors object that the argument only establishes a hypothetical judgment (if God exists, God exists necessarily).

MOKSHA (a.k.a. *Mukti*). Sanskrit, "release." *Moksha* is a term used in Indian religions to refer to the ultimate goal of release or liberation from the cycle of death and re-birth (*samsara*). It is similar to the Buddhist concept of *nirvana*.

MOLINA, LUIS DE (1535–1600). A Spanish philosophical theologian most noted for his theory of divine middle knowledge (*scientia media*) which was designed to reconcile the belief in divine foreknowledge and freedom. According to Molina, God knows what all creatures would freely choose to do under all possible circumstances. By knowing which circumstances obtain, God thereby knows how a free creature acts. *See also* MOLINISM.

MOLINISM. A theory of divine knowledge originated by the Jesuit theologian Luis de Molina. What is distinctive about the theory is its claim that God knows certain propositions, now usually termed counterfactuals of creaturely freedom (CCFs). These are propositions concerning each actual and possible free creature, stating what that creature would choose to do in any logically possible situation of libertarian free choice with which that creature might be confronted. God's knowledge of these propositions is termed middle knowledge (*scientia media*) because it is thought of as intermediate between God's "natural knowledge" of necessary truths and God's "free knowledge" of truths that depend on

152

God's own creative actions. The CCFs are contingent, yet are true prior to any creative decision on God's part, and their truth or falsity is not under divine control. Knowledge of the CCFs is of immense value to God in God's providential governing of the world, since it enables God to arrange circumstances in such a way as to elicit precisely the responses from free creatures that are most conducive to God's providential purposes, without at all abridging their freedom. Critics of middle knowledge claim that these truths which God is alleged to know do not exist to be known; there is no "grounding in reality" for their truth in the innumerable cases in which the choices in question are never actually made. Thomists, furthermore, insist that the existence of such truths is an unacceptable infringement on divine sovereignty. The defenders of Molinism have ingenious replies to these objections, and they point with satisfaction to the advantages for the doctrine of providence if their views are accepted.

MOLTMANN, JÜRGEN (1926–). A German Protestant theologian whose work stresses hope in the resurrection of Christ. Brought up in a secular education, Moltmann served in the German army in World War II. During his time as a prisoner of war, Moltmann converted to Christianity. Moltmann argued on historical grounds for the reliability of belief in the resurrection of Christ, and he built his theology on the grounds of eschatology. An important further development of his theology included a strong stance on God's identification and solidarity with the oppressed. His works include *Theology of Hope* (1964), *The Crucified God* (1972), *The Church in the Power of the Spirit* (1975), *The Trinity and the Kingdom* (1980), *God in Creation* (1985), *The Way of Jesus Christ* (1989), *The Spirit of Life* (1992), and *The Coming of God* (1996).

MONISM. Traditionally, the thesis that all is matter. More recently defined as: all is matter and energy. A current alternative is the thesis that all that exists will be described and explained by an ideal physics.

MONOTHEISM. The belief that there is only one God. *See also* CHRISTIANITY; ISLAM; and JUDAISM.

MONTAIGNE, MICHEL DE (1533– 1592). A highly influential French thinker who developed his philosophical positions in the form of essays. Against what he saw as the dogmatism and intolerance of his age, Montaigne advanced a form of skepticism that ruled out both religious bigotry and the secular dismissal of all religion. His famous motto was "What do I know?" (*Que sais-je?*). He thought that cruelty was the most grave vice.

MORAL ARGUMENTS FOR THEISM. A family of arguments that variously urge that certain features of human moral experience are best accommodated on a theistic worldview. In particular, the common claim is that moral realism, the view that there are objective or mind- independent moral facts, calls for theistic metaphysical or epistemological underpinnings. Immanuel Kant reasoned, for instance, that if there is no God then there are objective moral requirements that are not possibly met, namely, that the moral good of virtue and the natural good of happiness embrace and become perfect in a "highest good." The early twentieth-century idealist philosophers Hastings Rashdall and W. R. Sorley argued that an objective moral law requires an infinite mind in which to reside if it is to have full ontological status. C. S. Lewis offered a popularized version of such an argument in a series of talks for the BBC during World War II, later published in his *Mere Christianity*. Lewis argued that conscience reveals to us a moral law whose source cannot be found in the natural world, thus pointing to a supernatural Lawgiver. Philosopher Robert Adams has argued that moral obligation is best explained by appeal to the commands of a loving God, and moral values in general may be thought to reflect God's nature. Atheist philosopher J. L. Mackie observed that objective moral facts and our epistemic access to them would be metaphysically and epistemically "queer" on

metaphysical naturalism. He thus rejected moral realism for a variety of nihilism. The argument invites reversal: Insofar as the belief in moral facts seems warranted, we have reason to reject naturalism for something akin to theism. Other arguments focus on the inadequacy of metaphysical naturalism for accommodating any robust form of moral realism. The naturalist's commitment to a Darwinian genealogy of morals might be thought to present the naturalist with an undercutting defeater for any and all moral beliefs, thus yielding moral skepticism. The theist may be thought to be in a position to maintain that human moral faculties are designed for the purpose of discerning moral facts and are thus "truth-aimed" in a way that they would not be on naturalism. Or one might argue that no adequate theory of normative ethics sits comfortably within the confines of a naturalistic worldview. For instance, one might argue that the belief in natural and inviolable rights is implicated by our considered moral judgments, but would prove to be "nonsense on stilts" given the metaphysics of naturalism. The inherent worth of persons, on the other hand, might best be understood within a theistic framework in which the axiological and metaphysical Ultimate is a Person.

MORAL REALISM. The thesis that there are objective truths about moral rightness and wrongness; these truths are not a function of subjective preference or dependent upon social customs of language. A moral realist may claim that slavery has always been morally wrong even if the majority of cultures believed slavery was natural and benign. *See also* ETHICS.

MORAL RELATIVISM. *See* RELATIVISM.

MORE, HENRY (1614–1687). A Cambridge Platonist who defended theism on the grounds of the ontological and design arguments, as well as the immortality of the soul. More was an early proponent of religious tolerance. His poetry is deeply philosophical, addressing the mind-body relationship. His works include *Psychodia Platonica* (1642), *Philosophical Poems* (1647), *An Antidote Against Atheism, Or an Appeal to the Natural Faculties of the Mind of Man, whether there be not a God* (1653), *An Explanation of the Grand Mystery of Godliness* (1660), and *Divine Dialogues, Containing Sundry Disquisitions and Instructions Concerning the Attributes and Providence of God in the World* (2 vols. 1668).

MORE, THOMAS (1477/8–1535). A highly gifted statesman (he served as Under-Sheriff to the City of London, was knighted, entered into service to King Henry VIII, became sub-treasurer, Speaker of the House of Commons, Chancellor of Duchy of Lancaster, and became Lord Chancellor), More was a Christian humanist who promoted classical (pagan) study. His *Utopia* (1516) is sometimes mistakenly read as a serious proposal of a future, ideal society rather than as an amusing, ironic, and experimental work. More was executed by the order of King Henry VIII for high treason. In 1935, he was canonized and his execution recognized as a martyrdom for faith by Pope Pius XI.

MUHAMMAD (c. 570–632 CE). According to Islamic tradition, Muhammad (sometimes transliterated as Muhammed or Mohammad) was the last (and the "seal") of God's prophets sent to humanity. He began receiving revelations from the angel Jibril (Gabriel) at the age of 40. These revelations were compiled to form the Qur'an, the holy scripture of Islam, which Muslims believe to be God's final and complete revelation. By the time Muhammad died in 632 CE, Islam was a clearly distinct and emerging world religion, and much of the Arabian Peninsula had converted. Muhammad is highly respected by Muslims and his sayings (*hadiths*) are second only to the Qur'an as a source of authority. Upon uttering his name, Muslims add the salutation "Peace be upon him."

MURTI. In Hinduism, an image or icon of a god.

MUSLIM. *See* **ISLAM.**

MYSTICISM. From the Greek *mystes*, meaning, "one initiated into the mysteries." Broadly speaking, a domain of experience of and reflection on the sacred that involves affective and cognitive states that are not empirical, or are not only empirical. While the term is sometimes used disparagingly, it has a stable usage as a legitimate, even rigorous study of religiously significant states of consciousness as demonstrated by, for example, Evelyn Underhill's classic study *Mysticism* (1911).

MYTH. From the Greek *mythos*, meaning "legend." The term usually refers to narratives that are either not literally true or not known to be true. In the twentieth century when some theologians set out to de-mythologize Christianity, they sought to expunge from it stories of the miraculous and supernatural.

N

NAGARJUNA (c. 150–200 CE). Founder of the Madhyamika school of Buddhism. His works include *Twenty Verses on the Great Vehicle, Treatise on the Middle Doctrine,* and *Treatise on Relativity.*

NARRATIVE THEOLOGY. Theology can be conducted as part of a systematic exposition of the faith in light of contemporary philosophy or it can be carried out in terms of historical reconstructions of past creeds. Among the many other ways to conduct theology, narrative theology stresses the ways in which religious teachings, insights, and values can be conveyed through stories. In the Christian tradition, this may include the story of Jesus as well as the stories (parables) that Jesus told, but also literature at large (what can we learn about the problem of evil from Dostoevsky's *Brothers Karamazov*?) and the way in which we convey our own identity (religious or secular) through stories.

NATIVE AMERICAN TRADITIONS. Native American beliefs stem from their culture and nature. They usually believe in a Creator or Great Spirit and many smaller spirits. Most of the Native American groups have many common beliefs, but their rites and ceremonies differ; the Lakota, for instance, have rites such as the Ghost Keeping, the Vision Quest, and the Sun Dance, while the Sioux have the Keeping of the Soul, the Making of Relatives, and the Throwing of the Ball. Native American spirituality includes many sacred narratives that are based in natural elements: earth, weather, seasons, and so on, and supernatural meaning is given to natural objects (trees, sun, moon). The Inuits (Eskimos) believe that souls exist in every living being. Post-Columbian missionaries attempted to "civilize" the Indians by introducing schools, European customs, and Christianity. During this time, there were people from both sides who expressed both politeness and hostility; most of the Native Americans were willing to converse but not to give up their beliefs, but some would attack the British. This rejection of Christianity was not solely based on religion, but rather those things that came along with Christianity: schooling, separation of clan and family, taxes, and so on. Some were willing, however, to talk and learn about the Christian God. The Native Americans who were not opposed to learning about Christianity were drawn to the missionaries that adopted their culture (eating the native food, walking around barefoot, not dressing up, and acting kindly) as opposed to the missionaries that came in lavish clothes and imposed threats. Along with Christianity, Native Americans also were exposed to diseases such as smallpox and measles; with no vaccinations or previous dealings with the diseases, the diseases spread like wildfire through the different tribes in North, Central, and South America, killing millions. The Native Americans who were able to survive the wave of pandemics that swept through their villages then had to survive the famine, constant relocation, and the results of the conflict with the Europeans.

NATURAL LAW. The theory that the nature of a being such as a human or a horse has a good or value. According to natural law, the goodness of human life consists of the fulfilling of the capacities and powers that befit a complete human being. Such powers may include the powers to think, sense, feel, love, act, and so on in ways that enhance human well-being.

NATURAL RELIGION. The religion that develops without revelation, special divine acts, or social manipulation. The idea of a natural religion was paramount in the Enlightenment, especially among deists.

NATURAL THEOLOGY. Reflection and argument on the natural world to learn about God's nature and will. Natural theology differs from revealed theology, which reflects on God and the world on the grounds of what is believed to be divine revelation, e.g., the Bible or the Qur'an.

NATURALISM. Strict naturalism holds that all of reality can be described and explained in the natural sciences. Strict naturalists tend either to reduce or eliminate consciousness and other mental states, or provide bridge laws on the level of psychology that are derived from and based on a materialistic base. Broader forms of naturalism may allow for states and facts beyond physics and chemistry, but there is a general stress on the sufficiency of science (including the social sciences) and the nonexistence of God, the soul, and an afterlife.

NATURALISTIC FALLACY. The so-called fallacy of reasoning from matters of fact (e.g., people desire happiness) to a value (e.g., people ought to desire happiness). Those advocating the recognition of such reasoning as fallacious uphold a strict distinction between facts and values.

Opponents counter that values (the goodness of human life) should be regarded as a fact and no less factual than standard facts such as the fact that this is a dictionary, 2 + 2 = 4, and water is H_2O.

NATURE. From the Latin *natura*. (The Greek word, *physis*, gives us terms such as physical.) Something has a nature if it has value as a kind of being or thing (e.g., human nature). Sometimes "nature" is used to refer to all that is not God. Such usage is in tension with some theists who claim that God has a nature, e.g., the divine nature is maximally excellent. "Nature" has also been defined as "everything," but such a broad characterization seems to rob the term of philosophical significance.

NECESSITY, THE NECESSARY. X is necessary if it is possible and not X is impossible. Theists often regard God's existence as necessary or non-contingent, while some diverge and claim that God's existence is, rather, uncaused or without beginning or end and yet not necessary. Necessity is sometimes conditional: given that you exist, it necessarily follows that at least one thing exists. But from the latter it does not follow that you necessarily exist.

NEGATIVE THEOLOGY. *See* **APO-PHATIC THEOLOGY.**

NEO-CONFUCIANISM. Neo-Confucianism is a broad term, with no precise Chinese analogue, referring to the revival of Confucianism beginning in the Song dynasty (960–1276), which hoped to recapture the original vision of an ideal Confucian society and a return to the study of the Confucian classics. The Confucian canon was studied with new questions in mind, in response to Buddhist intellectual domination during the Tang period (618–906). Neo-Confucian philosophers formulated a response to some Buddhist concerns and methods, and they created a new Confucian metaphysics meant to compete with Buddhism. At the same time they drew from Buddhist ideas: Zen ideas of enlightenment through meditation had a strong influence, as did Huayang cosmology. Neo-Confucianism was nevertheless always this-worldly and practical. It rejected Buddhism's search for *nirvana*, salvation, and an afterlife, as well as religious Daoism's quest for immortality. The Cheng brothers, Cheng Hao and Cheng Yi, were among the founders of Song Neo-Confucianism, but Zhu Xi was its greatest synthesizer. Zhu Xi's writings became the basis of Confucian orthodoxy, enforced through the civil service examination system until the examinations were abolished in 1905.

NEOORTHODOXY. A theological position indebted to Karl Barth's insistence on God's sovereignty, the primacy of the word of God in faith and morals, and a resistance to natural theology.

NEOPLATONISM. Modern term for the stage of Platonic philosophy from the third to the sixth century CE. The founding figure is Plotinus (205–270) whose meditation on Plato's *Parmenides* is an imaginative reading of the dialogue in which reality is defined as levels of unity. However, the ultimate unity is not a pantheistic totality but a transcendent and immaterial cause of all beings. All of metaphysics culminates in a philosophical theology of the One, and practical philosophy is concerned with the immaterial soul's return to this transcendent Source. Iamblichus (250–330) is the great watershed figure in Neoplatonism: he replaces philosophical theory with magical practices or theurgy. After Iamblichus, the return to the One is a ritual and liturgical rather than a purely contemplative exercise. Proclus (412–485) is the last major Neoplatonic philosopher in late antiquity. Neoplatonism has a strong religious dimension and it became a source of opposition to Christianity, especially under Emperor Julian (the Apostate, 331–363). However, it exerted a vast and lasting influence upon medieval Christian, Muslim, and Jewish theology. The term can also be used for the dominant philosophy of the Italian Renaissance under Ficino and for speculative developments in European Romanticism from Hegel to Emerson.

NEWTON, ISAAC (1642–1727). In philosophy of religion Newton is known for his correspondence with Samuel Clarke on whether God interferes with the creation. Newton also thought of absolute space as a divine property. On this view, we literally move and have our being in God insofar as we and the cosmos exist in space. Newton is the author of *Mathematical Principles of Natural Philosophy* (1687), usually referred to as the *Principia*.

NICAEA, COUNCIL OF (325 CE). The first of seven ecumenical councils in the early Christian Church. Organized by the Emperor Constantine, the Council of Nicaea was an attempt to form a consensus among all the churches on official teachings. Between 250 and 318 bishops attended.

The main topic was the relationship between the Father and the Son (Jesus). Arius argued that the Father and the Son were one in purpose only, while St. Alexander of Alexander and Athanasius (who was only a deacon at the time) argued that the Father and the Son were one in purpose and in being. According to Arius and his supporters, the Son was a creation of, and thus subsequent to, the Father. The *homoousians* (Gk, "same essence"), represented by St. Alexander of Alexander and Athanasius, on the other hand, believed that the Father and the Son were of the same substance and were co-eternal. The Council ruled almost unanimously against Arius, who was then exiled and had his books burned.

The Council formulated the original Nicene Creed (a later version was agreed upon at the Second Ecumenical Council in 381), which was the first uniform Christian doctrine. It described Jesus Christ as "the Son of God, begotten of the Father, the only-begotten; that is, of the essence of the Father, God of God, Light of Light, very God of very God, begotten, not made, being of one substance with the Father."

The Council also decided when to celebrate the Resurrection, addressed the Meletian schism, discussed the validity of baptism by heretics and the status of lapsed Christians during persecution by Licinius, and formulated a series of canon laws.

NICHOLAS OF CUSA (c. 1400–1464). A German cardinal and theologian who held that God is not, strictly speaking, knowable; our best claims to knowledge should be viewed as "learned ignorance," insofar as we need to appreciate our own limitations and fallibility. His principle writings include *On Catholic Harmony, On Learned Ignorance, On Conjecture, On the Hidden God, Apology for Learned Ignorance, The Idiot, On the Peace of Faith,* and *The Vision of God.* The latter contains a fascinating account of God as seeing the creation from all possible points of view.

NIEBUHR, HELMUT RICHARD (1894–1962). H. Richard Niebuhr was born into the German Evangelical Synod of North America. Trained at Elmhurst College, Eden Theological Seminary, Washington University and Yale University, Niebuhr returned to teach at Eden between 1919 and 1931 (serving for a time as dean), a period divided by his Presidency at Elmhurst between 1924 and 1927. He culminated his career by teaching theology and ethics at Yale for more than three decades, beginning in 1931. Taken together, this range of experience in higher education made Niebuhr somewhat of an authority in the role of theological education in the American church. Niebuhr was the younger brother of political philosopher and theologian Reinhold Niebuhr.

H. Richard Niebuhr spent significant intellectual energy on typological analyses of Christianity and its relationship to life and culture. In his typological analysis, he stood on the methodological shoulders of Max Weber and Ernst Troeltsch, the latter being the focus of his doctoral dissertation. This methodology informed his study of the roots of the variety of Christian denominations. It helped frame his work in pursuit of the range of ways in which theological traditions understand the relationship of Christ to the surrounding culture. It is the method he used to understand competing ideological systems (whether overtly religious or not) in the cultural-political-ideological clashes of the Cold War era. It provided a basis for distinguishing his construction of what he saw as the most compelling mode of ethical theory at the end of his life—that of responsibility—from both teleological and deontological approaches. Niebuhr's approach matured from one merely sociological to a sociology deeply informed by theology.

In his focus upon the relationship between religion and culture, he variously expressed this as the contrast between accommodation and transcendence or between withdrawal (from culture) and approach (of culture). His metaphors for this begin with the repetitious pendulum, but shift to the slowly progressing wave upon the beach. His focus upon both God's transcendence and human limits placed him fully within the Reformed theological camp.

Some of H. Richard Niebuhr's most significant works include: *The Social Sources of Denominationalism* (1929), *The Church Against the World* (1935, with Wilhelm Pauck and Francis P. Miller), *The Kingdom of God in America* (1937), *The Meaning of Revelation* (1941), *Christ and Culture* (1951), *The Purpose of the Church and Its Ministry* (1956), *Radical Monotheism and Western Culture* (1960), *The Responsible Self* (1963), and *Faith on Earth* (1989, essays from the 1950s).

NIEBUHR, REINHOLD (1892–1971). Reinhold Niebuhr was the father of political and Christian realism and the elder brother of theologian H. Richard Niebuhr. He was a product of the German Evangelical Synod of North America which was a hybrid of the Lutheran and Reformed traditions of Protestant Christianity. His life and work was summed up by one biographer in the phrase "the courage to change." Niebuhr began his career serving as pastor of Bethel Evangelical Church in the city of Detroit from 1915 through 1928. There, he repeatedly challenged the unjust business practices of automobile magnate Henry Ford. During this period, Niebuhr shifted away from liberal moralism, renouncing liberalism as an ideology promoting the illusion of human progress, using Marxist thought to do so. In 1928, he began his four-decade-long tenure of teaching Applied Christianity at nion Theological Seminary of New York. By then, he was a socialist. However, when socialism could muster nothing beyond pacifism in response to Nazism, he left the party to become a Democrat firmly in support of the policies of President Franklin Delano Roosevelt. At the close of World War II, he became a Cold War fighter siding against the tyranny of communism. He supported the civil rights and Great Society policies of Lyndon Johnson, but came to oppose the war in Vietnam. In this, he made a turn away from an all-out rejection of liberalism. He understood that he had earlier equated it simplistically with the nineteenth-century myth of human progress. By the end of his career, he perceived the social gains American political liberalism had made possible.

Niebuhr's realism was deeply rooted in Augustinian thought. He took human sin with great seriousness, particularly the sin of pride manifested in the use of political power. He perpetually aimed a critical eye at too lofty characterizations of human morality in the personal and social realms. Yet, he was an activist by nature, criticizing both his brother H. Richard Niebuhr as well as Swiss theologian Karl Barth (with whom he was often grouped under the category of neoorthodoxy) for their hesitance to engage in political activism. For Niebuhr, love had to bear fruit in justice. In the Cold War world, he believed the U.S. should take a leading role, however doing so with the humble and self-critical awareness of the inevitable temptations to overreach by the powerful.

Among the hundreds of articles and sermons, as well as the dozens of books penned by Reinhold Niebuhr, the following are of particular significance: *Does Civilization Need Religion?* (1927), *Moral Man and Immoral Society* (1932), *The Nature and Destiny of Man* (1941–1943), *The Children of Light and the Children of Darkness* (1944), *The Irony of American History* (1952), *The Structure of Nations and Empires* (1959), and *Man's Nature and His Communities* (1965).

NIETZSCHE, FRIEDRICH (1844–1900). In philosophy of religion, Nietzsche is most noted for his critique of Christian monotheism. He argued that Christian virtues such as compassion arose out of resentment when the weak devised an ethic that may restrain the strong.

Nietzsche sought a restoration of heroic, pre-Christian virtues but not recourse to a Platonism that shuns change and seeks consolation in a realm of abstract forms. Nietzsche's view of moral values has sometimes been seen as nihilistic, but this is a mistake. Running throughout his work is the thesis that life itself (what may be called vitality) is good. Nietzsche's aim to bring about a transvaluation of values was part of his case that we should subordinate virtues like empathy to a life-enhancing code of values. The primacy he gave to life itself is evident in an early essay *The Use and Abuse of History in Life* (1874), in which he argued that analytic and monumental approaches to the historical past should be evaluated in terms of whether they are life-enhancing. Linked to his critique of monotheism, but of more wide ranging importance, is Nietzsche's shunning the idea of truth as being objective or free-standing apart from human perspectives. Truth, rather, is a matter of shifting, contingent points of view. Nietzsche's works include *The Birth of Tragedy* (1872), *Untimely Meditations* (1873–1876), *Human, All too Human* (2 vols., 1878, 1880), *The Wanderer and His Shadow* (1880), *The Dawn: Reflections on Moral Prejudices* (1881), *The Gay Science* (1882), *Thus Spake Zarathrustra* (1883–1885), *Beyond Good and Evil* (1887), *The Genealogy of Morals* (1887), *The Case of Wagner* (1888), *Twilight of the Idols* (1888), *The Antichrist* (1888), *Nietzsche contra Wagner* (1888), *Ecce Homo* (1888), and *The Will to*

Power (his 1880s notebooks, published posthumously).

NIHILISM. From the Latin *nihil*, meaning "nothing." The denial of values. Advocates of radical orthodoxy claim that the Western, Enlightenment tradition ultimately leads to nihilism.

NIRVANA. From the Pali *nibbāna*, meaning "to blow out" or "extinguish." According to Buddhism, *nirvana*, or Enlightenment, is the ultimate goal for which we ought to strive. It is the only way to overcome the suffering (*dukkha*) of life and end the cycle of death and rebirth (*samsara*). To attain *nirvana*, one must shed the illusion of selfhood and "blow out" all greed, hatred, and delusion. *Nirvana* is similar to the Hindu concept of *moksha*.

NOMINALISM. According to nominalism, there are no Platonic forms or universals or abstract objects like sets. There are concrete individual things that we classify linguistically into groups or classes of things, but "classes" do not refer to anything more than concrete individual things.

NON-REALISM. *See* **ANTI-REALISM.**

NON-THEISM. A philosophy that is described as non-theistic is usually one that does not entail or presuppose atheism; it is simply a philosophy that does not explicitly or implicitly imply theism.

NONMALEFICENCE. The precept that one should do no harm. Some philosophers (e.g., Karl Popper, W. D. Ross, and John Rawls) hold that the duty of nonmaleficence is more stringent than the duty to do good. The precept is pivotal to the Hippocratic Oath: First of all, do no harm (*Primum non nocere*).

NONVIOLENCE. The concept of violence is often taken to be the concept of that which violates another living thing either through torment, serious exploitation, or killing. An advocate of nonviolence repudiates intentionally causing or contributing to such violations. Advocates of nonviolence are commonly pacifists, but one may distinguish between the concepts of violence and force, according to which violence is an unjust use of force, thus allowing (at least in principle) some justified uses of force; e.g., a police force acting under principle of just governance.

NORMATIVITY. Normative requirements are authoritative or binding involving what one should do (normativity in ethics) or should believe (in epistemology and logic).

NOUMENAL. In Kant's philosophy, the noumenal world is the world as it is in itself as opposed to the phenomenal world which is the world of experience.

NOUVELLE THEOLOGIE. See **KARL RAHNER.**

O

OCCASIONALISM. A position advo-cated by Malebranche (among others) that natural causes (as in your willing to move your hand) are occasions when God exercises causal power to bring about the natural effect.

OCKHAM, WILLIAM OF (c. 1285–1349). An English philosophical theo-logian in the Franciscan tradition who championed nominalism, the view that there are no Platonic forms or Aristote-lian kinds. Ockham's rejection of these frameworks as unnecessary is the basis for subsequent reference to Ockham's razor (*see* OCKHAM'S RAZOR). His position on nominalism is sometimes seen as challenging medieval sacramental realism (the idea that Christ is present in the sacrament of the Eucharist), but there is no reason logically why nominalism should have that entailment. Ockham famously held that divine commands can overrule moral precepts, e.g., even if it is a moral precept that suicide is wrong, a suicide may be permissible or required if commanded by God. Ockham's works include *Four Books of the Sentences* (c. 1323), *Summa of Logic* (before 1329), and *Quodlibeta septem* (before 1333).

OCKHAM'S RAZOR. From the original Latin phrase *Entia non sunt multiplicanda praeter necessitatem,* meaning "Entities are not to be multiplied beyond necessity." Ockham writes, "*Frustra fit per plura quod potest fieri per pauciora,*" which is Latin for "It is pointless to do with more [things] what can be done with fewer." Ockham's razor has been used widely by both naturalists and theists to defend their own positions while indirectly opposing others by claiming to have the simplest theory about a given subject such as ontology.

OMISSION, SIN OF. Failing to do one's duty. An omission can be a matter of *negligence* when it involves a failure to act in a given role (e.g., an irresponsible lifeguard) or *reckless* if this is not tied to a role or vocation (e.g., reckless driving).

OMNIPOTENCE. A being is omnipotent if it is all-powerful. Philosophical attention to the divine attribute of omnipotence has involved such questions as: Is an omnipotent being restrained by logic or coherence? For example, can an omnipotent being make a square circle? Could a being be so powerful that it creates itself? Is there a conflict between the divine attributes of omnipotence and essential goodness?

A plausible analysis of essential goodness involves the property of being only able to do good and not evil. But if an omnipotent being can do *anything*, shouldn't an omnipotent being be able to do evil? If so, it seems that there cannot be an essentially good, omnipotent being. There are different replies historically to this argument. Some argue that an essentially good being may have the ability to do evil, but simply never does evil. Others argue that the ability to do evil is not itself a worthy, positive ability but a defect and unworthy of God.

OMNIPRESENCE. A being is omnipresent if there is no place where it is not. Theists traditionally believe that God is ubiquitous or omnipresent but allow there to be a sense in which God may be absent when, for example, people do evil in defiance of God's will and nature. In such events, God is still present insofar as God continues to be the omnipotent, omniscient Creator and sustainer of the cosmos, but God's reality is being deliberately ignored or shut out by evil agents.

OMNISCIENCE. A being is omniscient if it either knows all truths or knows all truth that it is possible to know.

ONTIC INQUIRY. The study of particular beings, things, or objects (God or gods, the soul, particular animals, and so on) rather than being itself. Heidegger lamented the fact that after the pre-Socratics, philosophers seemed to forget the topic of Being and focused instead on particular beings. Analytic critics such as Rudolf Carnap charged Heidegger's focus on being as conceptually absurd, but Heidegger's work has continued to have a good reception among continental philosophers.

ONTOLOGICAL ARGUMENT. Arguments for the existence of God based on the concept of God as maximally excellent or unsurpassably great. There are different versions of this form of argument, but most argue for the existence of God from the idea or concept of God. If successful, the argument would establish the actual existence of God based on reflection on concepts and ideas, and not on an a posteriori examination of the contingency and ordered nature of the cosmos.

ONTOLOGY. From the Greek *ontos* (being) + *logia* (study of). The study of being or an account of what exists. One engages in ontology in the course of inquiring into what exists, and the result of this inquiry (when successful) is called an ontology.

OPEN QUESTION ARGUMENT. An argument designed to test identity claims. If goodness is the very same thing as pleasure, then the question "Is pleasure good?" is not open. An analogy: the question "Is H_2O water?" is not open to those who know atomic theory.

OPEN THEISM. Open theism is a developing theological movement that is gaining credence in certain sectors of Protestantism. The view has attracted widespread attention since the publication of *The Openness of God* (Clark Pinnock et al.) in 1994, but essentially similar views were held by a number of earlier theologians and philosophers. Like more traditional versions of Christian theism, open theism affirms that God is the personal creator ex nihilo of all that exists other than God, and that God is omnipotent, omniscient, and morally perfect. (The affirmation of creation ex nihilo and of divine omnipotence clearly distinguish the view from process theism, with which it is sometimes confused.)

Open theism distinguishes itself from much of the tradition by affirming that God is temporally everlasting rather than timeless, and it emphasizes the continuing dynamic interaction between God and created persons that is so prominent in the Bible. It holds that humans are free in the libertarian sense and that much of the future is genuinely contingent and undetermined, from which it is held to follow that even a perfect Knower cannot have complete and detailed knowledge of that which is at present indeterminate. This last point is clearly in disagreement with the main theological tradition and has led to many and sometimes vituperative attacks on the view, especially by those of Calvinistic persuasion. Open theists claim, however, that their view is more consonant with a piety that emphasizes a personal relationship with God than are views that see God as all-determining and humans merely as the executors of God's foreordained plan for the world.

ORDINARY LANGUAGE. Normal discourse as opposed to recondite philosophical language. Ordinary language philosophy was popular in the mid-twentieth century when some philosophers (such as J. L. Austin) critiqued philosophical projects such as radical skepticism on the grounds that such philosophers were misusing ordinary language.

ORIGEN (c. 185–254). Origen believed that the ultimate overcoming of evil would occur in the *apokatastasis* when all of creation is restored to God. A student of Clement of Alexandria, Origen developed a highly Platonic form of Christianity in which the soul gradually comes to be in union with God. He advanced an allegorical reading of scripture, which sought to find meaning in the Bible that lay deeper than its literal significance. He developed a sustained defense of Christianity over against a pagan Platonic thinker, Celsus, in *Against Celsus*. According to Origen, God in Christ was not a proud aristocrat, but a profound lover of the created world who descended into the material world to draw us up and into the life of the divine. His key works include *Against Celsus, On First Principles, On Prayer,* and *An Exhortation to Martyrdom.*

ORIGINAL SIN. While not affirmed in the Apostle's or Nicene Creeds, prominent Christian theologians (especially Augustine) developed an account of the implications of the Fall of humanity. Partly based on the teaching about the Edenic disobedience and fall, as well as scripture passages such as Romans 5:12–21 and 1 Corinthians 15:22, theologians held that the descendants of Adam and Eve share in their ancestral guilt. One way to intuitively build a case for original sin is if we imagine one's ancestors in some way committed a moral violation in the course of procreation. From a moral point of view, their progeny should not exist; their mere existing is, in a sense, the effect (however remote) of something that should not have occurred.

Theological reflection on the implications of original sin has been contentious. A prominent argument against original sin is that guilt cannot be transferable. So, even if one's ancestors committed some punishable, blame-worthy wrong, it does not follow that their children should be punished or blamed for wrong-doing. Some theologians speculated that original sin was transmitted by male semen (hence Jesus did not inherit original sin, due to the virgin birth). Kant speculated that all humans in some sense are united with Adam in the fall through a kind of timeless, radical evil that we all freely elect. Jonathan Edwards speculated that God could treat all of us as united with Adam and Eve by fiat (viz. by God regarding all of us as one being, represented by our ancestors, we actually become organically united in guilt). Some theologians depict the nature of original sin in terms of human depravity, whereas others see original sin as simply marking a tendency among humans toward evil.

OSTENSIVE DEFINITION. Definitions by example, e.g., white is the color of snow. An example relevant to philosophy of religion is the proposal that "religion" should be defined as follows: R is a religion if it resembles Judaism, Islam, Christian, Hinduism, or Buddhism.

OTTO, RUDOLF (1869–1937). A German student of mysticism who proposed in his influential book, *The Idea of the Holy* (1917), that the encounter with God is a confrontation with that which is mysterious (Latin: *mysterium*), tremendous (*tremendum*), and fascinating (*fascinans*). His other works include *The Philosophy of Religion of Kant-Fries and its Application to Theology* (1909), *Darwinism and Religion* (1910), *Studies Relative to the Numinous* (1923), *Mysticism East and West* (1926), and *Freedom and Necessity* (1940).

P

PACIFISM. From the Latin *pax* (peace) + *facere* (to make). A strict pacifist believes all violence even if in self-defense is impermissible. More modest forms of pacifism hold that self-defense and the use of force or violence is *not morally required*. It has been argued that pacifism involves passive injustice insofar as a pacifist may not prevent wrongful killing. Strong pacifist traditions may be found in Jainism and the Society of Friends (Quakers). The Amish and Mennonites also have strong pacifist histories.

PAINE, THOMAS (1737–1809). An English political writer who came to the British colonies in America and played a key role in making the case of American independence. Paine argued fiercely against Christianity, though he was a deist who advocated a belief in individual immortality. His works include *Common Sense* (1776), *The Rights of Man* (1791–1792), and *The Age of Reason* (1794).

PALEY, WILLIAM (1743–1805). Most well known for his natural theology, especially an argument for theism based on the apparent design of the cosmos, Paley was also a utilitarian and an advocate of just social reform. His works include *The Principles of Moral and Political Philosophy* (1785), *Horae Paulinae* (1790), *A View of the Evidences of Christianity* (1794), and *Natural Theology* (1802).

PANENTHEISM. From the Greek *pan* + *en* + *theos,* meaning "everything in God" (cf. Acts 17:28). The belief that everything is in God. Panentheism is distinguished from pantheism insofar as it allows for the existence of God to extend beyond the world as well; God is in all things yet also beyond them.

PANPSYCHISM. From the Greek *pan-* + *psychē,* meaning "soul" or "mind." The belief that the world is a living organism, with a soul or mind of its own. Some panpsychists believe that every fundamental object in the cosmos has some mental or experiential property.

PANTHEISM. From the Greek *pan-* + *theos,* meaning "God is everything." The belief that everything is God. *Contrast with* PANENTHEISM.

PARADIGM. An ideal, governing case that serves to categorize similar cases. If, for example, Judaism, Christianity, Islam, Hinduism, and Buddhism are paradigm cases of religions, one can use them to assess whether other traditions count as religions.

PARADIGM CASE ARGUMENT. Arguments that appeal to ideal cases. So, someone might take an ideal case of when one person knows X and then use it to offer a full account of what it is to possess knowledge. *See also* PARADIGM.

PARADOX. From the Greek *paradoxos,* meaning "beyond belief." Often used to refer to an unacceptable thesis, the term can also refer to that which seems anomalous or mysterious, e.g., the paradox of omnipotence.

PARMENIDES OF ELEA (c. 6th/5th century BCE). Arguably the most important pre-Socratic philosopher, Parmenides was a pioneer in metaphysics. He was a monist, and he held that true being is unchanging, eternal, and indivisible. His one surviving work is a cosmological poem, written in Homeric hexameters. In it Parmenides contrasts

Doxa ("opinion" or "seeming") with Truth, arguing that the proper way to understand the world is through a priori reasoning. He argued, against earlier philosophers, that time, change, void, and plurality were all contrary to reason, since only that which is can be thought; non-being is unthinkable. Changes would require that which currently is to cease to be itself, or that which is not to come to be. Therefore, becoming and ceasing to be are not to be countenanced; either things are or they are not. While difficult to contemplate, this idea of the essential and unchanging unity of all being supported the notion that there is uniformity in nature that can be understood through reason. Parmenides exercised a strong influence on the development of Plato's thought, and his idea of the unity of being probably also supported early versions of the world-soul in Platonic philosophical theology.

PARSIS. *See* ZOROASTRIANISM.

PASCAL, BLAISE (1623–1662). A French philosopher, mathematician, physicist, and devout religious practitioner who sought to challenge the laxity of contemporary Jesuit teaching. Pascal offered a sustained, incisive portrait of human frailty, vanity, and weakness. He stressed the passionate and affective dimension of thought over against what he saw as an excessively intellectual, detached use of reason promoted by Descartes: "*Le coeur* *a ses raisons que le raison ne connaît point; on le sait en mille choses."* ("The heart has its reasons whereof reason knows nothing; one knows it in a thousand things.")

For those undecided about whether God exists, Pascal argued that there are prudential, personal reasons why a person should wager that the God of Christianity exists and seek salvation in that God rather than deny the veracity of Christianity and adopt atheism or agnosticism. As for the objection that one's beliefs about God or anything else are not under one's voluntary control, and thus not a matter one can wager, Pascal proposed that one can gradually cultivate belief through liturgical practice. His works include *Lettres provincials* (1656–1657), *De l'esprit géométrique* (1655), and *Pensées* (1670, published posthumously).

PAUL, THE APOSTLE. The Apostle Paul is a central writer and figure in early Christianity; when counting his letters and the letters written in his name, his writings comprise the majority of the books of the Christian New Testament. Very little is known about Paul's life outside of a few brief references in his authentic letters and from the account of his life given in the New Testament book of Acts. Though the details of Paul's life found in Acts are not necessarily entirely fictitious, they are highly idealized and at times conflict with details found in his authentic letters.

According to Acts, Paul was born "Saul" in the city of Tarsus in Asia Minor, and he was supposedly a citizen of the Roman Empire. As a devout Jew (though it is disputed to what extent Saul was involved in traditional Judaism: it has been suggested that Saul was already on the margins of Judaism), Saul was an avid persecutor of the early Christians (this comes from Paul's own letters and Acts). However, according to Acts, Saul received a vision of the risen Christ while on the road to Damascus and was struck blind. After this point, Saul "converted" to Christianity and changed his name to "Paul." (It should be noted that language of "conversion" is often applied to this story, but this language would not have been used—in our sense—by Paul himself. After his vision, he began to believe in Christ, thus changing from his previous mindset.)

After coming to believe in Christ, Paul traveled throughout the Roman Empire preaching the gospel and starting new churches in most of the cities he visited. As he traveled from city to city, he kept in correspondence with the Christian communities that he had helped to form. The result of this correspondence is a corpus of letters containing advice, answers to questions, and theological discourse. The seven original letters of Paul (Romans, 1&2 Corinthians, Galatians, Philippians, 1 Thessalonians, and Philemon) are thought to be the earliest Christian writings contained in the Bible.

Because Christianity was not recognized by the Roman Empire, Paul was often imprisoned for his teachings (again, mainly according to Acts). At his death, he is said to have been imprisoned in Rome, likely under the reign of Nero. The apocryphal *Acts of Paul* tells the story of his martyrdom under Nero, which is the only explicit story of Paul's death (Paul does not die in the book of Acts). In this story, when Paul is beheaded at the hands of Nero, milk flows from his head.

Paul quickly became an influential figure in early Christianity, and many who followed him tried to use his name to bolster the authority of their arguments. The result is a second corpus of "Pauline" letters written using Paul's name. Some of these texts, such as 3 Corinthians, were never placed in the biblical canon. Other letters were interspersed with Paul's original letters within the Bible and have only been found as forgeries since modern times. Scholars looking at word usage, Greek grammatical differences, style, and theological positions have determined fairly conclusively that these letters were not written by the same author who wrote the seven original letters. The Pauline forgeries found in the New Testament are Ephesians, Colossians, 2 Thessalonians, 1&2 Timothy, and Titus. Both the original Pauline and the pseudo-Pauline letters hold an important place in most Christian communities.

Pauline theology is both interesting and difficult to define because within his authentic letters, the early development of Christian theology is apparent. Paul's later letters often adapt the theology of earlier letters in order to refine his original thought or to reshape his argument for a different context. For example, Paul often references the *parousia* ("presence" or "coming") of Christ, which he believes is immanent within his own lifetime. This naturally influences his theology because he has little need to think about future church order and development beyond his death. While Paul does seem to take this more into account in his later letters, most "Pauline" writings that deal with church order can only be found within the Pseudo-Pauline corpus.

Paul is also concerned with the relationship between Judaism and Christianity, which were not two separate entities in the first century. Christians either came to believe in Jesus as Jews (thus, "Jewish Christians") or as non-Jews ("Gentile Christians"). It seems that Paul primarily saw himself as the "apostle to the Gentiles," but once these Gentiles converted to Christianity, Paul had to determine the relationship between Christianity and Jewish law (it appears that since Jewish Christians still saw themselves as Jews, they continued all forms of Jewish practice). In his letters, Paul clearly determines that Gentiles who come to believe in Christ are not required—nor should they be forced—to keep the Law, which often for Paul is narrowed to dietary laws and circumcision. However, as can be seen in Galatians, other early Christian leaders appear to have differed from Paul's opinions, particularly on this subject. Disputes like this often led Paul to defend his authenticity as an apostle; however, Paul's influence has remained strong through today while the arguments of most of his opponents have been lost.

PEIRCE, CHARLES SANDERS (1839–1914). A philosopher, semiotician, logician, and mathematician who defended pragmatism and a theistic metaphysic. He believed that truth is a matter of ideal inquiry as opposed to a matter of correspondence between theories and the way the world is. Peirce is the father of modern semiotics (the interpretation of signs and symbols) and of the logic of abduction. He wrote extensively on the relationship between religion and science. Peirce's writings argue for fallibilism in belief, the importance of community, the reality of God, the real possibility of miracles, the idea that miracles are a genuine part of any religion, and the likelihood that anyone who claims to be an atheist is in fact mistaken. Peirce held that creeds were largely written as tools of political exclusion and that what was needed was a religious community akin to the scientific community, i.e., one based on mutual respect, a desire to find things out, and a fallibilistic willingness to have one's pet theories proven wrong. Peirce was raised a Unitarian and was in frequent contact with prominent Transcendentalists in his youth, but in adulthood converted to the Episcopal Church and remained a Trinitarian

throughout his adult life. In his fifties he had what he described as a "mystical" experience, and he devoted some time to an attempted revision of the *Book of Common Prayer* and to notes for training clergy. In his "Neglected Argument for the Reality of God," Peirce offers a series of original arguments for the reality of God, concluding that God is real and has real effects in the world. Peirce claims that one may discover God through "musement" or the free play of the mind, and that it is not just the mind that perceives God, but also the "heart" which, he says, "is also a perceptive organ." His works include *The Collected Papers of C. S. Peirce* (vols. 1–6 ed. C. Hartshorne and P. Weiss (1931–1935); vols. 7–8, ed. A. Burks, (1958)), *Letters to Lady Welby* (ed. I. Lieb (1953)), *The Essential Peirce* (vols. 1–2, ed. Christian Kloesel and Nathan Houser, (1992, 1998)), *Writings of Charles S. Peirce: A Chronological Edition,* (vols. 1–6, 8; ed. Peirce Edition Project, (1982–2009)). *See also* ABDUCTION and REALITY.

PELAGIANISM. Pelagianism is a set of ideas on grace and human nature associated with the British monk Pelagius, opposed by St. Augustine, and condemned by the Church in the fifth century. According to Pelagius, the grace needed for salvation comes from God through creation (which gives humans the capacity to do good) and from revelation (which teaches and encourages them toward goodness). Sin does not invalidate these gifts, and baptism is not necessary for the forgiveness of original sin. Pelagius' associate Celestius taught that death is natural rather than a punishment for sin; that Adam's sin affected only him, not the entire human race, so that infants are born innocent; and that the Old Testament's law can lead humans to perfection as surely as the New Testament's gospel can, so that human perfection was possible even before Christ.

Against Pelagianism, Augustine taught that humans pass original sin to their children through reproduction, and that after Adam's sin they lost the divine gift of love that makes human actions effective for salvation. Without love, even things that seem to be virtues have evil motives. Nothing remains in humans that could naturally seek or respond to God: instead, an interior grace must prepare people before they can respond to the gospel. Thus human salvation is controlled by God's grace from start to finish, which led Augustine to the idea that God predestines humans to heaven or hell. These ideas provoked discontent even in Augustine's lifetime, but after a prolonged campaign he secured Pelagius' condemnation at Carthage in 418, and thereafter continued to fight Pelagius' most articulate defender, Julian of Eclanum.

A group which is now called the Semipelagians (represented by the monks John Cassian and Vincent of Lerins) agreed with Augustine on the necessity of interior grace and the effects of sin, but felt that predestination was dangerously close to some kind of destiny. In addition, Cassian argued that Scripture includes some cases in which humans turn to God before God bestows grace upon them; thus the question of initiative with regard to grace cannot be resolved. The debate continued into the sixth century, but in 529 Augustine's followers succeeded at having a moderated version of his teaching (downplaying some aspects of predestination but still asserting the initiative of God's grace) vindicated at the council of Orange. *See also* CHRISTIANITY.

PER SE NOTUM. From the Latin, meaning "known through itself." That which is self-evident. Arguably, one may know that the law of identity (A is A) is necessarily true or that wisdom is a virtue *per se notum*.

PERCEPTION. In philosophy of religion, there is attention to what we may perceive (is it possible to perceive God?) and the evidential significance of perceptual claims (e.g., assessing claims to perceive the sacred, miracles, the self). Perception is customarily thought to involve judgments, e.g., for someone to perceive that the Dalai Lama is present, she must judge that she is perceiving the Dalai Lama. By contrast, you may sense the Dalai Lama without knowing you are sensing (seeing) him.

PERFECTIONISM. Philosophers and theologians who believe that human beings should aspire and strive for perfection. A perfectionist need not believe that human beings can actually attain perfection, but they should still seek it. Most perfectionists are not utilitarians and they believe that perfection involves more than the cultivation of pleasure or happiness.

PERFORMATIVE UTTERANCE. An utterance that accomplishes an act such as the making of a vow. In a marriage ceremony, two people uttering, "I do," intentionally can bring about a marriage. Announcing that you forgive someone may also be performative, either actually conferring forgiveness on someone or announcing that you will come to a state in which you will bear no resentment toward the wrong-doer.

PERSONALISM. A movement which gives a central role to persons in philosophy of God, ethics, and theology. Borden Parker Bowne is considered a founding member. Other prominent personalists include Edgar Sheffield Brightman and Peter Bertocci at Boston University. Martin Luther King, Jr. was influenced by his personalist professors at Boston University.

PERSONS, PERSONAL IDENTITY. A philosophy of persons and personal identity is central to a philosophy of the trinity, human birth and death, and the standing of nonhuman animals. The concept of being a person is fraught with moral consequences. If personhood is not identical with being human, this opens the door to recognizing nonhuman animal and transcendent beings as persons, but it also opens the door to questioning whether all human beings are persons. An example of the concept of being a person not essentially linked to humans would be: a subject who can think, reason, desire, and act with a memory by which the subject may understand itself existing over time.

PERSPECTIVALISM. The view that truth and falsehood are features of perspectives or points of view. Nietzsche defended a form of perspectivalism. One challenge facing the theory is that it seems that the truth of perspectivalism cannot be a matter of perspectives, because from the perspective of many philosophers perspectivalism is false. *See also* ETHICS.

PHENOMENOLOGY. From the Greek *phainomenon*, meaning "that which appears or is seen," and *logos*, meaning "study." A disciplined method that gives central attention to experience and appearances. As a formal philosophical method, it was advanced by the German philosopher Edmund Husserl (1859–1938).

PHILO OF ALEXANDRIA (c. 20 BCE–c. 50 CE). A Jewish philosopher influenced by Plato who promoted an allegorical reading of the Hebrew Scriptures. He is especially noted for his recognition of the *logos*, a divine instrument of creation. Philo's view of the *logos* has a close resemblance to the Gospel of John's view of the *logos* except that the latter affirms the identity (incarnation) of the *logos* as Jesus.

PHILOSOPHER, THE. Honorific title for Aristotle.

PHILOSOPHER'S STONE. Turns base metal into gold. While the term had a central role in alchemy, one may also think of the philosopher's stone as that which can turn ordinary or unfortunate events into something valuable. A plausible candidate for the philosopher's stone is humility.

PHILOSOPHIA PERENNIS. Latin for "the perennial philosophy." The idea that philosophy as a discipline has an enduring set of themes such as: the Good, the True, and the Beautiful; or the problem of knowledge, being, and governance; or Being and Becoming; or God and nature.

PHILOSOPHER. One who engages in philosophical inquiry.

PHILOSOPHY. From the Greek *philo* + *sophia*, meaning "love of wisdom." Some philosophers have treated philosophy simply as the wisdom of love. There are multiple definitions of philosophy, but two have wide adherence:

(A) To have a philosophy is to have a view of reality (oneself, the world, God or gods, the sacred, good and evil, and so on), including a view on whether one can know anything at all about reality. In this usage, philosophy is difficult if not impossible to avoid among mature persons whether or not they have any formal education.

(B) Philosophy is practiced when persons engage in disciplined reflection on one or more views of reality, assessing which view (or worldview) is more reasonable or likely to be true or coherent or better. More specific demarcations of philosophy will depend on which framework is assumed.

So, for example, a philosopher in the canonical tradition of Plato, Aristotle, Kant, and so on would tend not to recognize a social history of philosophy as itself philosophical even if such a social history shed light on the conditions in which philosophy was practiced. On this view, such a history would be a case of sociology, not philosophy.

Philosophy has been practiced historically as a domain with its own questions (What is truth? What is good? What is beautiful?) as well as questions for virtually every domain of inquiry. Thus there is philosophy of religion, science, history, literature, language, and so on.

Philosophy of religion has been carried out from the beginning of philosophy insofar as philosophers have engaged religiously significant questions about gods or God, the sacred, and so on. As a special discipline or field, philosophy of religion emerged in the West in the seventeenth century when religious beliefs became a special focus of inquiry.

PHYSICALISM. The belief that everything is matter and / or energy, or that everything that exists is explainable by ideal physical sciences, usually identified as physics and chemistry. "Physicalism" and "materialism" are used equivalently today.

PICO DELLA MIRANDOLA, GIOVANNI (1493–1494). A Florentine Platonist who argued that while Christianity involved an ideal or paradigmatic case of divine revelation, most religions and philosophies contain some fragments and important hints of the divine as well as the truth, the good, and the beautiful. His works include *The 900 Theses* (1486), *Apology* (1487), *Heptaplus* (1489), *On Being and Unity* (1491), *Disputations against Astrology* (1496), and *Oration on the Dignity of Man* (1496).

PIETISM, CHRISTIAN. Initiated by Philipp J. Spener, author of *Earnest Desires for a Reform of the Evangelical Church*

(1675), pietism was a Protestant movement from the mid-seventeenth through the eighteenth centuries that stressed the interior life of the soul, the study of the Bible, and the affective life. The term "pietism" was originally (like the term "Quaker") used pejoratively to refer to this movement which (according to its critics) involved excessive preoccupation with the law (hence the link between pietism and legalism). But the movement also fostered communities which made grace, rather than the law, central.

PLATO (c. 429–347 BCE). Along with his student Aristotle, Plato has exercised a profound influence on philosophy in general, including metaphysics, epistemology, ethics, mathematics, and logic, as well the philosophy of religion. A student of Socrates, Plato's early work consisted of representing Socrates' defense of himself in a court case on the grounds that Socrates corrupted the young and was impious (*The Apology*), and the record of Socrates' famous search for knowledge. Socrates is described in dialogues seeking the proper understanding and thus the definitions of holiness, justice, courage, friendship, art, and so on.

Plato's later work involved a theory of forms according to which there are abstract ideal objects such as the form of justice, the good, the beautiful, the circle, and so on. Particular objects such as a concrete case of justice are justice because they participate in the ideal of justice.

Contemporary Platonic philosophers often articulate this view in terms of properties and exemplification. By their lights, there are indefinitely (perhaps infinitely) many properties, some of which are exemplified and some are not. Thus, the property of being a dictionary is exemplified and is actually multiply exemplified, but the property of being a unicorn is not.

Plato set forth one of the most powerful myths or stories in the history of ideas to represent his thinking: we are all like persons chained to a wall in a cave. Straight ahead of us we can see figures on a wall, shadows that we mistake for real life. One can (perhaps with the help of others) be released from one's chains and come to see the forms themselves in the light of day. On this view, our current life is like a shadowland. Plato constructed an ideal social order in the *Republic*, often taught to be deeply anti-democratic, but this can be disputed on many fronts. For example, some see the *Republic* itself as a rich blend of serious philosophy as well as irony.

In Plato's work one may find a defense of an individual afterlife, including reincarnation. Plato defended the idea that there is a single good God in the *Republic*, and some Christian theists have found theistic resources in the *Timaeus*, but Plato also discusses the gods and his actual views are difficult to discern. In his seventh letter Plato entertains what some see as a very mystical approach to the good. His early dialogues include *Hippias*

Minor, Laches, Charmides, Ion, Protagoras, Euthyphro, Apology, Crito, Gorgias, Meno, Cratylus, Hippias Major, Lysis, Menexenus, and *Euthydemus*; his middle dialogues include *Phaedo, Philebus, Symposium, Republic,* and *Theaetetus*; and his late dialogues include *Critias, Parmenides, Phaedrus, Sophist, Statesman, Timaeus,* and *Laws*.

PLENITUDE, PRINCIPLE OF. Every genuine possibility is actualized at some time. Some medievalists argued that because of the good of plenitude and God's omnipotence, all good types of being will exist at some time.

PLOTINUS (c. 204/5–270 CE). Perhaps the single most influential philosopher of Late antiquity. Plato and Aristotle were often read, by both the Muslim and Christian worlds, through a prism bequeathed by Plotinus. He fused the philosophical genius of the Hellenic tradition with the mystical and contemplative impulse of late antiquity and bequeathed an interpretation of Plato that was formative for the Medievals and Renaissance culture. In his own right, Plotinus' idiosyncratic hermeneutics, synthetic vision, speculative daring, and poetic fervor make Plotinus one of the most remarkable philosophers of the occidental tradition. He is a monist but not a pantheist. His philosophy of the One and the many is best thought of as the distant source of

Leibniz rather than of Spinoza. Immaterial souls are mirrors of the transcendent plenitude of the One and salvation is the return of the soul to its immaterial source. The whole of the physical universe reflects its transcendent immaterial cause and the cosmos is governed by Providence. The return of the soul to the One culminates in a communion of love and knowledge, not mere assimilation of the soul to the totality of being or, indeed, its annihilation. Plotinus' doctrine of the return to a transcendent source or principle made Platonism more congenial to later theists than Stoicism.

PLURALISM. The term is sometimes used descriptively to designate the presence of variety (e.g., the U.S. is a pluralistic society) and sometimes normatively (e.g., salvation or enlightenment may be found in multiple religions).

PLUTARCH (c. 48 CE–c. 122 CE). A Greek biographer who used his accounts of great historical figures to teach lessons of humility and integrity. His works include *Lives* and *Moralia*.

POLITICS. *See* **GOVERNMENT.**

POLYTHEISM. Belief in multiple gods. Sometimes polytheism is subordinate to an overriding monism or monotheism by which the multiple gods are seen as different manifestations of a Higher God.

PONS ASINORUM. From the Latin, meaning "the asses' bridge." The term's origin is obscure but it probably refers to a challenge that troubles or impedes someone of little intelligence, e.g., the fifth proposition in the first book of Euclid's *Elements*. A pluralist in today's philosophy of religion may claim that there is no current *pons asinorum*, viz., there are multiple options in philosophy of religion from feminism to Kantianism, no one of which is so prestigious and powerful that only an ass would fail to embrace it.

POSITIVISM. *See* **LOGICAL POSITIVISM.**

POSSIBILITY. Metaphysically, X is possible if it is not impossible. If X is possible it may be either contingent or necessary, but not both. Epistemic possibility is different and refers to what seems to be the case. Something metaphysically impossible (time-travel) may seem epistemically possible.

POSSIBLE WORLDS. A maximum possible state of affairs. In philosophical discussions of whether ours is the best possible world, the debate is over whether there could not be an alternative, maximum possible state of affairs. Our world is both possible and actual, but (arguably) there are other possible worlds that may have been actualized.

POST-MORTEM EXISTENCE OF THE SELF. *See* **LIFE AFTER DEATH.**

POSTMODERNITY, POSTMODERNISM. A movement that emerged in the 1950s that went against commonly accepted standards about the unity and coherence of artistic and narrative styles. It is seen as a reaction against naïve confidences in progress as well as mistrust in objective or scientific truths.

In philosophy, it abandons the modern or Enlightenment confidence in objective human knowledge through reliance on reason in pursuit of realism. Modernity is understood by postmodernists as offering a false, alienating, universal philosophy that tries to capture the essence of human life and value. They describe such modern projects as offering a "meta-narrative" that would capture truth from a "God's eye point of view."

Postmodernists express doubt about the possibility of universal, objective, "God's eye point of view" truth; they value instead irony and the particularity of language and life. Popular postmodernists include Foucault, Derrida, Lyotard, Haraway, and Rorty. These philosophers critique the possibility of pure, disinterested reason and the vision of a universal foundation and progressive unfolding of knowledge and morality. The question postmodernists ask is whether reason can establish a coherent and whole system of thought. Postmodernists strive to promote an active non-forceful receptivity to "the other," no matter how different it may appear.

Critics charge that the postmodernist embrace of uncertainty, ambiguity, and even the loss of identity, rationality, and ideology, in service of their rejection of the goal of impartial reflection, undermines the goal of identifying and protecting human rights across cultures. Critics have also raised the objection that postmodernism is self-refuting. If no reasoning is impartial, why think that postmodernism is reasonable? If postmodernism is not impartial, might it be simply partial or a reflection of what might be called a bias or prejudice?

PNEUMA. Greek word meaning "spirit," akin to Hebrew *ruach* and Latin *spiritus*, all of which also mean "breath." In ancient philosophy, *pneuma* refers to the breath that animates a living body, and so not just the physical breath but also the soul. Anaximenes and the Pythagoreans identify this with that which unites not just the body but the whole cosmos. In Aristotle, *pneuma* sometimes refers to warm air or to heat, and other times it refers to a substance that provides a link between the material body and the *psyche*. The Stoics took *pneuma* to be a combination of elemental air and fire. In all of these ancient philosophers, there is some analogy between the *pneuma* circulating in the human body and the divine circulating in and animating the cosmos. The word is sometimes used in the

New Testament and subsequent Christian theology to mean "soul." It is also used in Gnostic writings to distinguish those who had most liberated themselves from the material world by means of esoteric knowledge (the *pneumatics*) from those who were most in the grip of the material world (the *hylics* or *somatics*).

PRAGMATISM. American philosophical movement beginning in the mid-nineteenth century. Although a diverse philosophical tradition, pragmatists generally hold that beliefs get their meaning through their effects on action, that all thinking is problem solving, and that scientific inquiry provides the model for all knowledge. These views lead pragmatists to see beliefs as tools to be maintained as long as they are conducive to successful action. Any belief that holds no consequence for action is a meaningless belief. Pragmatists universally deny any representational theory of the mind, any strict dualism between mind and body or thought and action, and the intelligibility of speculating about what transcends experience. Pragmatists are often dismissive of religion. John Dewey thought it expressed the unreflective spirit of a people at a historical moment and William James took seriously the way certain forms of mystical experiences can shape actions, while denying that mystical experiences themselves provide evidence of a divine being. Josiah Royce, James' colleague at Harvard and a correspondent with Charles

Sanders Peirce, argued that pragmatist fallibilism only makes sense if it is supplemented with the belief in an Absolute Knower. He recasts this Absolute in his later works as an Infinite Community of Interpretation, toward which, he claims, Christianity uniquely aspires. Charles Sanders Peirce, who coined the name "Pragmatism," was hostile to creeds and to theologians in general, but he also held that evidential atheism and anti-religious sentiment were both abuses of science and impediments to human growth. Classical Pragmatism is most closely connected to the writings of Charles Sanders Peirce (1839–1914), William James (1842–1910), Josiah Royce (1855–1916), John Dewey (1859–1952), and George Herbert Mead (1863–1931). Later Pragmatists of note include Robert Brandom (1950–), Donald Davidson (1917–2003), Susan Haack (1945–), Jürgen Habermas (1929–), Joseph Margolis (1924–), Richard Rorty (1931–2007), and Cornel West (1953–). *See also* DEWEY; JAMES; PEIRCE; and ROYCE.

PRAYER. On a theistic understanding, prayer is how people commune with God. Prayer is also understood to be God-given, so that in prayer we give back to God the thoughts, words, or yearnings God has given to us. In Christianity the Lord's Prayer is the ultimate expression of this dynamic. In the New Testament (Romans 8.26–7; Ephesians 6.18), the Holy Spirit is said to pray through human beings.

The many forms of prayer include: repentance, confession, and prayers for forgiveness; praise and thanksgiving; petition and intercession; and meditation and contemplation.

"True repentance" is a genuine sharing of God's sorrow, rather than merely feeling sorry for oneself, or attempting to pay one's dues. Confession is articulation of the ways one understands oneself to be falling short of God's will. "Private confession" is made by an individual to a priest and is accompanied by a request for forgiveness and absolution (the absolving of one's sins). Corporate confession is made within the context of a congregational liturgy and is followed by a prayer of absolution pronounced upon the congregation.

Praise can take inarticulate forms, such as glossolalia (speaking in tongues), or articulate forms that marvel at the natural world insofar as it has no seeming relevance to human concerns. Thus, praise, as with all prayer, moves us from the center of our concerns. Thanksgiving is related: to thank is to think truly, to know that one's life is given and sustained by others.

Petitionary prayer is prayer in which desires are presented to God. Intercessory prayer is made on behalf of others. At face value, both types of prayer seem to be impetratory ("impetrate" is a theological term meaning to obtain things by request). The conviction behind impetratory prayer is that God gives us some things not only as we wish, but because we wish and ask for them.

This conviction raises a number of dilemmas in relation to traditional concepts of God. If God is immutable, prayer cannot change God's will or God's nature. If God is omniscient, omnibenevolent, and omnipotent, prayer cannot supplement God's knowledge, beneficence, or power in order to assist God in bringing about the good. Indeed, God ought to bring about the good regardless of prayer; otherwise God's own goodness is compromised. The doctrine of divine timelessness or eternality has been employed to address the dilemmas of immutability. Aquinas argued that by petitionary prayer those things are obtained that God has ordained to be obtained by prayer. The freely offered prayers of human beings therefore do not change God, but are taken up into God's dealings with the world, where God has ordained that this should be so. Alternative, post-Hegelian models of prayer emphasize divine immanence and abandon traditional concepts of immutability and timelessness. They present a temporal God who chooses to be influenced by the prayers of creatures. These models, such as are found in process theology, modify divine omnipotence, and configure God as persuading the world in a certain direction, aided by the free prayers of human beings insofar as they fall in with God's will.

Therapeutic models of prayer get around the theological dilemmas by interpreting impetration in terms of the effects it works within those who pray (and perhaps within those who know they are being prayed for), such as strengthening people's moral resolve (e.g., Immanuel Kant), bringing their will into line with God's will (e.g., D. Z. Phillips), or bringing them comfort. Such models are offered by both theists and atheists.

Meditation involves partially-structured rumination over scriptural words or the repeated chanting of simple forms of prayer. It is not synonymous with contemplation, which is prayer at its most radical level: silence and attention, in acknowledgment that all words, images, and gestures are inadequate religious expressions.

PRE-SOCRATICS. The philosophers before Socrates, a group that includes Anaximander, Anaximenes, Anaxagoras, Pythagoras, Heraclitus, Thales, Parmenides, and others. One of our principal resources in knowing about the pre-Socratics is Aristotle's overview of their contributions. Aristotle thought of the pre-Socratics as largely driven by a philosophy of nature, whereas Socrates was driven more by a concern for values.

PREDESTINATION. The belief that the salvation or damnation of all persons is determined by God, with the result that a person may be predetermined to be saved prior to the time when the person actually attains salvation. Supralapsarianism is the view that this predestination was elected by God before the fall, while infralapsarianism is the view that the divine decree occurred after the fall. Single predestination is the thesis that God only predetermines souls for salvation, but does not decree who are reprobate or damned. Predestination is sometimes advanced as not just a thesis about ultimate salvation, but about every detail in the created order. On this view, providence is determined by God. Some Christian philosophers have argued that predestination is compatible with freedom of the will of the creature. By their lights, God's predestination is linked to God's foreknowledge. By foreknowing what a creature will freely do, God's determination of the soul's end is made in virtue of what God knows the creature will freely do.

PREDICATE, PREDICATION. A predicate is an attribute; when you assign an attribute to something you predicate it of the thing. So, to claim a dog is brown is to predicate brownness of the dog. To predicate omniscience of God is to claim that omniscience is a divine attribute.

PRESENTISM. The view that only the present exists. Theistic presentists hold that God is temporal, existing in the present moment and is not timelessly eternal.

PRIMUM MOBILE. From the Latin, meaning "first mover." Primum Mobile is the outermost concentric sphere of the

Ptolemaic model of the universe. It is also known as the crystalline sphere, and it is the origin of time, motion, and life. God's love generates the sphere's rotation, which moves with incomprehensible velocity; it is the ultimate physical heaven. The sphere's perfect rotation and shape is representative of the self-contained nature of God. The *Primum Mobile* is enclosed only by the Empyrean Heaven, the mind of God. Dante Alighieri uses the term in his writings to demonstrate how a mingling of philosophical reflection on religious truths can reveal the obscure nature in biblical scriptures. He forms this conception by drawing on elements from both Aristotelian and Neoplatonist physics. Furthermore, *Primum Mobile* can be seen as an allegory that expresses Dante's belief in the value of philosophical engagement and intellectual contemplation for a happy life and closer relationship with God.

PRIOR PROBABILITY. Prior to some inquiry about whether X is true, there may be some independent reasons for thinking it is likely to be true.

PRIVATE LANGUAGE ARGUMENT. The meaning of language must be publicly confirmable and (in principle) its rules evident. Attributed to Wittgenstein, this argument has been used against Cartesianism and skepticism. D. Z. Phillips has used the argument that there can be no incorporeal divine being or consciousness.

Some philosophers have used skepticism to counter the private language argument. Arguably, a case could arise when, for example, one could not confirm or know with certainty whether a person's use of color terms is exactly the same as someone else's. Could an ostensibly unique case arise in which a person's use of the term "red" is precisely akin to all Anglophone subjects and yet she sees what most people call "blue"? This is called the problem of the inverted spectrum.

PROBABILISM. The thesis that the moral or religious precept that seems more probable to an agent is the one that is binding.

PROBLEM OF EVIL. *See* **EVIL, PROBLEM OF**.

PROCESS PHILOSOPHY. Philosophy inspired by Alfred North Whitehead (1861–1947) and Charles Hartshorne (1897–2000) that emphasizes God's *becoming* rather than God's *being*. Reality consists of events, not material substances. Panentheistic (God contains the world but is not identical with it) in its approach, process philosophy argues that by virtue of God's relationship to and interaction with the world, God is affected by the change within the world and experiences both suffering and joy alongside creation. Thus while certain things about

185

God's character may remain constant (God's goodness, wisdom, and so on), in some regards God changes. Hence God, along with creation, is in process, or becoming. Process philosophy has a strong commitment to the role of creaturely free will and self-determination. This changes the way that God's omnipotence is understood: God does not exercise power through coercion but rather influences our free will by offering possibilities that we may choose to actualize. Contemporary proponents include John B. Cobb, Jr., David Ray Griffin, and Marjorie Hewitt Suchocki.

PROPERLY BASIC. A term introduced by Alvin Plantinga to refer to beliefs that have epistemic merit but not on the basis of other beliefs or independent evidence. From Plantinga's perspective, examples may include the belief that one exists or that there is a God; these may be beliefs that may be proper for a person to hold without inference. Controversy has arisen over when proper beliefs may be undermined by contrary inferential arguments, sometimes called "defeaters."

PROPERTY. According to some theists, the whole cosmos is God's property. Passages in the Hebrew Bible, Christian New Testament, and the Qur'an support the idea that the natural world belongs to God as its Creator. Some theists maintain that this entails that creatures do not have absolute ownership rights even over themselves, but are called to be stewards or trustees of the created order. Other theists hold that the cosmos has been given to creatures, and thus the creature has been given itself and the things it makes as its possessions. Apart from the role of property in a philosophy of creation, philosophers of religion have debated the justification of property (to what extent are property rights a function of contracts and covenants?) and the limits of ownership (must I give surplus wealth away to those in chronic need?). At least among human beings, claims of property are customarily analyzed in terms of rights and duties. If you own this dictionary, for example, you may use it as you will, others have a duty not to use it without your consent, and if someone were to so use it, you would have a right for due compensation.

The term 'property' is also used to refer to 'attribute' as in being the color blue, being a square, and so on. Except in the case of haecceities, properties are multiply exemplifiable; that is, they can be exemplified by more than one thing.

PROPHET. A person inspired directly by the divine or through a messenger, such as an angel, to spread religious teachings about the divine.

PROPOSITION. Propositions are statements that are true or false and not identical with sentences. The two sentences, "It is raining," and in French, "Il pleut," both express the same proposition or statement.

PROVIDENCE. Synonym for God in Christian theology since the Middle Ages. The derivation of this word from the Latin *pro* + *videntia,* meaning "fore-sight," points to understandings of God as omniscient, or as foreseeing or foreordaining events. Self-identified theists customarily believe God to be provident.

PSEUDO-DIONYSIUS THE AREOPAGITE. The writer and theologian now known as Pseudo-Dionysius or Pseudo-Denys was probably a Syrian monk who lived and wrote circa 500 CE. He acquired this rather dubious title after later medieval theologians confused him with Dionysius the Areopagite, whose conversion by St. Paul is described in Acts 17:34. As a result, his writings gained great authority in the tradition of church scholarship. His extant writings include four books (*Divine Names, Mystical Theology, Celestial Hierarchy, Ecclesiastical Hierarchy*), and ten letters.

Pseudo-Dionysius espoused a sort of Neoplatonic, mystical Christianity characterized in large part by apophatic theology, also known as the *via negativa.* According to this method, one denies that anything can positively be known about God save that God is ineffable and transcendent. For Pseudo-Dionysius, the ultimate goal is unity with God, not knowledge of God. These and other Neoplatonic views have caused some to accuse him of heresy, but his writings are still, for the most part, accepted by the church.

PTOLEMAIC. Similar to or having to do with the natural philosophy of Ptolemy (c. 90–c. 168 CE). In his *Almagest,* Ptolemy developed the cosmology of earlier scientists and worked up a reliable system of sidereal navigation. The *Almagest* became the source of the dominant geocentric model of the universe until the time of Copernicus. Later medieval theology adopted a Ptolemaic and Aristotelian view of the cosmos, leading to controversy when heliocentric models of the universe were announced.

Philosopher of religion John Hick (1922–) argued that just as the Ptolemaic system of astronomy had to abandon the geocentric model to more closely match the truth, so religions ought to abandon models of belief that place one's own religion at the center. Instead, we should see the Divine at the center, with religions orbiting it as planets orbit the sun. *See also* PLURALISM.

PURE ACT. *See ACTUS PURUS.*

PURGATORY. From the Latin *purgatorium,* meaning "a place of purification or purging." Although the doctrine that purgatory is a place along with heaven and hell was not officially affirmed by the Roman Catholic Church until the Second Council of Lyons in 1274, seeds of the doctrine were evident much earlier. Church Fathers of the East as well as the West held that there would be a time of cleansing for many believers after death before they would be ready for heaven. The early practice of praying for the dead, which assumes the possibility of post-mortem spiritual growth and progress, played a significant role in the development of the doctrine.

The basic logic of the doctrine of purgatory is fairly straightforward. Nothing unclean or impure can enter heaven. So long as there is anything in our lives that keeps us from loving God perfectly, we cannot experience the full intimacy with God that heaven promises. However, many if not most believers die with various sins and imperfections in their lives and their characters. It is the need to make sense of these realities that leads to the basic concept of purgatory. Christians who reject the doctrine must have some alternative account of how these sins and imperfections are removed.

As the doctrine of purgatory was formalized and systematized, theologians generated more elaborate claims about what living persons could do to speed the release of their loved ones and help them enter heaven. In addition to prayers, they specified other acts of piety and service such as the offering of mass and the giving of alms. From this line of thinking, they developed the notion of indulgences, which in its crass form, held that souls could be sprung from purgatory for the right amount of money. This line of thinking readily lent itself to the worst sort of abuses that were easy targets for the Protestant Reformers.

The fact that some of the most notorious abuses of the time were associated with purgatory has no doubt contributed to the Protestant hostility to the doctrine and general rejection of it. Among the reasons Protestants have given for rejecting the doctrine, two have been persistent. First, the idea that fellow believers can do things (such as the purchase of indulgences) to get souls out of purgatory is alleged to be a form of salvation by works that devalues the work of Christ to save us and undermines the doctrine of justification by faith. Second, the doctrine is not clearly taught in scripture and has slender biblical warrant at best.

Defenders of the doctrine often concede that it lacks explicit scriptural support, but they argue that it coheres with things that are clearly taught in scripture and makes theological sense of how persons who die with character flaws can be perfected before they enter heaven. Likewise, the objection that purgatory is incompatible with the doctrine of justification by faith is dubious, for purgatory may be construed as a matter of completing the sanctification process. Whereas justification can be accepted by faith in an instant, sanctification still requires transformation over time. This understanding of purgatory can be advanced without accepting the Roman Catholic theology of indulgences.

PURITY. *See* **IMPURITY.**

PYRRHO OF ELIS (c. 365–275 BCE). Greek skeptic who gave rise to pyrrhonism, the view that for every opinion or thesis one can find as good a reason to oppose it as to accept it. Under such conditions, Pyrrho thought one should suspend judgment.

PYRRHONISM. *See* **PYRRHO OF ELIS.**

PYTHAGORAS (b. c. 570 BCE). One of the earliest Greek philosophers, attributed (probably wrongly) with the discovery of the Pythagorean theorem. He is believed to have practiced philosophy as not simply a matter of intellectual inquiry but as a way of life.

Q

QI. Literally air or breath, *qi* is the matter or material force that, along with *li* or principle, makes up all existence. The concept of *li* and *qi* was developed by the neo-Confucian philosophers Cheng Hao, Cheng Yi, and Zhu Xi. They taught that all things have a fundamental principle of form, called *li*. All *li* together constitute the limitless Supreme Ultimate, the principle underlying all existence. The Supreme Ultimate, a non-theistic transcendental order, is in all things. *Li* provides the form, but material existence comes from *qi*. The central issue of neo-Confucianism applies this scheme to human nature. Confucian orthodoxy held that human nature, the basis of all virtues, is good, but human nature as it really exists is a manifestation of *li* through *qi*. *Qi* can be impure, muddied, or dulled, and humans have an obligation to purify their *qi* through education and self-cultivation.

QUIETISM. A term first used in the seventeenth century to refer to Christians who stressed the primacy of quiet receptivity and the denial of self in the search for mystical union with God. Quietism was deemed heretical because of its denial of the trinity. Leaders included Miguel de Molinos, *Spiritual Guide* (1675), François Fénelon, *Explanations of the Maxims of the Saints* (1697), and Jeanne Marie Guyon.

QUR'AN. Arabic, "the recitation." The holy book of Islam. Muslims believe that God revealed it through the Angel Jibril (Gabriel) to the Prophet Muhammad over the course of 23 years. It contains 114 *suras* (chapters) offering divine guidance for human beings. The Qur'an includes many stories and characters from the Jewish and Christian scriptures, claiming that they also come from Allah (Arabic for "God"), but that the Qur'an is Allah's final and perfect revelation. Muslims consider the Qur'an to be the literal word of God and hence prefer to use only the original Arabic version. They treat physical copies of the Qur'an with great respect and take insults of it to be blasphemy.

R

RADHAKRISHNAN, SARVEPALLI (1888–1975). Indian philosopher and statesman. Radhakrishnan is one of the major twentieth-century philosophers of religion to comprehensively bridge Eastern and Western religious thought. He was the first Vice President of India (1952–1962) and the second President of India (1962–1967). He influenced the development of Indian philosophy through introducing Western Idealism and was instrumental in shaping Western understanding of Hinduism. Radhakrishnan's hierarchy of religions gives preference to Hinduism as the most unifying form of religious expression and defends *Advaita Vedanta*, the school of Hinduism to which he belonged. He ranks worship of the Absolute (*Brahman*) highest, followed in descending order by worship of the personal God, worshiping incarnations (e.g., Buddha), worship of ancestors and deities, and finally worshipers of forces and spirits. Radhakrishnan saw Western religious thought as flawed because it relied on purely intellectual thinking rather than intuition. In his view, the value of religious claims was supported by experience and spiritual intuition rather than biblical texts. His works include *Indian Philosophy* (2 vols., 1923–1927), *The Philosophy of the Upanishads* (1924), *An Ideal View of Life* (1929), *Freedom and Culture* (1936), *Eastern Religions in Western Thought* (1939), *Contemporary Indian Philosophy* (1950), *East and West: Some Reflections* (1956), *A Source Book in Indian Philosophy* (with C. A. Moore, 1957), and *Religion in a Changing World* (1967).

RADICAL ORTHODOXY. A movement involving high Anglican and Roman Catholic thinkers who contend that the form of secular reason that we today have inherited from the Enlightenment inevitably leads to a denial of values or nihilism. Radical orthodoxy seeks a concept of theological reason that is not held hostage to secular values or reasoning. Prominent advocates of radical orthodoxy include John Millbank and Graham Ward.

RAHNER, KARL (1904–1984). A twentieth-century German Jesuit and Roman

Catholic theologian. He was a proponent of a school of thought within Catholicism known as *Nouvelle Théologie*, which advocated for a reform of the Church's approach to theology. Such reforms included a return to biblical exegesis, the study of early Christian writers (or Patristics), as well as an openness to mystical theology, modernity, and contemporary issues in theology. This theology, and Rahner himself, greatly influenced the Second Vatican Council (1962–1965). Rahner was a well-known proponent of inclusivism and coined the term "Anonymous Christians" to describe those who had never heard of Jesus Christ or acknowledged him as their savior, but nevertheless received God's saving grace and had the effects of Jesus' atoning death applied to them.

His axiom that the immanent trinity (God in Godself) is strictly identical with the economic trinity (the way in which God communicates Godself to humanity in the economy of salvation) and vice versa, sparked a revival of trinitarian theology. In 1991, a group of scholars formed the Karl Rahner Society to promote the study of his work. His works include *Spirit in the World* (1939), *Hearers of the Word* (1941), *Mission and Grace* (3 vols., 1966), *Meditations on the Sacraments* (1974), *Foundations of Christian Faith* (1976), and *Theological Investigations* (23 vols., 1961–1992).

RATIONALISM. A philosophy that gives primary attention to rational introspective inquiry rather than empirical observation. Traditional rationalists include Descartes, Leibniz, and Spinoza, as opposed to empiricists like Locke.

RATIONALITY / REASONABLE. Some philosophers treat the word "rationality" as an instrumental form of thinking, such that it is rational to do X if it is the case that the agent desires to do Y and X is the most efficient means to bring about Y. The term "reasonable" is sometimes used by way of contrast to name the ability to assess the worthiness of the desires themselves. If you desire to go to Rome, it may be rational to go there by such and such means, but one may then ask the question of whether desiring to go to Rome is the most reasonable goal to have in the first place, given all other alternatives.

RAWLS, JOHN (1921–2002). Distinguished Harvard philosopher who defended a liberal political theory that entailed a substantial redistribution of wealth for the overall good. His theory gave a central role to impartiality. He is the author of *A Theory of Justice* (1971). Near the end of his life, Rawls turned his attention to global justice. In philosophy of religion, Rawls was an important advocate of liberalism according to which religious values and conceptions of the good should not be employed in law-making and legislation. He did not think it unjust for individuals to act on the grounds of comprehensive religious doctrine, but he believed that law-making should be essentially secular.

READING. Reading, for us, tends to be understood as one component of the technical skill of literacy. On this understanding, the reader interprets or decodes a written text, ordinarily in silence and alone, without intermediary or audience. The verb "to read" is, for us, used univocally of what we do with the Bible or Torah or Qur'an, and of what we do with the newspaper, a blog, or the airline timetable. Most contemporary nations aspire to make all their citizens capable of this technical skill, but none has achieved it, and recent evidence shows that literacy rates are in decline in the post-industrial nations of the West.

Before the sixteenth century, the activity of reading and responding to written texts was understood very differently. Sharing and absorbing knowledge was mostly through listening, and by people who could not decode graphs—which is to say written symbols. The text would be read aloud, heard, and stored in the memory (literacy, as Plato long ago predicted, is a memory-destroyer), later to be ruminated. Even by those who could decode graphs, doing so ordinarily meant vocalizing. Silent reading was, before the invention of printing, rare and worthy of remark. To know a text—to have read it—meant, therefore, to have heard it in such a way as to have it at memorial recall,

whether verbatim or digested. Well-read pre-modern Christians, Jews, Muslims, Buddhists, and Hindus were, therefore, often illiterate, and yet they were profoundly and communally intimate with large bodies of text. Their ways of using texts made it possible for them to be textualized—overwritten by their texts—in ways effectively impossible for us.

REAL, THE. A term John Hick uses to refer to the ultimate reality that is beyond the God or the sacred as conceived of in different religions. The God of theism, for example, is the Real as it is perceived through a theistic lens or from a theistic point of view.

REALISM. The thesis that there are true and false propositions and beliefs about reality and that these are not simply or entirely a matter of social convention. For most realists, truth is not a matter that is essentially linked to language. Hence, most realists think there were truths before language-speaking evolved.

REALITY. Some philosophers treat the concept of reality in a way that is independent of mind. On this view, often called realism, what is real does not depend upon and is not constituted by beliefs. Realism can allow, in principle, a radical form of skepticism, according to which no human persons may claim to know with certitude the nature of reality. Some realists distinguish the concept of reality from the concepts of delusion, illusion, and mere appearances.

Other philosophers, often called non-realists, treat 'reality' in epistemic terms. On one view, inspired by Peirce, what is real is what would be ultimately recognized as true by an ideal community of inquirers.

REASON. There is no consensus about a standard use of "reason," but it is frequently used as a contrast or complementary term for "faith." On this view, reason stands for the faculties of rational reflection, sensations and experience, memory and inference, and any a priori or a posteriori judgments that may be exercised without relying on a religious faith that is unsupported by reason. In this schema, faith is beyond reason, but it may or may not be incompatible with reason. Such usage is not, however, uniform, for some philosophers argue that the content of religious faith (e.g., there is a Creator God and Redeemer) is supported by reason.

REBIRTH. See **REINCARNATION; TRANSMIGRATION.**

REDEMPTION. See **ATONEMENT.**

REDUCTIO AD ABSURDUM. Latin, meaning "reduction to absurdity." Arguments that a given position is unacceptable because it leads to cases that are evidently preposterous, i.e., implying a contradiction. Someone who is led to the position that he believes he has no belief may be in a reduction to absurdity.

REFORMATION, THE. A protest movement (hence: Protestants) in Europe during the sixteenth and seventeenth centuries that sought to reform the Roman Catholic Church. Most date its inception to the publication of Martin Luther's *Ninety-Five Theses* (1517), although others, such as John Wycliffe and Johannes Hus, had been pushing for reform earlier. Among other things, Luther criticized the Church's practice of selling indulgences and its teachings about purgatory. He was soon joined by other reformers, such as Ulrich Zwingli and John Calvin. Although their original intention was to reform the Church, the reformers ultimately broke from the Roman Catholic Church and founded the Protestant Church. Disagreements among Protestants led to the formation of a variety of different denominations. Today, the Protestant Church includes Anglicans, Baptists, Calvinists, Lutherans, Methodists, Presbyterians, and many others.

REFORMED THEOLOGY. Theology inspired and influenced by early Protestants, especially John Calvin. Reformed theology tends to give primacy to scripture, recognize the sovereignty of God, and regard creation as a divine gift and act of grace and yet marred by the fall and human sin. Reformed theologians tend to be reserved in the use of natural theology, though Calvin himself seemed to allow natural theology a supportive role, pointing toward the need for revelation.

REID, THOMAS (1710–1796). Scottish philosopher who defended common sense over against the skepticism of David Hume. His "direct realism" served as a critique of mediational theories of perception judged by Reid as leading to skepticism. Father of the "Common Sense" school, Reid was a leading member in the Scottish Enlightenment. He moved from Abberdeen to Glasgow, occupying the position recently vacated by Adam Smith. His contributions to the topics of personal identity, causation, free will, and providentialism continue to be influential. Reid's major works include *An Inquiry into the Human Mind on the Principles of Common Sense* (1764), *Essays on the Intellectual Powers of Man* (1785), and *Essays on the Active Powers of Man* (1788).

REINCARNATION. Reincarnation refers to the belief in the rebirth or return of human souls or persons to life again in some form after death. It is one of the oldest and most widespread beliefs in human cultures, present in the indigenous cultures of Australia, West African, the Pacific Northwest, India, Egypt, and Greece. Reincarnation is often linked to ancestral cults since those who are born are considered to be a return of ancestors (in some cultures the identification is very precise, e.g., a recently deceased relative). While most often considered in tandem with the law of karma (respective fruits of good or evil deeds are generated causally in this life or the next), not all versions of reincarnation are linked to such an ethical component. Reincarnation is also occasionally linked to vegetarianism as in the case of Pythagorean reincarnation, since one ought to remain pure by not eating the flesh of those who may have been human persons in past lives. Reincarnation need not be limited to the human realm, and, indeed, in many of its forms, the human rebirth is just one of many possible realms of rebirth (including plants, insects, ghosts, animals, residents of hell, and gods, depending on the particular theory).

Belief in reincarnation (or a continuing cycle of rebirth-death-rebirth) is fundamental in Hinduism, Buddhism, and Jainism even though their respective accounts of how it occurs are quite different. Buddhism is often singled out as a special case since the historical Buddha also taught the doctrine of *anatman* (no-self, or no enduring substantial soul) which would seem to rule out reincarnation. But Buddhism accepts rebirths by considering succeeding lives (rebirths) to be part of the same causal stream. In Greek thought, along with Pythagoras the philosophers, Empedocles, Plato, and

Plotinus all held to some form of reincarnation. Platonic reincarnation in particular is characterized by a dualism of soul / mind and body with the goal of release of the soul / mind from the body. Indian thought also offers various methods of seeking release from the cycle of successive rebirths (*samsara*), since it is held that these continuous rebirths are characterized by a type of suffering.

When ethical considerations are tied to it (e.g., when karma is accepted), reincarnation allows one to extend the frame beyond this life for questions about justice and appropriate rewards and punishments. Unfair advantages or disadvantages in this life might be the fruits of previous good / evil actions one has done in a previous life, and similarly punishments and rewards for actions done in this life might not be realized in this life but in later reincarnations. Reincarnation need not be immediate between lives; some versions of reincarnation assume waiting periods between rebirths of a few days or even many years. *See also* TRANSMIGRATION.

RELATIVISM. The general system of thinking that there is no objective, impartial, or universal standard by which something can be judged. A conceptual relativist is a nonrealist who holds that truth and falsehood are dependent upon frameworks. This is closely related to perspectivalism. For a conceptual relativist, the thesis that water is H_2O may be true,

but only relative to the conceptual framework of atomic theory. Different frames of reference may produce convergent accounts; for example, a religious conceptual framework may see water differently than a secular one. Moral relativism is opposed to moral realism and holds that moral truths depend upon the community or individuals involved. Thus, in a community that finds slavery natural and permissible, slavery is (relative to that community) natural and permissible. Critics argue that moral relativism is unable to account for what seems like the fact that communities can be wrong; for example, even if all persons (enslaved and free) in a community thought that the human bondage of slavery was just, it does not follow that slavery is just. *See also* ETHICS.

RELIGION. Considerable controversy surrounds the definition of "religion." Definitions that explicitly identify the belief in a God as an essential feature of religion seem too narrow, as that would exclude some forms of Buddhism. A popular definition of "religion" today is through giving examples, e.g., a religion is a tradition such as Judaism, Christianity, Islam, Hinduism, or Buddhism, or those traditions like them. An alternative definition which aims at giving greater guidance is as follows: A religion is a body of teachings and prescribed practices about an ultimate, sacred reality or state of being that calls for reverence or awe, that guides its practitioners into what it describes as a saving, illuminating, or emancipatory relationship to this reality through a personally transformative life of prayer, ritualized meditations, and / or moral practices like repentance and moral and personal regeneration.

RELIGIOUS AMBIGUITY. A term introduced by John Hick for the thesis that the cosmos may be equally well described and explained from a religious or a secular, naturalistic point of view. If the cosmos is religiously ambiguous, then there is no independent conclusive evidence for embracing either naturalism or religion. While some would conclude that religious ambiguity entails agnosticism, others (such as Hick) defend the permissibility of embracing either religion or secularism. Hick's own position is that of a radical pluralism in which many ostensibly competing accounts of the cosmos may all turn out to be leading us to the same end, the Real.

RELIGIOUS EXPERIENCE. Apparent sensing or apprehending of a sacred reality. These may be monistic or monotheistic. Experiences that are part of Buddhist meditations on the self may also be seen as religious or philosophical experiences. A key issue in modern philosophy of religion relates to the evidential character of religious experience. When can, for example, an apparent experience or perception of God count as evidence that this experience is veridical? Philosophers reflect on the analogies and disanalogies between religious experiences and moral experiences (the ostensible experience of the goodness or evil of some act or event) and perceptual experiences of ordinary objects.

RELIGIOUS LANGUAGE. Language about the sacred and our relation to the sacred; for example, God, Brahman, Allah, karma, reincarnation, and so on. Religious texts and practices include almost all the main ways of using language: expressive, descriptive, referential, reformative, and so on. Terms may be used literally, metaphorically or analogously, or even equivocally. Some (such as John Duns Scotus) claim that terms like "cause" may be used univocally of God and creatures as in "God caused the cosmos to be" and "Lightning caused a forest fire." Calling God a "father," however, is more of a metaphorical or analogous attribution. Philosophers debate the extent to which religious language is analogous to other domains of discourse. In the aftermath or World War II and with the advance of positivism, there was a major debate over whether religious language is meaningful. Some philosophers today challenge the coherence of referring to God as a purposive reality or person or person-like subject that is nonphysical. In today's more pluralistic intellectual climate, religious language is not (as with positivism) usually considered incoherent until shown differently.

REPENTANCE. More than regret, repentance involves remorse for a past wrongdoing and the resolution not to do the wrong again. Theologians disagree about whether confession and repentance are necessary conditions for forgiveness.

RESURRECTION. The resurrection of Jesus is the central doctrine of the Christian faith and the ground of its ultimate hope. Christians hold that God raised Jesus to life after he had been dead for three days. The distinctively Christian doctrines hinge crucially on the truth of this claim. The resurrection is the most compelling demonstration for Jesus' divinity, which is essential not only for the doctrine of the atonement, but also for the incarnation and the trinity.

It is important to distinguish the doctrine of resurrection from two other notions that are sometimes confused with it. First, resurrection is not resuscitation. The New Testament records instances of Jesus and others raising people from dead, but these are all examples of resuscitation, for the persons were restored to mortal life and would consequently die again. Resurrection is more than mere resuscitation. Second, resurrection is not the survival of the soul after the death of the body. Resurrection pertains precisely to the body, not just the soul.

That resurrection is bodily is made clear in the gospels by the emphasis on the fact that Jesus' tomb was empty, along with the accounts of his performing physical acts like eating. That resurrection is not mere resuscitation is clear from the fact that the body of the risen Jesus does not have the sort of limitations that are typical of a mortal body. He can suddenly appear, he can pass through locked doors and the like. So resurrection is the raising of the body to immortality, to the kind of life that will be typical in the new order when there will be no more death, and all things will be made new. Jesus' resurrection was the prototype of what all persons who are saved may anticipate when heaven comes to earth and God's kingdom comes in its fullness. As such it was an eschatological event that portends the age to come.

A matter of debate among Christians is whether resurrection pertains only to the body, or to the whole person. The traditional view is that souls continue to survive in conscious form between death and resurrection. Although with Christ, separated souls are incomplete or damaged persons as they await the resurrection, which will reunite body and soul into one whole person. More recently, some biblical scholars and theologians have argued that there is no conscious survival between death and resurrection, that the entire person is destroyed at death and then restored to life at the resurrection. On this view, the "soul" is sometimes thought of as the form of the body (following Aquinas) or the information bearing pattern that organizes matter.

Part of what is at stake in this debate is the issue of personal identity. What is the source or carrier of continuity that makes the resurrected person the same person as the one who died? On the traditional view, it is the soul, a spiritual substance that retains not only consciousness, but also memory, character traits, and the like. On the other view, the carrier of identity would be the information bearing pattern that is retained in memory by God between death and resurrection.

REVEALED THEOLOGY. Theology based on a scripture that is taken to be normative or given or foundational. Revealed theology contrasts with natural theology, which seeks to offer knowledge or an awareness of God without appeal to special revelation.

REVELATION. In theology and philosophy of religion, revelation refers to a disclosure of God either through events (ostensible acts of God) or through language (which is special in that it differs from whatever general revelation of God is available through reflection on the cosmos). Paradigmatic cases of revelation are in the form of auditions (heard speech or sounds as when one appears to hear music "in one's mind" when there are no musicians or recordings being played) or mediated language through a prophet,

oracle, or some other human agent. The Qur'an is traditionally understood to be God's very words, dictated to the Prophet Muhammad through the Angel Gabriel.

RICHARD OF St. VICTOR (c.1123–1173). A student of Hugh of St. Victor, Richard further developed mystical theology in the late medieval era, juxtaposing it to moral theology. He believed that moral theology was a presupposition for approaching mysticism, but that the latter constituted a vital, new stage in the never ending journey of the human soul that ultimately seeks union with God.

RICOEUR, PAUL (1913–2005). French philosopher Paul Ricoeur wrote more than a dozen major books in philosophy and hundreds of articles; even before his death, Ricoeur's writings had been translated into more than 20 different languages. Although often found difficult to categorize, Ricoeur's contribution to twentieth-century philosophy is undeniable; interest in his ideas has continued to increase since his death in 2005. Highly distinctive is Ricoeur's own "hermeneutic phenomenology": a theory of interpretation of texts that is extended to actions and the meaning of lived experience more generally. Ricoeur's first major project is a philosophy of will, which begins with Kant's antinomy of freedom and determinism. The first volume of this project, his doctoral dissertation, was translated into English as *Freedom and Nature* (1966). In fact, we can recognize today how enduring the significance of this early project remains in Ricoeur, not only for the question of how to resolve "the conflict of interpretations" between two domains of discourse—for which "freedom" and "nature" represent only the first example of Ricoeur's attempts to mediate conflicting interpretations—but also for the phenomenological method which Ricoeur began to develop in the 1930s and 40s. During World War II, Ricoeur was a prisoner of war of Germany and was able to read Edmund Husserl in German. It is Husserl's method of phenomenological description that distinctively characterizes Ricoeur's account of acts of willing, while also developing as a crucial characteristic of the rest of his philosophical thinking.

English translations of Ricoeur's major works include *The Symbolism of Evil* (1967), *Freud and Philosophy* (1970), *The Conflict of Interpretations* (1974), *The Rule of Metaphor* (1977), *Hermeneutics and the Human Sciences* (1981), *Lectures on Ideology and Utopia* (1986), *Time and Narrative* (3 vols., 1984–1988), *From Text to Action* (1991), *Oneself as Another* (1993), *The Just* (2000), *Memory, History, Forgetting* (2004), and *The Course of Recognition* (2005). Although he strictly separated his religious and philosophical writings, these areas converge in his discussion of forgiveness as a private complement to public justice in his *Memory, History, Forgetting* (2004) and in his

discussion of agape as a love that incurs no debts in his *The Course of Recognition* (2005).

Ricoeur held a chair of general philosophy at the Sorbonne during the 1960s and was given an honorary Ph.D. in Divinity from the University of Chicago in 1967, after which he joined the Chicago faculty, holding positions in both Chicago and Paris until his retirement. Ricoeur was in demand as a lecturer in numerous countries and he received many honors (including one from the Pope) reflecting his contribution to philosophy, politics, and history-tradition-critical rationality, as well as to other social, religious, and intellectual concerns.

RITUAL / RITES. Religious rites are repeatable symbolic actions involving the sacred. Such rites include prayers involving praise (worship or adoration), petition and confession, vows, commissions such as ordination, rites of passage such as baptism, confirmation, marriage ceremonies, funeral rites and burials, communion or the Eucharist (also called Mass or the Lord's Supper), feasts, fasts, alms giving, vigils, lamentations, blessings, thanksgiving, grace before meals, and contemplative or meditative prayer.

ROMAN CATHOLICISM. Roman Catholicism is the style of Christianity found in the Roman Catholic Church (RCC). While this has much in common

200

with other styles of Christianity (such as Protestantism and Eastern Orthodoxy), it also has distinctive features, many of which pertain to the relationship between material and spiritual things—or more precisely, between created and divine realities. Thus, in Roman Catholicism, the will of the human being must cooperate with divine grace in salvation, rather than simply being acted upon. Furthermore, grace is primarily bestowed not directly upon the human soul, but rather is mediated through the material means of the sacraments; similarly, grace is found directly incorporated into exemplary Christians (saints) whose examples and even bodies (relics) are venerated after death. Moreover, the Christian Church *per se* exists not as a disembodied or abstract entity, but as found embodied in the RCC, where the bishops and the pope are heirs of the teaching of Christ (taking up the role of the apostles) and mediators of the sacramental grace (since they, assisted by the priests, celebrate the Eucharist). This relation of created and divine things is often justified by reference to the union of the divine and human in the incarnation, and it is taken to imply a positive view of God's presence in the material world. All of these factors foster among Roman Catholics a sense of reliance upon the RCC and upon Christian tradition that is not often found in Protestantism.

Furthermore, Roman Catholicism as a style of Christianity is tied to history of the RCC, which (though present throughout the world) has developed primarily in Western Europe. Many of the differences between the RCC and Eastern Orthodoxy can be attributed to this history. Thus, Latin rather than Greek has traditionally been associated with Roman Catholicism (though the RCC claims both heritages), Italian politics and art have shaped the papacy, and the circumstances of Western social history have influenced the structures, values, and expectations of the RCC. For example, the long reliance upon monasteries for priestly and Episcopal training may have contributed to the RCC's insistence upon priestly celibacy, and the isolation of the papacy from the other four prominent archbishops of ancient Christianity (all in the Eastern Mediterranean) may have advanced the papacy's singular authority in the RCC.

The doctrines of Roman Catholicism are elaborated primarily on the basis of two outstanding Latin theologians and saints: Augustine, a fourth / fifth-century North African bishop, and Thomas of Aquinas, a thirteenth-century Italian friar. However, neither theologian is followed completely, and many others have a significant voice. An extensive presentation of the teachings of the RCC can be found in the *Catechism of the Catholic Church*.

ROMANTICISM. The term generally denotes the period from 1760 to 1848. This was an age in which science was transforming the understanding of reality, and political revolution in the British colonies and France, along with industrial developments, was altering the structure of European society. Great advances and changes in society and technology were generating both excitement and anguish. The Enlightenment tended to embrace the benefits of reason and progress, whereas Romanticism tended to be more skeptical about the power of the new science to explain all phenomena. Romanticism was also wary of abstract universalism. The period was one of both erosion of and nostalgia for tradition and order. It was also marked by interest in folk cultures and particular human communities and practices. Romanticism attempted to fuse reason with emotion; thus, in music, poetry, and the arts we find a insistence upon the validity of feeling. For example, Schleiermacher's *Speeches* of 1799, defines religion as a "sense and taste for the infinite." For some Romantics, art became a substitute for religion, while for others it became a new handmaiden. The latter move became the basis for a revival of the "Gothic" Middle Ages.

ROUSSEAU, JEAN-JACQUES (1712–1778). Born in Geneva, Rousseau was equal in celebrity and cultural importance during his lifetime with his semi-rival Voltaire. Rousseau taught that humanity in a state of nature (before state and society) was fundamentally good, free, and uncorrupt. He believed that legitimate state power is created only when persons yield their natural rights to a greater community, but that political community can cease to have a right to political power if it violates the will of the people. Rousseau believed in a good, provident God, arguing that the evils of this world were not incompatible with God's goodness. He authored his *Confessions* (1782–1789), which is widely recognized as an important step in the development of autobiography (perhaps his *Confessions* was the biggest event in the genre of autobiography since Augustine's *Confessions*). His other works include *Discourses on the Sciences and the Arts* (1751, known as the First Discourse), *A Discourse upon the Origin and Foundation of the Inequality Among Mankind* (1755, known as the Second Discourse), *Letter to M. D'Alembert on the Theatre* (1758), *The Social Contract* (1762), *The New Héloïse* (1761), *Émile, or Education* (1762), *Government of Poland* (1772), *Essay on the Origin of Languages* (1781), and *Reveries of a Solitary Walker* (1782).

ROYCE, JOSIAH (1855–1916). An American pragmatist and idealist. Royce's form of theism involved human persons participating in and forming a divine community over time, notwithstanding world evils. His works include *The Religious Aspect of Philosophy* (1885), *The Spirit of Modern Philosophy* (1892), *The Conception of God* (1897), *Studies of Good and Evil* (1898), *The World and the Individual* (2 vols., 1900), *The Conception of Immortality* (1900), *The Philosophy of*

Loyalty (1908), *The Problem of Christianity* (1913), *Fugitive Essays* (ed. J. Loewenberg, 1920), and *Logical Essays* (ed. D. S. Robinson, 1951).

RUSSELL, BERTRAND ARTHUR WILLIAM (1872–1970). Prominent British philosopher who defended a myriad of positions. The most common conviction expressed throughout all of his charges was his atheism. In Russell's monumental history of Western philosophy, he positioned philosophy in what he called a "no man's land," in between science and religion or theology. In his view, religion and theology were too dogmatic and confident in their beliefs and values. Russell thought that reliable knowledge is best found in the sciences. In philosophy, however, the terrain is always less than scientific and less "dogmatic" (his term) than theology. Russell brought together some of his essays against theism and Christianity in a book called *Why I am not a Christian* (1927). He carried out an important debate about theism with Frederick Copleston on the BBC, which was frequently anthologized in late twentieth-century philosophy of religion texts. His works include *An Essay on the Foundations of Geometry* (1897), *A Critical Exposition of the Philosophy of Leibniz* (1900, new ed., 1937), *The Principles of Mathematics* (vol. 1, 1903, new ed., 1938), *Principia Mathematic* (with Alfred North Whitehead, vol. 1, 1910; vol. 2, 1912; vol. 3, 1913; new ed., 1925–1927), *Philosophical Essays* (1910), *The Problems of Philosophy* (1912), *Our Knowledge of the External World* (1914), *Principles of Social Reconstruction* (1916), *Road to Freedom: Social, Anarchism and Syndicalism* (1918), *Mysticism and Logic and other Essays* (1918), *Introduction to Mathematical Philosophy* (1919), *The Analysis of Mind* (1921), *What I Believe* (1925), *The Analysis of Matter* (1927), *An Outline of Philosophy* (1927), *Sceptical Essays* (1928), *The Scientific Outlook* (1931), *Education and the Social Order* (1932), *Freedom and Organisation* (1934), *Power: a New Social Analysis* (1938), *An Inquiry into Meaning and Truth* (1940), *A History of Western Philosophy* (1947), *Human Knowledge: its Scope and Limits* (1948), *Authority and the Individual* (1949), *Unpopular Essays* (1950), *The Impact of Science on Society* (1951), *New Hopes for a Changing World* (1952), *Satan in the Suburbs* (1953), *Human Society in Ethics and Politics* (1955), *Portraits from Memory and Other Essays* (1956), *Logic and Knowledge* (ed. R. C. Marsh, 1956), *My Philosophical Development* (1959), *Bertrand Russell Speaks his Mind* (1960), *Fact and Fiction* (1961), *Essays in Skepticism* (1962), and *The Autobiography of Bertrand Russell, 1872–1914* (3 vols., 1967).

S

SACRAMENT. Sacraments are liturgical rites that are both sensible signs and means by which divine grace is communicated to humans partaking in those rites. Sacraments were defined by Augustine as the "visible form of invisible grace," by Thomas of Aquinas as "a sign of a sacred thing inasmuch as it sanctifies humans," and by Richard Hooker as "outward and visible signs of an inward and spiritual grace." The word is derived from Latin *sacramentum*, which is a translation of the Greek *mysterion*.

Christian churches do not agree on the exact number or nature of the sacraments. The Roman Catholic Church acknowledges seven sacraments: Baptism, Confirmation, Eucharist, Penance, Extreme Unction (a.k.a. "Last Rites"), Orders, and Matrimony. Many Protestant churches name only two, Baptism and Eucharist, following the Augustinian definition of sacraments as *visible* signs, the others lacking a visible element. Some churches acknowledge no sacraments or do not enumerate them.

Sacramental theology raises certain philosophical questions about human nature, the nature of grace, and the means of its communication. Thomas of Aquinas effectively married Aristotelian hylomorphism (i.e., the doctrine that distinguishes the matter and form of a thing) to Christian theology resulting in the doctrine of transubstantiation. Sacraments are closely connected to the mystery of the incarnation, which is often taken to be the basis or example of all other sacraments. Many recent theologies prefer a symbolic, rather than a metaphysical, account of sacraments, in which sacraments are a means of symbolic participation in the mystery of the incarnation.

SACRED. *See* HOLINESS.

SACRIFICE. From the Latin *sacra facere* or "making holy." One can distinguish between the ritual of offering, usually an animal, and symbolic or figurative uses of the word. The first sense is interesting to philosophers in terms of anthropology or philosophical theology. The extended

204

figurative meaning is significant for questions of ethics: for example, the problem of altruism, or politics (e.g., theories of warfare or punishment).

Greek philosophy began with a critique of bloody sacrifice in the pre-Socratic period, though by late antiquity we find philosophers like Iamblichus (245–325) attempting to defend it. In Indian philosophy we find in the *Upanishads* the attempt to spiritualize and interiorize the Vedic rituals. In Judaism, the loss of the First Temple and then the destruction of the Second Temple meant that sacrifice was effectively ended, and in Islam it plays a minor role. It is through Christianity in particular that the language of sacrifice was retained for its theories of atonement, and eucharistic controversies kept the problem of sacrifice prominent in the West until the Enlightenment. In the Enlightenment, sacrifice was seen essentially as an aspect of the dark and violent side of Christianity. Various significant thinkers from Joseph de Maistre to Rene Girard have proposed theories of the human condition in which sacrifice is central, often with strong theological consequences. It can be argued that the idea of sacrifice plays an important role in a range of major thinkers including Kant, Hegel, Kierkegaard, and Nietzsche.

SALVATION, CHRISTIAN CONCEPTION OF. Christianity is first and foremost a scheme of salvation, not an explanatory account or a metaphysical system. To be sure, the Christian scheme of salvation involves truth claims, including metaphysical ones, of enormous magnitude, but the main message of Christianity is a diagnosis of the human condition and an account of how we can be saved from it.

The Christian diagnosis of the human condition is in terms of sin, a freely chosen condition that has separated us from God, subjected us to moral and spiritual bondage, and death. The Christian account of how we are delivered from this condition centers on the death and resurrection of Christ, but his entire life has saving significance. As the Nicene Creed professes: "For us and for our salvation he came down from heaven . . . and was made man." He became incarnate, took on human nature, in order to provide salvation for the entire fallen creation. His whole life, including his victory over all temptation and perfect obedience to his Father, was crucial for his work of defeating evil and breaking the power of sin.

The climax of his perfect obedience was his willing submission to death by crucifixion, which Christians believe has atoned for human sin. How exactly to understand the atonement ("at-one-ment") is one of the great debates in the history of theology, and several famous theories have been formulated. What is agreed, however, is that the death of Christ is the means by which God provides forgiveness for our sin and reconciles us to God. Again, the various Christian traditions disagree about the details, but there is broad consensus that faith in the atonement secures our salvation and makes us "at one" with God.

The death of Christ, however, cannot be understood apart from his resurrection. The resurrection is not only God's definitive victory over death, it is also the vindication of Christ and his perfect life. The resurrection of Christ confirms the fact that the one who died on the cross was not a mere man, and that his death was for our sins, not his.

Salvation is much more, however, than forgiveness for the wrongs we have done. To be saved from sin we must also be delivered from our moral and spiritual bondage, which requires regeneration and sanctification. This aspect of salvation is accomplished by the Holy Spirit, and it is carried forward as we are gradually transformed and fully renewed in God's moral image.

Salvation is not complete, however, until the final resurrection and redemption of the created order. So understood, salvation is a holistic matter that embraces the physical as well as the spiritual. The holistic nature of salvation is reflected in the fact that the New Testament speaks of salvation as past, present, and future. Christians believe that we have been saved by the death and resurrection of Christ, through faith; that we are being saved as God continues the work of transformation and renewal; and we shall be saved when our bodies are raised

incorruptible and all effects of sin have been overcome.

SALVATION, NON-CHRISTIAN CONCEPTIONS OF. Although "salvation" in Western philosophy of religion is largely a concept in Christian contexts, this grew out of Jewish notions of atonement and reconciliation in which persons come to be delivered from sin or the effects of sin. The term also has a general usage to describe any process by which persons are relieved and delivered from undesirable states whether these be conditions of ignorance, illusion, vices, or evil. In this broader context, enlightenment in Buddhist tradition may be considered a kind of salvation, but the use of that term should not gloss over the differences between Buddhism and, say, Christianity.

SAMSARA. See **REINCARNATION, TRANSMIGRATION.**

SANTAYANA, GEORGE (1863–1952). A Spanish philosopher, active in North America at Harvard and elsewhere. Santayana cultivated a nonrealist view of religious belief, once claiming that while there is no God, Mary is his mother. Santayana's great focus was on the relationship of mind and matter, consciousness and that which undergirds consciousness. His works include *Sense of Beauty* (1896), *Life of Reason* (5 vols.

1905–1906), *Scepticism and Animal Faith* (1923), *Realms of Being* (4 vols. 1927–1940), *The Idea of Christ in the Gospels* (1946), and *Dominations and Powers* (1949).

SARTRE, JEAN-PAUL (1905–1980). French existentialist, Sartre defined existentialism as the view that existence precedes essence. In Platonism, forms or truths about the essence of things are abstract and fixed, whereas a Sartrian existentialist treats existence itself as a brute fact. If there are any essences or definitions these are a consequence of what exists in concrete terms. Sartre defended atheism and the radical freedom of human beings. He and his partner, Simone de Beauvoir (1908–1986), had grave reservation about whether romantic love was compatible with human freedom. He coined the term "bad faith" in his discussion about self-deception. Sartre wrote many plays and novels in addition to his formal philosophical prose. A dramatic thinker (two of his more famous lines: "Hell is other people" and "Man is a useless passion"), Sartre was briefly drawn to Soviet Marxism. His writings include *The Transcendence of the Ego* (1936), *Nausea* (1938), *Sketch of a Theory of the Emotions* (1939), *The Psychology of the Imagination* (1940), *Being and Nothingness* (1943), *The Roads to Freedom* (4 vols. projected, only 3 published, 1945–1949), *Existentialism is a Humanism* (1946), *The Flies* (1946), *No*

Exit (1946), *What is Literature?* (1949), *Saint Genet* (1953), *Critique of Dialectical Reason* (1960), and *Situations I–X* (1947–1975). English translations of *Situations* under separate titles include *Literary and Philosophical Essays* (1955), *Between Existentialism and Marxism* (1975), and *Life / Situations* (1977).

SATAN. The Hebrew word *satan* (rendered in the Greek New Testament as *satanas*) means "adversary," or "one who plots against" another. The word appears only rarely in the earliest Hebrew literature, but appears more frequently in the later wisdom literature, notably *Job*, where Satan is Job's invisible tormentor. In the Septuagint, it is usually translated into Greek as *diabolé*, from which our word "devil" is derived. In the New Testament, this sense of Satan as accuser is contrasted with the idea that the Holy Spirit is *parakletos* or defender of the faithful. In later philosophy and theology "Satan" is synonymous with "Lucifer" and "the Devil."

SCHELER, MAX (1874–1928). German philosopher who defended an objective order of values. Scheler articulated the Augustinian idea that there is a proper order of love (*ordo amoris*). Scheler developed a compelling reply to Nietzsche's charge that Christianity is rooted in resentment. He distinguished between cases of when someone seeks the good out of resentment rather than out of a sense of the vitality of the good. Scheler's early work employed phenomenology in a general, theistic worldview, though his final work was marked by pantheism.

SCHELLING, FRIEDRICH WILHELM JOSEPH VON (1775–1854). German idealist philosopher. A fellow-student of Hegel and the poet Friedrich Holderlin at Tubingen theological seminary, the precociously brilliant Schelling established his philosophical reputation with a rapid succession of publications beginning in 1794. All of these works—which explored a bewildering variety of sometimes contradictory ideas—revolved around one central problem: how to reconcile the moral autonomy of the individual, stressed by Kant and Fichte, with Spinoza's pantheistic sense of the continuity of the human spirit with nature. Struggling with this problem, Schelling developed *Naturphilosophie* (an attempt to reintroduce teleology to modern science) and a pioneering account of artistic creativity as the synthesis of conscious and unconscious mental activity. His essay *On Human Freedom* (1809) began a new phase in his thinking, which involved a turn toward a (very unorthodox) form of theism and a recognition (polemically directed at his former friend Hegel) that reality may be ultimately ungraspable by reason. These ideas were subsequently explored in lectures and in extensive manuscripts, which, however, remained unpublished in his lifetime. His works include *Ideas for a Philosophy of Nature* (1797), *System of Transcendental Idealism* (1800), *Philosophical Inquiries into the Essence of Human Freedom* (1809), and *The Ages of the World* (1811–1815).

SCHILLER, JOHANN CRISTOPH FRIEDRICH VON (1759–1805). German poet, dramatist, and philosopher. Schiller became famous with his first play, *The Robbers* (1781), which explored (in a highly melodramatic style) ideas of freedom, rebellion, solidarity, and the corruption of ideals. These themes found a more mature expression in his later historical dramas, such as *Wallenstein* (1800). Interested in contemporary philosophical developments and deeply influenced by Kant, Schiller wrote important theoretical essays on aesthetics, distinguishing, for instance, between the "Naive" (spontaneous) poetry of his friend Goethe and his own "Sentimental" (more consciously articulated) style in *On Naive and Sentimental Poetry* (1795). In his major philosophical work, *Letters on the Aesthetic Education of Mankind* (1794–1795), Schiller develops an ambiguous but richly suggestive argument that it is the aesthetic sensibility that can close the gap between nature and spirit, inclination and duty, which he felt Kant had left open.

SCHLEIERMACHER, FRIEDRICH ERNST DANIEL (1768–1834). Often

labeled "the father of modern theology," Schleiermacher was a German theologian, philosopher, and classicist. He was born to a Reformed clergyman and was initially educated at institutions of the Moravian Brethren before enrolling at the University of Halle. He passed his theological exams in Berlin and served as a pastor for several churches in Germany. Influenced by his pietistic education, Schleiermacher's thought is also deeply indebted to the work of Immanuel Kant and the Romantic movement. His understanding of religion as a "feeling of absolute dependence" on the divine countered Kant and rationalist reductions of religion to the will or reason. Schleiermacher turned specifically to religious "consciousness" as an awareness of the unitive ground of human activity and passivity. In so doing, he married experience and religion, freeing it from a reduction to morality (contra Kant) or knowledge (contra Hegel). His ethics, theology, and philosophy were important for shaping nineteenth- and twentieth-century liberal theologies and sparked reactive arguments from neoorthodox Christian thinkers like Karl Barth. More recently, Schleiermacher's contributions to hermeneutics have been recognized by philosophers like Dilthey, Gadamer, and Ricoeur. While Schleiermacher was primarily concerned with issues in biblical exegesis, he also proposed a general (or universal) hermeneutics, one in which *mis*understanding was assumed between the author and the later interpreter of a text. His concern for the subjectivity of the author and "understanding" through rigorous interpretive strategies was a decisive moment in the history of hermeneutical philosophy. Schleiermacher's key works include *On Religion: Speeches to its Cultured Despisers* (1799) and *The Christian Faith* (1820–1821). After his death, one of his students published *Hermeneutics and Criticism* (1838), an overview of his hermeneutics based on his lecture notes.

SCHOLASTICISM. From the Greek *scholasticos*, implied as being substantive: a learned person or scholar. Scholasticism refers to the systematic philosophy and doctrines cultivated in the Middle Ages from the works of Aristotle and Augustine and their Jewish and Arab commentators, which was advanced by St. Thomas of Aquinas and is measured to conform to orthodox Catholic belief. "Schoolmen" is a term for the adherents of Scholasticism; they were typically scholars of the Christian university schools who came before or resisted the Modern or Enlightenment philosophies á la Descartes. The scholastic method is continued by Catholic philosophers who respect and commune with their tradition and stress humility above individual brilliance.

SCHOPENHAUER, ARTHUR (1788–1860). Confirmed atheist and pessimist, Schopenhauer is among the most important figures of post-Kantian German idealism.

Schopenhauer accepts Immanuel Kant's distinction between the world as it appears to perception and as thing- in-itself, existing independently of the mind. Unlike Kant, Schopenhauer further believes that thing-in-itself, the world in reality outside of thought, is not entirely unknowable, but can be grasped non-descriptively as Will. Schopenhauer characterizes the world as Will as uncaused, objectless, and therefore subjectless, pure willing, which is also sometimes identified as blind urging or undirected desire. Schopenhauer maintains that the world we experience is the objectification of ceaseless conflict, in that the world is constantly trying to achieve every incompatible desire through its manifestations. The result is the inevitable strife that results in individual lives, from the collision of social groups in competition and war, struggles for dominance and survival in the animal kingdom, and in the forces and events of inanimate nature. Schopenhauer's pessimism is based on the fact that the world in reality is necessarily the source of perpetual conflict, from which there can never be lasting peace. To live is to suffer, Schopenhauer concludes, citing the first principle of Buddhism as a religious anticipation of the same conception he arrives at through philosophical inquiry. Schopenhauer believes that there are nevertheless two paths to limited salvation from suffering, both of which involve denying or overcoming the individual empirical will experienced as desire in our mental lives.

The two methods of salvation involve either saintly religious asceticism, the monk's way; or self-transcending aesthetic contemplation of the beautiful and sublime, the way of the aesthetic genius, in which all persons can also participate at least to a limited extent. Schopenhauer rejects the existence of God, because there is nowhere in his metaphysics of the world as Will and representation, thing-in-itself and as it appears to the mind, where God as a divine personality might intelligibly be said to belong. As a result, despite praising certain religious doctrines as glimpses of more penetrating philosophical truths, Schopenhauer considers all conventional religion to be a poor substitute for rigorous metaphysics, suitable only for persons incapable of engaging in deep philosophical study. His works include *Fourfold Root of the Principle of Sufficient Reason* (1813), *On Sight and Colors* (1816), *The World as Will and Idea* (1818), *On the Will in Nature* (1836), *The Two Basic Problems of Ethics* (1841), and *Parerga und Paralipomena* (roughly translated as *Comments and Omissions*, 2 vols., 1851).

SCHWEITZER, ALBERT (1875–1965). A German philosopher, theologian, and doctor, distinguished by his advocacy of a reverence for life principle (that made vegetarianism essential) and his study of the historical Jesus. According to Schweitzer, Jesus lived in earnest expectation of the historical intervention by the

Father in bringing about the end of history. Jesus' radical ethic is to be understood on the grounds that it is an interim ethic, useful during the brief interim between the first coming of Jesus and the eschaton. His works include *The Quest of the Historical Jesus* (1906), *Paul and His Interpreters* (1911), *The Psychiatric Study of Jesus* (1913), *On the Edge of the Primeval Forest* (1920), *Cultural Philosophy* (2 vols. 1923), *Christianity and the Religions of the World* (1924), *Memoirs of Childhood and Youth* (1924), *Mysticism of Paul the Apostle* (1930), *More from the Primeval Forest* (1931), *Out of My Life and Thought: An Autobiography* (1931), *Indian Thought and Its Development* (1935), *From My African Notebook* (1938), and *Peace or Atomic War?* (1958).

SCIENCE AND RELIGION. In the West, the relationship between science and religion can be viewed in three ways. Probably most widely represented in popular culture is the conflict thesis, according to which religion has often served to impede scientific progress. The conflict thesis was advanced by John William Draper and Andrew Dickson White in the nineteenth century, who highlighted the church's resistance to Copernicus, Galileo, and Darwin. A second thesis is that religion provides an essential foundation for the practice of science. Acknowledging the regrettable times when the church failed to recognize good science, Alfred North Whitehead and others argued that theism provided early modern scientists a philosophical foundation for expecting the world to have a natural order that was rationally intelligible and explainable. Newton's claim that as a scientist he sought to think God's thoughts after him supports this positive stance. A third position may simply be called the complexity thesis, which neither sees science and religion in essential conflict nor sees religion as foundational to science. Such an outlook was articulated by William Whewell in the nineteenth century and Stephen Jay Gould in the twentieth century. Questions that arise in the literature on science and religion include: Does big bang cosmology support a theistic understanding of the cosmos? Does it appear that the emergence of life in the solar system rests on fine-tuning and is this best explained naturalistically or in terms of theism? Is evolutionary biology able to account for the emergence of consciousness, morality, and religion? Is evolutionary biology compatible with traditional Christianity? What impact might contemporary neurology have on the assessment of religious experience? Does contemporary physics support presentism (the idea that all times are equally real) and does this support the thesis that there may be a divine, eternal being for whom all times are present? Does science support or undermine concepts of freedom and responsibility?

SECULAR. Today the term is used frequently as "nonreligious," but originally it simply meant "worldly" and was used in contrast with living the monastic life. So, a priest who was active in the world was described as a secular priest.

SELF-DECEPTION. An important topic for Sartre's existentialism as well as what some call the methodology of suspicion in which questions are asked about a person's or institution's real, underlying motives. Nietzsche raised the question of whether the profession by Christians of a self-giving love for others was as it seems or, rather, stemmed from resentment. One of the paradoxes of self-deception is that it appears that a person cannot fully and self-consciously believe a contradiction. When one person, A, deceives another, B, then A gets B to believe something that A believes is false. This may be an unproblematic case of one person lying to another. But when you lie to yourself (and A is B), it seems that a subject has to simultaneously believe something she believes is false (e.g., Christians love the good because it is good) while realizing all along that she believes the contrary is true (e.g., Christians love what they call "good" not because it is good, but because in their weakness this allows them to control the powerful). To avoid this problem, accounts of self-deception often involve a division between the conscious and the unconscious, or they hold that self- deception occurs over time so that it is not carried out in a single moment of simultaneous deceiving and deception. *See also* BAD FAITH.

SELF, SELFHOOD. *See* SOUL.

SENECA, LUCIUS ANNEAUS (c. 1 BCE– 65 CE). Roman philosopher whose moral writings touch on proper living, the importance of restraint, and practical wisdom. He was an eclectic thinker, employing Stoic as well as Epicurean ideas. He had the misfortune of having his former student, the Emperor Nero, command that he commit suicide, which he did. Seneca was also a gifted dramatist and satirist.

SEPARATION OF CHURCH AND STATE. A political theory concerning religion, articulated in 1802 by U.S. President Thomas Jefferson. Jefferson wrote a letter to the Baptist Association of Danbury, Connecticut, explaining that the "establishment clause" of the First Amendment to the U.S. Constitution democratically built "a wall of separation between Church and State." Jefferson wrote, "religion is a matter which lies solely between man and his God," and "the legislative powers of government reach actions only, and not opinions." In consequence, the state shall not establish a church, nor privilege a church in matters of legislation. In this, Jefferson was drawing on the work of both Hobbes and Locke. Hobbes held that the church was not sovereign over the state, and that it therefore had no right to legislate. Locke argued that the state had no right to legislate concerning matters of conscience, but only concerning actions. Roger Williams, in the seventeenth century, and Thomas Paine, in the eighteenth, also articulated views akin to Jefferson's. The French political doctrine of *laïcité* (or secularism) and the U.N.'s Universal Declaration of Human Rights offer similar (though not identical) views of the relationship between religion and politics. Some contemporary political philosophers, notably René Girard and Gianni Vattimo, argue that while secularism has its roots in modern political liberalism, liberalism has its roots in Christianity, leading to the ironic conclusion that the separation of church and state is made possible by the influence of a church on the state. *See also* HOBBES and LOCKE.

SEVEN DEADLY SINS. The Seven Deadly Sins are the capital vices in Christianity. They are listed in increasing increments of evil: (1) Lust (*luxuria*), excessive thoughts and desires of a sexual nature, (2) Gluttony (*gula*), the over-indulgence in something, especially food, to the point of waste, (3) Greed (*avaritia*), acquisition of excessive wealth, (4) Sloth (*acedia*), spiritual or physical apathy by discontent, leading to failure to appreciate and act, (5) Wrath (*ira*), uncontrolled feelings of hatred and anger, (6) Envy (*invidia*), an insatiable coveting of the goods of others, and the wish to deprive them of their goods, (7) Pride (*superbia*), an undue idea of one's own greatness and ability, interfering with the individual's recognition of the grace of God. Pride is considered the sin from which other sins arise. This list of the seven was established by Gregory the Great. The Seven Deadly Sins were promoted through Dante's *Divine Comedy*, in which each wicked soul was punished for his sin accordingly by contrapasso (symbolic, poetic justice).

SEXTUS EMPIRICUS (c. 200 CE). Born in Greece, he is among the best known of the ancient Greco-Roman skeptics. He developed arguments against both the goodness of God and the intelligibility of the concept of God. His skepticism of our knowledge of the world was often structured on the basis of balancing counter-arguments. An argument for X (whatever it is) is only acceptable if there is not an equally good argument for not-X. The role of the skeptic is thus simply to provide good counter-arguments, and not to directly show why some positive arguments fail due to some internal logical problems. His works include *Outlines of Pyrrhonism* and *Adversos Mathematicos* (against the Professors, or Dogmatists).

SHAFTESBURY, ANTHONY ASHLEY COOPER, THIRD EARL OF (1671–1713). He defended a moral sense theory of ethics, according to which our sense of right and wrong as well as beauty and ugliness is grounded in our sensibilities. This school of thought, sometimes disparaged as sentimentalist, provided a rich account of values that, through an overriding theistic understanding of God as a beneficent creator, united ethics and aesthetics. His works include *Characteristics of Men, Manners, Opinions, and Times* (1711), *Soliloquy: or, Advice to an Author* (1710), and *Speeches of the Earl of Shaftesbury in Glasgow, August 1871* (1871).

SHAME. A feeling or emotion of embarrassment, dishonor, or a sense of regrettable failure. Shame need not be due to a moral failure for which one is personally responsible. So, while one may feel guilt as well as shame, a person can feel shame without feeling guilt. For example, a person may feel shame about being small of stature, but not feel guilty over his or her size. *See also* GUILT.

SHANKARA (a.k.a. Śaṅkara Bhagavatpādācārya or Ādi Śaṅkarācārya) (c. 788–820 CE). Shankara was the most influential proponent of the *Advaita Vedanta* school of Hinduism. He was born in Kalady (in the southwestern Indian state of Kerala) and reportedly mastered the Vedas by the age of eight. He became a *sannyasin* (itinerant holy man) and travelled to North India, where he became a disciple of Govinda Bhagavatpada. Shankara travelled throughout India, preaching Advaita and debating with philosophers of opposing schools of thought. Drawing mainly upon the *Upanishads*, the *Brahma Sutras*, and the *Bhagavad*

Gita, Shankara taught the unity of the infinite and indivisible *Brahman* and *atman* (the self). Since Brahman is the only ontological reality, the world does not have a separate or independent existence from Brahman. The essence of Shankara's interpretation is that Brahman is everything. While the Vedas, as *shruti* (revealed texts), are the ultimate source of knowledge, Shankara understands liberation to mean the direct and immediate understanding, with the help of the Vedas, of the identity of atman and Brahman. He opposed the ritualistic Mimamsa school and accorded importance to the wisdom teachings of the *Upanishads* (final sections of the Vedas). He founded four monasteries (*mathas*) for the dissemination of the teachings of Advaita. His works include commentaries (*Bhashyas*) on the *Upanishads*, the *Brahma Sutras*, and the *Bhagavad Gita*, in addition to a philosophical treatise (*Upadeshasahasri*) and devotional hymns.

SHINTOISM. Shintoism or Shinto, from the Sino-Japanese *shin* (gods) and *tō* (way or *dao*) refers to the indigenous religion that existed in Japan before the introduction of Buddhism and has coexisted with Buddhism to the present. It originated as a form of prehistoric animism and polytheism, emcompassing the worship of spirits representing different phenomena of nature and ancestors of clans. Eventually local religious cults were integrated with mythology. The Sun Goddess

Amaterasu, as the putative ancestor of the imperial family, emerged as the most important deity for the purposes of political legitimization. Yet Shinto is primarily concerned with nature. All great works of nature—waterfalls, huge trees, unusual rocks, and so on—are *kami* or sacred beings. *Kami* does not mean "god" or divinity in the Western sense, but suggests awesomeness and special powers. Emperors themselves came to be regarded as *kami*, but the distinction between humans and divinities was not clearly drawn. Shinto lacks any clear moral code—that came later with Buddhism. The stress in Shinto is not so much ethics or morality as it is ritual purity, which is tarnished by physical dirtiness, disease, menstruation, childbirth, wounds, and contact with death. Such defilement must be overcome by exorcism and cleansing ceremonies.

SIDGWICK, HENRY (1838–1900). British philosopher who advanced a systematic utilitarian ethic and developed an ideal observer theory, according to which right and wrong reflect the judgments of an observer, ideally situated in terms of knowledge, impartiality, and an affective awareness of all the involved parties. As a non-theist, Sidgwick thought there was no actual ideal observer (God), but he thought that ideally we should seek out such an ideal vantage point. His masterpiece, *Methods of Ethics*, was first published in 1874.

SIKHISM. A monotheistic religion that emerged in the Punjab region of India in the 1600s, based on the teachings of Guru Nanak (1469–1538) and the nine Gurus who followed him. Following the execution of the ninth Guru, Tegh Bahadur, by the Mughals in Delhi, the Sikh community or *Panth* became further solidified and militarized by the tenth Guru, Gobind Rai (a.k.a. Gobind Singh, meaning "lion"). In 1699, Gobind Singh established the *Khalsa*, a community of initiated (*amritdhari*) Sikhs who would defend the Guru and the Sikh Panth. Members of the *Khalsa* keep the five Ks: *kesh* (uncut hair), *kangha* (a steel comb in one's hair), *kach* (knee-length pants), *kara* (a steel bracelet on one's right wrist), and *kirpan* (a sword or dagger at one's side). After the death of Gobind Singh in 1708, Adi Guru (literally, the "original" or "first" Guru), the *Guru Granth Sahib*, which is a collection prayers and hymns, was established as the eleventh and final Guru. Today, the *Guru Granth Sahib* remains the sacred scripture of the Sikhs and plays a key role in their worship practices.

Sikhism drew upon the teachings of the two main religions in the Punjab region, Hinduism and Islam, but understands itself to be a separate and distinct religion. The central teaching of Sikhism is the oneness of God: the *Mul Mantra*, from Guru Nanak's first composition, begins with "*Ek Onkar*"—"There is one God." This God, who has many names but is most commonly referred to as *Waheguru* (a.k.a. *Vahiguru*, meaning "Wonderful

Lord" in the Gurmukhi language), is the formless and genderless creator of the universe who is the eternal truth (*ad sach*).

Sikhs believe in reincarnation and seek to overcome the painful cycle of death and rebirth (*chaurasi*) by following the teachings of the Sikh Gurus. Ultimately, it is only God's grace which may allow one to attain *mukti* (liberation), but one should strive to become more Guru-oriented (*gursikh*) and less self-oriented (*manmukh*). The name Sikh itself means "disciple" or "learner." Sikhs stress the importance of *nam* (the Name), *dan* (giving), and *isnan* (keeping clean). They believe in the equality of all people and reject the hierarchy intrinsic to the caste system, offering *langar*, a free meal, to all who come to their houses of worship, which are known as *gurudwaras* (literally, "Gate of the Guru"). Sikhs view religious diversity as a gift from God, understanding different forms of worship and religious traditions as contextual articulations of the one universal truth. In the *Dasam Granth*, Guru Gobind Singh wrote, "Recognize all human kind, whether Muslim or Hindu as one. The same God is the Creator and Nourisher of all. Recognize no distinction among them. The temple and the mosque are the same. So are Hindu worship and Muslim prayer. Human beings are all one." Today, there are about 20 million Sikhs in the world, most of whom live in the Punjab region of India.

SIMPLICITY. *See* **DIVINE SIMPLICITY.**

SIN. The concept of sin is principally found in theistic traditions and refers to a violation of God's will or commands. In traditions without a Godhead, such as early Buddhism, there is little room for the concept of sin. In theistic traditions, sin can be grounds for punishment or blame by God (even if sin is not a sufficient condition for a civil magistrate to impose punishment) and sins can be removed or covered (no longer constituting a barrier to relationship with God) by divine and human forgiveness and mercy. *See also* ORIGINAL SIN and SEVEN DEADLY SINS.

SINCERITY. Sincerity is closely associated with truth-telling. One fundamental sense of sincerity focuses on congruence between motivations and other internal states with external speech and action. The connection with truth is that one's speech or action is a true reflection of motivations or other internal states. Sincerity is not identical with truth in a wider sense (one can be sincerely mistaken). Another sense of sincerity has to do with congruence among or between internal states. This sense emphasizes that one is not internally conflicted with contradictory mental states which are allowed to exist as they are. In both of these senses of sincerity, related terms such as authenticity, purity, and openness carry something of the meaning of sincerity. To be insincere is to speak or act with a lack of openness because the world of inner states is hidden from the conversation partner or the external observer. An inauthentic person similarly exhibits a kind of deceitfulness, either toward others (internal states are deliberately hidden and incongruent external states are exhibited), or within oneself by permitting self-deception (an inconsistency among internal states which is masked either deliberately or unconsciously). Sincerity is considered a virtue, but in much contemporary usage it is a fairly "thin" or "flat" virtue without much robust content. One could fail in terms of many more important virtues but still be accorded the virtue of sincerity (with the implication that in most other ways the person fails and is misguided). But not just any congruence between inner and outer states can be called sincere. Thus, it would be odd to speak of someone as "sincerely cruel." This suggests an additional factor of some type of purity which is a grounding for sincerity or to which sincerity as a virtue is tethered. This condition of purity (in some relevant sense) seems to be invoked when, instead of individual actions, a person is characterized as sincere. Sincerity has waxed and waned as an aesthetic virtue in Western literature. In the eighteenth century it began to be prized as an aesthetic quality so that poetry, for example, was judged to be better if it possessed sincerity in the sense that it matched inner states of the poet, or arose from appropriate authentic inner states. Later, due in part to the notoriously difficult business of ascertaining authorial intention, sincerity became much less important aesthetically.

SKEPTICISM. There is a sense in which no philosophy, let alone philosophy of religion, is possible without some skepticism. When Augustine professed to believe in the God of Christianity he was, in essence, being skeptical about the gods of Imperial Rome. As Augustine and Descartes noted, there are degrees of skepticism. Modest forms of skepticism make sense in certain contexts, but it is more problematic when skepticism is projected universally. For example, if someone who claims to be a skeptic charges that no person knows anything, it appears that the "skeptic" is not really skeptical, but is making a radical claim that reaches almost breath-taking proportions. Can one know that no one has ever known anything? To answer this in the negative would seem to require a Herculean task of examining every possible knower. And then if the person did claim to know that no one knows anything, the person would seem to refute her own position for (if she is right) then she knows something (and thus she is wrong).

SMITH, ADAM (1723–1790). Scottish economist and philosopher, Smith

217

developed an account of the wealth of nations. He advocated small scale, free trade and a free market in which rational individuals seek their self-interest. He held that, ideally, if all seek their self-interest, they will be guided by "an invisible hand" to bring about the best outcome for all involved. Smith also articulated an ideal observer theory. He thought that moral evaluations are grounded in knowledge and sympathy with others as we consider their welfare from an impartial point of view. His works include *The Theory of the Moral Sentiments* (1759) and *An Inquiry into the Nature and Causes of the Wealth of Nations* (1776).

SOCRATES (c. 470–399 BCE). A classical Greek philosopher recognized as one of the primary founders of Western philosophy. We have no writings from Socrates himself, but we know about him through accounts from Aristophanes, Xenophon, and Plato. Socrates was a staunch believer in examining and reexamining one's life. He professed that wisdom can only come about through the admittance that one is not omniscient and actually ignorant of all the information. This would be necessary to be ethically virtuous, which held more importance than living to Socrates. Socrates was charged with irreverence for failing to treat the gods of Athens with due respect, thereby corrupting the youth. The tale of his death in Plato's *Phaedo* promotes a foundational view of this life

as transient. He stood firm with his beliefs at the cost of his life, and he accepted his death as the release or freeing of his soul from his body.

SOLIPSISM. Someone is a solipsist if she thinks only she exists. Old joke: There once was a person who adapted solipsism and was curious why more people aren't solipsists. While the "joke" is based on confusion, there is a kind of moral solipsism that can be shared by more than one person. A solipsist in morality acts only on the assumption that she exists as a person; others function only to use for private reason.

SOPHISM. An early school of thinkers who specialized in the art of arguments and often provided lessons in the art of arguments for fees. Sophism was critiqued by some early philosophers who contended that the sophists were not driven by the love of wisdom, but more by a love for winning disputes.

SORCERY. The practice of black magick and channeling of evil forces to have unnatural effects on the world. There is some mention of sorcery in the Bible: Leviticus 19:26 states, ". . . Do not practice divination or sorcery." Deuteronomy 18:10 declares "Let no one be found among you who sacrifices his son or daughter in the fire, who practices divination or sorcery,

SPINOZA, BENEDICT DE

interprets omens, engages in witchcraft." And Acts 8:9–11 says: "Now for some time a man named Simon had practiced sorcery in the city and amazed all the people of Samaria. He boasted that he was someone great, and all the people, both high and low, gave him their attention and exclaimed, 'This man is the divine power known as the Great Power.' They followed him because he had amazed them for a long time with his magic." *See also* WICCA.

SORLEY, WILLIAM R. (1855–1935). A British philosopher, strongly opposed to utilitarianism and a mechanical view of the natural world. Sorley developed a theistic argument on the grounds of objective moral values. He reasoned that objective moral values were, by nature, dependent upon mind, and that merely human minds could not secure such objective value. Rather, only an unchanging, omnipotent God can provide a secure grounding for objective values. His works include *The Ethics of Naturalism* (1885), *Recent Tendencies in Ethics* (1904), *Moral Values and the Idea of God* (1918), and *A History of English Philosophy* (1920).

SOTERIOLOGY. From the Greek *soterion* meaning "salvation" (*soter* means "savior" or "redeemer") + *logos* meaning "study." Thus, soteriology refers to the theology of salvation. For instance, Christian soteriology focuses on the salvific

nature of Jesus Christ, Buddhist soteriology emphasizes liberation from suffering, and so on. *See also* UNIVERSALISM.

SOUL. Sometimes used interchangeably with self or selfhood, "soul" is often used informally to refer to someone's integrity ("he lost his soul by getting an academic post through selective, sycophantish praise of the appointment committee") or technically, as a nonphysical locus of personal identity ("when he dies, his soul will be with the Lord"). Aristotle used the term we translate as "soul" in a more general sense to refer to the form or principle of life of an organism. On this view, plants have souls.

SPACE. In some religious traditions, particular places have religious significance: Mecca (for Muslims), for example, and Jerusalem (for all three Abrahamic traditions). Classical theism holds that God is omnipresent and so there is no place where God is absent. Newton proposed that space itself is a divine attribute so that we (literally) live and move in God. Some late twentieth-century theologians such as Sallie McFague have proposed that the spatial cosmos should (at least metaphorically) be regarded as God's body.

SPINOZA, BENEDICT DE (a.k.a. Baruch de Spinoza) (1632–1677). Rationalist philosopher of Portuguese Jewish

219

descent born in Amsterdam. He was excommunicated from the synagogue in 1656 for heretical views such as the belief that God has a body and the denial of the immortality of the soul. Spinoza believed that philosophy should be done in a deductive method like geometry, and his principle work, the posthumous *Ethica Ordine Geometrico Demonstrata* (1677), reflects this view. Spinoza's philosophy draws on classical Stoicism, medieval Jewish thought, and Cartesian philosophy. Spinoza found Cartesian dualism unintelligible and embraced substance monism, the belief that all particular things are merely finite modes of one substance. In Spinoza's view, this substance is God, and it is infinite and consists of infinite attributes. God is the only free cause, though whether God is considered as the active *natura naturans* or the passive *natura naturata*, God is determined by his essential nature, and the result is Spinoza's affirmation of determinism. Spinoza's rejection of Descartes' views of substance simplified the mind-body problem, as he only had to deal with one substance rather than with two totally distinct ones. Spinoza understood the mind as the idea of the body, so that the body is a finite mode explicated under the attribute of extension, while the mind is the same mode explicated under the attribute of thought. Salvation for Spinoza consists of the medieval concept of the intellectual love of God (*amor intellectualis Dei*), though without the Jewish and Christian conception of God as a being subject to the passions and with a will, combined with a Stoic acceptance of the necessity of all things however they occur. His works include *Descartes' Principles of Philosophy* (1663), and *Theological-Political Treatise* (1670).

SPIRIT. *See PNEUMA.*

SPIRITUAL / SPIRITUALITY. That which has to do with matters of the spirit, often conceived of in opposition to the physical or material world. Spirituality emphasizes the connection between one's own inner spirit and the divine. Spiritual practices include prayer, meditation, and so on. Traditionally, the spiritual was contrasted with the secular, but today it is often contrasted with religion: e.g., "I'm spiritual but not religious." This use of the term highlights the personal, non-dogmatic nature of spirituality. Many religious practitioners, however, cultivate a deep spirituality within a particular religious tradition.

STEINER, RUDOLF (1861–1925). A German philosopher who developed an organic view of human history, according to which human life is evolving into the realm of spiritual freedom and fulfillment. Initially drawn to theosophy (a late nineteenth-century movement that centered on God and spirituality but not as limited to any one religion), he came to see Jesus Christ as having a more vital cosmic role than theosophy allowed. He called his more Christ-centered spirituality "anthroposophy." Steiner promoted the arts as well as philosophy, and his work inspired the Woldorff school movement.

STOICISM. A school of philosophy founded in the late second century BCE in Athens by Zeno of Citium. The name "Stoic" comes from the Greek for "porch," as that names the area in which they met. Stoicism became a broad movement, defined by adherents' allegiance to *logos* or reason, the subordination of passion to reason, their conviction in a single, good God or divine being, and natural law. It is from Stoic sources that we derive the vision of the whole world as (ideally) constituting a singe polis or city (hence: cosmopolitanism). Tillich thought that Stoicism was a major competing alternative to Christianity. In fact, many Christians have had strong Stoical tendencies, as may be seen in the work of Boethius or even Richard Swinburne. Some of Swinburne's defense of the goodness of God has roots in Stoic arguments that the good of a natural world had to come with some liabilities.

SUÁREZ, FRANCISCO (1548–1617). A Spanish philosopher who, like Molina, developed a middle-knowledge account of God's prescience. His works include *Disputationes Metaphysicae* (1597) and *De legibus, ac Deo legislatore* (1612).

SUB SPECIE AETERNITATIS. Latin, meaning "under the aspect of eternity." Phrase used by Spinoza in his *Ethics* to refer to the highest form of knowledge. As a term, it can also apply to Boethius' project of coming to understand worldly, temporal goods and fate from the standpoint of the eternal God.

SUBJECT / SUBJECTIVITY. "Subject" usually refers to persons and "subjectivity" usually refers to the emotions, feelings, and psychological states of persons. Sometimes a judgment may be said to be subjective when it reflects the personal preferences of a subject and not a matter of impartial reflection.

SUBLIME. Early modern European philosophers used the term in contrast to the beautiful; the sublime involves a feeling of awe, dread, possibly even terror, though from a position of safety.

SUI GENERIS. A thing or event is sui generis when it is a unique kind of thing. According to many theologians, God is sui generis.

SUICIDE. Literally means self-killing. For some philosophers, suicide is a form of self-murder; the mere fact that the killer and the one killed are the same person does not excuse the murder.

Christian ethics traditionally forbids suicide as part of the general prohibition against homicide as well as on the grounds that suicide abrogates divine providence and the prerogatives of God, viz. the time of your death is not up to you. In the face of evidence that some kill themselves in states of insanity or chronic depression that robs them of the power of free agency, some Christians recognize exculpatory conditions that disassociate suicide and murder. Controversy has emerged when persons may undertake an act that will end their lives in an honorable fashion, as (for example) when morphine is administered to a person terminally ill and this will in turn hasten (or cause) death. Jewish ethics allows that some acts are permissible involving self-sacrifice that are akin to suicide, in a just cause.

SUMMUM BONUM. Latin, "the highest good." The term has been used to refer to that which is of the greatest value. This greatest value may be a single thing (e.g., pleasure) or it may be complex (e.g., a combination of practical, aesthetic, cognitive, and sensory activities and states).

SUPERNATURAL. From the Latin *super,* "above" and *natura,* "nature." Refers to God or gods or incorporeal agents such as angels or demons. Because "supernatural" is sometimes associated with the "superstitious," some use the term

"supra-natural" to refer to God and / or other realities that are beyond corporeal, cosmic agents.

SUPERSTITION. From the Latin *super,* meaning "above" and *stare* meaning "to stand;" superstition means "to stand over." Used as a term of disapprobation. A belief is superstition if it is held in the face of strong counter-evidence, based on fear, or based on an inadequate amount of evidence.

SUSPICION. Like skepticism, suspicion involves withholding assent to propositions. However, whereas skepticism is directed toward truth, facts, or evidence offered in support of truth, suspicion is directed toward the people offering the evidence, or toward their motives for offering them. Suspicion is thus a matter of hermeneutics, or of the art of interpretation.

Suspicion is a useful took for critiquing religion, because it allows the critic to set aside evidential claims and to focus instead on an examination of the reasons why people have religious belief in the first place. Examples can be found in Feuerbach's argument that God is a projection of human self-consciousness or in Marx's idea that religion is ultimately a political ideology. Similarly, Nietzsche and Freud offer accounts of religion based in the psychology of resentment or desire. More recently, Daniel Dennett has argued that religion is the result of an evolutionary process. In each case, religion's truth-claims may be dismissed once it is seen why these claims are proffered.

Others have suggested that the hermeneutics of suspicion is beneficial to both philosophical theology and to the practice of religion. Merold Westphal and Bruce Benson, for example, have argued that suspicion helps expose self-deception and idolatry, especially the idolizing of ideologies. *See also* FEUERBACH; FREUD; MARX; and NIETZSCHE.

SYMBOL. The word "symbol" is derived from two Greek words meaning "bringing together," suggesting the bringing together of two otherwise unrelated things so that one comes to signify the other. In theology, sacraments are sometimes taken as symbols of the mystery of Christ's incarnation. In philosophy, the most important figure for understanding symbols is Charles Peirce. Peirce's semiotics distinguishes between three classes of signs: icons, indices, and symbols. An icon signifies by being somehow like the thing signified, as a picture of the sun might be an icon for the sun itself. An index signifies not by similarity but dynamically, as pointing with one's finger at the sun is an index of the direction in which it lies, or as a sundial indicates the time of day. A symbol signifies by being a general rule, as for instance words regularly signify the things they name; so the words "sun," "soleil," "sol," and "helios," all symbolize the star nearest our planet. Symbols may thus have an arbitrary relation to the thing signified, and they do not need to be like or dynamically related to it.

SYNCRETISM. The combination of various beliefs and practices to form new ones. The term is usually applied to religions, but it may also be applied to philosophies. The Caribbean religion of *Santería*, for example, combines elements of Roman Catholicism and of Yoruba religious practice. Similarly, Augustine's thought displays syncretism in its combining of Christian theology, Ciceronian rhetorical theory, and Neoplatonist metaphysics.

T

TAOISM. *See* DAOISM.

TAWHID. The Islamic belief in God's oneness. This is often held up in discussions with Christians about Jesus, who Muslims believe to be a prophet and not a "partner with God." *See also* MONOTHEISM.

TEILHARD DE CHARDIN, PIERRE (1881–1955). Teilhard was born near Clermont-Ferrand, France, the fourth of eleven children to the great grandniece of Voltaire and a man interested in natural science. He attended Notre Dame de Mongre boarding school where he decided to become a Jesuit. Although he had a passion for Jesuit scholarship, his passion for geology and paleontology (inspired by his father) played a strong role in his life. He had a teaching internship at the Jesuit college in Cairo in 1905, lived as a Jesuit scholar for four years in France from 1908 to 1912, served in World War I, and after returning to France he completed his Ph.D. in geology. He spent several years in China studying fossils where he and a Jesuit friend founded the Institute of Geobiology in Peking, and then he traveled to the Far East for his study of natural history. Teilhard moved to New York with the permission of the Jesuit Superiors for the last years of his life; he died Easter morning of 1955.

Teilhard's philosophy was formed on his passions for both science and religion, of which his Jesuit leaders were not fond. He claimed that consciousness and matter are of the same reality and that evolution is the growth of consciousness and complexity of beings. He argued that a belief in evolution does not mean a denial of Christianity because as human beings (and life in general) evolved, consciousness evolved as well, and, quoting the Bible passage "I am the Alpha and the Omega" (Revelation 1:8), he said that humans become more divine through evolution as consciousness grew from alpha to omega. His most famous work is *The Phenomenon of Man* (1955).

TELEOLOGICAL ARGUMENT FOR THE EXISTENCE OF GOD. Approaches that stress the apparent value and purposive nature of the cosmos, arguing that this provides some reason to believe there is an intentional, powerful, good, and creative reality that creates and sustains the cosmos.

TELOS. Greek for "end." The purpose or end of a goal directed process or, more broadly, the good or use of an object. The *telos* of a tree may include growth; the *telos* or end of human life may include multiple goods.

TERTULLIAN (c. 160–c. 220 CE). A North African theologian deeply opposed to the bonding between revealed theology and pre-Christian, pagan philosophy. He construed Christian truths as apparent absurdities from the point of view of pagan thought. Tertullian was deeply opposed to Gnostic forms of Christianity and he upheld what may be described as a materialist account of human persons. His works include *Treatise against Hermongenes* and *De Anima* (On the soul).

THALES (fl. 580s BCE). Pre-Socratic philosopher from Miletus in Asia Minor. Seeking a single material cause for all being, Thales posited that it was water. Thales appears to have advocated hylozoism, the doctrine that all matter is alive, or has a soul. *See also* PRE-SOCRATICS.

THEISM. A term that was introduced in the seventeenth century in English to refer to the belief in a single Creator-God who is omniscient, omnipotent, all good, omnipresent, eternal or everlasting, and a being that does not depend on any other being for its existence. Theists believe that the cosmos exists due to the causal conserving power of God and, if the cosmos had a beginning, it originated by God's creating it. As opposed to deists, theists believe that God is revealed in human history. Theism is not limited to Judaism, Christianity, and Islam. Theistic elements may be found in Hinduism and elsewhere. *See also* ABRAHAMIC FAITHS and MONOTHEISM.

THEODICY. From the Greek *theos* "god" + *dikē* "judgment" or "right." A theodicy is an account of why an all-good, all-powerful, all-loving God allows (or does not prevent) what appears to be the evil of or in creation. *See also* EVIL, THE PROBLEM OF.

THEOLOGIAN. One who engages in theological inquiry.

THEOLOGY. From the Greek *theos* + *logos* ("God" + "word"). Theology is study of the nature of God and the relationship between God and the world. The term was first used by Plato in the *Republic* (Book II, Ch. 18). Theology is divided into two main categories: historical theology, wherein one describes the theology articulated by previous thinkers, and constructive theology, wherein one articulates one's own picture and understanding of God. *See also* NATURAL THEOLOGY and REVEALED THEOLOGY.

THOMISM. *See* **AQUINAS, THOMAS OF.**

TILLICH, PAUL (1886–1965). Tillich is perhaps the most important Protestant theologian of the twentieth century. More appropriately labeled, he is a historical theologian as well as a philosopher. At the core of his work is the "method of correlation," developed in his three-volume work titled *Systematic Theology* (1951–1963). The "method of correlation" combined philosophy and theology by posing existential questions and then looking to Christian revelation and its symbols for the answers to these existential questions. This method gave theology a more universal applicability. While this method is defined in the aforementioned work, his most popular work is *The Courage to Be* (1952).

The Courage to Be discusses the anxiety of the current age, defining the predominant anxiety of the time as anxiety of meaningless, which is to say we are worried about losing all meaning. In response to this, Tillich proposes absolute faith as the answer, meaning we accept the fact that we are not accepted by anyone or anything. Under this absolute faith, God is not tied to any particular symbol of a deity—God beyond the God tied up in the symbol. With absolute faith, God beyond God grabs control of us and gives on the courage to be.

Tillich's work is highly important in the field of philosophy of religion. He defines religion as when the unconditioned grasps us out of a state of purely being. The philosophy of religion, for Tillich, has a problem in that philosophy cannot define areas closed off to it and those that need reflection. In response to this, Tillich discusses the subject / object relationship, which is a form of conditioned being. In discussing God, we bring God into our finite world, which is a paradox. Philosophy of religion, then, is not based upon a decision we make regarding the nature of religion, but about a paradox. Now we can experience a critical moment where we experience the unconditioned. Tillich's other works include *The Religious Situation* (1932), *The Interpretation of History* (1936), *The Protestant Era* (1948), *The Shaking of the Foundations* (1948), *Love, Power, and Justice* (1955), *Dynamics of Faith* (1957), *Theology of Culture* (1959), *Christianity and the Encounter of the World Religions* (1963), and *Morality and Beyond* (1963).

TIME. The perceived continuous change in the world which is denoted by changes in objects or states. Most people assume that time is a basic part of reality. However, the theory of the unreality of time, most notably advanced by Kant, argues that time is simply a construct or framework through which people view the world but actually only exists in the mind. The world itself does not have a temporal component.

Beyond the reality / unreality of time debate, there is also a debate between the "A" theory of time and the "B" theory of time. The "A" theory of time argues that time is like a string stretched out with a knife being dragged across it. Where the knife has already been is the past, where the knife will go is the future, and where the knife currently is is the present. The present is real while the past is what was real and the future is what will be real. The "B" theory of time argues that time is more like a tapestry that shows all things happening at once. This means that all different times are equally real and no time can be argued to be past, present, or future. Thus, the "B" theory of time is sometimes called the tenseless theory of time. Another dispute that involves time is the argument of God's place in time. Some think that God is in the same time as us and can change, just like everything else. Others think that God is outside of time, existing eternally in one unchanging instant and viewing all of time at once. Also, some argue that God was outside of time until God created time. God then entered into our time, but will be outside of our time again after the created universe has ended.

TOLERATION. The enduring of that which is deemed wrong or disagreeable. Toleration is distinct from respect. A person may tolerate what he or she respects and deems socially important or a person may tolerate what she does not respect. An example of the former might be a society which tolerates (does not prosecute) pacifists on the grounds that it is good for persons to follow their conscience even if that conflicts with the majority decisions of the society. An example of the second may be "soft pornography" which a society may not respect, but it judges that to prohibit such pornography would create great damage, e.g., giving rise to an even more intolerable underground movement is sex trafficking. Alternatively, someone may respect what they do not tolerate. Someone might admire the determination and love that a Jehovah Witness displays for her child, but not tolerate her religiously motivated refusal to let her child receive a blood transfusion when necessary to save the child's life.

TOLSTOY, LEO (1828–1910). Chiefly known as an outstanding Russian novelist, Tolstoy also defended a form of

Christianity that included a creed of nonviolence. Tolstoy approached Christian faith as the answer to a fundamental question: What is the meaning of life? His personal life led him to think his own choice was finding meaning in Christ or meaninglessness. Tolstoy was a stern opponent of patriotism, which he saw as the root of much European violence. He held that a mark of excellence in works of art include the moral concert of the works themselves; a work of art that promoted unjust cruelty as part of its content is bad as a work of art. In addition to his major novels such as *War and Peace* (1869), Tolstoy wrote multiple short stories involving angels and the miraculous. His works include *A Confession* (1879–1882), *What I Believe* (1882–1884), *What Then Must We Do?* (1882–1886), *The Kingdom of God Is Within You* (1890–1893), *The Christian Teaching* (1894–1896), and *What Is Art?* (1897–1898).

TRANSCEND / TRANSCENDENCE. To transcend is to go beyond or to be beyond. In theism, God is ascribed with transcendence insofar as God is not identical to (and is thus beyond) the cosmos.

TRANSCENDENTALISM. Transcendentalism was a nineteenth-century American movement reacting to materialist and mechanistic philosophies of the Enlightenment including the sensationalist psychology of Locke, the physics of Newton, and mechanistic philosophies like that of de la Mettrie. Inspired by European Romanticism and by the writings of Coleridge, Wordsworth, Carlyle, Swedenborg, and Cousin, transcendentalists urged self-culture and self-reliance, personal liberty and social transformation, and an original and personal relationship with the divine, sometimes including mysticism. Some transcendentalists, encouraged by Charles Fourier's social philosophy, engaged in utopian social experiments like the Fruitlands and Brook Farm. Others engaged in polemics against social ills like war, slavery, and the mistreatment of Native Americans.

Ralph Waldo Emerson claimed that the name "transcendentalism" was taken from Kant, though it is plain that Emerson and Kant use the word quite differently. Whereas Kant was referring to the attempt to establish an a priori basis for reason (hence "transcending" experience), Emerson used it in a way reminiscent of the Neoplatonist drive to transcend nature in order to perceive the spiritual unity that lies behind all nature.

From its earliest days, transcendentalism has been criticized as not sufficiently rigorous to count as philosophy. Transcendentalist writings are often impassioned and lyrical, freely mixing the language of poetry, philosophy, and religion. The transcendentalists countered that they had no need to write or live according to the traditions of those who preceded them. While they drew broadly on the Western philosophical tradition—from Plato and the Stoics to Boehme and Kant—both Emerson and Henry David Thoreau also actively sought new sources of inspiration in the sacred texts of Asia. Later transcendentalists turned their attention increasingly to the observation of natural phenomena or of current politics.

Prominent transcendentalist figures include, in addition to Emerson, Henry David Thoreau, Orestes Brownson, James Marsh, Amos Bronson Alcott, George Ripley, Margaret Fuller, and Frederick Henry Hedge. Transcendentalism was a significant influence on the development of both American Pragmatism and environmentalism. *See also* EMERSON.

TRANSFER OF MERIT. Merit is that which accrues to one as a result of performing morally good actions. At times this is construed as a reward or standing. Merit can accrue both in the case of obligatory actions and in non-obligatory (supererogatory) actions. The notion of merit appears in a wide range of traditions. In the Buddhist tradition, merit is associated with the karmic benefits of morally good actions; however, merit can also be attained by various ritual actions beyond the scope of normal morality. *Bodhisattvas*, as they develop, create virtually infinite storehouses of merit which they intend to use compassionately to assist sentient beings. The transfer of merit under the strict interpretation of the law

of karma would seem to be impossible since karmic doctrine is that karmic effects must be worked out in each individual's causal stream. However, Buddhist practice developed a variety of methods of transfer of merit. The merit from a ritual action or good deed could intentionally be directed toward the benefit of some other being (e.g., an ancestor, a hungry ghost, a family member). Fields of merit—where the merit is sown, so to speak—are also significant in Buddhism. Thus, meritorious deeds to help the religious community (*sangha*) create more merit than similar deeds done outside of that context. The transfer of merit itself is a meritorious action, so there is no net loss of one's own accrued merit when one intentionally directs the fruits of an action to another. Spells and incantations (*dharani*) in some traditions are recited to invoke the transfer of merit from the merit storehouses of buddhas, etc. when one is in distress.

In the Christian tradition, the concept of merit is associated with rewards received from God due to God's promises; in addition, meritorious action is usually held to be possible due to the assistance of God's grace. Merit (in the sense of good works) was part of the controversy which led to the split between Catholics and Protestants. In the Roman Catholic Church, transfer of merit is possible through prayer requesting aid from Christ, Mary, and the saints, due to the surplus merit they possess. *See also* FORGIVENESS.

TRANSMIGRATION. Also called metempsychosis, the transmigration of souls is a belief held by many different cultures and religious groups. It is a belief in a soul's ability to pass from a person to another person, animal, or other object after death. Australian Aboriginal people believe the souls of their ancestors enter into newborns, so that the soul is repeatedly reborn. Hinduism believes the soul's rebirth is determined by its moral behavior in the past. Pythagoras was a believer in the transmigration of souls, which is where Plato obtained some of his ideas on metempsychosis.

TRANSUBSTANTIATION. Transubstantiation is a way of expressing the Real Presence of Christ in the Eucharist settled upon in medieval Western Christianity and presently held by the Roman Catholic Church. Assertions or suggestions that Christ was present in the Eucharist can be found in ancient Christian thinkers, but theological reflection at that time focused on baptism as the rite of initiation and salvation. The first controversy on the Eucharist to provoke treatises on the subject occurred in the ninth century, when Paschasius Radbertus argued that Christ's body and blood were physically present in the Eucharist, against the idea that Christ was present in divine power. Radbertus prevailed and was widely cited when another controversy broke out in the eleventh century. At that time, Berengar of Tours insisted that the body of Christ in the Eucharist could not be the same body born from Mary and raised to God's right hand; instead, Christ's body and blood became present with the bread and wine in a mysterious way comparable to the incarnation. His opponents drew on the common view that the mass participates in Christ's sacrifice on the Cross to say that Christ—and Christ alone—must therefore be physically present at the sacrifice. In the twelfth century, as philosophical vocabulary became more precise, the term "transubstantiation" was introduced to describe the conversion of bread and wine into Christ's body and blood without changing their appearance. (The unchanged appearance was seen as a challenge to Christians' faith and a way to avoid the horror of cannibalism.) The term appeared formally in 1215 in the Fourth Lateran Council's first constitution.

In the Reformation, different views on the presence of Christ in the Eucharist were proposed: it was a memorial (Zwingli); it was a spiritual rather than physical conveyance of the power of Christ's body (Calvin); it was a physical presence that didn't replace the bread and wine but was there with them, sometimes called "consubstantiation" (Wyclif). Only in 1551 did the Roman Catholic Church formally define its doctrine of the Eucharist at the 13th session of the Council of Trent: there, the complete conversion of the substance of bread and wine into the substance of Christ's body and blood at the consecration was "fittingly called transubstantiation." Related ideas include (1) the presence of Christ's entire body, blood, soul, and divinity in each fragment of the bread and wine, and (2) the endurance of Christ's presence in the Eucharist even after the mass, so that the Eucharist should be worshiped in the same way t hat God is worshiped. These views are still taught in the recent Catechism of the Catholic Church. *See also* EUCHARIST.

TRINITY, DOCTRINE OF. In Christianity, the belief that God is not a homogenous or undifferentiated being but rather that God is one in substance and three in persons: Father, Son, and Holy Spirit. The triune nature of God has been treated in the Western church as involving the Father begetting the Son and the Holy Spirit proceeding from the Father and the Son. For the Orthodox in the East, the Holy Spirit is understood as proceeding from the Father and who, together with the Father and the Son, is to be worshiped and glorified. Traditional, canonical views of the trinity in the Church (both East and West) have sought a middle ground, avoiding what are generally seen as unacceptable alternatives. Among the views that traditional Christianity seeks to avoid is modalism, which sees the Father, Son, and Holy Spirit as three modes or ways in which God is revealed to creation. In some churches, modalism is suggested when a blessing is offered in the name of God, as creator redeemer, and sanctifier. These three titles refer to God as revealed in human history as opposed to referring to the Godhead without reference to modes of divine action in the world. Another unacceptable position is some form of tri-theism in which Christians wind up acknowledging three Gods. A recent project among some Christian philosophers is to defend what is called a social theory of the trinity according to which there are three divine centers of consciousness but not three distinct Gods.

TRUTH & FALSEHOOD. According to realism, truth and falsehood are propositional values. Propositions like $2 + 2 = 4$ or "There are planets," are true when the state of affairs they refer to obtain. Arguably, the first proposition has always and will always obtain, whereas the second obtains now but did not obtain 14.5 billion years ago at what is believed to be the Big Bang. The propositions "There are unicorns" and "Napoleon won the Battle of Waterloo" are false because the relevant states of affairs do not obtain. This form of realism is Platonic and allows that the existence of truth and falsehood does not depend on the existence of minds or language. A correspondence account, according to which truth and falsehood are a function of sentences that either correspond or do not correspond with reality, faces the problem of holding that there are no truths if there are no sentences. A coherent, epistemic theory of truth is that a sentence or proposition is true if it coheres with an ideal body of

U

UBIQUITY. *See* OMNIPRESENCE.

UNCLEAN. *See* IMPURITY.

UNDERHILL, EVELYN (1875–1941). A British poet and scholar whose work on mysticism caused a revival of interest in mysticism throughout the West, especially in the English-speaking world. Her short book, *Practical Mysticism* (first published in 1911), was hugely popular, and her extensive study, *Mysticism* (also published in 1911), was and is regarded as a masterpiece.

UNITARIANISM. The name of an anti-Trinitarian movement with elements going back to the sixteenth century. For much of its history, the movement recognized Jesus as the Messiah, but not as the second member of the trinity. Today, the religious body of Unitarianism is more comprehensive and not committed to Jesus as Messiah or Redeemer.

UNITY OF SPACE. The thesis that all spatial objects are some distance from any (and thus every) spatial object. Some believe that there may be objects (dreams) or realms (heaven) that are spatial but not some distance from the spatial objects in our cosmos.

UNIVERSALISM. Universalism is the doctrine that eventually all persons will be reconciled to God and finally saved. Although this view has been largely rejected in the Christian tradition, if not considered a heresy, it was defended by a few Church Fathers, most notably Origen. Most Christian theologians and biblical scholars have held that the Bible clearly rules out universalism, teaching that some persons will be eternally lost. More recently, universalism has been defended as at least a possibility, if not a probability, by some noted theologians and philosophers. A few have taken a stronger view and have argued that universalism is the only view that is compatible with God's perfect power and goodness, and is therefore the only position that is possibly true. Although the advocates of universalism are perhaps increasing in number, it is still a distinctly minority position.

Two very different accounts have been given for why some will be lost. On one side, there is a significant Christian tradition that holds that God chooses unconditionally who will be saved and who will be lost, so it is God who determines that some persons will be eternally damned. On the other side, it is held that some people will, by their own free will, decisively reject God, and consequently be lost. On this view, God wills for all to be saved, so if any are not, it is entirely due to their own blameworthy choice. Advocates of universalism challenge key assumptions of both of these positions. With regard to the first, and in agreement with the second, they would contend that God truly loves all persons and would never determine anyone to be lost. Responding to the second position is more difficult, for if God has made us free in such a way that our choices are not determined, then it seems possible that some will be lost even if God desires to save them. This is recognized by those who hold to universalism tentatively, who argue that it is possibly or probably true, and we can rightly hope that it is. It is their view that human freedom does not necessarily rule out universalism: given enough time, we may hope that God will be able to win all persons and all will freely repent and be saved.

Those who hold that universalism is the only position that is possibly true contend that freedom, rightly understood, does not pose an obstacle. Two distinct moves have been made. First, it has been argued that there is no intelligible motive for anyone freely to choose eternal damnation. Such a choice would entail ever increasing misery, and at some point, all persons would be moved to repent and accept salvation. So the idea that any rational agent could freely choose eternal hell and be forever lost is simply incoherent. Second, it is argued that a loving God would, if necessary, override human freedom in order to assure the salvation of all persons. According to this view, the value and significance of human freedom have been overestimated, and it is wrongheaded to think God would be honoring us to give us the power to destroy ourselves in an ultimate sense. A loving God would not give us such a dangerous gift.

Clearly, the plausibility of universalism depends on one's judgments about the value of human freedom as well as one's assessment of whether a decisive choice of evil makes moral and psychological sense.

UNIVERSALS. Types or kinds of things such as human beings or animals. Universals are properties which may be multiply instantiated. Presumably, you and the authors of this entry exemplify the universal *human being* or property of being human. Christian philosophers have differed about whether Christ died for each human being as individuals or for a universal.

UPANISHADS. Philosophical discourses at the end of the Vedas. *See also* HINDU-ISM and VEDANTA.

UTILITARIANISM. A form of conse-quentialism, utilitarians measure good and evil, right and wrong, in terms of maximizing some end such as happiness, pleasure, or the satisfaction of prefer-ences. There is a difference between act utilitarianism and rule utilitarianism. According to act utilitarianism, an act is morally right if there is no other act available to the agent that will produce greater well-being. According to rule util-itarianism, an act is right if there is no alternative act that conforms to a right rule, and a right rule is such that confor-mity to it will produce maximal utility or well-being. Utilitarianism is distinct from egoism and may even require the heroic sacrifice of the agent. If the end to be sought is very general, as in pleasure or the minimization of pain, utilitarianism may justify ambitious practices of popu-lation growth or a re-examination of current use of animals for food, and so on. Utilitarianism faces objections in the name of justice; e.g., might cases arise when utilitarianism would warrant unjust punishment?

V

VALUES. *See* **AXIOLOGY.**

VEDANTA. Sanskrit, "the end of the Veda." One of the six schools of orthodox Hinduism, Vedanta privileges the *Upanishads*, which come at the end of the Veda. There are three main schools of thought within Vedanta: *Advaita Vedanta, Vishishtadvaita*, and *Dvaita*.

VEDAS. Sanskrit, "knowledge" or "sacred love." The Vedas are the earliest Hindu sacred texts and date back to the Vedic period (c. 1500–700 BCE). Combined, they contain over 10,000 verses in total. Along with the *Brahmanas*, they are considered *shruti*, which means "that which is heard," i.e., revelation, as opposed to other sacred texts, which are *smriti* ("that which is remembered"). They were originally transmitted orally using elaborate memorization techniques, and there is no scholarly consensus as to when they were first written down. The emergence of curses around the fifth century CE for those who use the written Vedas suggests that there must have been written copies of at least parts of the Vedas by that time. They were codified by at least the eighth century BCE (although whether in written or oral form is debated), so that, remarkably, no textual variants exist today. The Vedas are made up of four main collections: the *Rig-Veda* (book of hymns and prayers), the *Yajur-Veda* (book of sacrificial procedures), the *Sama-Veda* (book of chants to accompany sacrifices), and the *Athar-Veda* (book of magic and philosophical lore and musings). The Vedas are considered timeless and made up of wisdom that neither God nor humans created.

VERIFICATION PRINCIPLE. In the mid-twentieth century, philosophers in the Vienna Circle proposed that if a proposition is meaningful it has to be about either formal, conceptual relations (e.g., a square has four right angles) or it had to be verifiable in principle empirically. This principle was used to expose as meaningless propositions in metaphysics (such as the Absolute is timeless), ethics (lying is morally wrong), and religion (there is an incorporeal God transcending space and time) as they (ostensibly) did not yield empirically verifiable claims. Critics of the verification principle argued that the principle is itself meaningless for the principle is not itself about formal, conceptual relations, nor does it in principle yield empirically verifiable results. It also seemed to some critics that the principle would rule out important domains of science (e.g., cosmological theories about the big bang which might be built on some evidence but fall short of verification) and common sense (e.g., can a third person verify the mental states of another person?). *See also* LOGICAL POSITIVISM.

VICES. Corrosive, bad states of character leading to eventual self-destruction or blameworthy injury to others. In moral theory, "vices" refer to the motivations and dispositions of agents that give rise to immoral or wrong action. A vain person, for example, is likely to act selfishly and treat others unjustly if that advances her fame. *Contrast with* VIRTUES.

VICO, GIOVANNI BATISTA (1668–1744). An Italian philosopher of history who held that human history proceeds through stages in which we first are in an age of gods and heroes, progress through faith to a world of science, and then due to some calamity we return to the age of gods and heroes when the cycle begins again. Vico famously claimed that human beings principally know best that which we make. Because we make history, history is our primary domain of knowledge. His works include *On the Method of the Studies of Our Time* (1709), *On the Most Ancient Knowledge of the Indians* (1710), *Universal Right* (3 vols., 1720–1722), and *Principles of a New Science* (1725; 2nd rev. ed., 1730; 3rd rev. ed., 1744).

VIENNA CIRCLE (a.k.a. Wiener Kreis). The name for a group of philosophers who met in Vienna, Austria, from 1924 to 1936. The Vienna Circle was distinguished by a demanding, scientifically oriented philosophy that sought to rule out speculative metaphysics (as well as traditional religion). Prominent members included Moritz Schlick, Rudolf Carnap, Herbert Feigl, and Otto Neurath. The group fostered a movement called logical positivism, popularized by A. J. Ayer in his influential *Language, Truth, and Logic* (1936) which argued for a noncognitive view of religious and ethical beliefs. Such beliefs are noncognitive insofar as they are not such that they can be true or false. *See also* VERIFICATION PRINCIPLE.

VIRTUE THEORY. *See ARETĒ.*

VIRTUES. Excellence traits of character that motivate or dispose an agent to good acts. Someone with courage is likely to act bravely when the occasion warrants. *Contrast with* VICES.

VOLTAIRE, FRANÇOIS MARIE AROUET DE (1694–1778). Born Francois Marie Arouet, this prolific French writer later took Voltaire as his pen name. He was born into a wealthy family in Paris who wanted him to study law, but he decided to be a writer instead. A skeptic and a rationalist, he is often thought to be an atheist, but in fact his hostility was only directed toward formal religion and he identified as a deist. His satirical writings frequently criticized Catholic dogma, religious intolerance, and injustice. A social reformer and champion of liberty, he was imprisoned and exiled multiple times. He is best known for his novel *Candide* (1759), a satirical critique of philosophical optimism. His other works include *Letters Concerning the English Nation* (also entitled *Philosophical Letters*) (1733), and *Eléments de la philosophie de Newton* (1738).

VON BALTHASAR, HANS (1905–1988). Hans Urs von Balthasar is one of the most highly regarded Roman Catholic theologians of the twentieth century. Born in Lucerne, Switzerland, von Balthasar studied German language and literature at the universities of Vienna and Berlin before completing his doctorate at the University of Zurich in 1928. After entering the Society of Jesus in 1929 and being ordained to the priesthood in 1936, von Balthasar moved to Basel in 1940. In Basel, von Balthasar became friends with Karl Barth; this friendship was to have a profound influence on the theological work of both of these seminal representatives of twentieth-century Christian thought. Also in Basel, in collaboration with Adrienne von Speyr, he founded a secular institute called The Community of St. John. Von Balthasar regarded the foundation of this institute as one of his most significant contributions to the church of his day, and in 1949 he left the Society of Jesus to devote his attention to it.

Von Balthasar's theological writings secured him the reputation which he now enjoys. These writings range over numerous topics, notably including: theology and literature, prayer and the spiritual life, revelation, theological aesthetics, theology and drama, nature and grace. Von Balthasar's theology is distinctive in large part due to the prominence he accords to notions such as human holiness and mission, as well to his insistence that the saints of the church constitute a vital, if often overlooked, theological resource. He is most well known for his multi- volume theological trilogy: *The Glory of the Lord* (on theological aesthetics); *Theo-Drama* (on theological dramatic theory); and *Theo-Logic* (on truth, reason, and revelation). As well as being a free-lance writer and spiritual guide, von Balthasar founded the Johannes Verlag printing house and the international theological journal *Communio: International Catholic Review of Theology and Culture*. Pope John Paul II acknowledged von Balthasar's considerable contribution to twentieth-century Catholic life by his decision to nominate him a cardinal of the Roman Catholic Church. Von Balthasar died in Basel on June 26, 1988, just two days before the ceremony was to have taken place. Von Balthasar's theological legacy remains a dynamic force within twenty-first century Christian theology.

W

WEBER, MAX (1864–1920). German sociologist who claimed that with the waning of ancient beliefs in the gods we enter a period of disenchantment. Monotheism rid the forests and the natural world of spirits and, with the recession of monotheism in the light of modern science, we now face a more impersonal natural world which can fuel the human sense of alienation. Weber produced an extensive study that proposed that there were serious religious roots to capitalism in Northern Europe, and he offered one of the early naturalistic accounts of the origin and continuation of religion. One of his most influential works is *The Protestant Ethic and the Spirit of Capitalism* (1904–1905).

WEIL, SIMONE (1909–1943). French philosopher, mystic, and social activist. Weil was born into an agnostic Jewish family, but converted to Roman Catholicism after mystical experiences at Solesmes in 1938. Due to her distrust of institutional religion, however, she was never baptized. Weil taught philosophy at girls' schools from 1931 to 1938 and was active in worker's rights movements. An ardent socialist, she was critical of communism for its fascist and totalitarian tendencies. Her mysticism was world-rejecting and focused on the absence of God in the world. She sought detachment from self in order to achieve union with God. Weil died at the age of 34 due to tuberculosis and self-inflicted starvation mimicking French suffering during World War II. Her writings, published posthumously, include *Gravity and Grace* (1947), *The Need for Roots* (1949), *Waiting for God* (1950), and *Notebooks* (3 vols., 1951–1956), *Oppression and Liberty* (1958), and *Selected Essays, 1934–1943* (1962).

WHICHCOTE, BENJAMIN (1609–1683). One of the founding British leaders in a movement that has come to be recognized as Cambridge Platonism. Whichcote defended a form of Christian theism that gave a high role to reason and tolerance. His works (published posthumously) include *Select Notions of B. Whichcote* (1685), *Select Sermons*

(1689), *Discourses* (1701), and *Moral and Religious Aphorisms* (1703).

WHITEHEAD, ALFRED NORTH (1861–1947). A mathematician and philosopher who was highly influential in promoting what is called process theism or process philosophy. After co-authoring *Principia Mathematica* (1910–1913, with Bertrand Russell), a work that sought to derive mathematics from logic, Whitehead turned to metaphysics. He developed an account of God's relation to the world in and through processes as opposed to articulating a philosophical theology involving substances. In *Science and the Modern World* (1925), Whitehead defended the view that the emergence of modern science in the West was indebted to theism. His most important work for the philosophy of religion is *Process and Reality* (1929).

WICCA. An earth-based religion, Wicca involves working with the powers and spirits of the world to produce white magick. Wiccans worship both a Lord and a Lady (the God and the Goddess) and many lesser deities, including Diana, Brigid, Apollo, and many more who represent different aspects of the Lord and Lady. The Wiccan creed, ending "And it harm none, do as you will," provides a basis for the practice of magick; this is also referred to as karma. Wicca has no official doctrines that all must follow, but all practitioners subscribe to some variation of the Wiccan creed:

Bide The Wiccan Law Ye Must
In Perfect Love, In Perfect Trust
Eight Words The Wiccan Rede Fulfill:
An Ye Harm None, Do As Ye Will.
And Ever Mind The Rule Of Three:
What Ye Send Out, Comes Back To Thee.
Follow This With Mind And Heart,
And Merry Ye Meet, And Merry Ye Part.

Wiccans have eight holidays, or Sabbats, that center around the changing of the seasons: Imbolc (February 2), Ostara (March 21, the Spring Equinox), Beltane (May 1), Mid-summer (June 22, the Summer Solstice), Lammas (August 1), Mabon (September 21, the Autumn Equinox), Samhain (October 31), and Yule (December 22, the Winter Solstice).

When a person wants to begin practicing Wicca, he or she is expected to study the tradition solitarily and after a few years, if desired, seek out an experienced witch to further the his or her knowledge. Witches (referring to both men and women) can practice alone or in groups, called covens. Within a coven, the most experienced witch, known as the high priestess, leads the worship services. Because there is no doctrine or required beliefs or practices, each coven or witch practices differently. A typical worship or spellcasting will begin with creating a sacred circle and inviting in deities from the four directions (north, south, east, and west) to be a part of the service.

Then, prayers, thanks, or petitions are said to the Lord and Lady. Sometimes there is anointing of oil (different oils have different meanings). If it is a worship ritual, some kind of sweet cake and drink (such as juice or water) is consumed inside the circle in celebration of the deities. If it is a spellcasting ritual, the spell is performed using herbs, candles, string, oils, fire, or anything else for which that specific spell calls. At the end, the deities are thanked for being present and the sacred circle is broken.

Spells that are cast are thought out carefully beforehand. The witch considers whether the spell honors the Wiccan creed and whether it will harm anyone indirectly (if a spell is cast for rain, then somewhere else in the world will be deprived of the rain). The day is carefully chosen: if the witch is casting a good luck spell, then it is important to cast it when the moon is waxing (growing bigger so the good luck grows). The spell, then, requires different objects that have different meaning. With the good luck spell, for example, the witch, in the sacred circle, would light a candle that represents him or her (perhaps a blue candle representing the depth of the self), saying "This is me." Then the witch would light a black candle (representing bad luck), saying "This bad luck is draining from me;" then light a grey candle (representing neutrality), saying "The bad luck is neutral;" and finally light an orange candle (representing energy), saying "This energy is coming to me to work through better luck."

Once the candles have burned down, the circle is broken and the spell is complete.

Some witches keep an herb garden for their own personal growth or to use in rituals and so they plant the herbs that will help them. For example, basil is used in love and prosperity spells, chamomile is used for relaxation, dill is used for protection, peppermint for purification, and so on. Keeping an herb garden, for witches, requires tending to it and thanking the Mother Earth for the growth and health of the plants. Of course, just like most things in Wicca, you don't have to have a herb garden in order to be a witch. The herbs, along with oils, candles, stones, and anything else needed for rituals can be found almost anywhere: plant stores, convenience stores, and, of course, Witchcraft stores.

Some witches find it easier to practice with some kind of animal, as they believe animals are powerful spirits. The common animal is the cat, but other animals are kept as well. These pets, along with small children and other animals, are the only beings (besides the deities, of course) that can enter the sacred circle without destroying the ritual. All animals that aid in rituals or spiritual advancement are known as familiars (but they can be cats, frogs, birds, dogs, and so on). Even wild animals can be familiars; for example, if a witch is casting a spell or performing a ritual outside, any animal may wander up and come and go within the circle acting as a spirit aide. Contrary to popular belief, Wiccans do not perform any kind of animal sacrifice as they respect every life-form and the sacrifice would go against their creed of "And it harm none, do as you will."

WILL. In philosophy of religion, focus on the will is often in relation to questions of freedom (viz. Do human beings have free will?), value (Is it good that we are creatures with wills of our own?), and the philosophy of God (If God wills that persons do X, is X morally required)? *See* DIVINE COMMAND THEORY.

WISDOM. Wisdom (or *sophia*) was considered both a practical and theoretical virtue in ancient Greek philosophy. "Philosophy" literally means "the love of wisdom" and was considered by Greco-Roman moralists in ancient philosophy to be an enterprise which took practical life and values seriously.

There is also a body of literature called Wisdom literature, a popular genre in ancient Near Eastern cultures. Wisdom (Hebrew: *chochmah*) is practical and empirical in its focus, addressing everyday issues of life, often from a secular standpoint that seeks to understand the principles of order in the world and organize human life accordingly. It is considered international in scope and thus applicable to all. In the Hebrew Bible, books such as Proverbs, Job, and Qohelet (Ecclesiastes) are categorized as wisdom literature.

In Jewish-Christian dialogue, wisdom literature is often given prominence, for there is some similarity between the Hebrew Wisdom literature in which wisdom is characterized as a person (in Proverbs, wisdom cries out to the people) and Christian tradition in which the person Jesus Christ is seen as the embodiment of wisdom.

WITCHCRAFT. *See* **WICCA.**

WITTGENSTEIN, LUDWIG (1889–1951). An Austrian philosopher who had a major influence on philosophy of language and the general practice of philosophy itself. His dynamic life included studying under Bertrand Russell at Cambridge University, serving as a soldier in World War I on behalf of the Axis powers, enduring a time as a prisoner of war, being a schoolteacher in Austria, and working philosophically at Cambridge University surrounded by outstanding students such as Elizabeth Anscombe. There are two general periods of his life. In the first he developed a logical framework by which one can understand the world and truth. His chief work of this period, published as *The Tractatus-Logico-Philosophicus* (1921), was recognized by Russell and G. E. Moore as a work of genius. Wittgenstein believed he had solved all philosophical problems in this early work. Wittgenstein then repudiated this work, arguing that its underlying foundation (the picture theory of language) was unsuccessful. In his second, mature work, he contended that philosophical problems arise when we are bewitched by language; the traditional arena of philosophy (Can we know about the external world? How is the mind related to the body? What is time? Why believe God exists?) can be dissolved once we lead terms like "world," "mind," "body," "time," "God," and so on back to their proper home in ordinary discourse. His later views are captured in his highly influential *The Philosophical Investigations* (1953). *See also* RELIGIOUS LANGUAGE.

WOLFF, CHRISTIAN (1679–1750). German Enlightenment and rationalist philosopher and mathematician, Wolff was the link between the philosophies of Leibniz and Kant. His conviction that theological truths must be based upon mathematical certitude led to conflict with the Pietists. Wolff promoted the use of the German language in education and research.

WOMEN. *See* **FEMINIST PHILOSOPHY OF RELIGION.**

WORSHIP. Homage, praise, awesome reverence owed to the divine. In some cases, worship may involve fear and joy. In classical theism, the idea that God is worthy of worship is considered foundational to the very concept of God.

X

XENOPHANES (c. 570–c. 475 BCE). Greek pre-Socratic philosopher, poet, and social critic. Xenophanes criticized anthropomorphic portrayals of the gods, claiming that if it were possible "horses would draw their gods like horses, and cattle like cattle." He argued instead for an incorporeal universal god, advancing a partial monotheism. Yet in his view this supreme deity was only the greatest among many gods. With regards to epistemology, he regarded the human capacity to grasp the truth as inhibited by the limited nature of human experience.

XIONG SHILI (a.k.a. HSIUNG SHIH-LI) (1885–1968). Xiong Shili was a leading Chinese philosopher who synthesized Buddhism, Confucianism, Western analytic philosophy, and the theory of evolution. Originally an adherent of the idealist school of the Yogacara tradition of Mahayana Buddhism, he later turned to the metaphysical Confucian classic Book of Changes (Yijing) and the Neo-Confucian idealism of Wang Yangming (1472–1529). In 1944 he completed his major work, A New Theory of Consciousness-Only (Xin weishi lun). Xiong accepted Buddhist explanations for the causes of human suffering, but considered Confucianism superior as a guide for moral behavior. Xiong taught at Beijing University from 1922 until 1954. He continued to write until his death in 1968, generally unaffected by changing political circumstances.

XUANZANG (c. 602–664). Xuanzang was a Chinese Buddhist scholar, translator, and traveler who journeyed through Central Asia to India between 629 and 645 in order to acquire Buddhist scriptures. Upon his return he began a project to translate the 657 Sanskrit texts he had gathered. Xuanzang was a proponent of the idealist Yogacara or Consciousness-Only School. He also wrote an account of his travels, the Xiyuji (A Record of Western Regions). His 16-year journal was the basis of the sixteenth-century novel Xiyouji (Journey to the West), a religious allegory that can be compared to a combination of Pilgrim's Progress and The Wizard of Oz.

XUNZI (c. 312–230 BCE). Xunzi was a Confucian philosopher in the late classical period. Unlike Mencius, who believed that human nature was intrinsically good, Xunzi argued that human nature was basically selfish. He was the teacher of Han Feizi and Li Si, two founders of the anti-Confucian Legalist school that promoted state power as the ultimate political good. Unlike the Legalists, however, Xunzi remained basically Confucian in his belief that human beings have the capacity for goodness and discipline their behavior through ritual and education. Nonetheless, Xunzi deeply influenced Legalist philosophers, who rejected ritual and emphasized the necessity of a coercive legal system based on punishment.

Y

YHWH. Also known as the Tetragramaton (Greek, "four letters"). These four Hebrew consonants (*Yodh He Waw He*) constitute the sacred name of the God of the Israelites as revealed to Moses (Exodus 3:14) and are connected with the verb *hayah*, "to be." Jewish tradition prohibits the vocalization of the divine name and observant Jews substitute *Adonai* (Hebrew for "Lord") when reading the scriptures aloud. It is usually rendered as "Yahweh" or "Jehovah" in English.

YIN-YANG. In Chinese philosophy, a concept indicating the interconnected and interdependent nature of ostensibly opposite forces. The characters *yin* and *yang* originally meant dark and bright sides of a sunlit bank, but by the time of Confucius they referred to the duality inherent in all things. The *yin-yang* theory gained prominence toward the end of the Chou Dynasty, resulting in the *Yin-Yang* School (attributed to Tsou Yen, c. 305–240 BCE). The theory was further developed by philosophers in the Han Dynasty, especially Tung Chung-shu (c. 179–104 BCE). It influenced virtually all aspects of Chinese life (metaphysics, cosmology, government, art, and so on). *Yin* is characterized as non-being, negative, passive, slow, weak, destructive, earth, dark, female, mother, soft, and wet. *Yang* is characterized as being, positive, active, fast, strong, constructive, heaven, light, male, father, hard, and bright. *Yin* and *Yang* are balanced in a dynamic equilibrium and represent the principle of unity in duality. Their interaction is the cause of all life.

YOGA. From the Sanskrit, meaning "yoking" or "harnessing" of one's mind and body. In Hindu philosophy, *yoga* is one of six orthodox (*āstika*) schools of thought and is closely associated with Samkhya. It is divided into *Hatha Yoga* (the physiological aspect) and *Raja* (Royal) *Yoga* (contemplation). The classical account in the *Yoga-sūtra* of Patanjali includes eight elements or stages: restraint (*yama*), disciplines (*niyama*), postures (*asana*), breathing control (*pranayama*), elimination of perception of outer objects (*pratyāhāra*), concentration (*dhārana*), meditation (*dhyāna*), and absorption (*samādhi*). In the *Bhagavad Gita*, *yoga* is understood as comprised of three paths that lead to spiritual fulfillment: *jñānayoga* (wisdom or knowledge), *karmayoga* (action), and *bhaktiyoga* (ecstatic or loving devotion).

Z

ZEN BUDDHISM. A branch of Mahāyāna Buddhism that developed in China as Ch'an beginning in the seventh century CE. It later spread to Vietnam (where it is known as Thiền Buddhism), Korea, and Japan. Zen Buddhism stresses a form of sitting meditation known as zazen and other practices in order to cultivate experiential wisdom, believing that excessive focus on texts and theoretical knowledge can deter one from experientially realizing bodhi (enlightenment or awakening). Chinese and Vietnamese Zen are much gentler compared to the shocking Japanese Rinzai. Within Japanese Zen, the two main schools are Soto and Rinzai. Soto Zen is a calm version of Japanese Zen where practitioners spend most of their time in sitting meditation and wait to realize enlightenment. In Soto Zen, the meditator does not focus on anything, so if a thought arises, they are to acknowledge it and let it fade away. Rinzai Zen, on the other hand, is the school that the West has adopted. Rinzai has a strong focus on the koan (a statement or question-and-answer that does not make any logical sense, such as "What is the

Buddha? The rooster crows at daybreak.") and the awakening stick (a flat wooden rod that is used on meditators as a reminder to stay focused or to encourage "sudden enlightenment"). The Rinzai meditator focuses on breathing and the koan in hopes of attaining satori, or "sudden enlightenment." Zen, as a whole, is a very individualistic tradition, meaning that it is up to the individual to decide how to practice Zen and there are no set rules on how to practice; the individual or the school can pick and choose which, if any, Buddhist doctrines to accept. Zen does, however, emphasize the importance of questioning everything, otherwise the follower is no better than a parrot who repeats words without knowing the significance. Zen prides itself on being illogical, and the use of the koan and the awakening stick are examples of non- rational ways of reaching enlightenment.

ZENO OF CITIUM (344–262 BCE). A stoic philosopher from Citium in Cyprus, Zeno is considered the founder of the

Stoic school in Athens. As a Stoic, Zeno advocated "a good flow of life," and concerned himself with practical philosophy. According to Diogenes Laertius, Zeno was a pantheist who held that the universe and God were identical. (He also names God as "fate," "unity," and "mind," among other things.) The aim of life, then, is to live in accord with the universe, which one does by practicing the virtues and giving assent only to those propositions that merit it by their stability. Zeno viewed philosophy as a system, and gave logic a high place in the Stoic system. Zeno viewed reality as composed of a passive element, matter, and an active one, the *logos,* reason. The divine *logos* is the principle of change, and matter is the substrate in which that change occurs. The cosmos undergoes precisely the same changes again and again eternally, governed by the *logos,* and activated by the fire that permeates the cosmos. The fire in the cosmos corresponds to the *pneuma* in the human body. His doctrine of the soul, therefore, appears to be materialist. Zeno was reputedly a prolific writer, but none of his writings survive. *See also* PNEUMA and STOICISM.

ZENO OF ELEA (c. 490–c. 430 BCE). Philosopher, follower of Parmenides, famed for his paradoxes designed to show that motion is impossible. A student of Parmenides, Zeno's work was designed to establish that there is only unchanging being. His most famous paradox concerns the impossibility of completing an infinite sequence of movements. For you to cross a field with a border you must go halfway. Then you must go another quarter of the distance. Then you must go another fraction of the distance and so on, ad infinitum. Given this formulation of the problem of motion, you would never get to the other side of the field.

ZHANG DONGSUN (1886–1973). Zhang Dongsun was a Chinese philosopher, translator, and political figure. Zhang sought to integrate the insights of Kant into modern Confucianism. He also was a proponent of both the metaphysics of Henri Bergson and the ideas of Bertrand Russell, finding no contradiction between the two. Zhang, a professor at Yenching University in Beijing, became a prominent liberal critic of the Nationalist regime of Jiang Jieshi (Chiang Kai-shek) and was a leader of the China Democratic League. Zhang was imprisoned during the Japanese occupation of Beijing in World War II. In 1949 he helped negotiate the peaceful occupation of the city by the Chinese Communists. After the establishment of the Communist regime Zhang was forced into retirement.

ZHANG ZAI (a.k.a. CHANG TSAI) (1020–1077). Zhang Zai was an early Neo-Confucian cosmologist and moral philosopher. Disillusioned with classical Confucianism, Zhang explored Buddhism and Daoism before returning to Confucianism, ultimately concentrating on the metaphysical Confucian classic *Book of Changes* (*Yijing*). Influenced by his contemporary Zhou Dunyi (1017–1073), Zhang's work examined the concept of the Supreme Ultimate (*Taiji*), a non-theistic order or principle mentioned in the *Book of Changes* and elaborated by Zhou Dunyi. Unlike Zhou, who believed that the Supreme Ultimate was a combination of *li* (principle) and *qi* (matter), Zhang believed that the Supreme Ultimate consisted solely of *qi*. In his moral philosophy Zhang emphasized *ren* (benevolence or humanity) as the basis of all human relationships. Zhang was the uncle of the Neo-Confucian philosophers Cheng Hao and Cheng Yi.

ZHU XI (1130–1200). Zhu Xi was an official, a historian, and the greatest commentator on the Confucian classics, probably the greatest Confucian philosopher after the classical age. Zhu Xi believed in seeking truth through *gewu*—the investigation of things, a phrase he found in one of the Confucian classics, the *Great Learning*. In his case, he sought truth through investigation of Confucian classics. He interpreted them, however, with metaphysical issues on his mind, and he drew ideas from them that others had not. He taught that all things have a fundamental principle of form, called *li*. All *li* together constitute the limitless Supreme Ultimate, the non-theistic

principle underlying all existence and manifested in all things. *Li* provides the form, but material existence comes from *qi* (matter). Neo-Confucianism applies this scheme to human nature. Confucius—or more specifically Mencius—argued that human nature was intrinsically good and that human goodness is the basis of all virtues. Nonetheless, human nature as it really exists is a manifestation of *li* through *qi*. *Qi* can be impure, muddied, and dulled. Human beings can purify their *qi* through education and self-cultivation. Zhu Xi's philosophy, like classical Confucianism, is primarily concerned with social harmony and personal ethics. Zhu Xi emphasized a particularist, family-centered social ethic based on the five relations of authority and obedience (ruler-subject, father-son, husband-wife, elder brother-younger brother, and friend-friend). His philosophy supported the political status quo, regarding the state as a large family and the ruler as a father whose authority is essentially ethical. After Zhu Xi's death, his Neo-Confucian synthesis became orthodox. His commentaries were the standard interpretation of the classics considered authoritative for the civil service examinations until they were abolished in 1905.

ZHUANGZI. Zhuangzi refers both to a Daoist philosopher said to have lived in the fourth century BCE and to the book attributed to him. The *Zhuangzi*, along with the *Daodejing* or *Laozi*, is one of the two primary texts of philosophical Daoism. The text in fact appears to draw from at least two sources, and the relationship between the book and the eponymous philosopher is unclear. The *Zhuangzi* consists largely of anecdotes with philosophical meaning. It articulates the notion of *wuwei* or effortless action, the unfixed nature of language, the relativity of existence, and the natural place of death in the cycle of life. Probably the most famous anecdote is about Zhuangzi's dream that he was a butterfly. Upon awakening, he was unsure whether he was a human who had dreamed he was a butterfly, or if he was not a butterfly dreaming he was a human.

ZOROASTER. *See* **ZOROASTRIANISM.**

ZOROASTRIANISM. The main religion in Persia (now Iran) prior to the advent of Islam, founded by Zarathustra (Greek, Zoroaster). Most scholars believe Zarathustra was born around 570 BCE, although some date his birth as far back as the fifteenth century BCE. His sayings are preserved in the *Gāthās*, which are part of the *Avesta* ("Book of the Law"). Zoroastrianism teaches a mixture of monotheism and dualism. Ahura Mazdah is the supreme deity, but he has an evil and slightly less powerful opponent, Aura Mainyu. Zoroastrians interpret the world in terms of a cosmic battle between good and evil at present, but believe that Ahura Mazdah (good) will ultimately triumph over Aura Mainyu (evil). Human beings have free will, and their actions determine their eternal destiny. Zoroastrianism influenced Judaism, Mithraism, Gnosticism, and Manichaeism. After the fall of the Sassanid Empire in 651 CE, many Zoroastrians migrated to India. Today, the majority of Zoroastrians live in India, where they are known as Parsis. The small remnant of believers in Iran are known as Garbars.

Bibliography

Surveys and Introductions

Abraham, William J. *An Introduction to the Philosophy of Religion*. Englewood Cliffs, NJ: Prentice-Hall, 1985.

Bertocci, Peter. *Introduction to the Philosophy of Religion*. New York: Prentice-Hall, 1951.

Cahn, Steven M. *Exploring Philosophy of Religion*. New York: Oxford University Press, 2009.

Caird, John. *An Introduction to the Philosophy of Religion*. New York: Macmillan, 1891.

Clack, Beverly, and Brian R. Clack. *The Philosophy of Religion*. Malden, MA: Polity, 2008.

Clark, Kelly James. *Return to Reason*. Grand Rapids, MI: Eerdmans, 1990.

Copan, Paul, and Chad Meister, eds. *Philosophy of Religion: Classic and Contemporary Issues*. Malden, MA: Blackwell, 2008.

—, eds. *The Routledge Companion to Philosophy of Religion*. New York: Routledge, 2007.

Davies, Brian. *Philosophy of Religion*. New York: Oxford University Press, 2000.

—. *An Introduction to the Philosophy of Religion*. 3rd ed. New York: Oxford University Press, 2003.

Eshleman, Andrew. *Readings on Philosophy of Religion*. Malden, MA: Blackwell, 2008.

Flint, Thomas P., and Michael C. Rea, eds. *The Oxford Handbook of Philosophical Theology*. Oxford: Oxford University Press, 2009.

Harrison, Victoria. *Religion and Modern Thought*. London: SCM, 2007.

Hick, John, ed. *Classical and Contemporary Readings in the Philosophy of Religion*. 3rd ed. Englewood Cliffs, NJ: Prentice-Hall, 1990.

—, ed. *The Existence of God*. New York: Macmillan, 1964.

—. *Philosophy of Religion*. Englewood Cliffs, NJ: Prentice-Hall, 1983.

Meister, Chad. *Introducing Philosophy of Religion*. New York: Routledge, 2009.

Mitchell, Basil, ed. *Philosophy of Religion*. Oxford: Oxford University Press, 1971.

Morris, Thomas V. *Our Idea of God*. Downers Grove, IL: InterVarsity Press, 1991.

Murray, Michael, and Michael C. Rea. *Introduction to the Philosophy of Religion*. Cambridge: Cambridge University Press, 2008.

O'Hear, Anthony. *Experience, Explanation, and Faith: An Introduction to the Philosophy Religion*. London: Routledge and Kegan Paul, 1984.

Perett, Roy W. *Indian Philosophy: A Collection of Readings*. New York: Garland, 2001.

Peterson, Michael L., and Raymond J. VanArragon, eds. *Contemporary Debates in Philosophy of Religion*. Malden, MA: Blackwell, 2004.

Peterson, Michael, William Hasker, Bruce Reichenbach, and David Basinger, eds. *Philosophy of Religion: Selected Readings*. 3rd ed. New York: Oxford University Press, 2007.

Pojman, Louis P., and Michael Rea, eds. *Philosophy of Religion: An Anthology*. 5th ed. Belmont, CA: Wadsworth, 2007.

Quinn, Philip L., and Charles Taliaferro, eds. *A Companion to Philosophy of Religion*. 1st ed. Cambridge, MA: Blackwell, 1999.

Rea, Michael C., ed. *Oxford Readings in Philosophical Theology*. 2 vols. Oxford: Oxford University Press, 2009.

Rowe, William L. *Philosophy of Religion*. Belmont, CA: Wadsworth, 1993.

Taliaferro, Charles. *Contemporary Philosophy of Religion*. Oxford: Blackwell, 1998.

—. *Philosophy of Religion: A Beginner's Guide*. Oxford: Oneworld, 2009.

Taliaferro, Charles, and Paul Griffiths, eds. *Philosophy of Religion: An Anthology*. Malden, MA: Blackwell, 2003.

Taliaferro, Charles, Paul Draper, and Philip L. Quinn, eds. *A Companion to Philosophy of Religion*. 2nd ed. Oxford: Blackwell, 2010.

Wainwright, William J. *Philosophy of Religion*. Belmont, CA: Wadsworth, 1988.

Religious Language

Alston, William P. *Divine Nature and Human Language: Essays in Philosophical Theology*. Ithaca, NY: Cornell University Press, 1989.

—. "Ineffability." *Philosophical Review* 65 (1956): 506–22.

—. *Perceiving God: The Epistemology of Religious Experience*. Ithaca, NY: Cornell University Press, 1991.

Bevan, Edwin. *Symbolism and Belief*. Boston: Beacon Press, 1957.

Donovan, Peter. *Religious Language*. New York: Hawthorn Books, 1976.

Ferre, Frederick. *Language, Logic, and God*. London: Eyre & Spottiswoode, 1962.

Flew, Antony, and Alasdair MacIntyre, eds. *New Essays in Philosophical Theology*. London: SCM Press, 1955.

Griffin, David Ray. *Reenchantment Without Supernaturalism: A Process Philosophy of Religion*. Ithaca, NY: Cornell University Press, 2001.

Mitchell, Basil, ed. *Faith and Logic*. London: Allen & Unwin, 1957.

Mondin, Battista. *Models and Mystery*. Oxford: Oxford University Press, 1964.

—. *The Principle of Analogy in Protestant and Catholic Theology*. The Hague: Martinus Nijhoff, 1968.

Ramsey, Ian T. *Religious Language: An Empirical Placing of Theological Phrases*. London: SCM Press, 1957.

Rowe, William L. *Religious Symbols and God*. Chicago: University of Chicago Press, 1968.

Santioni, Ronald E. *Religious Language and the Problem of Religious Knowledge*. Bloomington, IN: Indiana University Press, 1968.

Soskice, Janet M. *Metaphor and Religious Language*. Oxford: Oxford University Press, 1984.

Stiver, Dan R. *The Philosophy of Religious Language*. Oxford: Blackwell, 1996.

Religious Experience

Almond, Philip C. *Mystical Experience and Religious Doctrine: An Investigation of the Study of Mysticism in World Religions.* New York: Mouton, 1982.

Alston, William P. "Do Mystics See God?" In *Contemporary Debates in Philosophy of Religion*, edited by Michael L. Peterson and Raymond J. VanArragon, 145–58. Oxford: Blackwell, 2004.

—. "Literal and Nonliteral Reports of Mystical Experience." In *Mysticism and Language*, edited by Steven T. Katz, 80–102. New York: Oxford University Press, 1992.

—. *Perceiving God, The Epistemology of Religious Experience.* Ithaca, NY: Cornell University Press, 1991.

Appleby, Peter C. "Mysticism and Ineffability." *International Journal for Philosophy of Religion* 11 (1980): 143–65.

Bagger, Matthew C. *Religious Experience, Justification, and History.* New York: Cambridge University Press, 1999.

Barnard, G. William. *Exploring Unseen Worlds: William James and the Philosophy of Mysticism.* Albany: State University of New York Press, 1997.

Batson, C. Daniel, and W. Larry Ventis. *The Religious Experience: A Social-Psychological Perspective.* New York: Oxford University Press, 1982.

Beer, Frances. *Women and Mystical Experience in the Middle Ages.* Woodbridge, Suffolk: Boydell Press, 1992.

Borchert, Bruno. *Mysticism, Its History and Challenge.* York Beach, ME: Samuel Weiser, 1994.

Bowker, John. *The Religious Imagination and the Sense of God.* Oxford: Claredon Press, 1978.

Clark, Walter H., H. Newton Malony, James Daane, and Alan R. Tippett. *Religious Experience: Its Nature and Function in the Human Psyche.* Springfield, IL: Charles C. Thomas, 1973.

Davis, Caroline Franks. *The Evidential Force of Religious Experience.* Oxford: Oxford University Press, 1989.

Dupré, Louis. *Transcendent Selfhood: The Loos and Rediscovery of the Inner Life.* New York: Seabury, 1976.

Edward, Kenneth. *Religious Experience: Its Nature and Truth.* Edinburgh: T & T Clark, 1926.

Fales, Evan. "Do Mystics See God?" In *Contemporary Debates in Philosophy of Religion*, edited by Michael L. Peterson and Raymond J. VanArragon, 145–57. Oxford: Blackwell, 2001.

—. "Scientific Explanations of Mystical Experience, Part I: The Case of St. Teresa." *Religious Studies* 32 (1996): 143–63.

—. "Scientific Explanations of Mystical Experience, Part II: The Challenge to Theism." *Religious Studies* 32 (1996): 297–313.

Gellman, Jerome I. *Experience of God and the Rationality of Theistic Belief.* Ithaca, NY: Cornell University Press, 1997.

—. *Mystical Experience of God: A Philosophical Inquiry.* Burlington, VT: Ashgate, 2001.

Griffiths, Paul J. "Pure Consciousness and Indian Buddhism." In *The Problem of Pure Consciousness, Mysticism, and Philosophy*, edited by Robert Forman, 121–59. New York: Oxford University Press, 1993.

Hollenback, Jess Byron. *Mysticism: Experience, Response, and Empowerment.* University Park: Pennsylvania State University Press, 1996.

James, William. *The Varieties of Religious Experience.* New York: Collier, 1961.

Katz, Steven T. *Mysticism and Philosophical Analysis.* New York: Oxford University Press, 1978.

Moore, Peter G. "Recent Studies of Mysticism: A Critical Survey." *Religion*, 3 (1973): 146–56.

Bibliography

Otto, Rudolf. *The Idea of the Holy.* New York: Oxford University Press, 1958.

Proudfoot, Wayne L. *Religious Experience.* Berkeley: University of California Press, 1985.

Scharfstein, Ben-Ami. *Mystical Experience.* New York: Bobbs-Merrill, 1973.

Sells, Michael Anthony. *Mystical Languages of Unsaying.* Chicago: Chicago University Press, 1994.

Staal, Frits. *Exploring Mysticism.* Harmondsworth: Penguin, 1975.

Stace, Walter Terence. *Mysticism and Philosophy.* London: Macmillan, 1961.

Underhill, Evelyn. *Mysticism: A Study in the Nature and Development of Man's Spiritual Consciousness.* London: Methuen, 1911.

Wainwright, William J. *Mysticism, A Study of its Nature, Cognitive Value, and Moral Implications.* Madison: University of Wisconsin Press, 1981.

Yandell, Keith E. *The Epistemology of Religious Experience.* New York: Cambridge University Press, 1973

Zaehner, Robert Charles. *Mysticism, Sacred and Profane.* New York: Oxford University Press, 1961.

Religious Epistemology

Alston, William P. *Perceiving God: The Epistemology of Religious Experience.* Ithaca, NY: Cornell University Press, 1991.

Bird, Graham. *William James.* London: Routledge & Kegan Paul, 1987.

Braine, David. *The Reality of Time and the Existence of God: The Project of Proving God's Existence.* Oxford: Clarendon Press, 1988.

Bouwsma, O. K. *Without Proof or Evidence: Essays of O.K. Bouwsma.* Lincoln, NE: University of Nebraska Press, 1984.

Clark, Kelly J. *Return to Reason.* Grand Rapids, MI: Eerdmans, 1990.

Clifford, W. K. *The Ethics of Belief and Other Essays.* Amherst, NY: Prometheus Books, 1999.

Conee, Earl, and Richard Feldman. *Evidentialism: Essays in Epistemology.* Amherst, NY: Prometheus Books, 2004.

Davis, Caroline Franks. *The Evidential Forces of Religious Experience.* Oxford: Oxford University Press, 1989.

Evans, C. Stephen. *Faith Beyond Reason.* Grand Rapids, MI: Eerdmans, 1998.

—. *Why Believe: Reason and Mystery as Pointers to God.* Grand Rapids, MI: Eerdmans, 1996.

Evans, C. Stephen, and Merold Westphal, eds. *Christian Perspectives on Religious Knowledge.* Grand Rapids, MI: Eerdmans, 1993.

Frankenberry, Nancy. *Religion and Radical Empiricism.* Albany, NY: State University of New York Press, 1987.

Geivett, R. Douglas, and Brendan Sweetman, eds. *Contemporary Perspectives on Religious Epistemology.* Oxford: Oxford University Press, 1992.

Gellman, Jerome I. *Experience of God and the Rationality of Theistic Belief.* Ithaca, NY: Cornell University Press, 1997.

—. *Mystical Experience of God: A Philosophical Inquiry.* Burlington, VT: Ashgate, 2001.

Griffith-Dickson, Gwen. *Human and Divine: An Introduction to the Philosophy of Religious Experience.* London: Gerald Duckworth, 2000.

Hoitenga, Dewey J., Jr. *From Plato to Plantinga: An Introduction to Reformed Epistemology.* Albany, NY: State University of New York Press, 1991.

James, William. *Essays in Pragmatism*. New York: Hafner, 1948.

—. *The Varieties of Religious Experience*. New York: Collier, 1961.

Kelly, Thomas. "The Epistemic Significance of Disagreement." In *Oxford Studies in Epistemology*, vol. 1, edited by John Hawthorne and Tamar Gendler Szabo, 167–196. Oxford: Oxford University Press, 2005.

Martin, Michael. "Pascal's Wager as an Argument for Not Believing in God." *Religious Studies* 19 (1983): 57–64.

Moser, Paul K. *The Elusive God: Reorienting Religious Epistemology*. New York: Cambridge University Press, 2008.

—. *The Evidence for God: Religious Knowledge Reexamined*. New York: Cambridge University Press, 2010.

Pascal, Blaise. *Pensées*. Translated by A. J. Krailsheimer. New York: Penguin, 1995.

Phillips, D. Z. *Belief, Change, and Forms of Life*. Atlantic Highlands, NJ: Humanities Press, 1986.

—. *Religion Without Explanation*. Oxford: Basil Blackwell, 1976.

Plantinga, Alvin. "Religion and Epistemology." In *Routledge Encyclopedia of Philosophy*, vol. 8, edited by Edward Craig, 209–18. London: Routledge, 1998.

—. *Warranted Christian Belief*. New York: Oxford University Press, 2000.

Putnam, Ruth Anna, ed. *The Cambridge Companion to William James*. Cambridge: Cambridge University Press, 1997.

Rescher, Nicholas. *Pascal's Wager: A Study of Practical Reasoning in Philosophical Theology*. Notre Dame: University of Notre Dame Press, 1985.

Swinburne, Richard. *The Existence of God*. 2nd ed. Oxford: Clarendon, 2004.

—. *Faith and Reason*. 2nd ed. Oxford: Clarendon, 2005.

—. *Is There a God?* Oxford: Oxford University Press, 1996.

—. *Revelation: From Metaphor to Analogy*. 2nd ed. Oxford: Clarendon, 2007.

Wainwright, William J., ed. *The Oxford Handbook of Philosophy of Religion*. Oxford: Oxford University Press, 2005.

Wittgenstein, Ludwig. *Culture and Value*. Edited by Georg Henrik von Wright and translated by Peter Winch. Chicago: University of Chicago Press, 1980.

—. *Lectures and Conversations on Aesthetics, Psychology and Religious Belief*. Edited by Cyril Barrett. Berkeley: University of California Press, 1966.

—. *Remarks on Frazer's* Golden Bough Translated by A. C. Miles and Rush Rhees. *Human World* 3 (1971): 28–41.

Wolterstorff, Nicholas. *John Locke and the Ethics of Belief*. Cambridge, England: Cambridge University Press, 1996.

Yandell, Keith. *The Epistemology of Religious Experience*. Cambridge: Cambridge University Press, 2004.

Zagzebski, Linda T., ed. *Rational Faith: Catholic Responses to Reformed Epistemology*, Notre Dame: University of Notre Dame, 1993. See esp. her chapter, "Religious Knowledge and the Virtues of the Mind," 199–225.

Theism

General

Adams, Robert Merrihew. *Finite and Infinite Goods: A Framework for Ethics*. New York: Oxford University Press, 1999.

Augustine. *The City of God*. Translated by Henry Bettenson. Harmondsworth: Penguin, 1972.

Bibliography

Barnes, Jonathan. *The Ontological Argument.* New York: St. Martin's Press, 1972.

Barrow, John D., and Frank J. Tipler. *The Anthropic Cosmological Principle.* Oxford: Oxford University Press, 1986.

Carr, B. J., and M. J. Rees. "The Anthropic Cosmological Principle and the Structure of the Physical World." *Nature* 278 (1979): 605–12.

Collins, Robin. "The Evidence for Fine-Tuning." In *God and Design*, edited by Neil Manson, 178–99. London: Routledge, 2003.

—. "Hume, Fine-Tuning and the Who Designed God? Objection." In *In Defense of Natural Theory: A Post-Humean Assesment*, edited by James Sennett and Douglas Groothius, 175–99. Downers Grove, IL: InterVarsity, 2005.

—. "The Multiverse Hypothesis: A Theistic Perspective." In *Universe or Multiverse?*, edited by Bernard Carr, 459–80. Cambridge: Cambridge University Press, 2007.

Craig, William Lane. *The Cosmological Argument from Plato to Leibniz.* Eugene, OR: Wipf and Stock, 2001.

Craig, William Lane, and Quentin Smith, eds. *Theism, Atheism, and Big Bang Cosmology.* Oxford: Clarendon, 1993.

Dawkins, Richard. *The Blind Watchmaker.* New York: W. W. Norton, 1987.

Dombrowski, Daniel A. *Rethinking the Ontological Argument: A Neoclassical Theistic Response.* Cambridge: Cambridge University Press, 2006.

Dore, Clement. *Theism.* Dordrecht: D. Reidel, 1984.

Everitt, Nicholas. *The Non-Existence of God.* London: Routledge, 2004.

Gale, Richard M. *On The Nature and Existence of God.* Cambridge: Cambridge University Press, 1991.

Hartshorne, Charles. *The Logic of Perfection: And Other Essays in Neoclassical Metaphysics.* LaSalle, IL: Open Court, 1962.

Hick, John. *God and the Universe of Faiths.* London: Macmillan, 1973.

Hughes, Gerard. *The Nature of God.* London: Routledge, 1995.

Hume, David. *A Treatise of Human Nature.* Edited by L. A. Selby-Bigge, 1888. 2nd ed., with text revisions by P. H. Nidditch. Oxford: Clarendon, 1978. Originally published 1739.

—. *Dialogues Concerning Natural Religion.* Edited by Richard H. Popkin. 2nd ed. Indianapolis, IN: Hackett, 1998. Originally published 1779.

Kant, Immanuel. *Critique of Pure Reason.* Translated by Norman Kemp Smith. New York: St. Martin's Press, 1965. Originally published 1781.

Lewis, David. *On The Plurality of Worlds.* New York: Basil Blackwell, 1986.

Mackie, John Leslie. *The Miracle of Theism: Arguments for and Against the Existence of God.* Oxford: Clarendon, 1982.

Manson, Neil A., ed. *God and Design: The Teleological Argument and Modern Science.* London: Routledge, 2003.

Martin, Michael. *Atheism: A Philosophical Justification.* Philadelphia, PA: Temple University Press, 1990.

Martin, Michael, and Ricki Monnier, eds. *The Impossibility of God.* Buffalo, NY: Prometheus Books, 2003.

O'Connor, Timothy. *Theism and Ultimate Explanation.* Malden, MA: Blackwell, 2008.

Oppy, Graham. *Ontological Arguments on the Belief in God.* Cambridge: Cambridge University Press, 1996.

Plantinga, Alvin. *God and Other Minds.* Ithaca, NY: Cornell University Press, 1967.

—. *Does God Have a Nature?* Milwaukee: Marquette University Press, 1980.

—. *The Nature of Necessity.* Oxford: Oxford University Press, 1974.

—. *The Ontological Argument: from St. Anselm to Contemporary Philosophers.* London: Macmillan, 1968.

—. *Warrant and Proper Function.* Oxford: Oxford University Press, 1993.

Quinn, Philip L. "Divine Conservation, Continuous Creation, and Human Action." In *The Existence and Nature of God*, edited by Alfred J. Freddoso, 55–79. Notre Dame: University of Notre Dame Press, 1983.

—. "Moral Objections to Pascalian Wagering." In *Gambling on God: Essays on Pascal's Wager*, edited by Jeffrey Jordan, 61–82. Littlefield, MD: Rowman & Littlefield, 1994.

Rescher, Nicholas. *Pascal's Wager: A Study of Practical Reasoning in Philosophical Theology.* Notre Dame, IN: University of Notre Dame Press, 1985.

Rowe, William L. *The Cosmological Argument.* Princeton, NJ: Princeton University Press, 1975.

Russell, Bertrand and Frederick Copleston. "Debate on the Existence of God." In *The Existence of God*, edited by John Hick, 167–90. New York: Macmillan, 1964.

Schlesinger, George. "A Central Theistic Argument." In *Gambling on God: Essays on Pascal's Wager*, edited by Jeffrey Jordan, 83–100. Littlefield, MD: Rowman & Littlefield, 1994.

—. "Possible Worlds and the Mystery of Existence." *Ratio* 26 (1984): 1–18.

Smart, Ninian. *Doctrine and Argument in Indian Philosophy.* London: Allen and Unwin, 1964.

Swinburne, Richard. *The Coherence of Theism.* Oxford: Clarendon, 1977.

Taliaferro, Charles. *Dialogues about God.* Rowman and Littlefield, 2009.

Taliaferro, Charles, Victoria Harrison, and Stewart Goetz, eds. *The Routledge Companion to Theism.* London: Routledge, forthcoming.

Taylor, Richard. *Metaphysics.* Englewood Cliffs, NJ: Prentice Hall, 1992.

The Concept of God

Beaty, Michael, and Charles Taliaferro. "God and Concept Empiricism." *Southwest Philosophy Review* 6:2 (1990): 97–105.

Craig, William Lane and J.P. Moreland. *The Blackwell Companion To Natural Theology.* Malden, MA: Wiley Blackwell, 2009.

Hartshorne, Charles. *The Divine Relativity: A Social Conception of God.* New Haven, CT: Yale University Press, 1948.

Hastings, Adrian, Alistair Mason, Hugh Pyper, eds., with Ingrid Lawrie and Cecily Bennett. *The Oxford Companion to Christian Thought.* New York: Oxford University Press, 2000.

Hill, Daniel J. *Divinity and Maximal Greatness.* New York: Routledge, 2005.

Hoffman, Joshua, and Gary S. Rosenkrantz. *The Divine Attributes.* Oxford: Blackwell, 2002.

Jeanrond, Werner G., and Aasulv Lande, eds., *The Concept of God in Global Dialogue.* New York: Orbis Books, 2005.

Lott, Eric J. *Vedantic Approaches to God.* London: Macmillan, 1980.

Marion, Jean-Luc. *God Without Being.* Translated by Thomas A. Carlson. Chicago: University of Chicago Press, 1991.

Morris, T.V., ed. *The Concept of God.* Oxford: Oxford University Press, 1987.

—. "Defining the Divine." In *Definitions and Definability: Philosophical Perspectives*, edited by James H. Fetzer, David Shatz, and George N. Schlesinger, 135–59. Dordrecht: Kluwer, 1991.

—. *Our Idea of God.* Downers Grove: InterVarsity, 1991.

Bibliography

Nash, Ronald H. *The Concept of God*. Grand Rapids, MI: Zondervan, 1983.

Owen, H. P. *Concepts of Deity*. New York: Herder and Herder, 1971.

Sorabji, Richard. *Time, Creation, & the Continuum*. London: Duckworth, 1983.

Wierenga, Edward R. *The Nature of God*. Ithaca, NY: Cornell University Press, 1989.

The Existence of God

Broad, Charlie Dunbar. "Arguments for the Existence of God, II." *Journal of Theological Studies* 40 (1939): 156–67.

Craig, William Lane. *The Kalam Cosmological Argument*. New York: Barnes and Noble, 1979.

Davis, Stephen T. *God, Reason, and Theistic Proofs*. Edinburgh: University of Edinburgh Press, 1997.

Dombrowski, Daniel A. *Rethinking the Ontological Argument*. Cambridge: Cambridge University Press, 2006.

Gale, Richard M. *On the Nature and Existence of God*. New York: Cambridge University Press, 1991.

Hick, John. *Rational Theistic Belief without Proof*. London: Macmillan, 1966.

Hick, John and Arthur C. McGill, eds. *The Many Faced Argument*. New York: Macmillan, 1967.

Moreland, J. P. *Consciousness and the Existence of God*. London: Routledge, 2008.

Oppy, Graham. *Arguing About Gods*. Cambridge: Cambridge University Press, 2006.

Reichenbach, Bruce. *The Cosmological Argument*. Springfield, IL: Charles C. Thomas, 1972.

Swinburne, Richard. *The Existence of God*. 2nd ed. Oxford: Clarendon, 2004.

Taliaferro, Charles. *Consciousness and the Mind of God*. Cambridge: Cambridge University Press, 1994.

God and Evil

Adams, Marilyn McCord. *Horrendous Evils and the Goodness of God*. Ithaca, NY: Cornell University Press, 1999.

—. *Christ and Horrors: The Coherence of Christology*. Cambridge: Cambridge University Press, 2006.

Adams, Marilyn McCord, and Robert Merrihew Adams. *The Problem of Evil*. Oxford: Oxford University Press, 1990.

Davies, Brian. *The Reality of God and the Problem of Evil*. London: Continuum, 2006.

Davis, Stephen T., ed. *Encountering Evil: Live Options in Theodicy*. Atlanta, GA: John Knox Press, 1981.

Draper, Paul. "Evil and the Proper Basicality of Belief in God." *Faith and Philosophy* 8 (1991): 135–47.

—. "Pain and Pleasure: An Evidential Problem for Theists." *Nous* 23 (1989): 331–50.

—. "Probabilistic Arguments from Evil." *Religious Studies* 28 (1992), 303–17.

Geivett, R. Douglas. *Evil and the Evidence for God: The Challenge of John Hick's Theodicy*. Philadelphia, PA: Temple University Press, 1993.

Graham, Gordon. *Evil and Christian Ethics*. Cambridge: Cambridge University Press, 2001.

Hasker, William. *The Triumph of Good over Evil: Theodicy for a World of Suffering*. Downers Grove, IL: InterVarsity, 2008.

Hick, John. *Evil and the God of Love*. New York: Harper and Row, 1978.

Hoffman, Joshua. "Can God Do Evil?" *Southern Journal of Philosophy* 17 (1979): 213–20.

Howard-Snyder, Daniel, ed. *The Evidential Argument From Evil*. Indianapolis: Indiana University Press, 1996.

Mackie, J.L. "Evil and Omnipotence." *Mind* 64 (1955): 200–12.

Martin, Michael. *Atheism: A Philosophical Justification.* Philadelphia, PA: Temple University Press, 1990.

Peterson, Michael L. *God and Evil: An Introduction to the Issues.* Boulder, CO: Westview Press, 1998.

Reichenbach, Bruce. *Evil and a Good God.* New York: Fordham University Press, 1982.

Ricoeur, Paul. *The Symbolism of Evil.* Translated by Emerson Buchanan. New York: Harper & Row, 1967.

Rowe, William L. "*The Problem of Evil and Some Varieties of Atheism.*" *American Philosophical Quarterly* 16 *(1979):* *335–41.* Reprinted in The Evidential Argument from Evil, edited by Daniel Howard-Snyder. Bloomington: Indiana University Press, 1996.

—. "Ruminations About Evil." *Philosophical Perspectives* 5 (1991): 69–88.

Swinburne, Richard. *Providence and the Problem of Evil.* Oxford: Clarendon, 1998.

Van Inwagen, Peter. *The Problem of Evil.* Oxford: Oxford University Press, 2006.

Divine Attributes

Craig, William Lane. *Time and Eternity: Exploring God's Relationship to Time.* Wheaton, IL: Crossway, 2001.

Fisher, John Martin, ed. *God, Foreknowledge, and Freedom.* Stanford, CA: Stanford University Press, 1989.

Flew, Antony. *God, Freedom and Immortality.* Buffalo, NY: Prometheus, 1984.

Hasker, William. *God, Time, and Knowledge.* Ithaca, NY: Cornell University Press, 1989.

Helm, Paul. *Eternal God.* Oxford: Oxford University Press, 1988.

—. *The Providence of God.* Downers Grove, IL: InterVarsity, 1994.

Hoffman, Joshua and Gary S. Rosenkrantz. *The Divine Attributes.* Oxford: Blackwell, 2002.

Kvanvig, Jonathan. *The Possibility of an All-Knowing God.* London: Macmillan, 1986.

Leftow, Brian. *Time and Eternity.* Ithaca, NY: Cornell University Press, 1991.

Mann, William E. "Divine Simplicity." *Religious Studies* 18 (1982): 451–71.

—. "Necessity." In *A Companion to Philosophy of Religion,* edited by Philip L. Quinn and Charles Taliaferro, 264–70. Oxford: Blackwell, 1997.

Stump, Eleonore, and Norman Kretzmann. "Eternity." *Journal of Philosophy* 78 (1981): 429–58.

Swinburne, Richard. *The Coherence of Theism.* Oxford: Clarendon, 1977.

Taliaferro, Charles. *Consciousness and the Mind of God.* Cambridge: Cambridge University Press, 1994.

Wierenga, Edward R. *The Nature of God: An Inquiry into Divine Attributes.* Ithaca, NY: Cornell University Press, 1989.

—. "Omnipresence." In *A Companion to the Philosophy of Religion,* edited by Philip L. Quinn and Charles Taliaferro, 286–90. Oxford: Blackwell, 1997.

Zagzebski, Linda T. *The Dilemma of Freedom and Foreknowledge.* New York: Oxford University Press, 1991.

Skepticism

Allen, Don Cameron. *Doubt's Boundless Sea: Skepticism and Faith in the Renaissance.* Baltimore, MD: Johns Hopkins Press, 1964.

Bergmann, Michael. "Externalism and Skepticism." *The Philosophical Review* 109 (2000), 159–94.

Bibliography

—. "Skeptical Theism and Rowe's New Evidential Argument from Evil." *Noûs* 35 (2001): 278–96.

—. "Skeptical Theism and the Problem of Evil." In *The Oxford Handbook of Philosophical Theology*, edited by Thomas Flint and Michael C. Rea. Oxford University Press, forthcoming.

Bergmann, Michael, and Michael Rea. "In Defense of Skeptical Theism: A Reply to Almeida and Oppy." *Australasian Journal of Philosophy* 83 (2005): 241–51.

Ferreira, M. Jamie. *Scepticism and Reasonable Doubt: the British Naturalist Tradition in Wilkins, Hume, Reid and Newman.* Oxford: Clarendon, 1986.

Jordan, Jeffrey. "Duff and the Wager." *Analysis* 51 (1991): 174–6.

—. *Gambling on God: Essay's on Pascal's Wager.* Lanham, MD: Rowman & Littlefield, 1994.

—. "Pascal's Wager and the Problem of Infinite Utilities." *Faith and Philosophy* 10 (1993): 49–59.

—. "Pascal's Wager Revisited." *Religious Studies* 34 (1998): 419–31.

—. "Pragmatic Arguments and Belief." *American Philosophical Quarterly* 33 (1996): 409–20.

—. "The St. Petersburg Paradox and Pascal's Wager." *Philosophia* 23 (1994): 226–40.

Meiland, Jack W. "What Ought We to Believe? Or the Ethics of Belief Revisited." *American Philosophical Quarterly* 17 (1980): 15–24.

Penelhum, Terence. *God and Skepticism: A Study in Skepticism and Fideism.* Boston, MA: D. Reidel, 1983.

Roth, Michael, and Glenn Ross, eds. *Doubting: Contemporary Perspectives on Skepticism.* Boston, MA: Kluwer, 1990.

Schellenberg, John L. *Divine Hiddenness and Human Reason.* Ithaca, NY: Cornell University Press, 1993.

—. *Prolegomena to a Philosophy of Religion.* Ithaca, NY: Cornell University Press, 2005.

—. *The Will to Imagine: A Justification of Skeptical Religion.* Ithaca, NY: Cornell University Press, 2009.

—. *The Wisdom to Doubt: A Justification of Religious Skepticism.* Ithaca, NY: Cornell University Press, 2007.

Unger, Peter. *Ignorance: A Case for Skepticism.* Oxford: Oxford University Press, 1975.

Atheism / Agnosticism

Antony, Louise M. *Philosophers Without Gods: Meditations on Atheism and the Secular Life.* New York: Oxford University Press, 2007.

Clifford, W. K. "The Ethics of Belief (1877)." In *The Ethics of Belief and Other Essays*, 70–96.Amherst, NY: Prometheus, 1999.

Everitt, Nicholas. *The Non-Existence of God.* London: Routledge, 2004.

Findlay, J. N. "Can God's Existence be Disproved?" *Mind* 37 (1948): 176–83. Reprinted in *New Essays in Philosophical Theology*, edited by Antony Flew and Alasdair MacIntyre. London: SCM Press, 1955. See also replies by G. E. Hughes and A. C. A. Rainer and final comment by Findlay.

Freud, Sigmund. *The Future of an Illusion.* Translated by James Strachey. New York: W. W. Norton, 1961. First published 1927 by Hogarth Press.

Gettier, Edmund L. "Is Justified True Belief Knowledge?" *Analysis*, 23 (1963): 121–3.

Hedge, Frederic Henry. *Atheism in Philosophy, and Other Essays.* Boston, MA: Roberts Brothers, 1884.

Kenny, Anthony. *The Unknown God: Agnostic Essays.* London: Continuum, 2005.

Levine, Michael P. *Pantheism: A Non-Theistic Concept of Deity*, London: Routledge, 1994.

Lilje, Hanns. *Atheism, Humanism, and Christianity: Today's Struggle for the Mind of Man*. Minneapolis: Augsburg, 1964.

Martin, Michael. *Atheism: A Philosophical Justification*. Philadelphia: Temple University Press, 1990.

—. *Atheism, Morality, and Meaning*, NY: Prometheus, 2002.

Rinaldo, Peter M. *Atheists, Agnostics, and Deists in America: A Brief History*. Briarcliff Manor, New York: DorPete Press, 2000.

Rundle, Bede. *Why There is Something Rather Than Nothing*. Oxford: Oxford University Press, 2004.

Smart, J. J. C., and J. J. Haldane. *Atheism and Theism*. Oxford: Blackwell, 1996.

Smith, George H. *Atheism: The Case Against God*. Los Angeles, Nash: 1974.

Sutherland, Stuart R. *Atheism and the Rejection of God: Contemporary Philosophy and the Brothers Karamazov*. Oxford: Blackwell, 1977.

Westphal, Merold. *Suspicion and Faith: The Religious Uses of Modern Atheism*. New York: Fordham University Press, 1998.

Religion and Science

Baker, Stuart E. *Bernard Shaw's Remarkable Religion: A Faith that Fits the Facts*. Gainesville, University Press of Florida, 2002.

Barbour, Ian. *Myths, Models, and Paradigms*. New York: Harper and Row, 1974.

Beilby, James, ed. *Naturalism Defeated: Essays on Plantinga's Evolutionary Argument Against Naturalism*. Ithaca, NY: Cornell University Press, 2002.

Berger, Peter. *The Social Construction of Reality*. New York: Doubleday Anchor, 1967.

Brooke, John Hedley, ed. *Science and Religion: Some Historical Perspectives*. Cambridge: Cambridge University Press, 1991.

Craig, William Lane, and J. P. Moreland, eds. *Naturalism: A Critical Analysis*. London: Routledge, 2000.

The Dalai Lama. *The Universe in a Single Atom: The Convergence of Science and Spirituality*, New York: Morgan Road Books, 2005.

Dembski, William A. "On the Very Possibility of Intelligent Design." In *The Creation Hypothesis*, edited by J. P. Moreland, 113–38. Downers Grove, IL: InterVarsity, 1994.

Dobzhansky, Theodosius. *The Biology of Ultimate Concern*. London: Fontana, 1971.

Draper, John William. *History of the Conflict between Religion and Science*. New York: D. Appleton, 1875.

Ferngren, Gary B., ed. *The History of Science and Religion in the Western Tradition: An Encyclopedia*. New York: Garland, 2000.

Forrest, Peter. *God without the Supernatural: A Defense of Scientific Theism*. Ithaca, NY: Cornell University Press, 1996.

Fuller, Steve. *Science vs. Religion? Intelligent Design and the Problem of Evolution*. Malden, MA: Polity, 2007.

Henderson, Charles P. *God and Science: the Death and Rebirth of Theism*. Atlanta, GA: John Knox, 1986.

Bibliography

Leslie, John. "How To Draw Conclusions From a Fine-Tuned Cosmos." In *Physics, Philosophy and Theology: A Common Quest for Understanding*, edited by Robert J. Russell, William R. Stoeger, S. J., and George V. Coyne, S. J., 297–312. Vatican City State: Vatican Observatory Press, 1988.

McMullin, Ernan. "Introduction: Evolution and Creation." In *Evolution and Creation*, edited by Ernan McMullin, 1–56. Notre Dame, IN: University of Notre Dame Press, 1985.

—. "Plantinga's Defense of Special Creation." *Christian Scholar's Review* 21.1 (1991): 55–79.

Midgley, Mary. *Evolution as a Religion: Strange Hopes and Stranger Fears*. London: Methuen, 1985.

Murphy, Nancey. "Divine Action in the Natural Order: Buridan's Ass and Schrodinger's Cat." In *Chaos and Complexity: Scientific Perspectives on Divine Action*, edited by Robert J. Russell, Nancey Murphy, and Arthur Peacocke, 325–57. Vatican City State: Vatican Observatory Publications, 1995.

—. 1998. "Nonreductive Physicalism: Philosophical Issues." In *Whatever Happened to the Soul? Scientific and Theological Portraits of Human Nature*, edited by Warren S. Brown, Nancey Murphy, and H. Newton Malony, 127–48. Minneapolis: Fortress, 1998.

—. *Theology in the Age of Scientific Reasoning*. Ithaca, NY: Cornell University Press, 1990.

O'Connor, Robert C. "Science on Trial: Exploring the Rationality of Methodological Naturalism." *Perspectives on Science and Christian Faith* 49 (Mar. 1997): 15–30.

Penrose, Roger. *The Emperor's New Mind: Concerning Computers, Minds, and the Laws of Physics*. New York: Oxford University Press, 1989.

Plantinga, Alvin. "Evolution, Neutrality, and Antecedent Probability: A Reply to McMullin and Van Till." *Christian Scholar's Review* 21.1 (Sept. 1991): 80–109.

—. "Methodological Naturalism?" *Perspectives on Science and Christian Faith* 49 (Sept. 1997): 143–54.

Polkinghorne, John. *Science and Providence: God's Interaction with the World*. Boston: Shambhala, 1989.

Pollard, William G. *Chance and Providence: God's Action in a World Governed by Scientific Law*. New York: Scribner, 1958.

Quinn, Philip L. "The Philosopher of Science as Expert Witness." In *But Is It Science? The Philosophical Question in the Creation/Evolution Controversy*, edited by Michael Ruse, 367–85. Buffalo, N.Y.: Prometheus, 1996. Reprinted from *Science and Reality: Recent Work in the Philosophy of Science*, edited by James T. Cushing, C. F. Delaney, and Gary M. Gutting, 32–53. Notre Dame, IN: University of Notre Dame Press, 1984.

Rea, Michael C. *World Without Design: The Ontological Consequences of Naturalism*. Oxford: Oxford University Press, 2002.

Ricard, Matthieu, and Trinh Xuan Thuan. *The Quantum and the Lotus: A Journey to the Frontiers Where Science and Buddhism Meet*. New York: Crown Publishers, 2001.

Rolston, Holmes, III. *Genes, Genesis and God: Values and Their Origins in Natural and Human History*. Cambridge: Cambridge University Press, 1999.

—. *Science and Religion: A Critical Survey*. Philadelphia, PA: Templeton, 1987. With a new introduction, 2006.

Ruse, Michael. *Darwinism Defended: A Guide to the Evolution Controversies*. Reading, MA: Addison-Wesley, 1982.

Russell, Bertrand. *Religion and Science*. New York: Henry Holt, 1935.

Schlesinger, George. *Religion and Scientific Method*. Dordrecht: D. Reidel, 1977.

—. *The Sweep of Probability*. Notre Dame, IN: University of Notre Dame Press, 1991.

Sober, Elliott. *Philosophy of Biology*. 2nd ed. Boulder, CO: Westview, 2000.

Trigg, Roger. *Rationality and Science: Can Science Explain Everything?* Oxford: Blackwell, 1993.

Pluralism

Alston, William P. "Religious Diversity and the Perceptual Knowledge of God." *Faith and Philosophy* 5 (1988): 433–48.

Basinger, David. *Religious Diversity: A Philosophical Assessment.* Aldershot, UK: Ashgate, 2002.

Bryant, M. Darroll, ed. *Pluralism, Tolerance and Dialogue.* Ontario: University of Waterloo Press, 1989.

Byrne, Peter. *Prolegomena to Religious Pluralism: Reference and Realism in Religion.* New York: St. Martin's Press, 1995.

Clark, Kelly James. "Perils of Pluralism." *Faith and Philosophy* 14 (1997): 303–20.

D'Costa, Gavin. *Theology and Religious Pluralism: The Challenge of Other Religions.* Oxford: Blackwell, 1986.

de Vries, Hent, and Lawrence E. Sullivan, eds. *Political Theologies: Public Religions in a Post-Secular World.* New York: Fordham University Press, 2006.

Eck, Diana L. *A New Religious America: How a "Christian Country" Has Now Become the World's Most Religiously Diverse Nation.* New York: HarperSanFrancisco, 2001.

Griffiths, Paul J. "Comparative Philosophy of Religion." In *A Companion to Philosophy of Religion,* edited by Philip L. Quinn and Charles Taliaferro, 615–20. Oxford: Blackwell, 1997.

—. *Problems of Religious Diversity.* Malden, MA: Blackwell, 2001.

Gyatso, Tenzin. *Freedom in Exile: The Autobiography of the Dalai Lama of Tibet.* London: Abacus, 1998.

Hick, John. *God Has Many Names.* London: Macmillan, 1980.

—. *An Interpretation of Religion.* New Haven, CT: Yale University Press, 2004.

—. "The Philosophy of World Religions." *Scottish Journal of Theology* 37 (1984): 229–36.

Kekes, John. *Pluralism in Philosophy: Changing the Subject.* Ithaca, NY: Cornell University Press, 2000.

Knitter, Paul. *No Other Name? A Critical Survey of Christian Attitudes towards the World Religions.* Maryknoll, NY: Orbis Books, 1985.

McKim, Robert. *Religious Ambiguity and Religious Diversity.* New York: Oxford University Press, 2001.

Meister, Chad, ed. *The Oxford Handbook of Religious Diversity.* Oxford: Oxford University Press, forthcoming.

Netland, Harold. *Dissonant Voices: Christians and Religious Pluralism.* Grand Rapids, MI: Eerdmans, 1991.

—. *Encountering Religious Pluralism: The Challenge to Christian Faith and Mission.* Downers Grove, IL: InterVarsity, 2001.

Quinn, Philip L. and Kevin Meeker, eds. *The Philosophical Challenge of Religious Diversity.* New York: Oxford University Press, 2000.

Race, Alan. *Christians and Religious Pluralism: Patterns in the Christian Theology of Religions.* London: SCM, 1983.

Rescher, Nicholas. *Pluralism: Against the Demand for Consensus.* Oxford: Clarendon, 1993.

Runzo, Joseph. *Global Philosophy of Religion: A Short Introduction.* Oxford: Oneworld, 2001.

Smith, Wilfred Cantwell. *Religious Diversity.* New York: Harper and Row, 1976.

Solomon, Norman, Richard Harries, and Timothy J. Winter, eds. *Abraham's Children: Jews, Christians, and Muslims in Conversation.* New York: T & T Clark, 2005.

Tilley, Terrence W. *Religious Diversity and the American Experience: A Theological Approach.* New York: Continuum, 2007.

Wainwright, William J. "Religious Experience and Religious Pluralism." In *The Philosophical Challenge of Religious Diversity,* edited by Philip L. Quinn and Kevin Meeker, 218–25. New York: Oxford University Press, 2000.

Ward, Keith. *Religion and Revelation.* New York: Oxford University Press, 1994.

Zagorin, Perez. *How The Idea of Religious Toleration Came To The West.* Princeton, NJ: Princeton University Press, 2003.

Feminist Philosophy of Religion

Allen, Paula Gunn. *The Sacred Hoop: Recovering the Feminine in American Indian Traditions.* Boston: Beacon Press, 1986.

Anderson, Pamela Sue. *A Feminist Philosophy of Religion: The Rationality and Myths of Religious Belief.* Oxford: Blackwell, 1998.

Carmody, Denise Lardner. *Feminism and Christianity: A Two-Way Reflection.* Nashville: Abingdon, 1982.

Cooey, Paula M. *Religious Imagination and the Body: A Feminist Analysis.* New York: Oxford University Press, 1994.

Daly, Mary. *Beyond God the Father: Toward a Philosophy of Women's Liberation.* Boston: Beacon Press, 1973.

Ebest, Sally Barr, and Ron Ebest. *Reconciling Catholicism and Feminism?: Personal Reflections on Tradition and Change.* Notre Dame, IN: University of Notre Dame Press, 2003.

Erickson, Victoria Lee. *Where Silence Speaks: Feminism, Social Theory, and Religion.* Minneapolis: Fortress, 1993.

Fulkerson, Mary McClintock. *Changing the Subject: Women's Discourses and Feminist Theology.* Minneapolis: Fortress, 1994.

Gross, Rita M. *Feminism and Religion: An Introduction.* Boston: Beacon, 1996.

Jantzen, Grace M. *Becoming Divine: Towards a Feminist Philosophy of Religion.* Bloomington: Indiana University Press, 1999.

Krafte-Jacobs, Lori. *Feminism and Modern Jewish Theological Method.* New York: Peter Lang, 1996.

Nye, Andrea. *Feminism and Modern Philosophy: An Introduction.* New York: Routledge, 2004.

Yamani, Mai, ed. *Feminism and Islam: Legal and Literary Persepctives.* New York: New York University Press, 1996.

Miracles

Basinger, David and Randall Basinger. *Philosophy and Miracle: The Contemporary Debate.* Lewiston, NY: Edwin Mellen, 1986.

Brown, Colin. *That You May Believe: Miracles and Faith: Then and Now.* Grand Rapids, MI: Eerdmans, 1985.

Cavadini, John C., ed. *Miracles in Jewish and Christian Antiquity: Imagining Truth.* Notre Dame, IN: University of Notre Dame Press, 1999.

Cotter, Wendy. *Miracles in Greco-Roman Antiquity: A Sourcebook for the Study of New Testament Miracle Stories.* New York: Routledge, 1999.

Flew, Antony. *Hume's Philosophy of Belief: A Study of His First Inquiry*. New York: Humanities Press, 1961.

Fogelin, Robert J. *A Defense of Hume on Miracles*. Princeton, NJ: Princeton University Press, 2003.

Fuller, Reginald H. *Interpreting the Miracles*. London: SCM Press, 1963.

Geivett, Douglas R. and Gary R.Habermas, eds. *In Defense of Miracles: A Comprehensive Case for God's Action in History*. Downers Grove, IL: InterVarsity, 1997.

Gross, Don H. *The Case for Spiritual Healing*. New York: Thomas Nelson, 1958.

Houston, Joseph. *Reported Miracles: A Critique of Hume*. Cambridge: Cambridge University Press, 1994.

Hume, David. "Of Miracles." In *An Enquiry Concerning Human Understanding*, edited by Eric Steinberg, 76–95. Indianapolis, IN: Hackett, 1993. New York: Oxford University Press, 2000.

Kallas, James G. *The Significance of the Synoptic Miracles*. Greenwich: CT, Seabury, 1961.

Kee, Howard Clarke. *Medicine, Miracle, and Magic in New Testament Times*. New York: Cambridge University Press, 1988.

Lewis, C. S. *Miracles*. New York: Harper Collins, 2001.

McInerny, Ralph. *Miracles: A Catholic View*. Huntington, IN: Our Sunday Visitor, 1986.

McKinnon, Alastair. "'Miracles' and 'Paradox.'" *American Philosophical Quarterly* 4 (1967): 308–14.

Swinburne, Richard. *The Concept of Miracle*. New York: St. Martin's Press, 1970.

—, ed. *Miracles*. New York: Macmillan, 1989.

Wenham, David, and Craig L. Blomberg, eds. *The Miracles of Jesus*. Sheffield: JSOT Press, 1986.

Faith and Revelation

Abraham, William J. *Crossing the Threshold of Divine Revelation*. Grand Rapids, MI: Eerdmans, 2007.

—. Divine Revelation and the Limits of Historical Criticism. Oxford: Oxford University Press, 2000.

Adams, Robert Merrihew. *The Virtue of Faith and Other Essays in Philosophical Theology*. Oxford: Oxford University Press, 1987.

Chappell, Tim. "Why is Faith a Virtue?" *Religious Studies* 32 (1996): 27–36.

Evans, C. Stephen. *Faith Beyond Reason: A Kierkegaardian Account*. Edinburgh: Edinburgh University Press, 1998.

—. *Kierkegaard's* Fragments *and* Postscript: *The Religious Philosophy of Johannes Climacus*. Atlantic Highlands, NJ: Humanities Press, 1983.

—. *Passionate Reason: Making Sense of Kierkegaard's* Philosophical Fragments. Bloomington: Indiana University Press, 1992.

Kierkegaard, Søren. *Concluding Unscientific Postscript*. Edited and translated by Howard V. Hong and Edna H. Hong. Princeton, NJ: Princeton University Press, 1992. Originally published 1846.

—. *For Self-Examination/Judge for Yourself*. Edited and translated by Howard V. Hong and Edna H. Hong. Princeton, NJ: Princeton University Press, 1990. *Judge for Yourself* written in 1851–1852 and published posthumously in 1876.

—. *Philosophical Fragments*. Edited and translated by Howard V. Hong and Edna H. Hong. Princeton, NJ: Princeton University Press, 1985. Originally published 1844.

—. *The Sickness Unto Death*. Edited and translated by Howard V. Hong and Edna H. Hong. Princeton, NJ: Princeton University Press, 1980. Originally published 1849.

Locke, John. *An Essay Concerning Human Understanding*. Edited by Peter H. Nidditch. Oxford: Oxford University Press, 1975. Originally published 1689.

Mavrodes, George I. *Revelation in Religious Belief*. Philadelphia: Temple University Press, 1988.

Price, Theron. *Revelation and Faith: Theological Reflections on the Knowing and Doing of Truth*. Macon, GA: Mercer University Press, 1987.

Swinburne, Richard. *Revelation: From Metaphor to Analogy*. 2nd ed. Oxford: Clarendon, 2007.

—. *Faith and Reason*. 2nd ed. Oxford: Clarendon, 2005.

Wolterstorff, Nicholas. *Divine Discourse: Philosophical Reflections on the Claim that God Speaks*. Cambridge: Cambridge University Press, 1995.

—. *John Locke and the Ethics of Belief*. Cambridge: Cambridge University Press, 1996.

Greco-Roman Theology

Colvin, Stephen, ed. *The Greco-Roman East: Politics, Culture, Society*. New York: Cambridge University Press, 2004.

Craig, William Lane. *The Cosmological Argument from Plato to Leibniz*. London: Macmillan, 1980.

Dombrowski, Daniel A. *A Platonic Philosophy of Religion: A Process Perspective*. Albany, NY: State University of New York, 2005.

Jeffers, James S. *The Greco-Roman World of the New Testament Era: Exploring the Background of Early Christianity*. Downers Grove, IL: InterVarsity, 1999.

Lapin, Hayim, ed. *Religious and Ethnic Communities in Later Roman Palestine*. Potomac, MD: University Press of Maryland, 1998.

Mesopotamian and Egypt Theology

Chavalas, Mark W. and K. Lawson Younger, eds. *Mesopotamia and the Bible: Comparative Explorations*. Grand Rapids, MI: Baker, 2002.

Downey, Susan B. *Mesopotamian Religious Architecture: Alexander through the Parthians*. Princeton, NJ: Princeton University Press, 1988.

Levtow, Nathaniel B. *Images of Others: Iconic Politics in Ancient Israel*. Winona Lake, IN: Eisenbrauns, 2008.

Snell, Daniel C., ed. *A Companion to the Ancient Near East*. Malden, MA: Blackwell, 2005.

Zoroastrianism

Bharucha, Ervad Sheriarji Dadabhai. *A Brief Sketch of the Zoroastrian Religion and Customs: An Essay*. Bombay: D. B. Taraporevala Sons, 1928.

Clark, Peter. *Zoroastrianism: An Introduction to an Ancient Faith*. Portland, OR: Sussex, 1998.

Dhalla, Maneckji Nusservanji. *History of Zoroastrianism*. New York: Oxford University Press, 1938.

Duchesne-Guillemin, Jacques. *Symbols and Values in Zoroastrianism: Their Survival and Renewal.* New York: Harper & Row, 1966.

Masani, Rustom Pestonji. *The Religion of the Good Life, Zoroastrianism.* London: George Allen & Unwin, 1938. Reprinted in 1954.

Moulton, James Hope. *The Treasure of the Magi: A Study of Modern Zoroastrianism.* London: Oxford University Press, 1917.

Judaism

Albo, Joseph. *Sefer ha-'Ikkarim [Book of Principles].* Edited and translated by Isaac Husik. Philadelphia: Jewish Publication Society, 1929. Written in 1425.

Berger, David. "Judaism and general culture in medieval and Early Modern times." In *Judaism's Encounter With Other Cultures: Rejection or Integration,* edited by Jacob J. Schacter, 133–5. Northvale, NJ: Jason Aronson, 1997.

Cohen, Arthur A. and Paul Mendes-Flohr, eds. *Contemporary Jewish Religious Thought.* New York: Free Press, 1987.

Frank, Daniel H., and Oliver Leaman, eds. *History of Jewish Philosophy.* London: Routledge, 1997.

Gordis, Daniel. *God Was Not in the Fire: The Search for a Spiritual Judaism.* New York: Scribner, 1995.

Hertzberg, Arthur. *Judaism.* New York: George Braziller, 1961.

Heschel, Abraham Joshua. *God in Search of Man: A Philosophy of Judaism.* New York: Farrar, Straus, and Cudahy, 1955.

Idelsohn, Abraham Z. *The Ceremonies of Judaism.* Cincinnati, IN: The National Federation of Temple Brotherhoods, 1930.

Kellner, Menachem. *Contemporary Jewish Ethics.* New York: Sanhedrin Press, 1978.

Maimonides, Moses. *The Guide of the Perplexed.* Translated by Shlomo Pines. Chicago: University of Chicago Press, 1963.

Noveck, Simon. *Contemporary Jewish Thought: A Reader.* Washington, DC: Bnai Brith Department of Adult Jewish Education, 1963.

Plaut, W. Gunther. *The Case for the Chosen People.* New York: Doubleday, 1965.

Satlow, Michael L. *Creating Judaism: History, Tradition, Practice.* New York: Columbia University Press, 2006.

Christianity

Abraham, William J. *Canon and Criterion in Christian Theology: From the Fathers to Feminism.* Oxford: Clarendon, 1998.

Beaty, Michael D., ed. *Christian Theism and the Problems of Philosophy.* Notre Dame, IN: University of Notre Dame Press, 1990.

Beilby, James, and Paul R. Eddy, eds. *Divine Foreknowledge: Four Views.* Downers Grove, IL: InterVarsity, 2001.

Brown, David. *God and Enchantment of Place: Reclaiming Human Experience.* Oxford: Oxford University Press, 2004.

—. *God and Grace of Body: Sacrament in Ordinary.* Oxford: Oxford University Press, 2007.

—. *God and Mystery in Words: Experience Through Metaphor and Drama.* Oxford University Press, 2008.

—. *Discipleship and Imagination: Christian Tradition and Truth.* Oxford: Oxford University Press, 2000.

—. *The Divine Trinity.* London: Duckworth, 1985.

—. *Tradition and Imagination: Revelation and Change.* Oxford: Oxford University Press, 1999.

Craig, William Lane. *The Only Wise God: The Compatibility of Divine Foreknowledge and Human Freedom.* Eugene, OR: Wipf and Stock, 2000.

Davis, Stephen T. *Christian Philosophical Theology.* Oxford: Oxford University Press, 2006.

Davis, Stephen T., Daniel Kendall, and Gerald O'Collins, eds. *The Incarnation: An Interdisciplinary Symposium on the Incarnation of the Son of God.* Oxford: Oxford University Press, 2002.

—, eds. *The Trinity: An Interdisciplinary Symposium on the Trinity.* Oxford: Oxford University Press, 2002.

Evans, C. Stephen. *The Historical Christ and the Jesus of Faith: The Incarnational Narrative as History.* Oxford: Clarendon, 1996.

Fisher, John Martin, ed. *God, Foreknowledge, and Freedom.* Stanford, CA: Stanford University Press, 1989.

Flint, Thomas P., and Michael C. Rea, eds. *The Oxford Handbook of Philosophical Theology.* New York: Oxford University Press, 2009.

Hasker, William. *God, Time, and Knowledge.* Ithaca, NY: Cornell University Press, 1989.

Hutchinson, Paul, and Winfred E. Garrison. *20 Centuries of Christianity: A Concise History.* New York: Harcourt, Brace, and World, 1959.

Lewis, C. S. *Christian Reflections.* Grand Rapids, MI: Eerdmans, 1967.

—. *The Case for Christianity.* New York: Macmillan, 1948.

McGrath, Alister E. *Christian Theology: An Introduction.* Oxford: Blackwell, 1994.

More, Paul Elmer. *The Catholic Faith.* Princeton, NJ: Princeton University Press, 1931.

Morris, Thomas V. *The Logic of God Incarnate.* Ithaca, NY: Cornell University Press, 1986.

Taliaferro, Charles and Chad Meister, eds. *The Cambridge Companion to Christian Philosophical Theology.* Cambridge: Cambridge University Press, 2009.

Westphal, Merold. *Overcoming Onto-Theology: Towards a Postmodern Christian Faith.* New York: Fordham University Press, 2001.

Islam

Armstrong, Karen. *Islam: A Short History.* New York: Modern Library, 2000.

Arnold, Thomas, and Alfred Guillaume, eds. *The Legacy of Islam.* London: Oxford University Press, 1945.

Averroes. *Faith and Reason in Islam.* Translated by Ibrahim Y. Najjar. Oxford: Oneworld, 2001.

Cragg, Kenneth. *The House of Islam.* Belmount, CA: Dickenson, 1969.

Craig, William Lane. *The* Kalam *Cosmological Argument.* London: Macmillan, 1979.

Fakhry, Majid. *Islamic Philosophy, Theology, and Mysticis.* Oxford: Oneworld, 1997.

Fry, C. George. *Islam, A Survey of the Muslim Faith*. Grand Rapids, MI: Baker, 1980.

Geaves, Ron. *Aspects of Islam*. Washington, D.C.: Georgetown University Press, 2005.

Lunde, Paul. *Islam*. New York: Dorling Kindersley, 2002.

Maimonides, Moses. *The Guide of the Perplexed*. Translated by Shlomo Pines. Chicago: University of Chicago Press, 1963.

Nasr, Seyyed Hossein. *Ideals and Realities of Islam*. Boston: Beacon, 1972.

Nigosian, Solomon Alexander. *Islam: Its History, Teaching, and Practices*. Bloomington: Indiana University Press, 2004.

Hinduism

Anonymous. *The Bhagavad Gita*. New York: Penguin Classics, 2003.

—. *The Upanishads*. Translated by Juan Mascaro. New York: Penguin, 1965.

Bartley, Christopher J. *The Theology of Ramanuja: Realism and Religion*. London: Routledge Curzon, 2002.

Chaudhuri, Nirad C. *Hinduism, a Religion to Live By*. New York: Oxford University Press, 1979.

Deutsch, Eliot S. *Advaita Vedanta: A Philosophical Reconstruction*. Honolulu: East West Center, 1969.

Deutsch, Eliot S., and Rohit Dalvi, eds. *The Essential Vedanta: A New Source Book of Advaita Vedanta*. Bloomington, IN: World Wisdom, 2004.

Ganeri, Jonardon. *Philosophy in Classical India*. New York: Routledge, 2001.

George Thibaut. *The Vedanta Sutras with the Commentary by Ramanuja*. Whitefish, MT: Kessinger, 2004.

Flood, Gavin D. *An Introduction to Hinduism*. Cambridge: Cambridge University Press, 1996.

Fowler, Jeaneane. *Hinduism: Beliefs and Practices*. Portland, OR: Sussex, 1997.

Kinsley, David R. *Hinduism, a Cultural Perspective*. Englewood, NJ: Prentice-Hall, 1982.

Matilal, Bimal Krishna. *The Character of Logic in India*. Edited by Jonardon Ganeri and Heeraman Tiwari. Albany, NY: State University of New York Press, 1998.

—. *Epistemology, Logic, and Grammar in Indian Philosophical Analysis*. The Hague: Mouton, 1971.

—. *Logic, Language and Reality: An Introduction to Indian Philosophical Studies*. Delhi: Matilal Banarsidass, 1985.

—. *Perception: An Essay on Classical Indian Theories of Knowledge*. Oxford: Clarendon, 1986.

Matilal, Bimal Krishna and Arindam Chakrabarti, eds. *Knowing From Words: Western and Indian Philosophical Analysis of Understanding and Testimony*. Dordrecht: Kluwer, 1994.

Mayeda, Sengaku, ed. *A Thousand Teachings: The Upadesasahasri of Sankara*. Tokyo: University of Tokyo Press, 1979. Reprinted in 1992.

Mohanty, Jitendranath Nath. *Classical Indian Philosophy*. Landham, MD: Rowman and Littlefield, 2000.

—. *Reason and Tradition in Indian Thought: An Essay on the Nature of Indian Philosophical Thinking*. Oxford: Clarendon, 1992.

—. *The Self and Its Other: Philosophical Essays*. Oxford: Oxford University Press, 2000.

Rambachan, Anantanand. *The Hindu Vision*. Delhi: Motilal Banarsidass Publishers, 1992.

—. *The Advaita Worldview: God, World, and Humanity*. New York: State University of New York Press, 2006.

Rodrigues, Hillary P. *Introducing Hinduism*. London: Routledge, 2006.

Sen, Kshitmohan M. *Hinduism*. Baltimore, MD: Penguin, 1961.

Shankara. *Shankara's Crest-Jewel of Discrimination*. Translated by Swami Prabhavananda and Christopher Isherwood. Hollywood, CA: Vedanta Press, 1947.

—. *The Vedanta Sutras of Badarayana, with Commentary by Sankara*. 2 vols. Translated by George Thibaut. New York: Dover, 1962

Sharma, Arvind. *Classical Hindu Thought: An Introduction*. New York: Oxford University Press, 2000.

—. *A Hindu Perspective on the Philosophy of Religion*. New York: St. Martin's Press, 1990.

—. *The Philosophy of Religion and Advaita Vedanta: A Comparative Study in Religion and Reason*. University Park: Pennsylvania State University Press, 1995.

—. *The Study of Hinduism*. Columbia: University of South Carolina Press, 2003.

Wainwright, William J. "Monotheism." In *Rationality, Religious Belief, and Moral Commitment: New Essays in the Philosophy of Religion*, edited by Robert Audi and William J. Wainwright, 289–314. Ithaca, NY: Cornell University Press, 1986.

Buddhism

Abe, Masao. *Zen and the Western Thought*. Edited by William R. Lafleur. Honolulu: The University of Hawaii Press, 1989.

Anonymous. *The Dhammapada: A New Translation of the Buddhist Classic with Annotations*. Edited and translated by Gil Fronsdal. Boston, MA: Shambhala, 2005.

Austin, James H. *Zen and the Brain: Toward an Understanding of Meditation and Consciousness*. Cambridge, MA: MIT Press, 1998.

Batchelor, Stephen. *Buddhism without Beliefs: A Contemporary Guide to Awakening*. New York: Riverhead, 1997.

Buddhaghosa, Bhadantacariya. *The Path of Purification: Visuddhimagga*. Translated by Bhikkhu Nanamoli. Onalaska, WA: Pariyatti, 2003.

Carrithers, Michael. *The Buddha: A Very Short Introduction*. Oxford: Oxford University Press, 2001.

Collins, Steven. *Nirvana and Other Buddhist Felicities*. Cambridge: Cambridge University Press, 1998.

Conze, Edward. *Buddhism: Its Essence and Development*. New York: Harper & Row, 1975.

Dumoulin, Heinrich. *Zen Buddhism: A History*. 2 vols. Bloomington, IN: World Wisdom, 2005.

Dutt, Nalinaksha. *Buddhist Sects in India*. Delhi: Motilal Banarsidass, 1978.

Fowler, Merv. *Buddhism: Beliefs and Practices*. Portland, OR: Sussex, 1999.

Gethin, Rupert. *The Foundations of Buddhism*. Oxford: Oxford University Press, 1998.

Griffiths, Paul J. *On Being Buddha: The Classical Doctrine of Buddhahood*. Albany: State University Press of New York, 1994.

Griffiths, Paul J., Noriaki Hakamaya, John P. Keenan, and Paul L. Swanson, eds. and trans. *The Realm of Awakening: A Translation and Study of Chapter Ten of Asanga's Mahayanasangraha*. New York: Oxford University Press, 1989.

Hayes, Richard P. "Principal Atheism in the Buddhist Scholastic Tradition." *Journal of Indian Philosophy* 16 (1988): 5–28.

Hesse, Hermann. *Siddhartha: An Indian Tale.* New York: Penguin, 1999.

Huntington, C. W. *The Emptiness of Emptiness: An Introduction to Early Indian Madhyamika.* Honolulu: University of Hawaii Press, 1989.

Jackson, Roger R. "Dharmakirti's Refutation of Theism." *Philosophy East and West* 36 (1986): 315–48.

Jayatilleke, Kulatissa Nanda. *The Message of the Buddha.* Edited by Ninian Smart. New York: The Free Press, 1975.

Kalupahana, David J. *Nagarjuna: The Philosophy of the Middle Way.* Albany: State University of New York Press, 1986.

—. *The Principle of Buddhist Psychology.* Albany: State University of New York Press, 1987.

King, Richard. *Indian Philosophy: An Introduction to Hindu and Buddhist Thought.* Washington, DC: Georgetown University Press, 1999.

—. *Orientalism and Religion: Postcolonial Theory, India and 'The Mystic East'.* London: Routledge, 1999.

Lillie, Arthur. *Buddha and Early Buddhism.* London: Trubner, 1881.

Lusthaus, Dan. *Buddhist Phenomenology: A Philosophical Investigation of Yogacara Buddhism and the* Ch'eng Wet-shih Lun. London: RoutledgeCurzon, 2002.

Matilal, Bimal Krishna. *Perception: An Essay on Classical Indian Theories of Knowledge.* Oxford: Clarendon, 1986.

McCagney, Nancy. *Nagarjuna and the Philosophy of Openess.* Lanham, MD: Rowman & Littlefield, 1997.

Nagarjuna. *The Fundamental Wisdom of the Middle Way. Nagarjuna's Mulamadhyamakakarika.* Translated by Jay L. Garfield. Oxford: Oxford University Press, 1995.

Oldenberg, Hermann. *Buddha: His Life, His Doctrine, His Order.* Translated by William Hoey. Whitefish, MT: Kessinger, 2003. Originally published 1882.

Percheron, Maurice. *Buddha and Buddhism.* New York: Harper, 1957.

Potter, Karl H., et. al., eds. *Encyclopedia of Indian Philosophies.* Vol. 7, *Abhidharma Buddhism to 150 A.D.* Delhi: Motilal Banarsidass, 1996.

Queen, Christopher, Charles Prebish, and Damien Keown, eds. *Action Dharma: New Studies in Engaged Buddhism.* London: Routledge Curzon, 2003.

Ross, Nancy Wilson. *Buddhism, a Way of Life and Thought.* New York: Vintage Books, 1980.

Streng, Frederick J. *Emptiness: A Study in Religious Meaning.* Nashville, TN: Abingdon, 1967.

Suzuki, D. T. *Zen Buddhism: Selected Writings of D.T. Suzuki.* Edited by William Barrett. Garden City, NY: Doubleday, 1956.

—. *An Introduction to Zen Buddhism.* New York: Grove/Atlantic, 1991.

von Glasenapp, Helmuth. *Buddhism: A Non-Theistic Religion.* New York: George Braziller, 1971.

Walshe, Maurice O'Connell. *Buddhism for Today.* New York: Philosophical Library, 1963.

Watts, Alan W. *The Way of Zen.* New York: Vintage, 1999.

Williams, Paul. *Mahayana Buddhism: The Doctrinal Foundations.* London: Routledge, 1989.

Williams, Paul and Anthony J. Tribe. *Buddhist Thought: A Complete Introduction to the Indian Tradition.* London: Routledge, 2000.

Daoism

Bokenkamp, Stephen R. *Ancestors and Anxiety: Daoism and the Birth of Rebirth in China*. Berkeley: University of California Press, 2007.

Chan, Wing-tsit. *A Source Book in Chinese Philosophy*. Princeton, NJ: Princeton University Press, 1963.

Chiu, Milton M. *The Tao of Chinese Religion*. Lanham, MD: University Press of America, 1984.

Clarke, John James. *The Tao of the West: Western Transformations of Taoist Thought*. New York: Routledge, 2000.

Hansen, Chad. *A Daoist Theory of Chinese Thought: A Philosophical Interpretation*. New York: Oxford University Press, 1992.

—. *Language and Logic in Ancient China*. Ann Arbor: University of Michigan Press 1983.

Kohn, Livia and Harold D. Roth, eds. *Daoist Identity: History, Lineage, and Ritual*. Honolulu: University of Hawaii Press, 2002.

Lau, D. C., trans. *Lao Tzu Tao Te Ching*. Baltimore, MD: Penguin, 1963.

Loy, David. *Nonduality: A Study in Comparative Philosophy*. Amherst, NY: Humanity Books, 1998.

Makransky, John J. *Buddhahood Embodied: Sources of Controversy in India and Tibet*. Albany: State University Press of New York, 1997.

Mayeda, Sengaku, trans. *A Thousand Teachings: The Upadesasahasri of Sankara*. Tokyo: University of Tokyo Press, 1979.

Miller, James. *Daoism: A Short Introduction*. Oxford: Oneworld, 2003.

Mohanty, Jitendra Nath. *Indian Classical Philosophy*. Oxford: Rowman and Littlefield, 2000.

Palmer, Martin. *The Elements of Taoism*. Rockport, MA: Element, 1993.

Pas, Julian F., ed. *The Wisdom of the Tao*. Oxford: Oneworld, 2000.

Smullyan, Raymond M. *The Tao is Silent*. New York: Harper and Row, 1977.

Welch, Holmes. *The Parting of the Way: Lao Tzu and the Taoist Movement*. London: Methuen, 1957.

Confucianism

Armstrong, Robert Cornell. *Light from the East: Studies in Japanese Confucianism*. Toronto: University of Toronto, 1914.

Edwards, Evangeline Dora. *Confucius*. London: Blackie & Son, 1940.

Jensen, Lionel M. *Manufacturing Confucianism: Chinese Traditions and Universal Civilization*.Durham, NC: Duke University Press, 1997.

Legge, James, trans. *The Chinese Classics: Translated into English with Preliminary Essays and Explanatory Notes*. Vol. 1, *The Life and Teachings of Confucius*. 2nd ed. London: J. B. Lippincott, 1869.

Rosenlee, Li-Hsiang L. *Confucianism and Women: A Philosophical Interpretation*. Albany: State University of New York Press, 2006.

Shun, Kwong-Loi and David B. Wong, eds. *Confucian Ethics: A Comparative Study of Self, Autonomy, and Community*. New York: Cambridge University Press, 2004.

Weiming, Tu and Mary Evely Tucker, eds. *Confucian Spirituality*. 2 vols. New York: Crossroad, 2003–2004.

Wilhelm, Richard. *Confucius and Confucianism.* New York: Harcourt Brace Jovanovich, 1931.

Wright, Arthur F. *Confucianism and Chinese Civilization.* New York: Atheneum, 1964.

Yao, Xinzhong. *An Introduction to Confucianism.* New York: Cambridge University Press, 2000.

African Religions

Abraham, William E. *The Mind of Africa.* Chicago: University of Chicago Press, 1962.

Appiah, Kwame Anthony. *In My Father's House: Africa in the Philosophy of Culture.* New York: Oxford University Press, 1992.

Bodunrin, Peter. "The Question of African Philosophy." *Philosophy: The Journal of the Royal Institute of Philosophy* 56 (1981): 161–79. Also in *African Philosophy: An Introduction,* edited by Richard A. Wright, 1–24. Lanham, MD: University Press of America, 1984.

Busia, K. A. "The African World View." *Présence Africaine* 4 (1965): 16–23.

—. "The Ashanti of the Gold Coast." In *African Worlds: Studies in the Cosmological Ideas and Social Values of African Peoples,* edited by C. Daryll Forde, 190–209. Oxford: Oxford University Press, 1954.

Danquah, J. B. *The Akan Doctrine of God: A Fragment of Gold Coast Ethics and Religion.* London: Frank Cass, 1968. Originally published 1944.

—. "Obligation in Akan Society." *West African Affairs* 8 (1952).

Griaule, Marcel, and Germaine Dieterlen. "The Dogon of the French Sudan." In *African Worlds: Studies in the Cosmological Ideas and Social Values of African Peoples,* edited by C. Daryll Forde, 83–110. Oxford: Oxford University Press, 1954.

Gyekye, Kwame. *An Essay on African Philosophical Thought: The Akan Conceptual Scheme,* Cambridge, Cambridge University Press, 1987. Revised second edition, Philadelphia: Temple University Press, 1995.

Idowu, E. Bolaji. *African Traditional Religion: A Definition,* Maryknoll, NY: Orbis Books, 1973.

—. *Olodumare: God in Yoruba Belief.* London: Longman, 1962.

Imbo, Samuel Oluoch. *An Introduction to African Philosophy.* Lanham, MD: Rowman and Littlefield, 1998.

Kagame, Alexis. "The Empirical Acceptance of Time and the Conception of History in Bantu Thought." In *Cultures and Time,* edited by L. Gardet, A. J. Gurevich, A. Kagame, C. Larre, G. E. R. Lloyd, A. Neher, P. Panikkar, G. Pattaro and P. Ricoeur, 89–116. Paris: UNESCO, 1976.

Keita, Lansana. "Contemporary African Philosophy: The Search for a Method." In *Praxis International* 5:2 (1985): 145–161.

Little, Kenneth Lindsay. "The Mende in Sierra Leone." In *African Worlds: Studies in the Cosmological Ideas and Social Values of African Peoples,* edited by C. Daryll Forde, 111–37.Oxford: Oxford University Press, 1954.

Mbiti, John Samuel. *African Religions and Philosophy.* London Heinemann, 1969. Second edition 1990.

—. *Concepts of God in Africa.* New York: Praeger, 1970.

Minkus, Helaine K. "Causal Theory in Akwapim Akan Philosophy." In *African Philosophy: An Introduction,* edited by Richard A. Wright, 107–63. Lanham, MD: University of America Press, 1984.

Oladipo, Olusegun. "Religion in African Culture: Some Conceptual Issues." In *A Companion to Philosophy,* edited by Kwasi Wiredu, 355–63. Malden, MA: Blackwell, 2004.

p'Bitek, O. *African Religions in Western Scholarship*. Nairobi, Kenya: East African Literature Bureau, 1971.

—. *Religion of the Central Lao*. Nairobi, Kenya: East African Literature Bureau, 1971.

Sawyerr, Harry. *God: Ancestor or Creator*. London: Longman. 1970.

Wiredu, Kwasi. *Cultural Universals and Particulars: An African Perspective*. Bloomington: Indiana University Press, 1996.

—. "Death and the Afterlife in African Culture." In *Person and Community: Ghanaian Philosophical Studies I*, edited by Kwasi Wiredu and Kwame Gyekye, 137–52. Washington, DC: Council for Research in Values and Philosophy, 1992.

—. "Determinism and Human Destiny in an African Philosophy." *The Hamline Review* 25 (2001): 10–22.

—. "On Decolonizing African Religions." In *Decolonizing the Mind: Proceedings of the Colloquium held at UNISA*, edited by Jeanette Malherbe, 178–93. Pretoria, South Africa: Research Unit for African Philosophy, 1995.

—. *Philosophy and an African Culture*. Cambridge: Cambridge University Press, 1980.

Sikhism

Cole, W. Owen, and Piara Singh Sambhi. *The Sikhs: Their Religious Beliefs and Practices*. 2nd ed. Brighton: Sussex, 1995.

Khazan Singh, Sardar. *History and Philosophy of the Sikh Religion*. 2 vols. Patiala, India: Punjab Languages Department, 1970. Originally published 1914.

Macauliffe, Max Arthur. *The Sikh Religion: Its Gurus, Sacred Writings, and Authors*. 3 vols. Delhi: S. Chand, 1963. Originally published in 6 vols. by Oxford University Press, 1909.

McLeod, W. H. *Exploring Sikhism: Aspects of Sikh Identity, Culture and Thought*. Oxford: Oxford University Press, 2000.

—. *The Sikhs: History, Religion, and Society*. New York: Columbia University Press, 1989.

—. *Who Is a Sikh: The Problem of Sikh Identity*. Oxford: Clarendon, 1989.

Nesbitt, Eleanor M. *Sikhism: A Very Short Introduction*. Oxford: Oxford University Press, 2005.

Uberoi, J. Pal Singh. *Religion, Civil Society and the State: A Study of Sikhism*. Delhi: Oxford University Press, 1996.

Native American Religions

Bierhorst, John. *The Sacred Path: Spells, Prayers, and Power Songs of the American Indians*. New York: Morrow, 1983.

Carmichael, David, Jane Hubert, Brian Reeves, and Audhild Schanche, eds. *Sacred Sites, Sacred Places*. New York: Routledge, 1994.

Carmody, Denise L., and John Tully Carmody. *Native American Religions: An Introduction*. New York: Paulist, 1993.

Gossen, Gary H. *South and Meso-American Native Spirituality: from the Cult of the Feathered Serpent to the Theology of Liberation.* New York: Crossroad, 1993.

Griffiths, Nicholas, and Fernando Cervantes, eds. *Spiritual Encounters: Interactions Between Christianity and Native Religions in Colonial America.* Lincoln: University of Nebraska Press, 1999.

Irwin, Lee. *Native American Spirituality: A Critical Reader.* Lincoln: University of Nebraska Press, 2000.

Kehoe, Alice Beck. *Shamans and Religion: An Anthropological Exploration in Critical Thinking.*Prospect Heights, IL: Waveland, 2000.

Torrance, Robert M. *The Spiritual Quest: Transcendence in Myth, Religion, and Science.* Berkeley: University of California Press, 1994.

Wicca

Conway, D. J. *Wicca: The Complete Craft.* Freedom, CA: Crossing, 2001.

Crowley, Vivianne. *Wicca, New Edition: A Comprehensive Guide to the Old Religion in the Modern World.* Shaftesbury: Element, 2003.

Grimassi, Raven. *Encyclopedia of Wicca and Witchcraft.* St. Paul, MN: Llewellyn, 2000.

Lipp, Deborah. *The Study of Witchcraft: A Guidebook to Advanced Wicca.* San Francisco: Weiser, 2007.

Murphy-Hiscock, Arin. *Solitary Wicca for Life: Complete Guide to Mastering the Craft on Your Own.* Avon, MA: Provenance, 2005.

RavenWolf, Silver. *To Ride a Silver Broomstick: New Generational Witchcraft.* St. Paul, MN: Llewellyn, 1993.

Sabin, Thea. *Wicca for Beginners: Fundamentals of Philosophy and Practice.* St. Paul, MN: Llewellyn, 2006.

Sylvan, Diane. *The Circle Within: Creating a Wiccan Spiritual Tradition.* St. Paul, MN: Llewellyn, 2003.

Resources in Modern Philosophy of Religion

Clack, Beverly and Brian R Clack. *The Philosophy of Religion: A Critical Introduction.* Revised 2nd ed. Malden, MA: Polity, 2008.

Davies, Brian. *An Introduction to the Philosophy of Religion.* Oxford: Oxford University Press, 1993.

—. *Philosophy of Religion: A Guide and Anthology.* Oxford: Oxford University Press, 2000.

—. *Philosophy of Religion: A Guide to the Subject.* London: Geoffrey Chapman, 1998.

Harrison, Victoria S. *Religion and Modern Thought.* London: SCM, 2007.

Kenny, Anthony. *A New History of Western Philosophy.* Vol 4, *Philosophy In The Modern World.* New York: Oxford University Press, 2007.

Long, Eugene Thomas. *Twentieth-Century Western Philosophy of Religion 1900–2000.* Dordrecht, The Netherlands: Kluwer, 2003.

Meister, Chad, ed. *The Philosophy of Religion Reader.* New York: Routledge, 2008.

Ricoeur, Paul. *Freud and Philosophy: An Essay on Interpretation*. Translated by Denis Savage. New Haven, CT: Yale University Press, 1970.

Taliaferro, Charles. *Contemporary Philosophy of Religion*. Oxford: Blackwell, 1998.

—. *Evidence and Faith: Philosophy and Religion Since the Seventeenth Century*. Cambridge: Cambridge University Press, 2005.

Tilghman, Benjamin R. *An Introduction to Philosophy of Religion*. Oxford: Blackwell, 1993.

World Religions

Archer, John Clark. *The Sikhs in Relation to Hindus, Moslems, Christians, and Ahmadiyyas: A Study in Comparative Religion*. New York: Russell & Russell, 1971.

Bowker, John, ed. *The Cambridge Illustrated History of Religions*. New York: Cambridge University Press, 2002.

Farles, Margaret N. "Feminism and Universal Morality." In *Prospects for a Common Morality*, edited by Gene Outka and John P. Reeder, Jr., 170–90. Princeton, NJ: Princeton University Press, 1993.

Foltz, Richard C., ed. *Worldviews, Religion, and the Environment: A Global Anthology*. Belmont, CA: Thomson/Wadsworth, 2003.

King, Sallie B. "It's a Long Way to a Global Ethic: A Response to Leonard Swidler." *Buddhist Christian Studies* 15 (1995): 213–19.

—. "A Buddhist Perspective on a Global Ethic and Human Rights." *Journal of Dharma* 20 (1995): 122–36.

Knitter, Paul F. "Pitfalls and Promises for a Global Ethics." *Buddhist-Christian Studies* 15 (1995): 221–9.

Kung, Hans. "History, Significance, and Method of the Declaration Toward a Global Ethic." In *A Global Ethic: The Declaration of the Parliament of the World's Religions*, edited by Hans Kung and Karl-Josef Kuschel, 71–2. New York: Continuum, 1993.

Neusner, Jacob, ed. *World Religions in America: An Introduction*. Louisville: Westminster John Knox, 2003.

Outka, Gene, and John P. Reeder, Jr., eds. *Prospects for a Common Morality*. Princeton, NJ: Princeton University Press, 1993.

Peters, Francis Edward. *The Children of Abraham: Judaism, Christianity, Islam*. Princeton, NJ: Princeton, 2004.

Quinn, Philip L. "Toward Thinner Theologies: Hick and Alston on Religious Diversity." In *The Philosophical Challenge of Religious Diversity*, edited by Philip L. Quinn and Kevin Meeker, 226–43. New York: Oxford University Press, 2000.

—. "Religious Diversity and Religious Toleration." *International Journal for Philosophy of Religion* 50 (2001): 57–80.

Smart, Ninian. *The World's Religions*. Englewood Cliffs, NJ: Prentice Hall, 1989.

Swidler, Leonard, and Hans Kung. "Editorial: Toward a 'Universal Declaration of Global Ethos.'" *Journal of Ecumenical Studies* 28 (1991): 123–5.

Environmental Philosophy of Religion

Gottlieb, Roger S. *Greener Faith: Religious Environmentalism and Our Planet's Future.* New York: Oxford University Press, 2006.

—. *Joining Hands: Politics and Religion Together for Social Change.* Boulder, CO: Westview, 2004.

—, ed. *The Oxford Handbook of Religion and Ecology.* New York: Oxford University Press, 2006.

—, ed. *This Sacred Earth: Religion, Nature, Environment.* 2nd ed. London: Routledge, 2003.

Light, Andrew and Holmes Rolston, III, eds. *Environmental Ethics: An Anthology.* Oxford: Blackwell, 2003.

Rolston, Homles, III. *Environmental Ethics: Values in and Duties to the Natural World.* Philadelphia, PA: Temple University Press, 1988.

Taylor, Bron. *Encyclopedia of Religion and Nature.* New York: Continuum, 2005.

Afterlife

Bailey, Lee W., and Jenny Yates, eds. *The Near Death Experience: A Reader.* New York: Routledge, 1996.

Baker, Lynne Rudder. "Need a Christian Be a Mind/Body Dualist." *Faith and Philosophy* 12 (1995): 489–504.

—. *Persons and Bodies: A Constitution View.* Cambridge: Cambridge University Press, 2000.

Bynum, Caroline Walker. *The Resurrection of the Body in Western Christianity , 200–1336.* New York: Columbia University Press, 1995.

Cooper, John W. *Body, Soul and Life Everlasting: Biblical Anthropology and the Monism-Dualism Debate.* Grand Rapids, MI: Eerdmans, 1989.

Cullman, Oscar. "Immortality of the Soul or Resurrection of the Dead: The Witness of the New Testament." In *Immortality and Resurrection: Death in the Western World: Two Conflicting Currents of Thought,* edited by Krister Stendahl, 9–53. New York: Macmillan, 1965.

Davis, Stephen T., ed. *Death and Afterlife.* London: Macmillan, 1989.

—. *Risen Indeed: Making Sense of the Resurrection.* Grand Rapids, MI: Eerdmans, 1993.

Edwards, Paul, ed. *Immortality.* New York: Macmillan, 1992.

Geach, Peter. *God and the Soul.* London: Routledge and Kegan Paul, 1969.

Habermas, Gary R. "Near Death Experiences and the Evidence: A Review Essay." *Christian Scholar's Review* 26:1 (1996): 78–85.

Hick, John. *Death and Eternal Life.* Louisville, KY: Westminster/John Knox, 1994.

Kvanvig, Jonathan L. *The Problem of Hell.* New York: Oxford University Press, 1993.

Moody, Raymond A. *Life After Life.* New York: Bantam/Mockingbird, 1975.

Moreland, J. P., and Gary Habermas. *Beyond Death: Exploring the Evidence for Immortality.* Wheaton, IL: Crossway, 1998.

Penelhum, Terence. *Survival and Disembodied Existence.* London: Routledge and Kegan Paul, 1970.

Perry, John. *A Dialogue on Personal Identity and Immortality.* Indianapolis, IN. Hackett, 1978.

Price, H. H. "Personal Survival and the Idea of Another World." In *Classical and Contemporary Readings in the Philosophy of Religion,* edited by John Hick, 364–86. Englewood Cliffs, NJ: Prentice-Hall, 1964.

—. "The Possibility of Resurrection." In *Immortality,* edited by Paul Edwards, 242–6. New York: Macmillan, 1992. Reprinted from the *International Journal for Philosophy of Religion* 9 (1978): 114–21.

Rea, Michael C. *Oxford Readings in Philosophical Theology.* 2 vols. New York: Oxford University Press, 2009.

Ring, Kenneth. *Life at Death: A Scientific Investigation of the Near-Death Experience.* New York: Coward, McCann, and Geoghegan, 1980.

Russell, Bertrand. *Mysticism and Logic.* Garden City, NY. Doubleday, 1957.

Russell, Jeffrey Burton. *A History of Heaven.* Princeton, NJ: Princeton University Press, 1997.

Schellenberg, John L. *Divine Hiddenness and Human Reason.* Ithaca, NY: Cornell University Press, 1993.

Stendahl, Krister. *Immortality and Resurrection.* New York: Macmillan, 1965.

Swinburne, Richard. *The Evolution of the Soul.* Oxford: Clarendon, 1986. Revised edition 1997.

van Inwagen, Peter. "Dualism and Materialism: Athens and Jerusalem?" *Faith and Philosophy* 12 (1995): 475–88.

Walls, Jerry L. *Heaven: The Logic of Eternal Joy.* New York: Oxford University Press, 2002.

—. *The Logic of Damnation: A Defense of the Traditional Doctrine of Hell.* Notre Dame, IN: University of Notre Dame, 1989.

—, ed. *The Oxford Handbook of Eschatology.* New York: Oxford University Press, 2010.

Wolterstorff, Nicholas. *Lament for a Son.* Grand Rapids, MI: Eerdmans, 1987.

Zaleski, Carol. *Otherworld Journeys: Accounts of Near-Death Experiences in Medieval and Modern Times.* New York: Oxford University Press, 1987.

Zimmerman, Dean. "The Compatibility of Materialism and Survival: The 'Falling Elevator' Model." *Faith and Philosophy* 16 (1999): 194–212.

Naturalism

Armstrong, David Malet. *A Materialist Theory of the Mind.* London: Routledge and Kegan Paul, 1968.

Beilby, James. *Naturalism Defeated: Essays on Plantinga's Evolutionary Argument Against Naturalism.* Ithaca, NY: Cornell University Press, 2002.

De Caro, Mario, and David Macarthur, eds. *Naturalism in Question.* Cambridge, MA: Harvard University Press, 2004.

Draper, Paul. "God, Science, and Naturalism." In *The Oxford Handbook of Philosophy of Religion,* edited by William J. Wainwright, 272–303. Oxford: Oxford University Press, 2005.

Goetz, Stewart, and Charles Taliaferro. *Naturalism.* Grand Rapids, MI: Eerdmans, 2008.

Kim, Jaegwon. *Mind in a Physical World: An Essay on the Mind-Body Problem and Mental Causation.* Cambridge, MA: MIT Press, 1998.

Koons, Robert C. *Realism Regained: An Exact Theory of Causation, Teleology, and the Mind.* New York: Oxford University Press, 2000.

Mackie, John Leslie. *Ethics: Inventing Right and Wrong.* Harmondsworth, UK: Penguin, 1977.

Papineau, David. *Philosophical Naturalism.* Oxford: Basil Blackwell, 1993.

Sellars, Wilfrid. "Empiricism and the Philosophy of Mind." In *Minnesota Studies in the Philosophy of Science*. Vol. 1, *The Foundations of Science and the Concepts of Psychology and Psychoanalysis*, edited by Herbert Feigl and Michael Scriven, 253–329. Minneapolis: University of Minnesota Press, 1956.

Seymour, Michel, and Matthias Fritsch. *Reason & Emancipation: Essays in Honour of Kai Nielsen*. Amherst, NY: Humanity, 2007.

Politics and Religion

Audi, Robert. *Religious Commitment and Secular Reason*. Cambridge: Cambridge University Press, 2000.

Audi, Robert, and Nicholas Wolterstorff. *Religion in the Public Square: The Place of Religious Convictions in Political Debate*. Lanham: Rowman & Littlefield Publishers, 1997.

Dombrowski, Daniel. *Rawls and Religion: The Case for Political Liberalism*. Albany: State University of New York Press, 2001.

Eberle, Christopher. *Religious Conviction in Liberal Politics*. Cambridge: Cambridge University Press, 2002.

Gaus, Gerald. *Justificatory Liberalism: An Essay on Epistemology and Political Theory*. Oxford: Oxford University Press, 1996.

Habermas, Jurgen. "Discourse Ethics." In *Moral Consciousness and Communicative Action*. Translated by Christian Lenhardt and Shierry Weber Nicholsen, 43–115. Cambridge: MIT Press, 1990.

Hampshire, Stewart. *Justice is Conflict*. Princeton, NJ: Princeton University Press, 2000.

Langerak, Edward. "Theism and Toleration." In *A Companion to Philosophy of Religion*, edited by Philip L. Quinn and Charles Taliaferro, 514–21. London: Blackwell, 1997.

Lockhart, Ted. *Moral Uncertainty and Its Consequences*. Oxford: Oxford University Press, 2000.

MacIntyre, Alasdair. *After Virtue*. 2nd ed. Notre Dame, IN: University of Notre Dame Press, 1984.

Marty, Martin E. *Education, Religion, and the Common Good*. San Francisco: Jossey-Bass, 2000.

Rawls, John. *The Law of Peoples with "The Idea of Public Reason Revisited"*. Cambridge: Harvard University Press, 1999.

—. *Political Liberalism*. New York: Columbia University Press, 1996.

Scanlon, T. M. *What We Owe Each Other*. Cambridge, MA: Harvard University Press, 1998.

Stout, Jeffrey. *Democracy and Tradition*. Princeton, NJ: Princeton University Press, 2004.

Taylor, Charles. *Sources of the Self*. Cambridge: Harvard University Press, 1989.

Trigg, Roger. *Religion in Public Life: Must Faith be Privitized?* Oxford: Oxford University Press, 2007.

Weithman, Paul J. "Citizenship and Public Reason." In *Natural Law and Public Reason*, edited by Robert P. George and Christopher Wolfe, 125–70. Washington, DC: Georgetown University Press, 2000.

—. *Liberal Faith*. Notre Dame, IL: University of Notre Dame Press, 2008.

—, ed. *Religion and Contemporary Liberalism*. Notre Dame, IN: University of Notre Dame Press, 1997

—. *Religion and the Obligations of Citizenship*. Cambridge: Cambridge University Press, 2002.

Wolterstorff, Nicholas. "Why We Should Reject What Liberalism Tells Us about Speaking and Acting in Public for Religious Reasons." In *Religion and Contemporary Liberalism*, edited by Paul Weithman, 162–81. Notre Dame, IN: University of Notre Dame Press, 1997.

History of Philosophy of Religion

Harrison, Victoria. *Religion and Modern Thought.* London: SCM, 2007.

Long, Eugene Thomas. *Twentieth Century Western Philosophy of Religion 1900–2000.* Dordrecht: Kluwer, 2000.

Oppy, Graham, and Nick Trakakis, eds. *The History of Western Philosophy of Religion.* 5 vols. New York: Oxford University Press, 2009.

Zagzebski, Linda T. *Philosophy of Religion: A Historical Introduction.* Malden, MA: Blackwell, 2007.

Wittgenstein and Religion

Phillips, D. Z. "Advice to Philosophers Who Are Christians." In *Wittgenstein and Religion,* edited by D. Z. Phillips, 220–36. Basingstoke, England: Macmillan, 1993.

—. *Belief, Change and Forms of Life.* Basingstoke, England: Macmillan, 1986.

—. *The Concept of Prayer.* Oxford: Blackwell, 1981. First published London: Routledge, 1965.

—. *Death and Immortality.* London: Macmillan, 1970

—. "Epistemic Practices: The Retreat from Reality." In *Recovering Religious Concepts,* edited by D. Z. Phillips, 22–44. Basingstoke, England: Macmillan, 2000.

—. *From Fantasy to Faith.* Basingstoke, England: Macmillan, 1991.

—. "Is Hume's 'True Religion' a Religious Belief." In *Religion and Hume's Legacy,* edited by D. Z. Phillips and Timothy Tessin, 81–98. Basingstoke, England: Macmillan, 1999.

—. "On Not Understanding God." In *Wittgenstein and Religion,* edited by D. Z. Phillips, 153–70. Basingstoke, England: Macmillan, 1993.

—. *Philosophy's Cool Place.* Ithaca, N.Y.: Cornell University Press, 1999.

—. "The Problem of Evil." A symposium with Richard Swinburne. In *Reason and Religion,* edited by Stuart C. Brown, 103–21. Ithaca, NY: Cornell University Press, 1977.

—. *R. S. Thomas: Poet of the Hidden God.* Basingstoke, England: Macmillan, 1986.

—. "Religion, Philosophy and the Academy." *International Journal for Philosophy of Religion* 44 (1998): 129–44.

—. "Turning God into One Devil of a Problem." In *Recovering Religious Concepts,* edited by D. Z. Phillips, 103–28. Basingstoke, England: Macmillan, 2000.

—. "The World and 'I.'" In *Recovering Religious Concepts,* edited by D. Z. Phillips, 157–70. Basingstoke, England: Macmillan, 2000.

Rhees, Rush. "Belief in God." In *On Religion and Philosophy,* edited by D. Z. Phillips, 50–64. Cambridge: Cambridge University Press, 1997.

—. "Death and Immortality." In *On Religion and Philosophy,* edited by D. Z. Phillips, 206–37. Cambridge: Cambridge University Press, 1997.

—. *In Dialogue with the Greeks.* Vol. 1, *The Presocratics and Reality.* Edited by D. Z. Phillips. Aldershot, England: Ashgate, 2004.

—. "Language as Emerging from Instinctive Behaviour." Edited by D. Z. Phillips. *Philosophical Investigations* 20 (1997): 1–14.

—. "Natural Theology." In *On Religion and Philosophy*, edited by D. Z. Phillips, 34–8. Cambridge: Cambridge University Press, 1997.

—. In *Discussions of Wittgenstein*, London: Routledge, 1970.

—. "The Ontological Argument and Proof." In *On Religion and Philosophy*, edited by D. Z. Phillips, 17–23. Cambridge: Cambridge University Press, 1997.

—. "Religion and Language." In *On Religion and Philosophy*, edited by D. Z. Phillips, 39–49. Cambridge: Cambridge University Press, 1997.

—. "Suffering." In *On Religion and Philosophy*, edited by D. Z. Phillips, 301–6. Cambridge: Cambridge University Press, 1997.

—. *Wittgenstein and the Possibility of Discourse*. Edited by D. Z. Phillips. Cambridge: Cambridge University Press, 1998.

—. *Wittgenstein's "On Certainty": There—Like Our Life*. Edited by D. Z. Phillips. Oxford: Blackwell, 2002.

Religion and Morality

Adams, Robert M. *Finite and Infinite Goods: A Framework for Ethics*. New York: Oxford University Press, 1999.

—. *The Virtue of Faith and Other Essays in Philosophical Theology*. New York: Oxford University Press, 1987.

George, Robert P. *In Defense of Natural Law*. Oxford: Clarendon Press, 1999.

Hare, John E. *The Moral Gap: Kantian Ethics, Human Limits, and God's Assistance*. Oxford: Clarendon Press, 1996.

Hauerwas, Stanley, and Alasdair MacIntyre, eds. *Revisions: Changing Perspectives in Moral Philosophy*. Notre Dame, IN: University of Notre Dame Press, 1983.

Helm, Paul, ed. *Divine Commands and Morality*. New York: Oxford University Press, 1981.

Idziak, Janine Marie, ed. *Divine Command Morality: Historical and Contemporary Readings*. Toronto: Edwin Mellen Press, 1980.

Kant, Immanuel. *Critique of Practical Reason*. Edited by Mary Gregor. Introduction by Andrews Reath. Cambridge: Cambridge University Press, 1997.

—. *Critique of Pure Reason*. Edited by Paul Geyer and Allen Wood. Cambridge: Cambridge University Press, 1999.

Lewis, C. S. *Mere Christianity*. New York: Macmillan, 1952.

MacDonald, Scott Charles, ed. *Being and Goodness: The Concept of the Good in Metaphysics and Philosophical Theology*. Ithaca, NY: Cornell University Press.

MacIntyre, Alasdair. *After Virtue*. Notre Dame, IN: University of Notre Dame Press, 1981.

Mitchell, Basil. *Morality, Religious and Secular: The Dilemma of the Traditional Conscience*. Oxford: Clarendon Press, 1980.

Mouw, Richard J. *The God Who Commands*. Notre Dame, IN: University of Notre Dame Press. 1990.

Quinn, Philip L. *Divine Commands and Moral Requirements*. Oxford: Clarendon Press, 1978.

Swinburne, Richard. *The Existence of God*. Oxford: Clarendon Press, 1979.

Vacek, E. C., S. J. *Love, Human and Divine: The Heart of Christian Ethics.* Washington, DC: Georgetown University Press, 1994.

Wainwright, William J. *Religion and Morality.* Aldershot, UK: Ashgate, 2005.

Zagzebski, Linda T. *Divine Motivation Theory.* Cambridge: Cambridge University Press, 2004.

—. "Emotion and Moral Judgment." *Philosophy and Phenomenological Research* 66 (2003): 104–24.

—. "Religious Diversity and Social Responsibility." *Logos* (Winter 2001): 135-55.

Postmodernism

Caputo, John D. *The Prayers and Tears of Jacques Derrida: Religion without Religion.* Bloomington: Indiana University Press, 1997.

Derrida, Jacques. "Difference." In *Margins of Philosophy.* Translated by Alan Bass, 1–28. Chicago: University of Chicago Press, 1982.

—. "Faith and Knowledge: The Two Sources of 'Religion' at the Limits of Reason Alone." In *Religion,* edited by Jacques Derrida and Gianni Vattimo, 1–78. Stanford: Stanford University Press, 1998.

—. "Force of Law: The 'Mystical Foundation of Authority'." In *Deconstruction and the Possibility of Justice,* edited by Drucilla Cornell, Michel Rosenfeld, and David Gray Carlson, 3–67. New York: Routledge, 1992.

—. "How to Avoid Speaking: Denials." In *Derrida and Negative Theology,* edited by Howard Coward and Toby Foshay, 73–141. Albany: State University of New York Press, 1992.

—. *On the Name.* Edited by Thomas Dutoit. Stanford: Stanford University Press, 1995.

—. "Psyche: Inventions of the Other." In *Reading de Man Reading,* edited by Lindsay Waters and Wlad Godzich, 25–65. Minneapolis: University of Minnesota Press, 1989.

—. *Specters of Marx: The State of the Debt, the Work of Mourning, and the New International.* Translated by Peggy Kamuf. New York: Routledge, 1994.

Marion, Jean-Luc. "Metaphysics and Phenomenology: A Summary for Theologians." In *The Postmodern God: A Theological Reader,* edited by Graham Ward, 279–96. Oxford: Blackwell, 1997.

—. *Idol and Distance.* Translated by Thomas A. Carlson, 20–41. New York: Fordham University Press, 2001.

—. "In the Name: How to Avoid Speaking of 'Negative Theology'." In *God, the Gift, and Postmodernism,* edited by John D. Caputo and Michael J. Scanlon, 20–41. Bloomington: Indiana University Press, 1999.

—. *Reduction and Givenness: Investigations of Husserl, Heidegger, and Phenomenology.* Translated by Thomas A Carlson. Evanston, IL: Northwestern University Press, 1998.

—. "The Saturated Phenomenon." In *Phenomenology and the "Theological Turn": The French Debate.* Translated by Thomas A. Carlson, 176–216. New York: Fordham University Press, 2000.

Ricoeur, Paul. *Fallible Man.* Translated by Charles Kelbley. Chicago: Henry Regnery, 1965.

Process Theology

Cobb, John B., Jr., and David Ray Griffin. *Process Theology: An Introductory Exposition.* Louisville, KY: Westminster John Knox, 1977.

Gray, James R., ed. *Modern Process Thought.* Washington, DC: University Press of America, 1982.

Hartshorne, Charles. *The Divine Relativity: A Social Conception of God.* New Haven, CT: Yale University Press, 1948.

Rescher, Nicholas. *Process Metaphysics: An Introduction to Process Philosophy.* Albany: State University of New York Press, 1996.

Whitehead, Alfred North. *Religion in the Making.* Cambridge: Cambridge University Press, 1926.

About the Authors

Charles Taliaferro, Professor of Philosophy, St. Olaf College, is the author of *Consciousness and the Mind of God* (Cambridge University Press), *Evidence and Faith: Philosophy and Religion Since the Seventeenth Century* (Cambridge University Press), *Contemporary Philosophy of Religion* (Blackwell), *Dialogues About God* (Rowman and Littlefield), *Philosophy of Religion: A Beginner's Guide* (OneWorld Press) and the co-author of *Naturalism* (Eerdmans). He is the co-editor of the first edition of the *Blackwell Companion to Philosophy of Religion* and the second edition, *Philosophy of Religion Reader* (Blackwell), *Cambridge Platonist Spirituality* (Paulist Press), and the *Cambridge Companion to Christian Philosophical Theology* (Cambridge University Press). He was the philosophy of religion area editor of the *Encyclopedia of Philosophy*, second edition (Macmillan) and is on the editorial board of *Religious Studies*, *Sophia*, *Blackwell's Philosophy Compass*, *American Philosophical Quarterly*, and *Ars Disputandi*. Taliaferro has lectured at Oxford, Cambridge, NYU, Columbia, Princeton, St. Andrews University (Scotland) and elsewhere.

Elsa J. Marty, a former student of Charles Taliaferro, is currently a graduate student in theology at University of Chicago Divinity School and a candidate for ordination in the Lutheran Church (ELCA). She has spent a significant amount of time in India studying interfaith relations. Her interests include theological anthropology and social ethics.

ADDENDUM to the entry FRIENDSHIP: Perhaps one of the more challenging ways of beginning and sustaining a friendship is through the co-authoring and co-editing of a dictionary, but this can be done with brilliant results as part of the cultivation of friendship, especially when helped out with the occasional cookie.

3 68 7